Till all our fight be fought

Till all our fight be fought

The Olavian 'Fallen' and the Great War
1914 to 1918

Peter J. Leonard

Reveille Press is an imprint of
Tommies Guides Military Booksellers & Publishers

Gemini House
136–140 Old Shoreham Road
Brighton
BN3 7BD

www.tommiesguides.co.uk

First published in Great Britain by
Reveille Press 2014

For more information please visit
www.reveillepress.com

© 2013 Peter J. Leonard

A catalogue record for this book is available
from the British Library

All rights reserved. Apart from any use under UK
copyright law no part of this publication may be reproduced,
stored in a retrieval system, or transmitted, in any form or
by any means, without prior written permission of the publisher,
nor be otherwise circulated in any form of binding or
cover other than that in which it is published and without
a similar condition being imposed on the subsequent publisher.

ISBN 978-1-908336-07-1

Cover design by Reveille Press
Typeset by Vivian@Bookscribe

Printed and bound in Great Britain

For my Grandfathers

Private Henry Edward Leonard no. A.774912/45
12th Battalion, East Surrey Regiment and no. 21011,
Royal Marines Light Infantry
Rifleman Joseph Sturmer no. 304648, 5th (City of London)
Battalion (London Rifle Brigade) and 28th (County of London)
Battalion (Artist's Rifles)

*Men of South London who were there and
returned as silent witnesses*

About the author

Peter Leonard was born in Farnborough, Kent in 1959 and attended St Olave's from 1970 to 1977. After graduating with a Bachelor of Arts (Honours) degree in Modern History and English Literature from The University of East Anglia in 1981, he commenced a career in sales and marketing for a global manufacturing company. Currently he is Global Market Development Manager, for their graphics business. Peter is married to Susan with two sons, Jake and Oscar and lives in Surrey.

Acknowledgements

Firstly I would like to thank my wife Susan and my sons, Jake and Oscar, without whose support this would not have been possible. I would also like to thank my father, Jack, and my grandfathers Joe and Harry for unintentionally inspiring me to become interested in both the history of my family and of the World Wars.

There are various people associated with St Olave's School who have helped and encouraged me in my research and writing. Amongst them are Susan Crocker, Christine Andrews, John Brown, Chris Davies, Rob Gardner, Roger Hards, Chris Harris, Tony Jarvis, Aydın Önaç, George Snelgrove and Jane Wells.

Thanks should also be expressed to those who have commented positively on the book – including Richard van Emden, John Silberrad, James Thurbin and Kenneth Eade, not to forget the many Pals and Old Sweats from the Great War Forum!

My special thanks go to Leon Brown, both a current student at St Olave's, and a talented creative responsible for all the centrepiece photography and the cover design.

I would like to thank the Western Front Association and, in particular, Ryan Gearing and his team at Reveille Press for their assistance and guidance in this new publication.

Staff at the National Archives in Kew have been, as ever, courteous, informative and helpful.

Finally, I would like to pay tribute to Larry Smy, John Burston, Alan Evans (long though my memory might be) – for they collectively were responsible for sending me off to University to read Modern History and English.

PJL

Contents

Dedication	5
About the Author	6
Acknowledgements	7
Contents	8
The Poems	10–11
The School Song	12
Armistice Day Speech 1930	13
Prologue	22
Foreword	24
Introduction	26

CHAPTER 1	Bermondsey and the School	30
CHAPTER 2	First Ypres (1914)	37
CHAPTER 3	The Royal Navy	44
CHAPTER 4	Gallipoli and the Dardanelles (1915)	59
CHAPTER 5	Second Ypres: Neuve Chapelle, Aubers Ridge and Festubert (1915)	69
CHAPTER 6	Loos, Hulluch and Ypres (1915)	83
CHAPTER 7	Royal Army Medical Corps	100
CHAPTER 8	The Battle of the Somme – The first two weeks (1916)	108
CHAPTER 9	The Somme: The Woods, Guillemont and Ginchy (1916)	121
CHAPTER 10	The Somme: Flers Courcelette, Morval, Transloy Ridge and the Ancre Heights (1916)	134
CHAPTER 11	The Arras Campaign: Vimy Ridge, Scarpe and Arleux (1917)	152
CHAPTER 12	The Royal Engineers	169
CHAPTER 13	Third Ypres: Messines, Pilckem Ridge and Langemarck (1917)	177
CHAPTER 14	The Artillery	188

CHAPTER 15 The Machine Gun and the Tank Corps **210**
CHAPTER 16 Third Ypres: Menin Road, Passchendaele
            and Poelcapelle (1917) **220**
CHAPTER 17 The Royal Flying Corps **229**
CHAPTER 18 Loos, Cambrai and Ypres (1917) **248**
CHAPTER 19 The Canadian Contingent **262**
CHAPTER 20 The Kaisers Offensive (1918) **273**
CHAPTER 21 The Balkans and the Middle Eastern Campaign **292**
CHAPTER 22 Bapaume and Peronne (1918) **310**
CHAPTER 23 Hindenburg Line, Armistice and Aftermath **330**

Bibliography **346**

Appendix 1 – Cemetery and Memorial Index **348**
Appendix 11 – Name Index **358**
Appendix 111 – Military Unit Index **370**
Appendix IV – Western Front location Index **380**
Appendix V – Battle Index **382**
Appendix V1 – Medal Awards Index **392**
Appendix V11 – School Years Index **403**
Appendix V111 – Fathers and Brothers Index **409**
Appendix IX – Date of Death Index **415**
Appendix X – Home Area Index **417**
Appendix XI – Epitaphs Index **423**

Dulce et Decorum Est

Bent double, like old beggars under sacks,
Knock-kneed, coughing like hags, we cursed through sludge,
Till on the haunting flares we turned our backs,
And towards our distant rest began to trudge.
Men marched asleep. Many had lost their boots,
But limped on, blood-shod. All went lame, all blind;
Drunk with fatigue; deaf even to the hoots
Of gas-shells dropping softly behind.

Gas! Gas! Quick, boys! – An ecstasy of fumbling,
fitting the clumsy helmets just in time,
But someone still was yelling out and stumbling
And floundering like a man in fire or lime. –
Dim through the misty panes and thick green light,
As under a green sea, I saw him drowning.

If in some smothering dreams, you too could pace
Behind the wagon that we flung him in,
And watch the white eyes writhing in his face,
His hanging face, like a devil's sick of sin;
If you could hear at every jolt, the blood
Come gargling from the froth-corrupted lungs
Bitter as the cud
Of vile, incurable sores on innocent tongues, –
My friend, you would not tell with such high zest
To children ardent for some desperate glory,
The old lie: *Dulce et decorum est
Pro patria mori.*

Wilfred Owen

The Soldier

If I should die, think only this of me:
That there's some corner of a foreign field
That is forever England. There shall be
In that rich earth a richer dust concealed:
A dust whom England bore, shaped, made aware,
Gave, once, her flowers to love, her ways to roam,
A body of England's, breathing English air,
Washed by the rivers, blest by suns of home.

And think, this heart, all evil shed away,
A pulse in the eternal mind, no less
Gives somewhere back the thoughts by England given:
Her sights and sounds: dreams happy as her day:
And laughter, learnt of friends: and gentleness,
In hearts at peace, under an English heaven.

Rupert Brooke

The School Song

Next to the land that's under us:
Our honour and our name,
For all the years that sunder us
We love her yet the same:
And all the loyal heart of us
Is one with her who wrought
Herself to be a part of us
Till all our fight be fought

She took us by the hand of us
And gave us to her sons,
She made a single band of us
While all time runs:
'Twas she who taught the game to us –
To rule and to obey –
And now her fame is fame to us
Her honour ours today

Though far away they seem to us,
The mighty days of youth,
And things may look a dream to us
That once were naked truth:
Though many suns have set for us,
Were none so bright as those
That light the long days yet for us,
And shall unto the close.

Olaf to raise the song –
Olaf to bear along –
Olaf to right the wrong
Till all our fight be fought.

H.F.B. Brett-Smith, 1902–03

Armistice Day – 1930

The Headmaster of St Olave's read the Roll of Honour of those Olavians who had given their lives for their Country. These were his words:

"We hear that pitiful long list of names of Old Olavians – many of them boys, going from school into the war-machine. It makes one hate the injustice of it all, those lads, mere schoolboys, radiant, full of hope, upon the threshold of the outer world, swept out of life, killed on the battlefield.

The solemn reading of their names recalls their faces as we knew them in the School, linked with some tone or glance, some incident of classroom, or the Corps, or cricket field. The name recalls the features: one by one, seen as of old, they pass before the mind, a living gallery of pictures, dearer made by pity, for the wanton sacrifice of their young lives to cruel war's demands.

Some had already shown their quality, earning high praise at college, and marked out for special service. Others were to find their places in the humbler tasks of life. Yet, whether slow or brilliant, each was loved, each of them lived within his mother's heart, each one was valued by his chum and friends, each one was fitted for some little part in all this many-sided life of ours.

And right across that love, across that life, insatiate war with blind stupidity has cut its way and torn them from their friends. A dozen years have passed and to most here, the names are strange.

Soon, it may be, the list no longer read, will rest, a vellum roll, within a drawer, mute witness of their willing sacrifice.

But while the youthful figure, sword in hand, calls through the years, our youth to take their stand, with heart ablaze to fight against the wrong, may these forgotten names live to declare to future generations of the School, the cruel injustice, senseless sacrifice of life, the misery, the desolation, wrought by war".

Saint Olaves School

The Record of Those our Beloved who for our sakes in the GREAT WAR of 1914-1918 Laboured and Fought and Fell.

The King's Tribute to each of his Fallen Soldiers.

He whom this Record commemorates was numbered among Those, who at the call of King and Country Left all that was dear to Them, Endured Hardness Faced Danger and finally, Passed out of the sight of men by the Path of Duty and Self Sacrifice giving up Their Lives that others might live in freedom.

Let Those who come after see to it that HIS NAME be not forgotten.

The Parish of Bermondsey before the War.

The Parish of Bermondsey before the War.

The Parish of Bermondsey before the War.

The Old School before the move to Tooley Street in 1893 and frequented by a few of the older Fallen.

St Olave's School Roll of Honour Volume One of three Volumes.

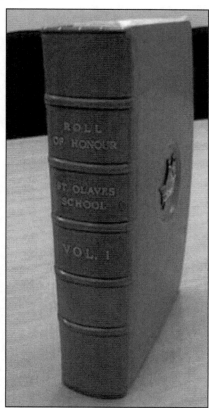

The St Olave's School Memorial, flanked by King George V and Queen Mary's portraits, a gift given following their visit to the School in Tooley Street during 1918.

1913 – Jack Gill (back row second from left) Fred Norris (front row second from left) Didi Maybrook (front row second from right) Sid Terry (front row far right)

The Main Hall at Tooley Street as the Olavian Fallen would have known it in the years leading up to the Great War.

Prologue

"He whom this scroll commemorates was numbered among those who, at the call of King and Country, left all that was dear to them, endured hardness, faced danger, and finally passed out of the sight of men by the path of duty and self sacrifice, giving up their own lives that others might live in freedom. Let those who come after, see to it that his name be not forgotten".

The tribute of King George V to the members of His Majesty's Forces that died as a result of the Great War 1914 to 1918, still arouses strong sentiments.

This book, originally written in preparation for the eightieth anniversary of the Armistice, attempts to go some distance to upholding that sentiment. In a time when most young people in our country, have no experience of war, when traditional ideas concerning duty, morality, national pride and religion are being questioned and sometimes undermined, it is important to reflect on what life was like for the 'Olavian Fallen'.

What sent them off to war with such enthusiasm, why did they not moan and reject the harshness of their lives, why did some resign themselves so readily to the loss of their young lives. How did they live, what kind of individuals were they, what might they have achieved if they had lived longer lives. What did they do to distinguish themselves in the short time that was allowed them. What were the circumstances of their deaths, and how can we, their 'collective' children, grandchildren, great nieces, nephews, and great grandchildren, live up to their hopes, their values, their standards? Certainly, by the end of this story of the Olavian's and the Great War, we should be motivated to try.

Times may change, but all Olavian's have a commonality with these men. We were all at one time their age, and took the opportunity to pass through the halls and corridors of a fine School with its own culture, history and expectations. Society in the world at large has changed, but an Olavian will always be an Olavian, despite the change in buildings, uniforms, sports and syllabi.

Brett-Smith's anthem, sung eagerly at Old Olavian dinners in London each year, continues that sense of pride endemic in the pre-war era. 'Olaf to raise the song, Olaf to bear along, Olaf to right the wrong...'

Till all our fight be fought... this is a tribute to the 'Fallen'.

Foreword

Dear reader

During its 453 year history, St Olave's Grammar School has seen some fascinating changes from Shakespeare's Elizabethan London to the vast, cosmopolitan city we know today. Few of its experiences, however, can have had such a profound impact as the First World War, which saw so many courageous Olavians sacrifice their lives for their country.

As I reflect on previous Headmasters, staff, students and families, it is almost impossible to conceive of their feelings at the loss of nearly 200 men, all linked by their attendance at St Olave's Grammar School. This book will give you a rare insight into their biographies, with individual details, passionate narratives, letters home and school-masters' reflections interwoven into the story alongside specialist chapters on different aspects of the Great War campaign from aerial to naval combat, medical support to artillery technology.

At the centenary of the commencement of The Great War it is a fitting tribute to these men that one of our own Old Olavians has researched and drawn together the details of this significant part of the school's history. Peter Leonard's Till all our fight be fought allows us, the current Olavians, to connect with and remember the 'fallen' and to take a glimpse into their lives, thoughts and feelings.

Aydın Önaç
Headmaster

Introduction

One hundred and ninety-two men died as far as the School was advised. Many others may have perished on the battlefields, who to date, are not commemorated. Seventy-five were officers, one hundred and seventeen were in the ranks. Three won the Military Medal – Stephen Bishopp, Fred Husk and Idwal Jones, and five, the Military Cross – William Halliwell, Robert Hearn, Douglas Oake, Sid Terry and Arthur Vernall.

There were twenty-three non-commissioned officers and four men were 'mentioned in despatches' – Fred Defries, William Oliver, John Hood and Fred Husk. The eldest Olavian to fall was Harold Ryley Senior, ex pupil and master, followed closely by journalist, Beaumont Fletcher, a friend of H.G.Abel, Rushbrooke's replacement as Head, both men well into their forties, and the youngest just sixteen years. Twenty-six of the Fallen didn't leave school until the War had commenced.

Three masters were gazetted as officers and died as a result of the conflict – Cecil Edmunds, Grantley Le Chavetois and Harold Ryley Senior. The highest ranked officer amongst the 'Fallen' was Major Fred Bennett; he was accompanied by fourteen captains, twenty-one lieutenants and thirty-six second lieutenants.

Nine school captains lost their lives; eight of them had held the post between 1911 and 1917. The practice at that time of appointing two school captains per year meant that between 1911 and 1915, all six had perished, with one from 1916 and one from 1917. Their combined intellect, sophistication, academic excellence and commitment had to be marvelled at; the names alone mean much to many Old Olavians throughout the twentieth century:

Howard Keesey 'the intellectual'; Leslie Sanders 'the realist'; Noel Hamilton 'the cultured Irishman'; Fred Norris the 'Hertford winner'; Didi Maybrook 'the archaelogist'; Olly Wade 'the scientist';

INTRODUCTION

Jimmy Jones 'the all rounder'; Teddy Cock 'the mercurial artist' and Vic Budd, 'the submarine chaser'.

As the War progressed and warfare became more static, whilst also introducing ever more destructive technological invention, unsurprisingly there was an increased frequency of Olavian deaths reported. In the final year of the War in 1918, twice as many of the School's own were killed, as in the first year in 1915. As final signs of victory appeared in the last nine weeks of hostilities, enemy desperation dramatically grew and 18 Olavians were to die during the last sixty days before the Armistice was signed.

Of the War's survivors, one received the Victoria Cross – Alf Pollard, two received the Distinguished Service Order – AJ Pelling and S.W.Bunker; The DSM went to A.W. Herbert and the DCM to H.E.Bowman, Pollard again and Monte Richardson.

Twenty-four surviving Olavians in total were awarded the Military Cross (including Pollard). Another ten received the Military Medal, and a further thirteen were mentioned in despatches.

Six Olavians received foreign honours for their part in various activities: the Order of Leopold 1 of Belgium to A.J.Pelling; the Belgian Croix de Guerre to Messr's Olivier and Pelling; the Cavaliere of the Order of St Maurice and St Lazarus, to S.W.Bunker; the Medaille Militaire to W.B.Betts, the French Croix de Guerre, to Messr's R.Barton and J.D.Bradly, and finally the Legion of Honour to J.D. Bradly.

Despite their many academic and athletic differences, the Olavians that joined the British Forces in the Great War, were attracted mainly to the Infantry, and were developed through the familiar process of Cadet Corps, London Regiment training and then on to other Regiments when commissioned. Seventy-nine recruits augmented the ranks of the thirty-three London regiments, before some left to gain commissions.

The cross section of Regimental choice for Olavians was broad, starting with 'Premier' line regiments like, the Grenadier Guards (the Harvard brothers), the Bedfordshires (Roeber and Stables) and the Royal Berkshires (Taffs and Lansdale), through to 'second ranks' like the Yorkshires (Dell), the Wiltshires (Maybrook, Terry and P.Grant) and the Royal Sussex (Knifton, Knox and Rings).

Some however, ventured into other spheres of highly technical work, and highly risky, but adventurous branches of the services.

Nine Olavian Fallen had been gradually seconded from the Infantry into the fledgling Royal Flying Corps. Seven of them were officers and pilots flying DH2s, Sobwith Strutters, BE2s and Nieuport 17s.

Fifteen joined the Artillery: Royal Garrison, Royal Field, Royal Horse and, the Honourable Artillery Company, in various capacities – seven were officers with Bennett, the Senior Olavian Officer, amongst them.

Five worked in the Royal Army Medical Corps, with either relevant experience or on religious grounds, as stretcher-bearers.

Seven were attached to the Royal Navy or the Volunteer Reserve; They served on a variety of ships including HMS *Lysander, Phaeton, Louvain, Queen Mary*. Some were at Jutland and some flew sea missions as part of the Royal Naval Air Service.

Two were in the early Tank Corps from Flers Courcelette in 1916 to Cambrai in later 1917 and after; five were in the new Machine Gun corps.

All in all, the Olavian Fallen served in over sixty-five different Regiments, Batteries, Squadrons, Ship's Companies, Tunnelling Companies, and Brigades. If ever a group of individuals were 'representative' of the War's entire experience, it was these men.

They served on the Home Front, in the mud, cold and rain of the Flanders plain and the French farmlands, in the hills and mountains of northern Italy, in the deserts of Palestine and Mesopotamia, on the beaches of Turkey, and the sparse countryside of Salonika.

Some Olavians stood out for their contribution to a specific arm of the services whether Engineers, Medics, Gunners, Seaman, Flyers, or exponents of the new Tank and Machine Gun technology.

INTRODUCTION

Others showed their courage, fortitude and commitment in the, by now, well known campaigns of the War.

Four died as a result of Gallipoli in summer 1915; eight in the Middle East in 1917/8; The several battles of the Ypres area between 1914 and 1917 took the lives of thirty-five. The Somme campaign of 1916 was responsible for the death of twenty-three men, three of whom were killed on the infamous 1st July (Hocking, Prout and S.Weatherston).

The Kaiser's Offensive in March 1918 led to the demise of another thirteen, with Bapaume, Peronne and the Hindenburg Line increasing the 'Pro Patria Mortui' lists in the School magazine, by another nineteen. Even after the signing of the Armistice, more returning and weakened boys and men added to the final number by another eleven – some claimed by the influenza virus circulating over the winter of 1918/9.

Overall, ten pairs of Old Olavian brothers sacrificed their lives during the conflict, with maybe more that are unknown from the combined total of over 250 male siblings of the Fallen; from the Walkers, Hollands and Weatherstons, to the Talbots, Berrows and Trotmans, not forgetting the Hamiltons, Harvards, Halliwells and, of course, the Ryleys.

During the long four years of war, barely a few days passed before news of another casualty reached the School, usually a victim of exploding artillery shells and shrapnel, sniper rifle fire or machine gun enfilade fire during attacks. The three bloodiest days of the conflict for Olavians, aside from the first day of the Somme in 1916, proved to be 18th September 1916 at Flers Courcelette, the 7th June, 1917 at Messines and Wytschaete, and the 28th March 1918 at Arras.

These were all clever, educated, committed boys and men; they were a cut above, and their lives, though short, provide strong example. We must remember what they gave up for us.

CHAPTER 1
Bermondsey and the School

St Olave's and St Saviour's Schools have always been inextricably linked with the urban south London riverside parish of Bermondsey and have been for their entire history since foundation in 1561. Even today, many years after St Olave's moved to Orpington, connections remain strong with Southwark Cathedral at the southern foot of London Bridge.

Many of the scholars attending the new School building, which had opened in 1893 replacing the 1855 version, resided with their families within the boundaries of Bermondsey, with the north side on the river, in the west, London Bridge and Borough High Street, in the east, Southwark Park, and on the south side, Great Dover Street and the Old Kent Road. Others travelled from the neighbouring parishes of Rotherhithe, Southwark, Walworth, Deptford, Lambeth and beyond.

Originally, most of the area surrounding the small island called 'Beormund's Ey' was uncultivated marsh lying below the high tide of the River Thames, until the Church, in the form of Bermondsey Abbey, built there. By the eleventh century, the area was first mentioned as a royal manor in the Domesday Book and the Abbey's creation of the 'Bermondsey Wall' with its dykes and drainage channels, had shored up the river's banks. The parish, of quite small geography – no more than one mile square, remained unchanged for centuries with tenant farmers ploughing corn, dairymen tending cows and pigs in meadowland and woodsmen storing nuts and acorns from the woods, all interspersed amongst the watery marsh fed by the river's tributary, the Neckinger.

Industrialisation and the development of the Thames Docklands, in the nineteenth century dramatically altered the area. The London to Greenwich Railway arrived in 1834 with its 878 brick arches hovering permanently over the network of terraced houses and streets. The population grew from 17,000 to 87,000 people between 1801 and 1881. Trade and industry flourished – leather making and its noxious odours together with hop brewing, had been there for centuries with well known brands, Courage, Noakes, Bevington's and Sarsons, but now the riverside wharves with famous names like 'Hays', Butler's and Yardley's , proliferated and both lightermen and watermen offloaded tea, butter, bacon and cheese from ocean going clipper ships and steamers, to store 'London's Larder' into their warehouses. Food processing and packaging commenced with Pearce Duff's Custard Powder, Lipton's Tea's, Crosse & Blackwell's Pickles, Southwell's and Hartley's Jams, Jacob's and Peek Frean's Biscuits.

Sadly, with industry, came poor living conditions, bad sanitation, killer diseases, over-crowding and poverty, immortalised for many by Dicken's descriptions of Jacob's Island in his fictional novel, Oliver Twist. Large families lived closely together, they knew their neighbours, who were usually poor like themselves, community spirit was strong, entertainment was in the corner pub, the music hall, the early cinema or the street-markets.

By 1900, Charles Booth's survey summed up Bermondsey's social geography saying the fairly comfortable, often railwaymen, commercial salesmen and travellers were to be found in the streets south of Southwark Park Road, and the poor, usually leather workers, glue makers and jam and sweet makers, were north of it around Neckinger Street and Spa Road.

However the housing stock was very similar across the area and the differences between class levels was often extremely delicate. A family could become destitute within weeks if a seasonal job was lost, or injuries like burning or scalding were sustained in the factories heavily staffed with local women.

Many remember Bermondsey by its blend of smells from leather dyeing, sugar used in food processing, brewing hops and, of course, poverty. But Bermondsey also benefitted from some great benefactors and social pioneers, from Charles Booth and his street by street social surveys, Dr Alfred Salter, Bermondsey MP and Doctor to the poor, and his 'garden city' developments for the parish, to the Reverend Scott Lidgett of the 'Bermondsey Settlement', Mr H.W. Butcher of the Wolseley Mission and Dr Selina Fox of the Grange Road Medical Mission for Women.

Some of these influential community social reformers joined with the owners of local businesses to give back to the community through governorship and wardenship of St Olave's school – Charles Oscar Gridley, a wealthy hop merchant, John and Robert Courage, of the brewing family, Leonard Shuter and Giles Pilcher, Adam Willson of Willson's Wharf, and Topham Richardson, also a hop merchant – all helped the school considerably at the turn of the century. Gridley, himself, supported Headmaster Rushbrooke's innovative and experimental educational ideas from the 1890's onwards. It was these ideas that helped form the intellect, confidence, physical fitness and sometime academic excellence of the 'Olavian Fallen' generation.

Elocution lessons were introduced into the syllabus, Science, English, Carpentry and Music were developed. French was taught by the direct 'Gouin' method and a French debating society was set up. Singing was encouraged and an orchestra became possible after the donation of an organ by the Courage family. Parent's open evenings were offered and an inter-classroom telephone system was installed.

Rushbrooke was most interested in the physical health of his scholars and developed physical activities by pushing for a swimming bath and fives courts on the one hand, and commencing annual school camps away at East Preston in Sussex, on the other. A School Doctor and Dentist were also later appointed and comparative physical development statistics were kept and constantly compared to the Public Schools. Specific 'Old Boys' were recruited to help with the camps – Grantley Le Chavetois and A.C. Wilson, the cricketer, amongst them, as well as Olavian Luminaries,

F.G. Forder, later Head of St Dunstan's and S.W. Grose, later a Don at Cambridge.

The Head spoke of going further – teaching Russian and introducing wireless telegraphy as early as 1910, and by 1918 he was considering teaching Aviation. In his attempt to lift the school to the level of the great Public Schools, he introduced extra-curricular shooting facilities at the playing fields in Dulwich, thanks to Gridley's generosity. Overall, Rushbrooke's initiatives built upon his predecessor Johnson's already impressive scholastic achievements, so much so that by 1910 it was reported that ten 'Old Boys' were Headmasters of English Grammar Schools.

When war broke out, both the School and the Parish of Bermondsey 'did its bit' according to the saying of the time. The School formed a Cadet Corps, used the Dulwich fields to grow vegetables, and made munitions in their metal-workshops. On 15th February 1918, Rushbrooke and the School were honoured by a visit from King George V and Queen Mary.

The parish under the mayoralties of Councillor's Fells, Hart, Vezey and Shearring also prepared for war. The 1/22nd Battalion of the County of London Territorials had been formed earlier in 1909 from their Abbey Street drill hall. The 12th (Service) Battalion of the East Surrey Regiment had been raised in May 1915 by the Mayor and Borough. John Veale-Williams, later father of a Fallen Olavian son, Managing Director of Messr's Austin's Ltd of Bermondsey, and also an Alderman on the Council, worked with the Government to make as much liquid ammonia as possible as the only neutraliser to the enemy's poison gas in use in 1915. This proved to be a supportive stop gap until effective gas-masks could be made in volume for the front.

Brandram Brothers, refiners of salt petre and sulphur, engaged with the Government to supply vast amounts of explosives made by a skilled workforce; Burt, Boulton & Hayward provided timber for bridge-building and aeroplane production on the one hand, whilst storing food in their warehouses on the other. Exempted staff spent their spare time on air-raid, anti-aircraft and motor transport work. RH & S Rogers in the south of the Parish, specialised in making 20,000 stokes mortar shell-caps and bases in the 1915-1916 year. In their clothing factories, they switched production to half a million cotton bandoliers, flannel body belts, flannel shirts and officer's collars. Peek Frean's 'Biscuit Town' produced many millions of biscuits for the troops in the trenches as well as releasing nearly 1500 men to join up, of which 134 died.

From the Bermondsey leather industry, businesses like Salomon & Co, Bevington and Sons, Harbord & Poole and many other smaller tanners, curriers, dressers and finisher firms converged together on massively reduced manpower, to supply most of the army's needs for Sam Brown belts, saddles, bootlaces, boots, harnesses, straps and wallets. At Surrey Docks, the stevedores and dockers of the Cunard Company unloaded shells and food from their 26 commercial liners throughout the war, and loaded fuel and soldiers to transport elsewhere, much of the work being done during night-time enemy air-raids.

In the local community, voluntary organisations also played an important role. Those local boys who had benefitted from the opportunity of attending the Boy's Brigade or the Boy Scouts, had learnt vital lessons in self-reliance, personal initiative, survival outdoors, map-reading and so on. Cecil Talbot was one of the local scout leaders and was also to become a Fallen Olavian. On the outbreak of war, scout troops acted as cyclist messengers, interpreters to Belgian refugees and as guides to troops. However, within a few months, all the leaders had enlisted and the troops were run by their patrol leaders. Boy's Brigades were similarly active from their Baptist Church bases under the organisation of Henry Morriss, an ex-Mayor.

Bermondsey's first Victoria Cross, and Medaille Militaire winner, Lance Corporal Fred Holmes of the King's Own Yorkshire Light Infantry, had a huge impact on the men of the borough and without doubt, encouraged more to enlist during 1915. Born in Abbey Street and attending Neckinger L.C.C. School, he had joined the army at 16, before the war started. At Le Cateau, having saved a wounded man, he drove an allied gun carriage with horses to safety by replacing the wounded driver. Seriously wounded himself a month later at Bethune, he was still recuperating in Millbank Hospital when the King had asked to see him and was given a public reception at Bermondsey Town Hall by Mayor Joseph Hart followed by a procession through his home streets.

The following war years saw a high level of committed municipal fund-raising activities by successive Mayors, Councillors and Aldermen – A division of V.A.D. workers was started with help from the Red Cross, Mayor Shearring acted as Chairman of the War Savings Committee and set up a 'Wounded Soldiers Day' in the Parish. Mayor Vezey opened Food Economy exhibitions and set up a 'Comfort's Fund' for Bermondsey men on active service. He and his wife supported many fund initiatives from 'Smoke's for Soldiers and Sailors' to 'Sick and Wounded Horses' to 'Church Army Huts'. Mayor Hart opened the Southwark Park Road Rifle Club and ran several Flag Days for Belgian orphans and to provide gramophones to 12th East Surrey men in training! Mayor Fells was involved in the formation of the 2nd Battalion, South London Regiment (Volunteer Training Corps) at the St Katherine Naval Brigade drill hall in Silwood Street. The unit acted as home defence, digging trenches, using machine guns for anti-aircraft work and manning gun stations locally through the night. By 1917, air-raids were occurring more frequently over Bermondsey as the machines became more reliable and more powerful. This culminated in three bombings on Spa Road, Keeton's Road and Southwark Park Road on a night in December.

Following the long war and the eventual armistice, the Borough initiated 'The Bermondsey and Rotherhithe War Memorial Fund' on March 12th 1919. Fells and Gridley were involved. Mill Pond Bridge was chosen as the location for a monument as it was the junction between Bermondsey and Rotherhithe. Two years later it was unveiled by Mrs Speer who had lost three sons in the conflict. Reverend Lidgett, who lost his own son John, an Olavian, offered prayers. Present that day was Arthur Carr, Chairman of Peek Frean & Co, and a generous donor to the Fund. He should have the last words....

"We must not forget the suffering of others in the war – those who suffered illness, were wounded, blinded, or crippled. But the men whose memory we honour today gave their ALL for us. They laid down their lives that we might live. Our hearts are full of sorrow at the loss of so many faithful friends. But full also, of gratitude and pride for all they have done for us. Each one of us, does indeed, owe them a debt of gratitude, a debt both deep and inextinguishable. Do we fully realise this? Do we realise that it was not worthwhile their dying for us, if we were not worth dying for? May we prove ourselves worthy of their sacrifice! Let us never forget what this monument commemorates!"

CHAPTER 2
First Ypres

The hectic first few months of the Great War saw the gradual annihilation of the small, professional and experienced British Army that had travelled so confidently to France in August 1914.

The 'Old Contemptibles' of the British Expeditionary Force (B.E.F) first clashed with the advancing German Army at a line drawn in the countryside near the Belgian town of Mons. The Germans had arrived at this point by following the ambitious 'Schlieffen Plan' (a tactic involving swooping down on Paris from the north east by moving swiftly through peaceful Belgium).

Troops, embarking for Le Havre or Rouen from Southampton, were at the front within less than two weeks, having route marched over sixty miles. At Mons, the regulars and the recalled reservists prepared their defences along the Mons/Conde Canal, under the direction of Generals Haig and Smith-Dorrien, whilst the volunteering civilians were queuing at the enlisting offices at home.

On the 23rd August, German Cavalry, followed by intensive artillery, started attacks and bombardments on II Corps commanded by Smith-Dorrien, but not on I Corps under Haig. Hours later, a massive enemy infantry charge – focused on the bridges at Nimy and at Obourg, protected by 3rd Division (4th Royal Fusiliers and 4th Middlesex) – broke through. The French infantry led by General Lanrezac planned to retreat, forcing the British under Sir John French to follow suit. The famous 'Retreat from Mons' had begun, caused by poor understanding and communication between the Allied chiefs and further upset by political intrigues between the British Generals. Sixteen hundred casualties gave a minor glimpse of what was to come.

Three days later, Smith-Dorrien's extremely fatigued, II Corps were routed again further south at Le Cateau, where, despite orders to continue the retreat, Smith-Dorrien decided to stand and fight, unknowingly saving the B.E.F. and halting the German advance, giving sufficient regrouping time, causing 3,000 casualties and disobeying orders all at the same time. Some months later, this very same decisive General was controversially sacked by his Commander-in-Chief.

The B.E.F's retreat through Compiegne to the Marne River, forced a link with the main body of the French Army. By the 5th September, the Germans had decided to 'wheel' inwards and stood between the Allies and Paris, at a distance of less than thirty miles. However they were out of position for the first time, and successive passionate French attacks at the flanks and communication junctions of the respective enemy armies, gave positive results. The Germans retreated forty miles to the Aisne River (where French General Joffre attacked again a few days later to little effect), German General Von Moltke was replaced with Von Falkenhayn, and the static war of trench life began, as a stable line started to be recognised.

Strong Allied defences now persuaded Von Falkenhayn to move north in the 'Race to the Sea' to attack Belgian and British Forces under Rawlinson near Antwerp in early October. The City fell on the 9th and encouraged the Germans to move on to Calais. But they had to get through the B.E.F at Ypres first.

First Corps were sent to Ypres to join the newly arrived 7th Division. They started to dig into the earth and prepare. From the 18th October, for three weeks, the Germans sent regular mass infantry attacks against the developing defences. More equipment was being transported in, more men were arriving, a 'hinterland' of communications was now possible, as the B.E.F was in one place.

The first battle of Ypres represented the five combined battles of Armentieres, Messines Ridge, Langemarck, Gheluvelt and Nonne Boschen – the B.E.F suffered over 58,000 casualties, German losses were double. Attrition warfare had begun.

Four Olavian infantrymen, serving in the Allied armies, died in

Flanders and France between November 1914 and March 1915 – the 'territorial', the 'observer', the 'legionnaire' and the Suffolk 'expeditionary'. The eldest, Gordon Ryder at twenty-nine, was a private in the London Scottish, the famous 14th, encamped south of Ypres on the Messines Ridge; the second eldest was Leonard Tait, a rifleman, at twenty-three, a few miles along the same line with the Queen's Westminster Rifles, the 16th Londons; the third, one day younger, also twenty-three and serving as a 'Caporal' in Joffre's French Army, was the English born, Len Bendixen. Finally, the youngest, James Roberts, a newly appointed second lieutenant in the 2nd Battalion, the Suffolk Regiment at only 18 years, stationed seven miles south west of Ypres at Locre.

Their school years at St Olaves suggest that certainly Tait and Bendixen may have known each other; they were the first of the Fallen, and of the few soldiers of real pre- war experience. Gordon Ryder and his brother Arthur, sons of Arthur and Helena from Wallington in Surrey, came from a long line of 'exiled' Scots, living in London; both attended St Olave's; Gordon left at 15 and apprenticed as a clerk in the London County and Midland Bank in the City. He had worked his way to a management position, when the outbreak of war put an end to his banking career. When he had started work, he enlisted as a part-time territorial in the London Scottish, possibly influenced by the level of press attention associated with the Boer War in South Africa, but more likely just to use the social facilities of the club for rugby, football, and the much awaited annual 'Burns night' parties. Six years later, he transferred to the 7th Middlesex Volunteers, but moved straight back to the Territorials in 1914.

As an early volunteer with some experience, he was kitted out and mobilised, reaching Le Havre on the 18th September. Training followed at St Omer and then the long march to Ypres. The London Scottish were the first territorial battalion in France. However, they were used on lines of communication for many weeks, as engineers, dockers, transporters, and for general policing. They were in Paris, whilst the Marne was fought. Ypres proved to be their first 'blooding' and much looked forward to by the educated, mature, kilted men in the ranks.

Leonard Sidney Tait was one of three sons and a daughter of warehouseman, Edward Tait and wife Emily, of Avenue Road, Anerley, born in 1890. He spent four years at St Olave's, leaving in 1906 aged sixteen to join the H.M. Education Department as a clerk, and in 1914, becoming one of the earliest volunteers, joining up from his home near Herne Hill. In August, he went to Westminster to enlist in the 1st Battalion of the 16th Londons as a private, and was aboard ship to Le Havre on 1st November. He missed the battles of First Ypres, but was part of the relieving and maintaining force that occupied the Armentieres sector, after the heavy fighting had ceased. What Private Tait witnessed was the rain, mud, cold, wind and the onset of winter in the first hastily built, poorly positioned trench systems built by the B.E.F.

Leonard Bendixen, son of a Bermondsey leather manufacturer had spent two years at the school, leaving in 1906 aged sixteen, in the romantic gesture of the times, following the image of P.C.Wren's 'Beau Geste', Len sailed for France and joined the French Foreign Legion as an ordinary soldier. It is unclear as to how many pre-war years he served, but he was involved in the early defence by Joffre's forces of the border from Verdun and Amiens to the Marne.

Born on 26th October, 1890 to Julius Carl Bendixen a leather merchant, born in Peckham and his wife, Alice from Hemel Hempstead, Leonard had an elder brother by six years called Charles Sidney who sadly had died at just 18 years in 1903 and two sisters, one elder, who died as an infant, Maud and another, Gladys a year younger. It was to his sister Gladys that he willed his estate on his death.

He was rewarded for conspicuous bravery in his first engagement with the 'Porte a l'ordre du regiment', and promoted to the rank of 'Caporal'. As the best rifleman in his company, he was awarded the distinctive badge, the 'Cor de chasse en or', and finally, was 'mentioned in despatches' by his captain for an honourable act.

James Roderick Trethowan Roberts was from a younger generation. He had attended the School from 1908 to 1913, a period of five years, leaving at seventeen to go to Sandhurst to become an army officer. Sixteen of the boys that joined St Olave's in his year were eventually slain on the battlefields. James was the first of his year to enlist, to become a serving officer, and to arrive in Flanders. Born on the 8th March 1896, he was the son of William and Adelaide Roberts of King's Avenue, Clapham Park.

The London Scottish, south of Ypres and Gheluvelt, fought off skirmishes, whilst the enemy, in unbelievably high numbers attacked the British 1st Division. Gheluvelt fell on the 31st October. General Lomax was badly wounded with other senior officers, by a shell landing at Hooge Chateau. Brigadier-General Fitzclarence pushed the men of the South Wales Borderers and the Worcesters to fix bayonets and charge across the open ground between Polygon and Gheluvelt and on to the Menin Road. Their courage stopped the enemy advance.

The London Scottish meanwhile, with Gordon Ryder in the line, were anxious and excited to get into the fight, and stop the enemy taking the village of Wytschaete, and more importantly, the Messines Ridge. Conflicting orders from above, coupled with the Battalions total inexperience of battle conditions, provoked grave consequences. As they advanced over the Ridge in formation to support the cavalry as ordered, they were mown down by enemy guns, with 50% casualties; some dropped into shell holes; the enemy attacked at night, and fought with those remaining, the British line retreated, without telling the Scottish remnants. They were eventually saved, by the smoke from a burning haystack. Ronald Colman, later a Hollywood actor, survived the attack, Gordon Ryder was declared missing, presumed killed.

Caporal Leonard Bendixen was killed in action on the 25th November 1914 at Kondiat el Biad in Morocco during the battle of El Herri against the Berber Zaian Confederation. His father Julius, in a letter informing the staff at St Olave's, concluded, 'May England find many sons as brave as my poor boy in this time of need'. Julius and Alice had lost both of their sons, but their daughter later married Reginald Nourse and had a daughter but not before both had passed themselves during the 1920s.

Shortly after the baptism of the London Scottish at Messines, the Queen's Westminsters arrived in the Ypres sector of Flanders. They were based at Armentieres where the Allies had survived furious fighting for possession of Ploegsteert Wood from the 13th October to 2nd November. Although the town of Armentieres had been occupied by the Germans in August 1914, the wood was never won, owing to the superhuman efforts of the protecting battalions, the Somersets and the Warwickshires. The Q.W.R's, with Len Tait, relieved these weary battalions, during the winter.

On Christmas Eve, early in the morning, with enemy activity at a low ebb, the day before the famed football match and the No Man's Land truce, Len Tait was shot by a sniper, whilst involved on an observation patrol. He died back in his trench shortly afterwards, attended by his officers, Lieutenant Henderson Scott and Captain Julian Henriques.

By the end of the year, casualties amounted to over 90,000 men; the opposing armies had lost their mobility, they sat in damp, waterlogged holes in the ground and waited for spring. 90% of the soldiers who had laughingly boarded ship for France, as if on a day trip, were either dead, maimed, wounded, captured or psychologically damaged.

The remaining few officers of experience now had to turn their minds to training the civilian army waiting at home. 1915 had arrived. Meanwhile, Second Lieutenant James Roberts of the 2nd Suffolks had just arrived in France on the 5th December. His Battalion had been attached to the 14th Brigade, of 5 Division, 2 Corps and sent to Belgium by day and night route march. Shortly before Christmas, the tired new arrivals, together with the survivors of the August battle of Le Cateau, engaged the enemy in the ferocious battle of Givenchy, which continued spasmodically until the end of January.

It had started on the 18th December, when the Indian Division based in Givenchy had been attacked by German troops from the direction of Cuinchy. Within two days the British 1st Division were there to give support. By the 22nd, the Germans had eased off, and previously lost trenches, were regained. The battle resumed on January 25th, 1915, with the 1st Division repulsing a major enemy attack. Four days later, another advance was blocked at Cuinchy. By the end of the month, the Germans had changed tactics, and the Suffolks, who had withstood the daily pressures in their first experience of the trenches in winter, were relieved. Two months later, James Roberts, seriously wounded by shell fire, died from his wounds on the 3rd March, five days before his 19th birthday. He is buried in the Churchyard at Locre.

CHAPTER 3
The Royal Navy

It was to be the ninth ship in the Royal Navy to have been given the name, the first having fought the Spanish Armada in 1573. Its launch at Portsmouth in February 1906, after a hurried spurt of building activity, had cataclysmic effects on the 'Arms race' already escalating between Great Britain and Germany. 'HMS *Dreadnought*', as a new breed of fighting ship, immediately outdated all existing technology, prompting the German Navy to redouble its efforts in the years approaching the Great War. By the time of the decisive battle of Jutland, just a decade later in 1916, Germany boasted over twenty similar battleships.

With the investment of such large sums of money and time, both national powers presumed that victory in any future conflict would be largely dependent on naval prowess. In fact, the opposite proved true. Although both navies were vital in the struggle to protect colonial possessions, and to maintain food supplies, their use to affect the outcome of the Great War, was negligible. A major reason for this was the inherent conservatism and caution of the naval leadership of both sides. Neither wished to risk all, in a major confrontation, thereby reducing the naval war to a series of side-shows against the backdrop of the trench war. Had the German Navy invested as much into its strikingly successful U-boat submarine programme, as it did in its surface vessels, the war at sea could have had a very different outcome.

The first six months of the war witnessed the battles of Coronel and the Falkland Islands, in which British Admirals Cradock and Sturdee routed the German Colonial Navy under Von Spee in the Pacific. Closer to home, the battle of Heligoland Bight, prompted by Admiral Beatty's daring raid into German waters, provoked Von Ingenohl's blockade of British east coast ports, from Hartlepool to Scarborough and Whitby. In addition to this, the entry of the German battle cruisers, 'Goeben' and 'Breslau' to the Dardanelles, presaged the entry of Turkey into the War against the British, and the disastrous amphibious campaign on the Gallipoli peninsula.

By the time winter had turned into springtime in 1915, three of seven Olavians, who all eventually gave their lives at sea for their country in the Great War, were already in the service of the Royal Navy. The remaining four would all be in action by 1917.

Even though the seven all had naval service in common, their respective roles were extremely diverse; two served in the Royal Naval Air Service as pilots, one, a flight sub lieutenant, Vic Budd, in the North Sea, and the other, an air mechanic second class, William Dodson, in the Mediterranean; two served in the Royal Naval Volunteer Reserve both as able seamen, Alwynne Fairlie on HMS *Queen Mary*, and John Weatherston ; two served in the Royal Navy, one as Ship's Writer second class, Roland Foreman on HMS *Phaeton*, and the other as a Surgeon Sub Lieutenant, Eugene Pearson on HMS *Lysander*; and the seventh, in the Royal Naval Fleet Auxiliary – Wireless Telegraphy section, William Dale-James, working from time to time on the 'Lusitania', the 'Marmora' and the 'Kaiser-I-hind' in the Atlantic and the Pacific.

The eldest was the kindly, whimsical William Rushbrooke Dale-James. He was born in 1883 to a brother, Kenneth, both sons of a Sheffield doctor of some literary distinction, who, in turn, was the son of a President of the Wesleyan Conference, and editor of 'The Watchman'. William's 'rapid observation', 'retentive memory' and 'even temper' helped him move comfortably through a school career of seven years, despite being disadvantaged with a weak constitution. In July 1900 he left the School to take a position as an apprentice at the Metallurgical Laboratory of the Bessemer works, in Rotherham, Yorkshire, at the age of seventeen years, where he began to indulge his love of the natural sciences.

Three years his junior was John Alwynne Fairlie, son of Percy and Blanche Fairlie of West Norwood. Born in September 1886, he attended St Olave's with his brother, Hugh. Within a year of commencing his studies, he contracted meningitis, which set him back considerably. He left the school at sixteen years in 1903 to go into business in the City, leaving behind him descriptions of a 'gentle, cheery and merry boy'. From here he worked as a clerk for a timber merchants and indulged his childhood dream of joining the Royal Navy by giving his leisure time to the 1st London Division of the Royal Naval Volunteer Reserve from 1908. In the six years that elapsed until the outbreak of war, Alwynne won eight prizes in naval competitions. His spare time involvement meant his immediate call up when the conflict commenced.

John Frederick Weatherston was two years younger than Alwynne, and three years older than his brother, Sidney, who fell in the advance of the London Scottish on the first day of the Somme in 1916; a third brother, Harold survived the conflict. The boys were sons of John Weatherston, foreman of a hop warehouse, and wife Clara from Clapham. John attended St Olave's for five years leaving in 1904 aged sixteen to join a London bank as an accountant. His masters spoke of his 'happy disposition' and 'unstained character'; in the years prior to the war, John married, with his wife bearing him a son towards the end of the war.

William Albert Dodson, son of Albert and Harriet of Shepherd's Bush, was born in June 1892, the eldest of seven siblings. Of his two brothers, one was killed in 1917 at Passchendaele, and the other invalided home. He studied at St Olave's for just three years leaving aged fifteen in 1906 to join a Solicitors Office, where he spent the next eight years.

'Painstaking perseverance marked his whole career'. 'His life has been marked by persistent determination in the face of difficulties and quiet assurance in an uphill fight'. Comments from Olavian staff on the struggles of 'Tot' Pearson. Christened Eugene Arthur, he was the youngest of five Pearson boys, born in 1894 to Rector J.G. and Mrs J.Pearson recently of Sydenham, formerly of the Rectory, Leguan, British Guiana. The brothers were often seen walking together over

Tower Bridge to the school, such was their closeness in age. Tot's poor health forced him to constantly battle to succeed; he left the school a fine footballer and cricketer despite his handicaps. Sincere and friendly, he began to study to be a doctor and surgeon in July 1912.

Roland Foreman was younger still, than the previous five; Born in 1896 to George and Elizabeth Foreman of Bermondsey, he spent six years at St Olave's creating an impression of a 'quiet and unassuming' student of 'warm-hearted disposition'. In 1911, aged sixteen, he apprenticed as a clerk in a local business, where he learned his trade as an administrator and book keeper, later becoming a private secretary. He enlisted on his eighteenth birthday in the Royal Navy.

The 'babe' of the group, was a boy of exceptional character. His school friends, teachers and even the Headmaster, all combined to praise his 'remarkable popularity'. Vice-Captain at Rugby, Sergeant-Major in the School Cadet Corps, opening bat for the first XI, first XV centre, and School Captain, Victor John Budd, known as 'Vic' was an original. Born in late October 1898 the eldest of three brothers born to Leonard and Lilian Budd, publicans of the Queens Head in Mortlake and later The Bridge House at the Borough in Southwark, he entered the School with a London County Council (L.C.C.) scholarship, at the age of twelve, bringing his 'love of fun' and his 'lightning repartee' with him. His leadership qualities became obvious along with his athleticism, but it was his foolhardy and fearless approach to life that frequently got him into daring situations, none more so than his training as a 'submarine chasing pilot' at Vendome in 1917.

With the mobile land war turning fast to one of static trench lines on the western front, the German navy planned one more raid to back up Von Ingenohl's efforts. Von Hipper's battle cruiser squadron encountered Beatty's force at Dogger Bank in January 1915 and was quickly defeated. The 'Blucher' was sunk, and the 'Seydlitz' damaged. A change of tactic was needed: Von Ingenohl was replaced by Von Pohl, and German submarines were briefed to destroy all, even neutral, merchant shipping in British waters.

The subsequent sinking of three quarters of a million tonnes of allied shipping in six months, culminating in the sinking of the Lusitania in May, provoked an outcry in America, whose citizens were frequently travelling on board the vessels attacked. By the time that these activities were suspended by Germany, much of the maritime focus had already moved to the Mediterranean where U-boats attacked extremely vulnerable allied battleships supporting the landings at Cape Helles and Suvla Bay.

The on-off submarine campaign began again in early 1916 accompanied by further blockades, this time of Yarmouth and Lowestoft in April. This fresh use of surface vessels soon led to the one great sea confrontation of the war: at Jutland on the 31st May and 1st June.

Admiral Von Hipper had moved north with 40 ships in the vanguard; Scheer's High Seas fleet followed with sixteen Dreadnoughts, six other battleships plus cruisers and destroyers. Jellicoe's Grand fleet at Scapa Flow, and Beatty's battlecruiser fleet at Firth of Forth were alerted by German radio traffic. Beatty's HMS *Lion* sighted the German vanguard which tried to draw Beatty onto the approaching High Seas fleet. Beatty's squadron followed and opened its long range guns. Von Hipper's vanguard responded. Despite heavy damage to the 'Lion', and the sinking of the 'Queen Mary' and the 'Indefatigable', Beatty gave pursuit, and on sighting Scheer's main fleet, turned towards Jellicoe's approach to pressure Scheer to follow, which he did. By 18.30 hours, they attacked each other. The 'Invincible' was sunk, amongst other ships on both sides; Facing complete destruction, Scheer began to look for a way to withdraw. Darkness and fear of torpedo attacks made Jellicoe hold from following. Scheer made base by morning, with heavy losses.

Jellicoe had strategic victory, despite much criticism for his decision to allow Scheer to 'get away'. Jutland effectively ended the activities of the German High Seas Fleet which stayed in port for the rest of the war.

Able Seaman Alwynne Fairlie of the 1st London Division, R.N.V.R was mobilised on the outbreak of war. He was one of the first hundred sailors to be sent to Thurso, where he was drafted firstly onto HMS *Pembroke* and then onto the HMS *Queen Mary*, flagship to Admiral Beatty's 'Lion'. On August 28th, he took part in the first offensive naval engagement of the Great War, at Heligoland Bight. Dreamt up by Commodore Reginald Tyrwhitt of the Harwich force and Roger Keyes, the submarine leader, the plan was approved by Churchill and Battenberg, the First Sea Lord; Jellicoe's fear that it was too risky with Grand Fleet support, led to Beatty (with Alwynne Fairlie) taking the 1st Light Cruiser Squadron and sailing to the destination of Heligoland Island.

'Weak, uncoordinated planning, poor communications, and ineptitude ashore and afloat were all revealed and were unfortunately a portent for the future' was the general opinion of the raid. Tyrwhitt, didn't know Beatty was in support until he'd been lured into a well laid trap engineered by the Germans who knew of allied plans in advance. Various British ships chased and attacked their own ships and submarines. Fortunately the sheer volume of Beatty's force won the day, sinking three enemy battle cruisers and a destroyer, damaging three light cruisers badly, and taking 1200 prisoners including the Flotilla Admiral and Destroyer Commodore. The Heligoland incident, coming, as it did, so early in the war, had a major affect on the morale of the German Navy and the Kaiser, who insisted on more caution in future, and instructed that the Fleet should only engage in a major action, if the odds were overwhelmingly on their side.

HMS *Queen Mary* had survived this first conflict. Built in 1912 as a battle cruiser, it sported eight of the new 13.5 inch guns; in comparison with its German counterparts, it was slower by 6 knots, and less well armoured to the tune of 33%. The addition of 'anti-flash doors' in German ships as a result of the severe damage to the Seydlitz at Dogger Bank, was not reciprocated by the British. If a ship was hit, the doors prevented the transmission of fire from gun turret to the magazine.

The HMS *Queen Mary*, not involved at Dogger or at the Dardanelles, next saw major action at Jutland. During its 'quiet' period, Alwynne received orders in late 1915 to go to Whale Island to take an advanced Gunnery course, having passed third in his ship's company in gunnery whilst on board. These orders were, however, revoked at the last moment by the Admiralty, and he was instructed instead to remain in the 'Director-Tower' of the Foretop, as 'Range-Transmitter' to the Guns. Whilst at sea, not during action, he was also 'Captain's man' on the Bridge and had won the Sleeve badge of 'two guns and a star' as a seaman gunner – second class.

The loss of Alwynne Fairlie in the Director-Tower during Jutland has something to do with the lack of 'anti-flash doors'. The 'Queen Mary' had begun to take the brunt of offensive fire from Von Hipper's Squadron, now that the 'Lion' was seemingly destroyed. The ship was hit several times, before a 'sheet of flame' was seen to 'shoot out from the stricken vessel, followed by a thunderous explosion as her magazine exploded'. The ship had been split in two by the cordite flash that had caused the magazine to explode. 1,265 men on board either died in the explosions or drowned in the cold sea, with a fine Olavian.

Stationed at Polegate, William Dodson, R.N.A.S, had come to accept that he would spend his war as an air mechanic working on new prototypes, as well as repairing the tried and tested models. The service had been held back by Jellicoe's inherent conservatism, despite the passionate plea's for 'Aircraft carriers' from influential men like Dunning, Murray Sueter and Hugh Williamson. After Jutland, however, the development by Sopwith of the 'Baby' seaplane and the 'Cuckoo' torpedo plane, led to the conversion of, not only the 'Campania', but also the 'Argus' and the 'Eagle'. Late in 1917, however, William was finally sent with the draft to the eastern Mediterranean. He was based on board HMS *Louvain*, which was torpedoed by a German U-boat on the 29th January 1918, the same day the 'Goeben' was beached and the 'Breslau' sunk at the entrance to the Dardanelles. He was twenty-five and less than three months later the Air Service, of which he was so proud, merged with the Royal Flying Corps, to become the Royal Air Force.

Exactly a month later, nineteen year old Flight Sub Lieutenant Budd, Williams' R.N.A.S compatriot, was also reported missing – in the North Sea. Having completed his pilot's training at Vendome, he had returned home, before drafting to his Squadron base in France. Harold Wensley, his best friend, also to perish in the fields around Caudry the following November, described best what happened.

> "Then at last there came the sad day when his plane (probably a Sopwith 'Pup' seaplane) failed to return from a trip over the North Sea, and, when, after hours of suspense, there arrived a pigeon bearing his pencilled message that his machine had come down and that he was floating upon the water. With characteristic presence of mind, he had indicated his approximate position, and search parties were immediately sent out. His plane was discovered, but its occupant was nowhere to be seen. There was just a bare chance that he had been rescued by some passing vessel".

Vic Budd was never found. It transpired that his machine had been chasing German U-boats and had been struck by surface turret fire.

Wensley has the last words. "His greatest gift was perhaps the gift of leadership. As a pilot he had all the gifts which make the British airman so formidable an antagonist. Of course he was rash, almost foolhardy. If he had known the meaning of fear, he might not have met the tragic end which fell to his lot".

Dale-James the telegraphist, trained by the Marconi Service, moved from London to Seaforth and then to Rosslare in County Wexford, all by the time he was twenty-five, in 1908. War was still a long way distant. After a spell at Crookhaven, and a 'romantic interlude', ending with a dispute with an armed Irishman, he joined the Liverpool to New York liners, and served as a wireless operator on both the 'Lusitania' and the old Cunard liner, the 'Carmania', soon to be converted as one of the first seaplane carriers. In 1910, William, still under contract to Marconi, boarded the flagship of the Infanta of Spain, destined for Brazil. He moved to work on P & O liner, 'Marmora' in April 1913, at which point, Marconi had promoted him to a 'Travelling Inspectorship'.

War brought the 'Marmora' home to be armed as a Light Cruiser. William stayed on the ship and became a Naval Officer of the Royal Naval Fleet Auxiliary – W/T (Wireless Telegraphy) branch. His undoubted, and rare skills as a telegraphist, brought him into contact with 'Blinker' Hall, Alfred Ewing and the extraordinary group of individuals that comprised the first code-breaking operations of 'Room 40' at the Admiralty. In 1914, the Germans recognised that the enemy was reading its wireless telegraphy, but believed that through regular changes, their codes would be secret. 'Room 40' proved them wrong, and were passed massive volumes of enemy radio traffic from men like William Dale-James.

He was, in fact on board the *Marmora* sailing off the coast of Lagos, when he sighted the chase to sink the SS *Karlsruhe*, a German light Cruiser which had enjoyed remarkable success in sinking allied Merchantmen in the West Indies and Atlantic. Wireless communication at this time was unreliable due to range variation and poor reception leading to misidentification. Soon after, they put to harbour in Malta and the ship's company recuperated from the effects of too much time at sea.

William took the opportunity to transfer in spring 1915, to troopships in the Pacific bringing the 'Anzacs' from Sydney to Lemnos and Cairo in the Mediterranean in preparation for the Gallipoli landings. The Union Castle's 'Saxon' and P&O' s 'Palermo' and 'Kaiser-i-hind' were amongst several vessels that he served on. Later in 1915, he move north again, into far colder climates, and spent much of 1916 in the north sea. By the end of that year, his health was suffering and he was moved ashore, where he took up a post as Marconi Instructor first at Newcastle, and then at Portsmouth, where he spent his time training wireless operators for the Mercantile Marine. In 1918, he found himself in Southampton, as Superintendent of the depot, and later as temporary manager of the East Ham stores. Most of these assignments were met with too little leave to see his wife, Mary in Amersham, not enough sleep and rest, and far from improving his physical constitution, he contracted pneumonia and died in hospital at Highgate just three weeks before peace was signed, on 18th October 1918, he was thirty-five years old.

Surgeon Sub Lieutenant Eugene Pearson had contracted influenza on board HMS *Lysander* at around the same time as William got pneumonia. The long war was coming to an end, most men were tired, mentally drained, and susceptible to the many viruses circulating. Clearly as a Surgeon on board,'Tot' was vulnerable. As news of his death reached his home, news also arrived of his success in the medical examinations the previous year for the M.R.C.S and L.R.C.P. His body was brought home, and he was buried at the Crystal Palace District Cemetery in London He was twenty-four years old.

Roland Foreman had spent most of the war years working his way from Ship's Writer 4th Class, to 1st Class, first on HMS *Pembroke*, then *Halcyon* and finally on HMS *Phaeton*. Enlisting in October 1914, he was first stationed at Lowestoft, where he was injured in the enemy bombardment of that port. Later, in 1917, he joined one of the most famous of ship's companies, one that had seen considerable action at both the Dardanelles and Jutland. It was, in fact, the 'Phaeton' that had conveyed Sir Ian Hamilton and his General Staff from Marseilles to Lemnos in preparation for the Gallipoli landings. A year later, on 31st May 1916, it was 'Phaeton' along with 'Galatea' that first met with Hipper's vanguard at Jutland. In late November of 1918, again the 'Phaeton', and Roland Foreman were present at the surrender of the Scheer's German High Seas fleet to Beatty, forty miles east of May Island.

'The weather was sunny, but misty. The filthy, neglected condition of the German ships, the scruffy, ill-disciplined state of the German crews on deck, told their own story of what had happened during the previous thirty months to one of the toughest, most professional, and skilful fighting forces in the world'. The *Phaeton* led the enemy cruisers and destroyers into the Firth of Forth harbour.

Whilst in Scotland, he was taken sick with influenza on board, and was taken to hospital in Rosyth in early February 1919. He survived here for only two days as pneumonia had developed, and was not strong enough to withstand the illness. He was buried in Plumstead Cemetery at Woolwich, in London. He was just twenty-two.

John Weatherston also succumbed to the influenza virus, a month later. He was thirty. He had enlisted in late 1916 and subsequently served on both HMS *Victory* and HMS *President* which were training ships, but his death marked the loss of a second son of three for his parents, with the saving grace of a small grandson.

Olavians had, once more, been found working hard, with firm eyes on duty, in interesting and varied parts of the service. They had been present at most of the major naval actions, had become instrumental parts of wireless communication, medical surgery and seaplane operations.

1910 – Fred Norris (back row far left) Sid Terry (back row second from right) Noel Hamilton (middle row third from right) Jack Gill (middle row second from right) Bay Ryley (middle row far left)

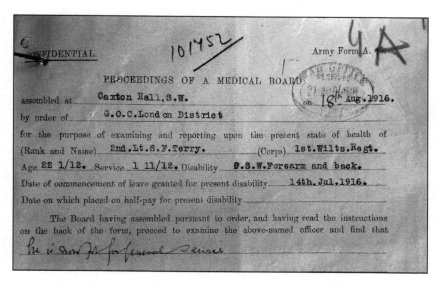

Medical Board report on the gun shot wounds received by Sid Terry.

1903 – Science Sixth – Howard Keesey (back row far left)

Charles Blencowe's memorial inscription on the wall at Tyne Cot in Belgium.

Class Photograph from 1914 with 5 of 28 in Cadet Corps uniform

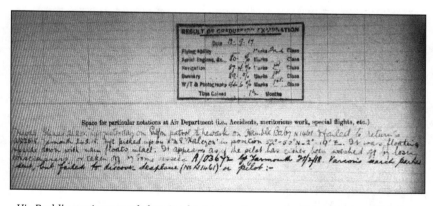

Vic Budd's service record showing his impressive examination scores, and his fate.

Chavvy as form master between 1912-1915 (back row far right)

ROBERTS, JAMES RHODERIC TRETHOWAN, 2nd Lieut., 2nd Battn. Suffolk Regt., elder *s.* of William Roberts, of Errington, 18, King's Avenue, Clapham Park, S.W., and Bridgestone House, Sheppey, Author and Journalist, a member of the literary staff of The Times since 1895; by his wife, Adelaide Rodder, dau. of the late James Trethowan, of Truro, Cornwall; *b.* London, S.W., 4 March, 1896; educ. St. Olave's Grammar School, London, and the Royal Military College, Sandhurst; gazetted 2nd Lieut, 2nd Suffolks, 1 Oct. 1914; went to Ypres, 1 Dec. following, and was killed in action near Ypres, 3 March, 1915, being shot near his trench by a sniper; *unm.* Buried Locre Churchyard.

ROBERTS, JOHN ALFRED, Private R.M.L.I., Ports. 14951, HM S. Good Hope: lost in action off Coronel, on the coast of Chili. 1 Nov. 1914.

James R. T. Roberts.

James Robert's Obituary entry in Duvigny's Roll of Honour.

CHAPTER 4
Gallipoli and the Dardanelles

It could be strongly argued that Asquith's Liberal Government lost the political initiative to maintain Turkey, the controller of the valuable Straits of Constantinople, as an ally, in the run up to the Great War. Six years before the commencement of hostilities, a *Coup d'Etat* in Turkey, brought the 'Young Turks' under Talaat Bey and Enver Pasha to power. They desired to establish stronger links with their old ally, friends since the days of the Crimean conflict, some sixty years earlier. The British Government, however, even though the threat of a German/ Austro-Hungarian presence in the area was a real possibility, acted with cool disdain to the new Turkish leadership, as it refused to initiate the constitutional reform Britain desired.

Things went from bad to worse from 1912. The finely balanced diplomatic situation illustrated by the political lobbying of both Admiral Limpus's British Naval Mission, and General Otto Liman Von Sanders German Military Mission, swung by 1914 towards the Germans. In August, a secret treaty was signed giving German protection to Turkey against the threat of Russian aggression; two Turkish battleships paid for by public subscription in Turkey and under construction in Britain, were appropriated by the British. The Germans saw the immediate opportunity to placate the Turkish people by paying for the building of two new German replacement ships. Finally, the last straw – Pasha, under pressure from Von Sanders, allowed two German cruisers through the Dardanelles, and refused access to the British Naval Squadron in pursuit.

The amphibious infantry landing on the Gallipoli peninsula, just north of the Dardanelles and the Straits, was a mere few political 'chess moves' away and with it a total casualty figure of half a million men, in a campaign that drifted on for nearly seven months through the summer months of 1915 in the Mediterranean.

Shortly after the reciprocal declaration of war on Turkey by the Allied Powers on November 5th 1914, the War Council had already considered a combined landing, but initially rejected the idea as unfeasible. Despite the attraction to Churchill, the Minister for War, Lt Colonel Hankey, Secretary of the War Council, and Admiral Jackie Fisher, it was decided to use Churchill's earlier plan to deploy a British naval blockade in the Mediterranean to bombard the entrance to the Straits.

The result, of course, was to cause limited damage to the existing land defences, but to draw the Turkish Army's attention to the need to move more troops into the area, and to build more impregnable fortifications. By the following April, unknown to the British, an Infantry landing would have a much tougher challenge for success.

Meanwhile, five Olavian's, who had been some of the first to volunteer for military service after the outbreak of war, were training for a campaign just beginning to take shape in the meeting rooms of Westminster.

The eldest, Neil Wells, born on Halloween 1885, one of five children, with two brothers, to Neil Wells Senior, a Bermondsey tan yard manager and his wife, Sarah, had joined the first Australian Expeditionary Force, leaving Melbourne for Egypt in late 1914. He was 29 years old. His brother, William, later joined the 14th Londons (the London Scottish) serving in France from July 1915 and surviving the War. Private Neil Wells, a Londoner, had attended St Olave's for seven years from 1895, leaving after matriculation at seventeen, to join his father's leather and tannery business in Bermondsey, deliberately resigning the rewards of his scholarship for someone else more in need. He moved after a while to another City company of hide and skin brokers, before chancing his luck, by moving to Melbourne, Australia as a commercial traveller.

Ralph Portland Akerman was three years younger than Neil. He was born on the 18th August 1888 one of two brothers of Portland and Ada from Osterley Park, and attended St Olave's for five years from 1901. Originally from Bridgwater in Somerset, the Akerman family were descendants of the Board family who created the famous Portland cement later used in the War Graves stones. Ralph, a man of introverted and cautious disposition, was reliable, quiet and steady. He won distinction in the School's shooting championship. He was a man of humour, but avoided fuss. In short, he was self disciplined and well suited to a military career. In 1906, he enlisted as a Private in the 28th London Regiment (the Artists Rifles) and three years later moved to South Africa, and joined the Natal Mounted Rifles. In May 1914, he was home on leave, and on the outbreak of hostilities, re-enlisted in August in the Artist's as a commissioned officer. As a professional soldier and still only 26 years old, he was ideal for the British Expeditionary Force, leaving any day for France. The fact that he was gazetted to the 1st Battalion, 11th Londons (Finsbury Rifles) meant he remained in England through the long winter of 1914, and set sail for the Mediterranean in July 1915, ready for the second wave of Gallipoli landings.

Charles George Ruggles, known as 'Jimmie', one of three brothers, studied at the School for the same time period as Ralph. He was a year younger, born on 26th June 1890, and left at sixteen in 1906. Seen as a diffident boy, he worked hard to develop fine leadership skills on the sports field. He apprenticed with the Gas Company, in Leighton Buzzard, and when his younger brother, Frank, finished at the School in 1908, the Ruggles family took an opportunity to relocate to Australia. In August 1914, Jimmie queued patiently with his brothers to enlist in the early colonial waves of jingoistic fervour. Frank, the youngest was first to join, the 4th Australian Infantry Brigade, followed by Bill and Jimmie in the 5th. All three set sail for the Mediterranean in late 1914. Jimmie was twenty-four.

Eric Halliday was the fourth and younger still. He was born on the 11th May 1896, and after four years of education at St Olave's, joined 'Messr's Cayser, Irvine and Co.' of the 'Clan Line' of Steamers in 1912. He enlisted six weeks after the declaration, and volunteered as a Private in the 24th Londons (The Queens Regiment). He was eighteen. After eight months of training during the winter and spring of Wiltshire and Hampshire, his battalion set sail for the Mediterranean in July 1915, like Ralph Akerman, to prepare for the second wave of Gallipoli landings.

Philip Grant, described as a boy of frankness, honesty and charm, spent five years at St Olave's leaving at Christmas 1912, aged sixteen. He was born in Stockwell to Philip and Isabel Grant on the 30th November 1896. Such was his boyish eagerness, it was obvious he would volunteer to serve at an early stage. Short of his eighteenth birthday, he enlisted as a Gunner in the Royal Field Artillery. After months of training, his skills and education selected him for an officer's commission. He was gazetted as a Second Lieutenant and transferred to the 5th Battalion, the Wiltshire Regiment in summer 1915. In September, he set sail for the Mediterranean for the last leg of the Gallipoli occupation.

After the abortive naval attack on the entrance to the Dardanelles on the 18th March, the Allies finally decided to open the waterways to the Black Sea by the landing of infantry troops. General Sir Ian Hamilton was selected by the War Council to lead the campaign and based his staff in Alexandria. Von Sanders, meanwhile, deployed 60,000 troops into the Gallipoli peninsula. The invasion was planned for April 25th, and four days earlier, all troops and ships were ready on the nearby island of Lemnos.

The first landings, in the south at Cape Helles and in the north at Ari Burun were unsuccessful, due to the quality and volume of the defensive forces and the strategic skills of Mustafa Kemal, better known as 'Ataturk', in the north against the Anzacs. Of the 52,000 men who landed, most were pinned down on the beaches with little cover, or evacuated as wounded. Stalemate ensued for several weeks, during which time, it became apparent that there had been little in the way of pre-planning for failure, evacuation, the treatment of casualties, the provision of food, drink, clothing, shoreline cover, and even the basics, sun protection.

The early loss of nearly a third of the invasion force, led to Churchill being dropped from the War Cabinet. As June approached,

GALLIPOLI AND THE DARDANELLES

the Government thought it too early to withdraw, and consigned more Army Infantry divisions to Lemnos, to act as a second wave invasion, destined to be at Suvla Bay, further north than Ari Burun, now designated 'Anzac Cove' by the troops based there.

Neil Wells was one of the Anzac's that had landed at Ari Burun on April 25th. Less than a week later, he wrote to his father in London assessing the day of invasion. " The first party to land were the 9th and 10th Battalions, who were rushed up to the shore by HMS 'Prince of Wales' boats; The Turks were in full force waiting, and as soon as the boats touched, everyone jumped up and charged at once with bayonet. There was a terrible fire from shrapnel and machine guns. The casualties were very heavy, boat-loads being killed."

Neil then proceeded to go ashore with the 6th Battalion. Their boat was one that landed safely, with men waist high in water, scrambling to get to the cover of the cliffs, avoiding the shrapnel shells emanating from the forts above. Neil continued, "as soon as we reached the cliff, over the top we went and down into a valley… Now we began to feel the hiss and ping of the bullets and could see the twigs of the 'ti-shrub' flutter and break. The bullets were like hail, and after a while, the Turks got their artillery to work, and it became the 2nd hell… anyhow, in rushes we continued to advance, some in the rear entrenching in… Whilst resting for another rush, I got hit in the left arm by shrapnel. It broke the upper arm and knocked me out. I lay there for a bit and then started to crawl back behind the firing line, laying down in a heap of wounded".

It had taken him five hours to crawl back to the line, and many more until he received a basic dressing to his wound. On the 26th April, Neil Wells was evacuated by boat to the 'Clan Macgilorney' where he lay between decks for 3 days untreated. Some days later, he reached hospital in Alexandria, from where he wrote his letter.

His father, on receiving the letter was expecting him home any day, but in early July received instead a notification that he had succumbed to his wounds in hospital on June 25th, aged 29 years. The Anzacs under the command of Colonel Ewen Sinclair-

MacLagan had begun to land at 04.30 hours. Neil Wells had been wounded less than seven hours into his first day of front line battle with a wound that he should have recovered from, had the medical facilities been available.

Beach personnel had been strictly instructed only to evacuate wounded in specific boats, so as not to interrupt the continuing landing of fresh troops. This was not carried out to the letter, and wounded men tried to get to one of the few hospital ships, thereby slowing down the disembarkation of new support troops. Boats full of wounded, had to tour the hospital ships to find spaces, as by early evening, most were full. Even though heaving with wounded below decks, the hospital ships were ordered to remain in position for the first 48 hours from the invasion time, in case a complete evacuation was necessary. Neil had found a place on a ship but had paid the price of the long delay with the onset of gangrene in his wound.

On August 6th, two fresh army divisions landed at Suvla Bay under the command of General Sir Frederick Stopford, whilst secondary 'pushes' occurred in the south at 'Anzac Cove' and at Helles. Turkish forces held firm in all areas, but at Suvla, the landings were made with little opposition and limited casualties, providing probably the single best opportunity for a quick thrust inland to get behind the enemy defending Anzac Cove. Once again, unclear orders, poor leadership, and general procrastination and hesitation, removed the advantage. When, three days later, the divisions did move inland, the Turks were ready.

Private Eric Halliday of the 24th Londons, was attached to the 29th Division and landed at Suvla Bay on August 18th. Hamilton had decided that evening to send the rest of 29 Division to Suvla to support an attack on West Hills on the 21st. De Lisle, Corps Commander, was optimistic as a result of tactical gains from a number of minor skirmishes. As it turned out, the men already ashore, needed time to reorganise and dig wells for water; the last thing that was needed was another invasion and attack immediately. Eric landed with little problem, and was involved in attacks with enemy troops later in the day. He obviously strayed, for some reason, from his Company, and was thought to have been taken prisoner, as some other forty odd men had been. On the 19th, a few men returned and none had information on his whereabouts. It is thought that he was killed by a shell and died where he fell. He was just nineteen.

H.W. Sims, an Olavian who survived the War, was also present on the 18th August as part of the 2nd Mounted (Yeomanry) Division. He wrote to his father, "Lighters put us ashore on 'A beach', Suvla Bay. We had a very comfortable three days stay, with casual shrapnel shells to keep us alive to the fact that we were in the enemy's country.....we advanced over a slight ridge and opened out into a line of troop columns on the plain between La La Baba and Chocolate Hill. Goodness knows why we were led across the open like that...common shell thumped and thundered in the earth around us, and the choking fumes got into our lungs. My Regiment had miraculous luck, only losing one N.C.O. killed, as against the thirties and forties of other Regiments that preceded us across the plain". He was later evacuated with dysentery, like thousands of others, who had caught the virus in Egypt.

Second Lieutenant Ralph Akerman, serving in 11th Londons, 162nd Brigade, 54th (East Anglian) Division, landed at Suvla Bay on August 10th primarily to fill the gap between existing forces already ashore. Stopford's orders were imprecise with no obvious objective. Future Field Marshal, and fellow officer of Ralph Akerman, on that day, was John Harding, who recorded his thoughts. "We set off in the dark, and we marched in column halting at frequent intervals. We seemed to go about 100 yards at a time....we were told to halt and lie down, there was an awful stench. At daylight, we saw that we'd being lying alongside four or five dead Turks. Then we were told to go back to the beach". Within a day, Stopford, under intense pressure for action from Hamilton, started blaming the quality of the troops and the junior officers, instead of his own pusillanimity.

Nine days later, Ralph recorded his own thoughts in a letter home. "The country is very mountainous, and is covered with boulders and thorn bush. It is terribly hot, and there is no water; every drop has to be carried by hand from the ships, which, I believe, bring it from Alexandria. The affair last Sunday was quite a big fight. Hundreds of wounded died from lack of attention and from thirst. I had so many narrow escapes that I thought it useless to try to take cover. I was taking a knife off a man's belt, when a shell burst and hit him in several places. A few moments after, another shell burst and hit the man who was next to me".

A few weeks later, dug in on the beaches of Suvla with his Battalion, Ralph was badly wounded by machine gun fire, and as an officer, received speedy evacuation to England, instead of Egypt like so many others. He was taken to Netley Military Hospital straight from the troopship docked at Southampton. He succumbed to his severe injuries three weeks after being shot at Suvla.

Both his C.O. and fellow officers seemed to bestow more than the usual accolades on Ralph. "We shall all miss him tremendously in mirth and work. He was always one to treat things as a joke, and compare them to his Natal experiences. We relied on him as our really safe man".

Jimmie Ruggles was the only one of the five Olavians to get through the Gallipoli campaign unscathed, only to succumb, seven months later to the ever increasing toll of 'the missing' at Pozieres on the Somme on the 25th June 1916, the day before his 26th birthday.

As part of the 5th Australians, he served in a composite brigade from the Anzac Corps under Brigadier General Cox. Their objective during the August landings at Suvla Bay, was to capture Hill 60. Its importance lay in its view across the enemy valleys. His Battalion, had been almost decimated in the attack on Sari Bair, and many of the remaining troops were affected by disease. The attack had some success, but was high in casualties on both sides, ending in another stalemate.

Jimmie Ruggles lived to fight another day, and when he finally fell in Pozieres, the flags were flown at half mast in Camperdown, Australia, his adopted home.

Whilst the landings at Suvla were in operation, newly commissioned Second Lieutenant Philip Grant of the 5th Wiltshire's was on board ship destined for Egypt to join his Battalion. As part of the 40th Brigade, 13th (Western) Division, the Wiltshires had been buttonholed for Gallipoli on June 8th, when the War Council agreed to Hamilton's demands for reinforcements after the initial landings.

Just a few weeks before his arrival, the Wiltshires had moved into Anzac Cove to relieve the New Zealanders around 'Chunuk Bair'. They became lost, however, en route, and took shelter, extremely fatigued, in Sazli Beit Dere. The men were almost without officers, thirsty, hungry, tired and in a vulnerable position. On 10th August, the Turks launched a perfectly timed counter attack, six battalions swarmed down from Chunuk Bair virtually wiping out the 5th. Corporal A.G. Scott wrote that "A and C Companies were nearly all done for in no time.... caught in the open and killed before we had time to get to our rifles even, but B and D were more fortunate as they were in a small trench and they made a good fight for it".

Philip, embarking in September from England, was one of many officer replacements for the 10th August massacre. By the time he landed at Anzac, it was early October, and he took his place, trying in his inexperience, to lead older, battle worn men in a military situation that had already been perceived by politicians and generals, as a lost hope.

He lasted for only a few days, in the entrenched positions on the lowland of Anzac Cove. On the morning of October 15th, he was engaged in special reconnaissance work. A fellow lieutenant advised him to keep low because of snipers. He replied that he wanted to live a little longer yet. Within 15 minutes, a shrapnel shell exploded close to him, he was stunned by the noise and impact, and wandered around the trenches in full view of the Turks on the hillside. His chest was riddled with machine gun bullets causing instant death. He was only eighteen. His colonel, who must have written many similar letters wrote "From the very first we all liked him. He was so bright and cheery and always ready for anything. I greatly deplore his loss".

The story of Gallipoli continued until the end of 1915. On November 22nd, Hamilton was relieved by General Sir Charles Monro, who promoted General Birdwood to take charge of the sea evacuation which took place between December 20th and January 9th. There was no loss of life in the withdrawal.

CHAPTER 5
Second Ypres:
Neuve Chapelle, Aubers Ridge and Festubert

By spring 1915, thoughts of an early victory had vanished into memory along with the Christmas Day truce; British troops had endured their first winter in makeshift trenches. French troops were stretched, from covering their complete eastern border down to Switzerland. Politically, the French Government were applying pressure for the British to enormously, and quickly, increase their number of trained infantrymen on the Western Front, to allow a diversion of French troops further towards the south. Furthermore, they wanted some evidence of British military action, not reliant on French support.

This 'evidence' started to be supplied over a three day period in March, near the Belgian village of 'Neuve Chapelle'. The area, situated south west of the town of Armentieres, was surrounded by other smaller villages, whose names act like a roll call of locations, where thousands of British soldiers laid down their lives in the first truly British fight against the enemy – Aubers Ridge, Fromelles and Pietre. On the 10th March, after a fierce thirty minute bombardment, utilising over 500 guns, the first of many such artillery preliminaries to follow throughout the war, the Garhwal Brigade of the Meerut Division, fresh from India, supported by the 8th Division north of the village, advanced taking their objectives with ease and penetrating to a depth of over 1,000 yards in some places.

Early enemy surprise had been supplanted with fast defensive manoeuvring, whilst poor communications between both the British corps commanders and General Haig, had led to a five hour delay, before the advance could continue. Even when it did, the soldiers were forced to retire through lack of ammunition and artillery cover. The resultant shell shortage rocked the Government at home, leading to the appointment of David Lloyd George as 'Minister of Munitions', however, the battle had exhibited a measure of military success and a clear political advantage in showing the French that 'British Commanders had shown their readiness to attack 'regardless of loss' even if loss was to be their only result'.

Of the fourteen Old Olavians either killed in action or dying from wounds resulting from combat, from that infamous Belgian springtime through to the middle of July, it appears that only two men served in the attacking Front line on the 10th March at Neuve Chapelle.

George Enoch Benson, 'the Missionary'. Born in December 1894 to three sisters and two brothers, Arthur and Joseph, he was a son of Joseph Benson, a local Bermondsey leather shaver and his wife Jane living at Storks Road. He spent eight full years at the School developing a quiet, amusing and unostentatious personality. He had experienced both love and tragedy in his life, helping his father to nurse his terminally ill mother for several years, whilst he was a mere schoolboy. He commenced studying theology at St John's, Cambridge in late 1913, but left to enlist in the first days of September 1914.

Rifleman Benson no. Z/2980, 2nd Battalion, The Rifle Brigade, embarked for France as part of the 25th Brigade, 8th Division arriving in Havre on the 16th March 1915 after three months of basic training in the peaceful English countryside. He had chosen the Rifle Brigade, as one of his childhood hero's, Lord Kitchener, had served his early days in the same regiment. Bearing this in mind, there was little chance that George Benson would have ignored designer Alfred Leete's famous recruiting poster. Owing to the minimal resistance encountered at Neuve Chapelle, George survived, to accompany his battalion moving northwards to defend Ypres against its second major attack, just a month later.

Charles Taffs was five years older than George Benson, born in 1889, one of the three children of Leslie Taffs, a schoolmaster. He left the School after six years, taking a position as an estate duty lawyer in the City of London. When war broke out, Charles, at just over 25 years of age, had ample maturity and experience to take an immediate commission and become a second Lieutenant, and posted to the 1st Battalion, the Royal Berkshire Regiment. Like Private Benson of the Rifle Brigade, Second Lieutenant Taffs advanced with the Berkshires, and Lincolnshires, in the vanguard on the 10th March, coming through unscathed, to fight again at Festubert.

Von Falkenhayn, the German General commanding on the Western Front, was coming under increasing pressure from his General Staff to start moving large numbers of trained, experienced troops to the Eastern Front, once it had become apparent that the quick defeat of France through Belgium, had failed. Russia was considered to be the weaker of the two protagonists, unsophisticated in technical weaponry, and in political turmoil in Moscow. As a result, he instructed his commanders to hold the line on the west, and only probe for weak points, and use the occasional attack to keep the 'entrenched' British and French soldiers constantly guessing.

The German Army desperately needed a new weapon which could potentially have devastating effects on the enemy, but replace the need to attack with thousands of men; At Kummersdorf, near Berlin, there was a artillery base, where the German chemical industry were working, to create a usable poisonous gas, that could be deployed in the Front line, and thereby breaking 'Article 23' of the 1907 Hague Convention, forbidding the use of such weapons.

The second battle of Ypres became infamous for the first use of gas in a mass attack. The Ypres Salient, still held by the British, was tactically key for the Germans, and the route to the Pas de Calais, it was seen as a sensitive spot to try out the new technology. The 4th (German) Army had almost broken through at Gheluvelt, the previous November, virtually destroying the British Expeditionary

Force. Hundreds of thousands of newly arrived and newly trained, British, Indian and Canadian reinforcements were piling into the area. Eighty-four British Army Regiments, eleven Indian, and forty-one Canadian, were engaged at the Front at the Ypres Salient over a period of thirty-three days enduring casualties of over sixty thousand men.

On the 20th April, British Tommies heard the constant clanking of metal, just across No Mans Land in the forward enemy trenches. But they didn't know that over thirty thousand cylinders of various lethal and irritant gases were being dug into launch positions for the 22nd. Most were not immediately lethal, they were delayed action respiratory irritants like phosgene, which if inhaled in quantity, could cause blindness, and years of breathing problems. The deliberate inclusion of lachrymators, sternutators and vesicants, targeted watering eyes, sneezing and blistering respectively.

With the benefit of hindsight, it is frustrating to see that the British missed regular clues to the first serious use of these gases in the war. Ordinary German infantrymen, who knew of the cylinders, informed British battalions, the French Army had written to the British General Staff telling them to expect such an attack, and to prepare some form of defence. All was ignored. Even when gas was smelt, it was thought to be tear gas shells which were commonplace.

By 17.00 hours on the afternoon of the 22nd April, the winds had changed to the right direction to take the gas across to the Allied trenches. The cylinder taps were turned on and the gas descended on the Canadian 3rd Brigade including the Lancashire Fusiliers and the French Algerian 45th Colonial Division. The latter infantrymen either turned and ran several thousand yards back to Ypres or clutched their throats and fell almost immediately. The former, under the command of Brigadier General Turner, stood their ground, fighting off German infantry attacks for several hours, despite their exposure to the poisonous fumes.

As the gas attack had been experimental, and not supported with massive infantry support, the Germans could not capitalise

SECOND YPRES

on the complete routing of the French Division, which had left the way to Ypres free. They contented themselves with the capture of the Pilckem Ridge. Counter attacks followed, with both Smith-Dorrien's Second Army moving into support. Three days later on the 25th, the Germans made a powerful effort to break through, but were contained. For six weeks, battles developed up and down the Salient at Gravenstafel, St Julien, Frezenberg and Bellewaerde.

Including Rifleman Benson of the 2nd Rifle Brigade, and Second Lieutenant Taffs of the 1st Berkshires, twelve other Olavians had been brought up to the line in the days after the gas attack. Seven of them were ranking territorial soldiers attached to London Regiment battalions – Rifleman Haseldine (5th Londons, the London Rifle Brigade), Corporal Schulz and Rifleman Edwards of the 12th (The Rangers), Private Glenn of the 20th (The Queen's Own), Rifleman Heron of the 21st (First Surrey Rifles), Lance Corporal Fitzgerald and Private Quixley of the 24th (The Queens).

Of the others, four were also ranking men in other regiments, Lance Corporal Dell of the 5th Yorkshires, Trooper Edgley of the Royal Horse Guards, Private Walker of the 6th Seaforth Highlanders, Private Halliwell of the 1st Rifle Brigade, and the fifth, an officer, Lieutenant Taylor of the 1/3rd East Kent Regiment (The Buffs).

Claude Dell was a shy, retiring boy, born in 1889 in London to two brothers, also Olavians, Charles and Guy. Their parents, Frederick and Emma Dell, moved their business to Scarborough in Yorkshire, when the boys left school, and Claude, like his brother, went into the family firm. He left St Olave's after four years in 1905, and joined the Territorial Force three years later. When the War arrived, he enlisted as a Private with his brother Charles, and both went to France in April 1915.

Harry Schulz was a couple of years younger, born in July 1891 to a brother, Frederick, both sons of a German immigrant fur skin dresser, Gottlieb and his wife Wilhelmina who resided at 11 Grange Walk, close to the School. He also spent four years at St Olave's, leaving in 1907 to enter the London clothing trade. In his spare time, he progressed from the School Cadet Corps in to the Territorials and in the summer of 1914, aged twenty-three, he went to enlist as a private. Training was absolutely minimal, with some basics covered on Barnes Common in October 1914 before a route-march to Southampton and embarkation on troopship for Le Havre on the 23rd December. His previous experience in the cadets, prompted his quick promotion, first to acting corporal, then full corporal. As part of the 12th Londons (The Rangers), he arrived at the French town of St Omer on New Year's Eve, moving on towards the Ypres Salient, by way of Hazebrouck in late January 1915.

Newton Woollcombe Haseldine was the only son of Hannah Haseldine of Balham. He was younger still, born in November 1895. After two and a half years as an Olavian, he left in summer 1912, aged sixteen to apprentice to a local business. Barely a year had gone by, when the War broke out, and he felt the immediate need to enlist. As a rifleman in the 5th Londons, he embarked on SS Chyebassa for Le Havre, earlier than Harry Schulz, on the 4th November 1914, as part of 'Army Troops' setting up supplies and working behind the lines. Once again, training had been virtually non-existent, but for some rifle drill at Bisley and Crowborough. On the 17th November, the London Rifle Brigade were transferred to the 11th Brigade, 4 Division and moved into the line around Ypres.

Albert Edwards, son of Frank and Mary from New Cross was a private in the same battalion as Corporal Harry Schulz. They had joined the School at the same time in 1903, with Albert leaving two years later, aged fifteen, to train as an auctioneer in London. Clearly they would have known each other well. In summer 1914, he enlisted and found himself in and around Busseboom, and Poperinghe, on the Salient by February.

Leslie Seymour Edgley was a twenty-three year old drapery wholesaler when war broke out. He and his brother Harold, were sons of Robert and Leopoldine Edgley of Tooting. He'd won a scholarship from a church school to attend St Olave's, and although only there for fifteen months, before beginning his apprenticeship,

SECOND YPRES

he excelled as an athlete winning regular prizes. His physique and fitness helped him become a competent cavalryman as Trooper no.1708 in the prestigious 'Royal Horse Guards' (the Blues). He arrived in Belgium shortly after the 8th April 1915.

Together with Taffs and Benson, these first seven died on the Belgian battlefields over a period of twenty-three days. Claude Dell and Harry Schulz both fell at St Julien on the 24th April, counter attacking the enemy advance. Claude had been rushed to the line on the 23rd in a fleet of motor buses, to take up position on the Yser Canal. The next morning, he had volunteered to go with a small party of men, to silence an enemy machine gun nest that was preventing further attack. Whilst moving forward with bayonet fixed to his Lee Enfield rifle, he was shot in the head by another machine gun, hidden further to the rear. He was killed instantly and fell in the enemy trench, his body was not recovered. He was twenty-six.

Harry Schulz's fate is best expressed by Arthur Conan-Doyle, the writer, describing the advance of 'Wallace's detachment': 'Their assault was a desperate one, since there was inadequate artillery support, they had to cross two miles of open ground under a dreadful fire. They went forward in the open British formation – the 1st Suffolks in the vanguard, then the 12th London Rangers. Numerous gassed Canadians covered the ground over which they advanced. The losses were very heavy'. Harry was shot by enfilade rifle fire, working to get through to the isolated surviving Canadians. He was twenty-three.

Albert Edwards was killed on the 2nd May, based at Verlorenhoek, on the Wieltje-Fortuin Road, during the battle to retain 'Hill 60' on the Salient. Having survived his friend, Harry, by a few days, he had to endure a fresh gas attack, followed by crippling shrapnel bombardment. Fighting alongside the Lancastrians, the Argylls, the Monmouths and the Royal Irish, some drew to one side to avoid the gas, others waited for it, and then ran swiftly through it, to attack the following enemy. Private Lynn VC of the Lancashire Fusiliers epitomised, on the one hand, the fierce resistance and on the other, the agonising death caused by such resistance. He had stood firing his machine gun, without any protection from the cloud of gas, mowing down the advancing enemy, until completely overcome with the fumes. Albert Edwards had been mortally wounded by flying pieces of shrapnel, he was twenty-four.

Newton Haseldine died three days after that, also as a result of the loss of 'Hill 60'. After a gas attack on the Dorsets on May 1st, a further final attack proceeded four days later. Newton was asphyxiated along with a rough total of over a thousand men at 'Hill 60'. He was nineteen.

Meanwhile, George Benson and the 2nd Rifle Brigade were defending Fromelles, south of Armentieres, near to the Aubers Ridge. On the 9th May, the Allied spring offensive began. Artillery had been brought up to the Front line, with the objective of concentrated, accurate fire on two enemy positions, adjacent to Fromelles and to Neuve Chapelle. Once the wire had been cut by the guns, the infantry, the Meerut and 8th Divisions, would advance through the gaps and attack Aubers Ridge from both sides.

George Benson's 2nd Rifle Brigade, part of 25 Brigade, 8 Division, succeeded in getting through the break in the line. Captain Berkeley M.C. of the same battalion, recorded that 'enemy machine gun fire was terrific, and (the companies) had many casualties. The battalion machine guns were unable to get across, the bombing and blocking parties were broken up. The Rifle Brigade were on the first objective. Where were the East Lancashires on the right, and the Sherwood Foresters beyond them ? They were lying out in No Mans Land, and most of them would never stand again'.

George was one of those mown down by deeply burrowed, sandbag protected, machine guns, as he climbed onto the parapet of his trench to move forward. He was twenty, and had written a few days earlier to a school friend to advise the School that, in the event of his death, that they should break the news to his father and his sisters. He wanted to save them the insensitive shock of being informed by the Army. Aubers Ridge had a casualty cost of

SECOND YPRES

over 4,500 officers and 11,000 men in just one day. It also further depleted the ammunition and shell stores, causing General Haig to suspend the attack, and move troops further south to Festubert to regroup.

Trooper Leslie Edgley of the 'Blues', 8th Brigade, 3rd Cavalry Division, was under the command of General De Lisle, who had been ordered by General Plumer to fill the infantry line near Bellewarde Lake from Velorenhoek to Hooge. It was a desperate move by the Allies, to use highly trained cavalrymen in this manner, signalling clearly to the enemy that suitable reinforcements were not available. The British were playing for time. On May 12th enemy shelling focused on the 3rd Division. Conan Doyle, later reported that 'the Germans appeared to have an inexhaustible supply of munitions, and from morning to night they blew to pieces the trenches in front, and the shelters behind'. The right hand attack was launched by the 3rd Cavalry Division in the midst of howling wind, driving rain and ceaseless fire from the Ypres-Roulers Road. 6 Brigade were 'blown into the air by a bombardment which continued for fourteen hours'.

Finally the Horse Guard troopers moved forward on foot, reclaiming the trenches they had lost earlier in the day, and taking several prisoners. Further progress was impossible without support under heavy shellfire. The line had yet again been held, but at high human cost. Leslie Edgley had been reported missing during the attack, and was presumed dead the next day. He was twenty-four.

Another four days passed when Lieutenant Charles Reginald Taffs of the Berkshires fell, during the later stages of the battle of Richebourg, part of the Festubert campaign. The initial attack had taken place on May 9th on a Front from Laventie to Richebourg. Taffs had been involved from the start. Once again, hordes of infantry were shot down as they clambered out of their trenches. A week later, a change in tactics brought improved results. Three Divisions made a night attack and bombers were used. Three miles of trenches were taken to half a mile depth. 'At 11.30, the word was passed, and they advanced at a walk. Flares were suddenly discharged from the German trenches, and a ghostly flickering radiance illuminated the long line of crouching men…. In three minutes, they had swarmed across the open, and poured into the trenches'. On the Sunday night, the 16th, the enemy counter attacked, and again in the rainy misty morning of the 17th, Lieutenant Taffs was killed in action holding the ground won during the night attack. He was twenty six.

From 25th May at Festubert to the 16th July at Mazingarbe, seven more Olavians died in action.

Joseph Solomon Heron was a twenty-seven year old estate agent and bachelor when war broke out in 1914. He had been educated at Tooley Street for five years until 1904 and lived near his widowed mother, Phoebe, in Cricklewood, his father, Albert, having died some years earlier. His time at the School coincided with that of Claude Dell and Charles Taffs. In August 1914, Joe enlisted as Rifleman No.1926, in the 21st (County of London) Battalion, the London Regiment (First Surrey Rifles). By February 1915, his Battalion was in the trenches to the south of Ypres, moving south to Richebourg in May. On May 24th, in the final stage of the Battle of Festubert, the 47th Division, the London Territorials, were brought up to the Front. They became involved immediately in heavy fighting at Givenchy.

Arhur Quixley, an 'educationalist', working for the Government, had enlisted in the 24th Londons (the Queens) as a Private aged just seventeen years. He was the son of widowed and remarried, Caroline Neale, and the late Arthur Quixley of Camberwell. He had spent four years at St Olave's leaving in 1911. His contemporaries included fellow soldier in the 24th – Robert Fitzgerald, and Reginald Glenn of the 20th.

Robert Fitzgerald's mother had also remarried and was known as Margaret Ball. His late father was David Fitzgerald. They had lived in Blackfriars. He was born on 8th September 1896, attending the School for three years until 1911, when he left to join the army as a regular. His choice was 'The Queens', the 24th Londons, and it was his pre-war experience that gave him rank status over his school friends in 1914.

SECOND YPRES

On the eve of the 25th May, the 142nd Brigade under Brigadier General Willoughby was ordered to attack. The 23rd and 24th Londons, Fitzgerald and Quixley included, in the vanguard, supported by the 21st, with Joe Heron and 22nd's.

The trenches were taken with minimal casualties, with each man carrying a sandbag for protection, once in the trench. A defensive traverse was built, three enemy counter attacks got to within ten yards of the 24th, but were beaten back each time. The Germans, operating from a ridge, commenced use of machine guns and bombs, to great effect. Private Quixley was most likely killed by bombs in the enemy trench before midnight. By 10.30 on the 26th, the 21st Londons had made good their support position in the trench. Rifleman Heron had been shot making his way to the trench the previous evening. At some time before the 24th Londons were relieved that afternoon at 16.30 hours, Lance Corporal Fitzgerald had also been struck down. The combined age of the three London soldiers was just over sixty. Their deaths were accompanied by those of 16,648 other British men, for a military gain of a thousand yards on a three thousand yard front.

Further north, as Festubert was coming to a close, Lieutenant William Frederick Taylor, of the 3rd Battalion, the East Kent Regiment (The Buffs), was in the line at Zillebeke, south of Ypres withstanding enemy attacks using, for the first time, flame throwers powered with liquid petrol. Hooge Chateau, close to Zillebeke, was a British headquarters in late 1914, and had been taken by the Germans in May 1915.

William was born in Bermondsey to a sister, Doris, in September 1891, children of WilliamTaylor, schoolteacher and his wife Mary Ann. He attended the School for five years, leaving in 1910 to become a L.C.C. student at London University. George Benson and Sid Walker were his contemporaries, fighting with him in Belgium. On the outbreak of war, he sought a commission and was gazetted as a Second Lieutenant in the East Kents. As an 'Old Contemptible', he had been 'bloodied' at the Aisne in September 1914, Armentieres in October and the second battle of Ypres in April 1915.

On the 7th June, he was shot suddenly by an enemy sniper whilst walking in his trench at Hooge, and was later buried at Perth Military cemetery, also known as China Wall, in Zillebeke. He was just twenty three and was one of the few who were posthumously awarded the 'Mons' Star.

Sid Walker, a friend of William and from a scottish family, had enlisted early as well, as a Private in the 6th Battalion, the Seaforth Highlanders. His brother, William, had opted for the 'famous' 14th – the London Scottish, and may have known Gordon Ryder, nine years his senior, through either the 'Caledonian' or 'Olavian' network. Sid was a year younger than William, both were killed in action leaving only a third brother, James; Sid died at Festubert on 6th July, aged eighteen, two days after his brother stepped on to French soil, and William, on the 25th September at Loo's, just eleven weeks later, aged twenty.

Sidney Herbert Walker had attacked the enemy lines at Givenchy with his battalion, as part of the 152nd brigade, 51st (Highland) Division. The attack had started at 05.58 hours, after two days of constant shelling; there was no surprise and an inadequate supply of grenades. The results were predictable. Sid Walker lost his life. There was little planned military action in Flanders until 3rd July, when the Germans raided trenches near Ypres. Three days later on the 6th, a British attack on the enemy line at Pilckem Ridge, between Boesinghe and Ypres, began. It claimed the life of Company Sergeant Major no. 228 William Halliwell M.C. – a decorated Old Olavian.

William and his elder brother Ernest, were sons of Thomas and Martha Halliwell of Bermondsey. William was born in January 1886 and spent two years at St Olave's, leaving at the end of his scholarship, aged thirteen. He decided to become a professional career soldier, entering the pre-war army just after the end of the Boer War, in 1902. Working his way up through the ranks to warrant officer class 11, he was one of the most experienced younger soldiers to survive the virtual annihilation of the Expeditionary Force in 1914.

SECOND YPRES

The 1st Rifle Brigade had seen action at Le Cateau in August, through the Mons retreat, and the Marne, to the Aisne in late September. For his gallantry he was awarded the Military Cross. The gazette date was 18th February 1915 and he was awarded the decoration on the 18th June. Sadly there was no citation of his award. However, the Rifle Brigade regimental history for the War states:

"Meanwhile the First Battalion worked away at German House, and continued to improve the breastworks in the wood, spending alternately three days in the line and three days in billets at Ploegsteert and Armentieres (where baths were available). C.S.M. Halliwell won the Military Cross and Sergeant B.Daldry, the D.C.M. for consistent good work".

The 1914 War record of the 1st Rifle Brigade states:

"On 18th February C.S.M. Halliwell was awarded the M.C., and Sergeant Daldry the D.C.M. The former did very good work throughout, especially on the 19th December".

On the 19th December, the Battalion attacked German posts around the German House area.

He was also mentioned in despatches as published in the London Gazette on the 17th February 1915. Just a few weeks after his decoration, on the 6th July, he was killed in action by machine gun fire, storming the Pilckem Ridge.

Ten days later, Reginald James Glenn, a Private in the 20th Londons, was killed in action at the village of Mazingarbe, near the Belgian mine area of 'Fosse 7'. He was also nineteen. Reginald was the second of four surviving children born in 1895 in Greenwich, to James Thompson Glenn, an Automobile collector from Chislehurst and his wife Isabella. He attended St Olave's, as did brothers, William and Horace, for five years from 1909 until 1913. The family resided comfortably in Manor Road, Brockley where younger sister Hilda and mother-in-law, Isabella Owens, also lived. When the War arrived, he enlisted immediately in the first wave of jingoistic excitement. By September 1914, he was Private No 2894, in the Blackheath and Woolwich battalion of the London Regiment – the 20th. His regiment was part of the 141st Brigade under Brigadier General Thwaites at the battle of Festubert, and had since fallen back to a defensive line near Bethune. His fate is uncertain, he may have been shot by a sniper or killed by a exploding shell on the 16th July. He was buried by his comrades at 'Fosse 7' Military Cemetery, near Bethune, in the Pas de Calais.

And so ends the involvement of the Olavians in the early campaigns of 1915; in the words of another who fell at their side in May…

'The Thundering line of battle stands,
And in the air, death moans and sings,
But day shall clasp him with strong hands,
and night shall fold him in soft wings'

Julian Grenfell 1888–1915.

CHAPTER 6
Loos, Hulluch and Ypres

Having soaked up the seemingly continual German offensives at Aubers Ridge, Frezenberg and St Julien earlier in the year, the British Army, together with the French, had begun to plan an autumn offensive of their own further south. After the heavy casualties caused by poisonous gas during the second battle of Ypres, the failure of the landings on the Gallipoli beaches, and the bad fortunes on the Russian Front, Field Marshal Sir John French desperately required an early strategic victory.

In June, the French General, Joffre, suggested a joint offensive, with the French Army attacking in the Champagne region, and the British, with some French support in Artois, to the north. The main attack on the enemy trench system would be based around the city of Lens, where the British 1st Army would advance northwards through the village of Loos-en-Gohelle, with the French 10th Army marching through Lens itself. Joffre believed that a successful break through the line at either point, could be successfully followed by a combined mass offensive along the whole line through Belgium and France, bringing the War to an early close.

The battlefield, chosen by Joffre, had some interesting characteristics; Lens had been captured by the enemy in October 1914, and a network of complex tunnels ran underneath the town, in which there was to be much hand to hand fighting. Loos and Hulluch, which were small villages both behind the German Front line by October 1915, witnessed much of the subsequent fighting. Haig, at that point, Commander of the 1st Army, had surveyed the field in depth as a prelude to commenting on Joffre and French's plans. His strong feelings that the flat open terrain was vastly unsuitable for an infantry attack, due to vulnerability to enfilade machine gun fire, prompted him to attempt changes in the plans. Joffre's refusal and

Kitchener and French's insistence to Haig, that politically the British needed to support the French Army, caused Haig to embark on certain decisions that would affect the forthcoming battle.

With memories of the Neuve Chapelle munitions shortage fresh in his memory, Douglas Haig initially opted for a very narrow Front to help concentrate artillery fire. For such an attack, he only needed two divisions, the 9th and the 15th. The sudden possibility of the use of poison gas cylinders, which had just arrived in France, encouraged the adoption of a wider Front, with six divisions supported by this new weapon, only recently introduced by the Germans in Ypres a few months earlier. The decision of whether to use gas was put on hold, pending weather conditions, and Haig's 'narrow Front – wide Front' strategy remained optional until the 25th September, the launch date.

Nine Old Olavians gave their lives trying to break the German line at Loos and further north at Ypres. Two were Officers – Cecil Melliar Talbot was a Lieutenant in the 4th Middlesex Regiment, 63rd Brigade 21st (Light) Division based at Brandhoek, west of Ypres. Jack Woodward Gill, his school contemporary, was a Second Lieutenant in the 6th (Kings Own) Yorkshire Light Infantry, 43 Brigade, 14th (Light) Division, in Ypres town.

Five of the six ranking men were based near to Loos amongst the mining pit-heads and slag heaps; Private Bill Walker of the London Scottish, at the town of Vermelles, brother of Sid; Rifleman Alleyne Cook fighting with the London Irish at Bethune, and Private Harry Bliss of the 7th Norfolks entrenched at Hulluch. Lance Corporal Norman Jones of the 6th Buffs, a shade older than Harry, also at Hulluch, with Sergeant Bob Howett of the 1/5th Sherwood Foresters at Loos. The final two men, were, Rifleman James Richardson of the 12th Rifle Brigade serving further north at Ploegsteert Wood, near Ypres and Rifleman Geoff Schooling of the 16th Londons, the Queens Westminster Rifles based on the northern ourskirts of Ypres.

The six front line divisions chosen for the wide front attack at Loos, comprised the 2nd, 9th (Scottish) 7th, 1st, 15th (Scottish) and 47th (London Territorial). Two further divisions, the 21st and 24th were to be held in reserve, but under John French's control, and not Haig's – a crucial factor in the poor follow up. Four days before the main infantry were to attack, the artillery bombardment, now with a much wider trajectory than originally planned, began along the German line. The transportation of British 'gas' to the line at Loos was supposed to be secret and all involved described the new weapon as 'the accessory'. Armed with Meteorological Office forecasts, trained gas officers at the Front tried to predict the wind direction hourly in the run up to the 25th. Finally, on extremely vague information, the order came from Haig to turn on the gas, despite the existence of areas along the line where there was clearly no wind. One infamous report sent to Brigade Headquarters from the Front, claimed 'Dead calm. Impossible discharge accessory'. The reply that came back simply said, 'Accessory to be discharged at all costs'. The gas officer of 6th Brigade at La Bassee canal, refused to turn on the gas for fear of it being blown back on his own men. He was outranked by his General, Horne, and sure enough, hundreds of British infantrymen were poisoned by their own gas.

Even the supposedly co-ordinated launch times went awry, with the French Divisions attacking over five hours later than the British. Despite these obstacles, the vanguard Divisions made good progress in some places, supported by the gas clouds hovering towards the enemy lines, with the 15th Division, full of assaulting Highlanders, sweeping north of Loos, capturing the town after a night of street fighting. The Londoners of 47 Division broke through the line completely, with Alleyne Cook's London Irish, the 1/18th, dribbling a football across No Man's Land, whilst receiving over 1,200 casualties within an hour. The men of the 20th Londons, the Blackheath and Woolwich Rifles, took over, moving swiftly through Loos Cemetery and Gardens and fighting their way into the enemy held, 'Chalk Pit Copse', before their numbers were so depleted they could not continue.

Two Olavians were killed in action on that first day of battle. Rifleman no. S/68 James Bert Richardson was twenty. He was the son of Joe and Sarah Richardson who managed the post office at 91 Union Road, Rotherhithe. James had won a scholarship to attend St Olave's for three years from 1908 to 1910, when he left to take an apprenticeship. He was a contemporary of Wee Cook, Richard Walsh, Arthur Hay and David Roeber. At the outbreak of War, he enlisted in the Rifle Brigade, following the example of other Olavians, Keesey, Blackman and Churcher. His early enlistment and appointment as his colonel's orderly, kept him away from the Front until the september campaign in Belgium. He was blown up by enemy shelling, and is commemorated on the Ploegsteert Memorial. Whilst in the trenches at Laventie, a fellow Rifleman, who later gave an oral history of the events, claimed that 'at about 8am, the order was passed down to move up to the Front line. Those ten hours of waiting, up to our knees in mud, had certainly dampened our fighting spirit. My Company Commander had been shot through the head whilst standing on the fire step. Duck boards, with every other bar knocked out, were being used as ladders. We could hear the bullets and splinters plopping into the mud around us, the safest place seemed to be the German trench. We slithered and scrambled across the long, long two hundred yards'. The 12th Service Battalion, of the Rifle Brigade had performed well, as the only battalion of 20th Division to go into battle, sustaining 329 casualties.

William Richard Walker was the elder brother of Sidney Walker, the machine gunner of the 6th Seaforth Highlanders who had died at Festubert months earlier. Sons of William and Mary Walker of Ilford, Essex, both boys attended St Olave's from 1907 until 1911. When War arrived, coming from a Scottish family, whereas the younger Sidney chose to join the Seaforths, William retained London connections enlisting with the 'Kilties', the London Scottish. Neither boy was to last long in Belgium. Private no. 3928 Walker, based in the French stronghold of Vermelles, was subjected to regular and fierce enemy attacks. Arriving in July 1915, the somewhat innocent young man, was shot and killed, during an advance on a German stronghold called the 'Lens Road Redoubt'. This part of the line was captured on the 25th by the 15th (Scottish) Division, and many of 'the Fallen' that day were buried close to where they fell. Bill Walker is buried in Dud Corner Cemetery, right on the spot of the stronghold. He was twenty-one.

A London Scottish comrade, also present on the 25th later reported his feelings, 'When you get out of the trench, you feel quite naked. The protection's gone. It's a queer feeling out in the open after being in the trench for about a week'. The same man, a survivor, continued, 'They told us it would be a bit of cake, and all we'd got to do for this attack was to dawdle along and take these trenches which we'd find pulverised by our guns. (But) every other blooming (shell) shot was a dud. Most of the stuff wasn't worth sending out. When we did start the attack, my battalion lost hundreds of men in the first hour or so. The whole thing was a waste of lives'.

Alleyne James Cook, born in June 1895, was the youngest of four brothers – Charles, Frank and George, all of whom entered the School on junior L.C.C. scholarships from Alexis Street School. The boys, sons of Edward and Ellen Cook, lived at St Mary's Road in Peckham. Their school years spanned eighteen years from 1894 to 1912. Alleyne, particularly, was fondly remembered by Masters at the School for his 'sense of fun and mischief making'. He first entered the gates at Tooley Street in 1907 along with fellow contemporaries, Leslie Sanders, Bay Ryley and the Walker brothers. Leaving school aged seventeen, he worked for a while in Bermondsey, before enlisting at Chelsea in the summer of 1914 as a Rifleman no. 2433 in 'A' Company, 18th Battalion, the London Regiment, better known as the London Irish Rifles.

Over the Christmas period, he was based at St Albans in Hertfordshire for basic infantry training, before eventually arriving in France in March 1915. Having survived the fighting at Festubert in May, his battalion, with fresh and naïve 'Citizen Soldiers' moved to Lapugnoy near Bethune, where, in the run up to the battle in late September, they were engaged, night after night, in working parties, digging new trench lines in the very unsuitable and very visible, chalky ground. Despite heavy casualties, orders insisted that the digging continued.

On the 25th, the role of the 47th (London) Division was to capture the 'Double Crassier' an area of high ground, south of the village. They were then to act as a 'hinge' on which the whole assault could pivot, but poor communication of tactics to the division on their left, the 15th Scottish, left the latter stranded, when the Londoners dug in, as advised, once they had taken the Crassier. Alleyne Cook was killed in action by machine gun fire whilst storming up the Crassier Ridge, (along with the now legendary 'footballs' being kicked along with the advancing troops), an action in which his comrades claimed he showed exemplary courage, and would have been recommended for a Distinguished Conduct Medal, had he lived. He was just twenty, and was buried at Lapugnoy Military Cemetery. Mercifully, for his parents, their other three sons survived the war.

In Hammertons's 'Popular History of the Great War', the story of the London Irish at Loos is described in detail, 'The London Irish, who had led the Territorial Division which closed the gap, west of Lens, seem to have had a good share in the taking of Loos. After these extraordinary footballers had kicked their leather into the German trenches crying 'Goal', and had captured three German lines, another regiment came up to relieve them. The Irish had done their work, and the taking of Loos was not their job, but they worked away all the rest of the day, clearing house after house, and stabbing, shooting and bombing until they felt ready to drop dead themselves. The 23rd Silesian regiment was wiped out by them'.

The 21st Division was one of the two divisions held in reserve by Sir John French, whilst Haig attacked at Loos. Haig was later to criticise French for not releasing the reserves to the front sooner, this being the only hope to reinforce his early successes. Cecil Talbot, a lieutenant in the 4th Middlesex, formed part of the 21st, based near Brandhoek. He was an officer in charge of new raw, 'Kitchener volunteers', with no previous experience in trenches, or battle conditions. The battalions had only arrived from the troopships at

Boulogne two weeks earlier, and since then, had marched all day, every day to get to the battle area. In the two days before the battle, the battalions had marched fifty miles in driving rain.

On the 26th, the tired reserves did engage the enemy, but were forced back by continuous counter-attacks. The arrival of the experienced professional soldiers of the Guards Division the next day, helped prevent a retreat of the novices. A day later, badly wounded by rifle fire, Cecil Talbot fell in the field of battle defending against heavy attack. He was twenty-five. The skills that young officers had had to employ during those few days, to enthuse, rally and manage their scared, fatigued troops, should never be underestimated.

Cecil was born in September 1890, the son of Francis Talbot, a bargebuilder from Deptford and his wife, Sarah. He had one sister, Lilian. He attended St Olave's for six years from 1902 to 1907, a contemporary of William Berrow, Miles Wardley and Sid Weatherston. He enlisted on the outbreak of war, taking an immediate commission and joining the 14th Battalion, the Middlesex Regiment, only to be transferred to the 4th, when in Belgium. As an experienced scout he made a fine officer and leader. His body was interred in Brandhoek Military Cemetery near the town of Vlamertinghe in Belgium.

The 7th Battalion, the Norfolk Regiment had formed up with the 7th Suffolks, 9th Essex and 5th Royal Berkshires to create the 35th Brigade, which in conjunction with the 36th and 37th went to France on the 29th May 1915 as the new 12th (Eastern) Division. They had not taken part in the initial attacks at Loos, but had formed reserves and, moved into the area, after the heavy losses sustained in the first three days. By the fourth day of battle, the 28th September, some further progress had been made to the south of Lens, and a prisoner count, revealed 3,000 taken with 21 guns and 40 machine guns.

Reports of advances by the French in Champagne, brought encouragement and on the 29th, 'Hill 140' on the crest of the Vimy Ridge, and overlooking Lens town, was captured by the Allies.

Skirmishes and counter attacks continued into October. On the 2nd, Sir John French announced the success of British counter attacks on the mine, 'Fosse 8' and other ground to the north west of Loos. Six days later, on the 8th, the Germans were repulsed, but with terrible casualties. The next day, British trenches pushed out saps continuously, north east of Loos between 'Hill 70' and Hulluch. Shortly after, the British generals received proof of the extent of the scale of the recent German offensive and its resulting demoralisation. In response, on the 13th October, Haig retaliated with a major gas attack; after a short bombardment, the British Divisions, including the Norfolks of 12 Division, moved forward behind a great cloud of smoke and gas, south west of Hulluch to storm the 'Hohenzollern Redoubt'.

Harold Edgar Bliss, an eager young man with 'unsullied record' had gone to France the previous month. He had entered the trenches at Hulluch for the first time on October 12th. He was a twenty-one year old, educated businessman, who had, the previous year, enlisted along with his brother, as a Private in the 7th Norfolks. His leadership potential marked him out for promotion to lance corporal whilst still training in England. On the morning of their arrival, both brothers had advanced to take their objectives, hoping against hope, that the wind wouldn't change and turn the gas back against them. According to reports later submitted by his surviving comrades, Harry clearly saw his brother's death by rifle fire, before receiving his own wounds in a fresh advance the following day. At this point, things become less clear; one source claimed to have seen him walking to the rear to receive attention at the nearest dressing station. An alternative story was given by a stretcher-bearer, who knew him, who claimed that he saw him lying dead on the battlefield, but before he could retrieve his body, a new wave of British attacks was under way, capturing several sections of enemy trench line. His body was not found later, and he was reported missing in action the same day.

Also moving forward on the 13th, was the other Eastern Division, the 18th, comprising 53rd, 54th and 55th Brigade. The 55th Brigade

LOOS, HULLUCH AND YPRES

were mostly men from the south east, from Kent and Surrey. On the 13th October 1915, the 6th Battalion, the 'Buffs' (East Kent Regiment), fought alongside the 8th East Surreys, the 7th Royal West Kents and 7th Queens, also at Hulluch.

Norman Jones fell with 'the Buffs' at Hulluch. His school years crossed with Harold Bliss. He was two years his senior, and spent five years at the School, leaving in 1907 to learn farming, firstly in Cheshire, and later in Cornwall. However, it was his experience as a scout master that had marked him out as a potential officer and leader.

Norman Aldman Jones was an only child, born on the 25th March 1892 to John Jones, a club steward from Bromley and his wife Emily. At Tooley Street, he was remembered as an affectionate boy with a great sense of determination to get what he wanted from life. He did not have an academic temperament, and yearned to become a farmer. After he had served his apprenticeship for three years in England, he became more adventurous moving to Saskatchewan to continue farming. However, later, he started working in an accounts office in Saskatoon. In early 1914, Norman caught rheumatic fever, and returned to England for treatment and recuperation. On returning to Canada, he caught the fever again, and again sailed for England. By the time, he was ready to return to Canada a second time, hopefully cured this time, War had been declared, and he decided to stay and enlist.

At first, due to his recent health record, he was rejected as being unfit for military service. However, on reapplying a few weeks later elsewhere, he was accepted without qualms. He became Private no. G/246 in the 7th Buffs, becoming a Lance Corporal within 3 months. The 7th Buffs embarked for France in May 1915, arriving on June 1st. By October they were entrenched at Hulluch. On the 13th, Norman was moving up in charge of his section to reinforce the Front line, when he, with several of his men, were killed instantly by a direct hit from an enemy shell. He was twenty-three years old. Norman Jones is commemorated on Panel 15 to 19 on the Loos Memorial at

Dud Corner Cemetery on the Lens Road Redoubt, an enemy strong point in 1915, not far from the commemoration of Harold Bliss on Panels 30 and 31.

The fighting at Hulluch was to continue for several days yet, with the Germans mounting a ferocious artillery and infantry counter attack on the 19th October. A few days earlier on the 14th, the pressure to capture the Hohenzollern redoubt was severe. More British brigades were being poured on to the battlefield to achieve the objective.

The modern traveller, driving along the D39 on the outskirts of Loos village, will find a specific memorial to the action by the 46th (Midland) Division on the 13th and 14th October to take Hohenzollern Redoubt. 138th and 139th Brigades set out with a strong belief in their ability to succeed where others had failed. But, as was to happen many, many times, they were let down by a very weak cloud of gas that had very little effect on the German defenders; furthermore, British artillery failed completely to cut the wire. The working men, from the fields and mill towns of Lincolnshire, Leicestershire and Nottinghamshire were gunned down whilst trapped and struggling on the wire. Those not shot, were poisoned by their own gas and shelled. The 46th Division lost 180 officers and 3,500 men.

Robert Plunkett Howett was one of them. Born in October 1883, one of an incredible thirteen children, of which seven were sons, surviving infancy born to Alice Howett and her husband, John, of Peckham, Robert spent four years studying at St Olave's from 1895, leaving to apprentice as a clerk. Later he moved to Derby, to work in the county education office, where he was married to Esther Taylor. By the end of 1910, he had progressed from solicitor's clerk to chief clerk to Buckinghamshire's Education Committee.

Robert had been a cheerful, sincere boy with a 'striking personality'. He was always enthusiastic, 'the embodiment of all that was manly'. In August 1914, he enlisted with his work colleagues, and became Private no. 1929, in the 1/5th Nottinghamshire and Derbyshire Regiment, otherwise, known as the 'Sherwood Foresters'.

Whilst at training camp, his authority and leadership skills ensured his rapid promotion, first to lance corporal, and then because of his obvious maturity and capability, to sergeant. As a married man of thirty-one, it is extremely likely that he would have taken a commission had he made it through to 1916. He embarked for the Front on 25th February 1915. Within a few weeks of his arrival, his brother Frank, a warrant officer in the 15th Londons, was killed in Belgium. Although the circumstances of Robert's death are not known, it is clear that he fell in the failed attempt on the Hohenzollern Redoubt on the 14th October.

Jack Woodward Gill was a fine Olavian. He was one of the select few who made the School Honour list, whilst not becoming school captain. He joined the school in 1903 as a nine year old boy, whilst Howard Keesey was captain. He left eleven years later in 1913 as a respected academic, alongside Sanders, Hamilton, Norris and Maybrook. He had three brothers, all Olavians and all older – Hugh, Norman and Laurance. They were the children of Robert and Helen Gill from Hatch End. A boy of 'singular variety and charm', Jack was liked by masters and colleagues. He was described as graceful, playful, with 'mercurial laughter' and a 'deep reverence for life'. As with the captains mentioned, Jack went up to Oxford in the fall of 1913, as an exhibitioner at St John's College, taking with him, his leisure time pursuit of botany.

When the War came, his brother Hugh took a commission in the Artillery in the hope that he could serve but would have a fair chance of survival. His wife had requested this on his enlistment. Furthermore, his parents had already lost one of the four boys as a child. Norman had died in 1903. Hugh tried very hard to convince Jack to take the same route, but Jack, as a bachelor, considered it his duty to join a Front line infantry battalion, fully aware of the dangers to junior officers in the trenches. He became a second lieutenant in the 6th Battalion, the (Kings Own) Yorkshire Light Infantry, part of 43 Brigade, 14 Division. From the trenches, he frequently sent home pressed flowers in his letters, a reminder both to his loved ones and himself, that the horror of war would not last forever. On the morning of 20th November 1915, whilst advancing against the German line near Ypres, he was shot directly through the heart and died within an hour. He was twenty-one.

The final Olavian to give his life in the 1915 campaigns at Loos and Ypres was Geoffrey Holt Schooling. Born on the 16th July 1891, to siblings Terence and Marjorie, he was the son of the late Henry Schooling and his widow, Lilian, of Hampstead in North London. Lilian Schooling, originally from Dublin, played a prominent role in the organisation of the nascent National Society for the Prevention of Cruelty against Chidren, from who she may well have encountered the young Jack Lidgett. Geoff spent four years at St Olave's from 1903 to 1906 rubbing shoulders with, amongst others, Jack Gill and Norman Jones.

He left to join the Prudential Assurance Company as a fifteen year old apprentice clerk, and later started to build a reputation as a published writer of stories for boys. He married just before the war, to Violet, and they lived in West Ealing. As a boy, his Masters remembered him as a 'quiet, unassuming youth with a gentle and wistful personality'. He enlisted in May 1915 as a Private no. 4084 in the 16th Londons and spent much of the year training in Richmond Park. On November 10th, he embarked by ship from Southampton for Le Havre, and was wounded within three weeks at the Front in Belgium. His wound, which was only slight, allowed him to recover, and he remained in the Front line into December. He was killed in action with two companions, three days after Christmas by an exploding shell. Geoff Schooling was twenty-four, and is buried in the Potijze Burial Ground Cemetery near Ypres.

The failure by Field Marshal French to capitalise on the early infantry successes of Haig's Army at Loos, eventually led to his departure, leaving the overall mantle of military power on the shoulders of the ambitious Douglas Haig, who had to wait over seven months before he could really find a suitable location and situation to test his strategy – in the Somme valley in France in July

1916. Loos was over, but not without terse critical comment from many quarters. Rudyard Kipling had lost his son, John in the Irish Guards. Robert Graves had taken part.

> 'If any ask us why we died,
> Tell them 'Because our Fathers lied'

A couplet written by Rudyard Kipling concerning the death in action of his son, John at Loos in October 1915.

> "What's happened ?" I asked.
> "Bloody Balls-up" was the most detailed answer I could get'

Robert Graves – *Goodbye to all That*.

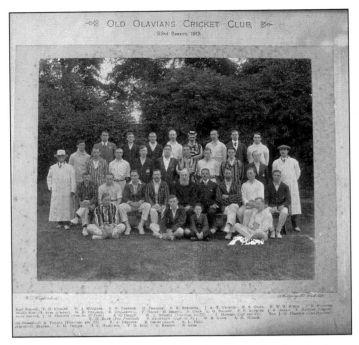

Len Stables, Clarence Falkner and the Pearson Brothers in the OO Cricket Club 1913.

Gilbert Doyle's Munitions Workers in the Midlands.

| 22.10.16 | 2/Lt.O.J.Wade. 2/Lt.W.J.Thusll. | P. O. | 45. 45. | M. M. | Sop. 2 str. 7786. | 1 Lewis & 1 Vickers guns. | Offensive Patrol. BAPAUME - PERONNE. | Left aerodrome 10.15 a.m. German message dropped in our lines states: "Lt.Oliver John Wade :- Born at Purley "on 1/5/96. Pilot's certificate numbered "3343. He and his observer are d* 1". |

Ollie Wade's fate as notified to the Flying Corps by the enemy.

Leslie Sander's posthumous book

1911 – Bay Ryley (back row third from left) Cecil Edmunds (front row far left) Teddy Cock (front row third from left) Jimmy Jones (front row fourth from left) Harry Kenyon (front row third from right)

HMS Queen Mary in which Alwynne Fairlie died in the Director-Tower during the Battle of Jutland

Noel Hamilton, Bay Ryley and Leslie Sanders 1911–1912 with the Head

Bay Ryley

Don Ryley

CHAPTER 7
Royal Army Medical Corps

At the beginning of the War in 1914, the Royal Army Medical Corps comprised less than twenty thousand individuals of all ranks. Within four years of terrible conflict, the service had grown seven fold, as a reaction to the increasing numbers of wounded soldiers. The Corps had no choice but to always be reactive, as it was nearly impossible to predict the medical effects and demands of a specific campaign. The doctors, nurses, voluntary aid detachments, stretcher bearers, sanitation staff, and ambulance drivers, constantly worked, until near exhaustion during campaigns, just to keep up with, not only the flow of wounded, but also to cope with the spread of infectious disease, rife in cold, damp and dirty environments, like the trenches of France and Flanders.

Another feature of the demands placed on the Medical Corps during the conflict was the complexity, severity and sheer revulsion and horror, towards some of the wounds inflicted on Allied soldiers. The unexpected effects of gas poisoning, heavy artillery shelling, 'gas gangrene' and enfilade machine gun fire, had to be addressed by medical staff, working largely on their wits, in poor conditions and with a lack of appropriate operating equipment and dressings. Such was the volume of injuries that, in the majority of cases, badly wounded soldiers, who had already been left for hours, if not days, before reaching a casualty clearing station, could only have their wounds cleaned, dressed and morphine, if available, given, to help reduce some of the agonising pain.

Four Old Olavians stand out, amongst others, that gave their services to the Medical Corps, because they also gave their lives in the pursuit to save the lives of others. More often than not, men of conscience, with a strong sense of religious belief and compassion, such individuals were torn between the call to serve their country, and their personal morality, not to take life, but to protect it. The four men, all born within five years of each other in the south east suburbs of London, attended St Olave's, before venturing into their respective careers, only to be thrown together again in the desire to keep the troops in the Front line.

Leslie Harold Hocking was the youngest of the four, and was born in September 1896, to two brothers, all sons of William Hocking C.V.O, C.B.E and his wife Agnes, later of Bristol House, Danbury, Essex. Leslie was described by his schoolmasters during his ten year tenure at the School as having 'visions of great enterprises', a personality of 'humour, idealism and unflagging energy'. Others commented on his shy sensitivity, his religious commitment and his love of natural beauty. He had joined the School in 1904 at the tender age of eight, at the same time as others that were to die in the war, Lionel Harvard, Don Ryley, George Castell and Fred Husk. He outstayed them all at the School. His only contemporary to spend an equal time in Tooley Street, was Olly Wade, 'the scientist', a head of School in his last year, 1915. Hocking, 'the naturalist' may have been good friends with 'the scientist', bearing in mind their common interest.

Just over a year younger than Leslie, was Douglas Charles Belcher, son of Charles Belcher, a greenhouse manufacturer and wife Mary Ann from Peckham, London. He was born on 22nd May 1895 adding to a sister Matilda and joined the School with a L.C.C. scholarship in 1906, where he spent six years. Colleagues, subsequently on the list of 'Fallen', at this time were numerous, and included, Brittain, Dawes, Dunkley, Foreman, Lorey, Lovekin and Stockins – all leaving together in 1911. Memories of his school years are limited to comments about his poor general health and resulting lack of athletic pursuits. In his spare time, he was more interested in following the Baptist religion at Rye Lane Church, near his Peckham home. He also began, as an adolescent, to take an unusually in depth interest in the activities of Doctor Barnardo's Homes for Orphans.

Harry Thomas Kenyon arrived at St Olave's a year before Douglas, but after Leslie. A few years older, he was born in November 1892 to Harry and Hannah Kenyon, his father, a schoolmaster, later took up a position at a village school in Suffolk at Leiston, having worked for many years with the London County Council. After a spell at Monmow Road Higher Grade School, he moved to St Olave's in January 1905, joining with Bliss, Dennis, Noel Hamilton, Norris and Sid Terry. In 1911, he left to take an appointment in the same profession as his father, as assistant teacher at Farncombe Street School. Two years later he moved to St Paul's Residential College in Cheltenham and then back to Brick Lane Church School in Spitalfields, East London, in 1914.

Son of a doctor, William Morris Lansdale made up the four Olavians. The eldest of them, born in July 1891 to Dr William Lansdale, a physician and surgeon and his wife Kate, of Newington, he attended the School for seven years until 1909, with contemporaries, Prout, Wardley and Cecil Talbot. He excelled academically in, amongst other subjects, classics and medicine and was described as 'one of those pupils who are good in so many subjects that it is difficult to make the final selection for their lifework' so said his schoolmasters. Only quite late in his school career, did he finally decide to choose medicine at Guy's Hospital, instead of reading classics at Oxbridge. Here he studied under Dr Thomas Stretton Robson who, usefully, happened to be his his maternal uncle.

All four were to find their place in the War, Lansdale as a medical officer attached first to artillery, then infantry in France; Kenyon, as a stretcher-bearer, assigned to battalions in action in the Front line in Belgium; Hocking, with the London Field Ambulance as both driver and stretcher-bearer in France; and Belcher, as non-commissioned sanitation officer in Salonika.

Medical success in returning injured men to active duty, was dependent on many factors outside the control of the R.A.M.C. With time, as the mobile war of 1914 developed into the more static line, characteristic of trench warfare, a well planned chain of medical facilities was created, behind the Front.

Battalion stretcher-bearers risked their lives daily, and nightly – men just like Private no. 510504 Harry Kenyon, to rescue the wounded from No Man's Land, usually under heavy shelling and rifle sniping. The wounded would then be taken from the trench system, where all they could be given was a drink, to the regimental aid post, often in a partially protected dug-out or building cellar in the support line structure, near the Front. These places were dark, unheated and damp, and the wounded would have their wounds diagnosed by the medical officer in charge, men like Captain and Adjutant William Lansdale, injections would be given and dressings, either improved, changed or, in many cases, given for the first time. For surgery to be given at the aid post was rare.

A line of relay and collecting posts linked the regimental aid post with the advanced, and main, dressing stations. In the early days of the conflict, wounded would be classified as 'walking cases' or 'stretcher cases' and would be relayed by men of the field ambulance units, like Private no. 678, Leslie Hocking.

At the dressing stations, the better equipped medical teams, concentrated their resources on temporary treatment, and more diagnosis, although amputations and other emergency surgery was carried out. The next stage was to transfer the wounded to the casualty clearing stations, further back from the Front lines, usually in railway sidings, but still sometimes within the range of enemy shelling. There was approximately one clearing station for each battalion in the line. By 1917, each station was dealing with over a thousand cases at one time in the most stressful of circumstances.

After the clearing station, for those who couldn't easily be returned to duty, wounded men were taken by ambulance train or barge to a 'base hospital' near the French coast, or, if in need of convalescence, to Southampton by ship. An analysis of the success of this network of facilities is best viewed in comparison to French and German systems, and in the ratio of those that returned to fight again, against the total wounded taken through the system. Allied reports claim that over 80% of wounded returned to the front, and that the system was better equipped and better organised that both allied and enemy alternatives.

Lansdale, the thoughtful, eager, gentle boy had won an entrance scholarship to Guy's Hospital in London in 1909, followed by the 'Wooldridge Memorial prize' for Physiology in 1911, the 'Beaney prize' for Pathology in 1914, and the 'Essay prize of the Physical Society', of which he was also its President. All by the time he was twenty-three. He did not enlist immediately in summer 1914, as he was preparing for the London University tests, but having taken the 'M.B. & B.S', he took a commission with the Royal Army Medical Corps and was gazetted in January 1916 as a lieutenant. He went to France on the 29th as medical officer of the 107th Field Ambulance.

Leslie Hocking, at nineteen, could have won a science scholarship to Oxford or Cambridge Univeristies, but preferred to stay in South Kensington with his father and brothers. Clearly, without the arrival of the War, he may well have become a senior academic in both natural history or science. In July 1915, having seen that the War was not be over quickly, he decided that he would enlist in the 2/1st London Field Ambulance as a private. In late 1915, he saw, at first hand, the results of the use of gas at Loo's in September. Dr J.S.Haldane, part of a Government trip to France to see the effects, reported that 'these men were lying, struggling for breath and blue in the face'. Both nurses and doctors didn't know how to cope with wards full of men, gasping for breath.

Harry Kenyon, the merry, generous hearted youth, left his third teaching post a month after the launch of gas at Loo's. He enlisted in the R.A.M.C. Territorial Force, 2/2nd London Field Ambulance as a private, and was sent to France in the middle of the Somme campaign in late 1916, attached to a battalion at the Front. Here he formed part of a team of up to thirty-two stretcher-bearers whose job it was to recover those that fell whilst advancing.

On leaving school in 1911, Douglas Belcher, apprenticed as a clerk in the City, for a while, until a better opportunity arose in the Public Health Office of the London County Council. His interest and aptitude for this type of work, led him to enlist in the Medical Corps, in the sanitation section in summer 1914. He was nineteen. Within a few months he found himself on board ship for Salonika with the 39th Sanitary Section.

Chronologically, the first to lose his life was Private Hocking of the London Field Ambulance. Having survived the Loo's campaign, his ambulance unit moved south with the London Territorial Regiment to the Somme Valley to a base near the village of Hebuterne, which is about twenty kilometres north of the French town of Albert. In the run up to the battle of the Somme, Hebuterne was turned into a British fortress, marking the end of the left flank of the attack on the 1st July, an area dominated by the anticipatory presence of 56 (1/1st London) Division. Ten battalions were defending this section of line from Gommecourt to Hebuterne. Wounded men of the Royal Fusiliers, Rangers, Kensingtons, Scottish, Queen's Victoria & Westminster Rifles and the London Rifle Brigade, were plucked off the battlefield in unacceptably high numbers by roving teams of stretcher-bearers, as realisation set in, that the pre-attack bombardment had neither succeeded in destroying the enemy machine gun nests, nor in cutting the barbed wire.

Leslie Hocking, operating as a temporary stretcher-bearer to boost the numbers, waited in the Front line trenches, whilst waves of London men climbed out of their trenches to attack the town of Gommecourt. The first two lines of trenches were taken with little trouble, but attempts to take the enemy stronghold at 'Nameless Farm' were repelled and prompted a counter-attack with intense artillery barrage and bombs. Gallant attempts to reinforce soldiers who had got cut off, all resulted in more casualties. By 10pm that night, all the land gained, had been retaken at astronomical cost. As part of a stretcher party picking up wounded, Leslie was killed instantly by the explosion of a shell. His senior officers, Captain Rice Oxley and Major Brebner later spoke of him as a cheerful and fearless man, who had been 'specially mentioned' in despatches. He was twenty-one, and is buried in the Hebuterne Military Cemetery. He was one of three Olavians to die on the first day of the Somme.

Meanwhile, Private Kenyon, known to his schoolfriends as 'K of C', had worked his way successfully through the French campaigns of 1916, and was in summer 1917, based with 56 Division near the Belgian village and lake of Dickebusch. The area, used for rest and recreation by troops, was a short distance from the town of St Eloi, south west of Ypres, and about three kilometres behind the Front, as it stood in June 1917 at the start of the third battle of Ypres. As the campaign developed through the localised battles of Messines, and Pilckem, Harry, whose unit had been working in the Front trenches at Zillebeke as a stretcher-bearing team, were, on the 16th August, relieved of their posts, and told to move to Dickebusch for a rest.

As they were making their way from the support trenches to the road, he was hit by a shell fragment from a nearby explosion. Although he had only been hit in the thigh, an artery had been severed, and by the time that his comrades could get him to an dressing station, he had lost too much blood. He died a day later, aged just twenty-four. His body was buried at 'The Huts' Cemetery in Dickebusch.

It was nearly a year later when newly promoted Lance Corporal Belcher, now of the 102nd Sanitary section, R.A.M.C. contracted dysentery in the searing summer heat of Salonika. He had been stationed in this theatre of war for nearly three years, supporting British infantry fighting the Turks at the battles of Kosturino, Struma and Doiran, and regularly volunteering for dangerous stretcher-bearing assignments, which he could easily have avoided, as a non-commissioned sanitation officer. In spring 1918, having contracted dysentery, with his slight physique, weakened by poor nutrition, and normal wartime privation, didn't help his recovery. He was nursed, with some care, for three months in a well equipped hospital in Salonika, but to no avail. He slipped away on the 5th July aged twenty-three. He is buried in the Lembet Road Cemetery on the road from Salonika to Seres.

Finally, Captain and Adjutant Lansdale. He had left the Field Ambulance in 1916, transferring to the Royal Field Artillery for a while, gaining experience of dealing with wounds caused by explosion, then becoming medical officer attached to the 5th Battalion, the Royal Berkshire Regiment based in the southern suburban area of the town of Albert on the Ancre River, at Meaulte Village. In spring 1918, the enemy had stormed the shell-ruined town, finally taking its possession, after four long years. In the summer, the Allies, armed with fresh American troops, planned to retake Albert in their general advance, part of the third battle of the Somme. William Lansdale was killed during its defence, by an exploding shell on the 26th August, snuffing out, in an instant, a potentially brilliant surgeon. He had just shouted a warning to some stretcher-bearer to take cover, when he himself was struck by direct hit. He was twenty-seven and is buried at Meaulte Military Cemetery.

And so, as the part of the Olavian 'Fallen' in the activities of the Medical Corps draws to a close, it is worth reflecting on the sad statistics of the War, left in millions of memories. Nearly two million British ordinary soldiers received near fatal wounds, with another seven hundred thousand officers. One in eight infantrymen were killed, 12% of all active troops were killed and 38 % wounded. The infantry received over 80% of the casualties, followed by the artillery, with less than 6%; When you add to this, the three and a half million cases of 'non battle' casualties from meningitis, pneumonia and frostbite, of which only forty thousand perished, the role and work of the medics, speaks volumes.

CHAPTER 8
The Battle of the Somme –
The first two weeks

Joffre, the French General, had for some months during 1915, been applying pressure to General Haig and the British Staff to commit more British soldiers to the Somme Valley sector of the French Front, thereby allowing French troops to move south, to defend the line near Verdun. The summer of 1916 witnessed the first major campaign of the War co-ordinated by the British command, employing sixteen British Infantry Divisions and only five French. Joffre meanwhile, enduring ridiculously high levels of casualties at Verdun, was secretly hoping that the 'blooding' of British troops on the Somme, would serve to commit Great Britain firmly, to the defence of the Front.

Not even he could have anticipated the impact of Haig's strategy on the British divisions, on the infamous 1st July and for several months afterwards. The plan that emerged in the spring of 1916 was to launch a fourteen mile wide infantry attack from the town of Serre in the north, right down to the town of Maricourt in the south, with a diversionary attack around Gommecourt, slightly above Serre. A heavy artillery bombardment would destroy the German Front lines, put their machine gun nests out of action and cut the barbed wire entanglements laid in No Mans Land.

Then, a hundred thousand Allied soldiers would advance slowly with bayonets fixed, to take their primary and secondary objectives. Further back, two cavalry divisions would wait to exploit the infantry success. Many Old Olavian soldiers served in the line or in reserve on the 1st July 1916. Five of them were killed in the space of six days, two of them on the first day. These five men typified and shared, the character, trust, loyalty, commitment and hope of the sixty thousand casualties that had occurred by the end of the first day of battle.

The two Olavians who were killed in action on the first day were members of two of the best trained Territorial Regiments at the Front at that time: Corporal no. 470551 Arthur Stanley Prout and Private no. 511402 Sidney Bowler Weatherston. Arthur served with the Rangers, the 12th Battalion, London Regiment, and Sidney with the London Scottish, the 14th Battalion, London Regiment. Both had enlisted as privates, both were twenty-five years old. They had been friends at St Olave's in their school years between 1902 and 1908, Arthur, an Englishman and Sidney, a Scot. Both took part in the Gommecourt 'diversion' as part of 168 Brigade, 56 (London) Division.

Working south down through the battalions, from Gommecourt in the north, down through Serre covered by the Yorkshiremen and Lancastrians, through Beaumont Hamel with the various Fusilier battalions of 29 Division, to Thiepval, fortified by the Ulstermen and the Borderers of 36 and 32, three other Olavians were stationed in the reserve trenches at Ovillers and La Boisselle.

The three were all commissioned officers. They had been gazetted in 1914 as second lieutenants. Herbert Cecil Harris served with the 6th Battalion, the Royal West Kent Regiment, part of 37 Brigade, 12 Division. He was 25 years old. Alex Duncan Guthrie Procter served in the same Division, in 36 Brigade, with the 8th Battalion, the Royal Fusiliers. He was a shade younger at 24 and had been commissioned out of the 16th Londons, where he had been Private no.3714. William John Mason commanded a company of 8th Gloucesters in 57 Brigade, 19 division. He was the senior man at 27. Two were promoted first to lieutenants, then to captains. Alex Procter would have been promoted too, had it not been for his early demise. Their school years also crossed in part.

The quiet early morning of Saturday July 1st was shattered at 06.25 hours with the usual artillery bombardment. Many of the fresh troops of 'Kitcheners New Army' that had moved up to the line the afternoon before, had not been so close to a bombardment before, and sat cheering its ferocity as if at a firework display. Enemy artillery was also active, particularly at Gommecourt. Less than an hour later, smoke was released from the left of the line and the front line infantry climbed out into 'No Mans Land' under the cover of the advancing smoke screen. Both the Rangers and the London Scottish took up the vanguard position for 168 Brigade. Next to them, advanced the Queen Victoria's Rifles and the London Rifle Brigade of 169. Fortunately, the bombardment had cut the wire sufficiently, to allow the troops to pass through unencumbered.

In a short time, the first two lines of trenches had been taken with few casualties. Much of this early success was put down to the London Division's reputation as experienced in battle, with a high proportion of trained, pre-war volunteers still in its ranks, plus a vast quantity of educated intelligent men from the commercial world, who would most likely have been made officers in other regiments. By 9am, all objectives had been secured, but at higher loss. Sid Weatherston's senior officer, Major Low reported that 'the German trenches were so badly smashed up, we didn't really know where we were. From my company of 150 men, there were only 35 who were not wounded'.

Deadlock ensued, when the Germans set up a counter barrage from 'Nameless Farm', eliminating a bombing party from the Queens Westminster Rifles (16th Londons), and cutting off other stranded casualties of 4th, 14th and 16th from rescue by stretcher parties. The combined effects of continuous enemy artillery barrage and bombs, with two light field guns 3,000 yards away in Puisieux Valley, was devastating to 56 Division. A German officer later spoke of the moment he first saw the London Scottish, or the 'Kilties' as they were known. 'The behaviour of the Highlanders seemed to us rather strange, for they came forward very slowly, either because of their heavy loads, or was it madness, without taking the slightest cover'. The men in kilts became a specific target for enemy guns. As one rifleman from the 4th Londons put it, 'the Germans kept hitting him (a London Scot) with rifles; they hated the 'Kilties'.

THE BATTLE OF THE SOMME

The Germans realised that 47 Division had failed to link up with the Londoners in their pincer strategy around Gommecourt town. A machine gun section of the London Scottish had managed to get across No Mans Land with a Company of the 13th, the Kensingtons, to join up with the first attack wave, but by late morning they had sustained heavy losses. As 56 Division gradually weakened, it's company commanders all became casualties. The battalion commanders had not been allowed to advance. The N.C.O.'s eventually ordered a reluctant retreat due to lack of ammunition. At 9.30 in the evening, fourteen hours after the initial attack, five officers and seventy other ranks were still holding out, dug into shell holes. Eventually, they formed a rearguard, whilst others escaped. The Londoners had fought with the utmost gallantry, but had suffered grievously. Of the division's seven participating battalions, 1,700 men were dead, 200 had been taken prisoner, with over 2,300 wounded, most in No Mans Land.

Sid Weatherston had perished with his fellow Scots. The London Scottish had lost 616 casualties from 871 men. The Westminster's lost more officers, twenty-eight, than any other battalion at the Front. Gommecourt had proved a most expensive diversion.

Sid Weatherston's remains were not located. He was commemorated on the Thiepval Memorial to the Missing of the Somme. He was 25 years old when he died. Born on the 27th January 1891 to John Thomas and Clara Weatherston of Clapham, London, he had an elder brother, John, who survived the war in the Royal Naval Volunteer Reserve, only to be struck down by influenza in March 1919, and another younger brother Harold. The boys had attended West Square School where they had won scholarships to St Olave's, with Sidney attending from 1902 until he left at 16 in 1907. His masters remember him for his sunny character, his keen sense of idealism, his reliability and devotion.

In 1905, he sat and successfully passed, the College of Preceptors examinations and when he finally left the School, he joined the London and South West Bank. In the years running up to the war, he had volunteered to join the Queen's Westminster Rifles, whilst also running the 83rd London Boys Brigade as a brigade 'lieutenant'.

As if this were not sufficient to occupy him, he was a bell ringer at Southwark Cathedral, member of the Cathedral Society and London County Association.

When war broke out, with his banking and military background, he immediately enlisted in the London Scottish as a Private no. 511402. It would only have been a matter of time, until he had been commissioned and transferred to a line regiment, had he survived the Somme. During training in late 1915, his mental strength, reliability and intensity marked him out for regular promotion. He became acting sergeant of the signalling section of 'B' Company. In March 1916, he had arrived in France ultimately to be based near St Amand, not knowing that he had only a few weeks to live.

Meanwhile, Arthur Prout had advanced on the same target with the Rangers. These were also tenacious men and, given the chance, 'survivors'. A week after the battle, an artillery officer spotted movement in a shell hole in No Mans Land. Two Rangers had been living there for a week, sharing water with overfed rats from the bottom of the shell holes. On July 1st, the Rangers had stumbled forward through the smoke screen with the Scots, had been immediately caught by an enemy barrage, and then had been driven back by enemy fire near Fable trench.

During the morning, Arthur had been killed by an exploding shell, whilst occupying enemy trenches. His body was not recovered, and like, Sid Weatherston, he was commemorated at Thiepval. He was also twenty-five years old, recently promoted to Corporal from Private no. 2593.

Arthur Prout was the fourth of five brothers from Denmark Hill. He was born on the 19th February 1891, following brothers George, Alf, Bert and Frank into Tooley Street. Arthur spent seven years at the School, leaving in 1908 with a reputation as a steady worker, making gradual progress to his objectives. He became a clerk in the City of London and trained to become a businessmen. He enlisted immediately in August 1914, and became a private in the 1st Battalion. After training, they embarked from Southampton for Le Havre arriving in February 1915. Based around Ypres in April, the Rangers prepared for the battle of Frezenberg. On the 8th May, Arthur Prout was badly wounded. The battalion war diary for the day reveals the scene.

> 'Arrived 4am. Enemy began to shell dugouts. A number of casualties. Order came to go forward and support Monmouths. Battalion about 200 strong, went in following order – A,B,C companies, D in support. Machine Gun section moving independently on the left with one gun. Many casualties sustained before ridge taken. Machine Gun enfiladed, enemy ascending hill, but then struck and disabled'.

Corporal Prout was taken from clearing station to hospital with a bad neck wound. The commanding officer of the Rangers, Lieutenant Colonel Bayliffe, published a 'Special Order of the day'. In it he 'congratulated all ranks...on a gallant performance, when after three weeks of continuous fighting, they delivered a counter attack in the face of overwhelming artillery fire, and in spite of heavy losses, succeeded in saving the situation, for the time being'. Arthur spent several months in England in late 1915, only returning to the Front in spring 1916. His men reportedly liked him and admired his sense of honour and trust. He was 'presumed missing' on 1st July.

The 'signaller' and the 'ranger' – Olavian rankers with the London Territorials, had gone. Gommecourt was not captured by the Allies, until the enemy relinquished it in their retreat to the Hindenburg Line in February 1917.

Herbert Harris was a popular boy, a probationer scholarship from Rotherhithe New Road School to St Olave's. He was big hearted, with a nature that gave and craved sympathy. His considerable natural ability made him an excellent cricketer and a brilliant full back at football. He was born in Rotherhithe on the 3rd September

1890, a few months before the birth of the Weatherstons and the Prouts. He spent five years working his way through St Olave's, from 1905 to 1909. Fellow Olavian friends, present between the same dates, included, Frank Dixson, the Royal Engineer's draughtsman and Harold Hunt, the ex patriate from Chile, who served and died at Ypres. In his last year, Herbert Harris's name was entered on the 'Honour List' along with twenty-one other boys, including fellow Somme soldier, William Mason.

After leaving St Olave's, Herbert studied successfully to become a teacher, whilst remaining regularly in contact with the School, its Masters, and its younger pupils. His steady perseverance and ambition had served him well. He was affectionately remembered for his tuneful rendition of various music hall songs at the school camp of 1914, literally weeks before the guns began to fire. In early 1915, he enlisted as a private in the Queen's Own Royal West Kent Regiment and was soon selected to train for a commission, mainly due to his teaching qualification. He was gazetted as a second lieutenant in charge of a platoon of the 6th Battalion.

His battalion was sent to France in late 1915, initially to work in the hinterland of the front, occasionally supplying reserves to the 1st battalion, which had fought at the second battle of Ypres. In the late spring of 1916, Herbert was promoted to lieutenant and moved with 37 Brigade, 12 Division south, to the Somme Valley, in preparation for the 'Big Push'. His regular letters home belied the circumstances of his life in the trenches. He joked of 'living in mud' and speculated on the goodies contained in his parcels from Kent.

12 Division were in reserve, west of Ovillers when the calamity of July 1st occurred. News travelled fast. 25 Brigade's Royal Irish Rifles (8 Division) had advanced towards Ovillers on an 800 yard Front under continuous machine gun fire, but had made the second enemy trench line regardless. To their right, the 2nd Middlesex with their Commanding Officer, Lieutenant-Colonel Sandys, had to traverse a stretch of No Mans Land with uncut wire, and with untouched enemy machine gun nests on higher ground, with their

THE BATTLE OF THE SOMME

guns trained on the muddy fields. Sandys had predicted as much. He saw his men mown down and having survived himself, could not live with the fact, and shot himself the following September.

To this situation, the 6th West Kents arrived early in the morning on July 2nd, 12 Division having relieved 8 Division. Herbert Harris, now a captain, and leading a company, found himself occupying the same line as had 25 Brigade the previous day.

There was no infantry attack on Ovillers that day, but the village was bombarded to confuse the enemy, while a separate attack took place south of La Boisselle, a neighbouring village. At 02.15am on the 3rd, the deafening bombardment resumed on the same targets as the 1st July with the infantry advance starting an hour later across a No Mans Land, now much narrower, due to the digging of rough assembly trenches. Captain Harris's West Kents were joined on their left by the Fusiliers, Sussex's and the Middlesex, and on their right by the Suffolks and the Royal Berkshires. The enemy were soon aware of the advance, and came out of their trenches with bombs and bayonets to meet the attack. All companies of the West Kents had gone over with the Buffs in support. Their flanks were poorly protected. Further reserves were held back for too long pending news of progress. There had been no surprise. The attack failed to gain a footing at a cost of 2,400 men to 12 Division. Herbert Harris was a casualty.

He had been encouraging his men through the smoke screen, urging them confidently to 'take the trench'. His company had made progress against the odds and he had been cut down by a bullet in the head as he mounted the lip of the enemy trench system. As the enemy were involved in hand to hand fighting, his men had to leave his prone body, but his N.C.O. managed to retrieve his pocket book and watch. Herbert was 25 and is commemorated on the Thiepval Memorial. His pocket book was overflowing with humour, endearments and messages from Olavian masters, pupils and old boys. The 'teacher' can still provide a powerful lesson.

There are some striking parallels between Alex Procter and Herbert Harris; Alex was eighteen months his junior and a year below him at School, but both men trained and became teachers, both exhibited strong, confident and ambitious personalities; they had been friends, and had found themselves selected, to become 'leaders' in Kitcheners New Army, destined for annihilation on the Somme; and finally, both had been shot in action cajoling their men to advance against crazy odds.

Alexander Duncan Guthrie Procter was nicknamed 'Muscles' whilst at St Olave's. He was the son of Charles and Janet Procter, and brother of two much older sisters, Janet and Isabella. All three children were left orphans at an early age by the untimely death of first their father, Charles and later their mother. Alex had been born on the 2nd April 1892 in Glasgow, Scotland and somehow managed to win a scholarship to attend St Olaves for five years leaving in 1910 aged 18 to train as a teacher. His personal circumstances may have moulded his character in certain ways. He is remembered by his tutors as being of 'high character, a boy devoted to duty, of unfailing courage and with both idealism and inspiration'. He spent the next three years, whilst living with his sisters in New Cross, working at Keeton's Road School, followed by a course at Goldsmiths College. By 1913, he received his first appointment as Master at the Ben Jonson School in Stepney. He managed two academic years there, before deciding to enlist in January 1915.

He chose the life of a private in the Royal Army Medical Corps, but later asked for a transfer to the Infantry, to the Queen's Westminster Rifles, the 16th Londons. He became Private no. 3714 and embarked for France with no infantry training in March. Within days he was in the Front line of Festubert and Hooge, dodging bullets, shells and avoiding gas. He was promoted to lance corporal and in the summer, he took the offer of a return home to take an officer's course. In August, he was gazetted as a second lieutenant and transferred to the 8th Battalion ,the Royal Fusiliers.

His new battalion required training, and he now had six months at home before, his embarkation to France and the Somme Valley in March 1916. He proved, during this time, very popular with his men, renowned for his coolness under pressure and his enthusiasm. In France, he served alongside a fellow Olavian, S.H. Clark, who won an M.C. and survived the war. Clark retained strong memories of 'Muscles' Procter. At the end of March, the 8th moved from their base near Vermelles, via Bethune and Enguinegatte, to Marles and Mazingarbe by June.

In support near Herbert Harris's 37 Brigade on the 3rd July, Second Lieutenant Procter and his platoon, prepared to move up to the line, replacing what was left of the depleted tired, hungry battalions who had been there previously. On the 7th July, 36 Brigade attacked Ovillers from the west, while 74 Brigade moved across from the south. The 8th Royal Fusiliers were on the right of the line. The battalion war diary reports five objectives – trenches, church and houses. Allied bombardment had started at 06.45am and lifted by 08.30am. The leading companies, including Alex Procter, started crawling into No Mans Land. All four Companies attacked at thirty yard intervals over a frontage of a hundred and twenty yards. As the gun emplacements had not been destroyed, the enemy commenced a barrage of shrapnel over the 500 yards of No Mans Land causing over 300 casualties. As the lines of infantry reached the enemy trenches, the respective waves got caught up.

The war diary continues: 'the line swept on still suffering heavy casualties; few officers were left, but the men gallantly led by their N.C.O.'s and reinforced by the 4th wave, carried the first enemy trench'. Further progress, bombing along the trench system, was delayed by deep clinging mud. The battalion had lost so heavily that the second objective was, with difficulty, put into a state of defence. There were now no officers left. The battalion had captured two strongly fortified lines of trenches and had finally established themselves on the edge of the village. Casualties among officers were, Captains, Featherstonhaugh, Chard, Franklin, Walker, Second Lieutenants, Procter and Arnold – 17 other officers were wounded. The battalion went into action 800 strong and came out 160 strong, a large proportion of the casualties were wounded'.

Within a few hours ,the 8th were relieved. During the attack, Alex had been cut down by rifle fire and died. He was twenty-four and is commemorated, like his comrades, at Thiepval.

Bowler George Mason and his wife lived in Loughton in Essex. They had seen their son, William achieve startlingly rapid academic and military success over a short period of time. They had also seen his potential and his future eliminated by machine gun fire on the 3rd July 1916. He had been twenty-seven years old, and had written to the School a month of so beforehand, advising that 'if anything happens to me, will you please let those dear people of mine at home, know that I have 'gone out' knowing full well that the sacrifice will not be in vain, and that it was for the future (that I fought and fell), for unborn generations of Englishmen, and the liberty of a Continent, and, that War by machinery may be banished forever'. The letter was never sent, remaining in his tunic and was found with his belongings.

Clearly an intelligent man, a man in a spot, with dwindling hope of survival, but with a burning belief that what he was part of was right and necessary, and for the greater good. William John Mason was a shy, principled boy who grew into a man of high intellect through hard work. He became a respected man of 'sterling character', whether as Captain in the 8th Battalion the Gloucester Regiment, or as Examiner in the Exchequer and Audit Dept of the Admiralty.

Born on the 19th May 1889, he was one of the exceptional few boys who stayed with their Olavian education for a full decade, from 1898 to 1908. He made the Honour list, was senior prefect and chaired the economics debates. Before joining the services of the Admiralty, he sat the intermediate examinations for the 'Gladstone Memorial' and the 'Gerstenberg' prizes, winning both with best papers on 'Economics and British Constitution' and 'Economic and Political Science'. He also gained a Bachelor of Science degree with first class Honours in Economics.

Whilst studying at the London School of Economics, he started lecturing, a position he made permanent in 1912, followed by a

THE BATTLE OF THE SOMME

spell at Bristol University. In 1910, he had enlisted as a volunteer soldier in the Civil Service Rifles, the 15th Londons, and when he moved to Bristol, joined the Bristol Officers Training Corps. Squeezed into any spare time available, was his role as tutor of the Worker's Educational Association. Naturally, when War broke out, this trained officer was immediately commissioned and transferred to the Gloucesters, probably because of his location in Bristol at the time. By February 1915, after intensive training, he was promoted to lieutenant. The battalion embarked for France in July arriving at Boulogne on the 18th. By the 1st September, they experienced their first flavour of the Front line trenches at Richebourg L'Avoue.

The battalion war diary reports that on the 6th September, 'Lieutenant Mason, Second Lieutenant Fitzgerald and a man from 'D' Company, patrolled an old German communication trench 100 yards in front of the first line trenches, and found several dead Germans. They brought back valuable information in the shape of articles of equipment and newspapers. At 8pm a signaller read a German signalling lamp and made out the words 'Kitchener. Transport. Halt. Officers'.

In October, the battalion moved to the reserve lines at Givenchy and Festubert where they remained up to Christmas. In early 1916, they moved south of Neuve Chapelle to Jericho and Salamanca Camps by March, and on to Bapaume and Bailleul in June.

On 1st July, William, by then a captain, moved with his battalion, now part of 57 Brigade and 19 Division, to Millencourt. On the day, they gradually moved up from the intermediate line, north of Albert, to the Pozieres Road, and finally into the trenches at the famous 'Tara-Usna Line' At 01.30am on the morning of the 3rd, the 8th Gloucesters moved forward to attack via St Andrew's trench. At exactly 03.15am, three of the companies, led by three captains, advanced to attack La Boisselle. Captains Cox, Crooke and Mason were all killed, plus three second lieutenants. The loss of all three battalion commanders threatened a serious reverse. Lieutenant-Colonel Adrian Carton de Wiart, the Battalion's commanding officer, took control, reorganised the companies and prevented disaster. A unique character, Carton de Wiart was awarded the Victoria Cross for this act of gallantry. He had already lost an eye in South Africa and a hand at Zonnebeke, and was to be wounded eight times during the War. He survived all, to negotiate the Italian Surrender in 1943 and to work alongside Chaing-Kai-Chek. He died in Cork aged 83 in 1963.

William Mason, the economist is commemorated on the Thiepval Memorial.

An old soldier, a survivor of the first two weeks on the Somme, was quoted as saying "it is easy to read that 20,000 men were killed in one day, but only when one sees the cemeteries on the old battlefield, with their rows and rows of white headstones, does the figure begin to mean anything. It is a hard heart that is not moved by the sadness of the graves".

CHAPTER 9

The Somme:
The Woods, Guillemont and Ginchy

After nearly two weeks of intense fighting along the Front line from Gommecourt to Maricourt, Allied corps commanders were basically being left to make their own decisions on localised attacks, while their General Headquarters considered what their adapted overall strategy for the campaign was now to be. Clearly, complete success had been anticipated on the 1st July, and no plans for a long drawn out battle of attrition had been drawn up.

Between mid July and mid September, hundreds of thousands of Allied troops continued to die of disease and wounds. Many were to suffer shell-shock and to break down mentally under the strain. During this period of the War, marked in the memory by the battles at Bazentin, Delville Wood, Fromelles, Pozieres. Guillemont and Ginchy, seven Old Olavians died serving their Country and the Army, on the fields of France. Five were officers, two, other ranks, with Captain Howard Keesey the eldest at thirty and Rifleman Austin Rule, the youngest at seventeen. Two had been captains of St Olave's, Keesey and Hamilton. Only one died of wounds in hospital, the rest fell on the field.

Eventually, General Rawlinson, leading 'X111 Corps', in the southern part of the line, began to argue that Field Marshal Haig, allow him to organise a major attack, to seize the clear opportunity of the three great woods behind the German trench system defences, north east from Montauban. On the left, Bazentin-Le-Petit Wood, south east of the town of Pozieres; on the right was Delville Wood, near the village of Longueval, and in the centre, set slightly back, was the dark, dense, High Wood.

Rawlinson appeared to have learnt some lessons from the

disastrous attack at the start of the month. Firstly, he planned to surprise the enemy with this initiative, by moving his troops up to the Front at Caterpillar Valley at night. Secondly, he ordered the advance, after only a short bombardment of less than five minutes, instead of the prolonged affairs previously. Finally, all of his troops also attacked at night, clambering out of their trenches at 03.25am.

Twenty thousand men from four of the divisions of 'XV and X111 Corps' were involved in the dramatic effect. They pushed through the German line; and continued for five miles. Bazentin Le Petit Wood was promptly taken by the 7th and 21st Divisions. Further to the right, the terrible six day battle for Delville Wood started, with the 3rd and 9th Divisions at the Front. The 9th (Scottish) Divisions recent new brigade of South Africans, would forever more, be associated with this struggle.

Meanwhile on the day, before the morning attack on Bazentin Le Petit Wood, the 18th (Eastern) Division had been ordered to take yet one more final attempt to take Trones Wood, to the right of the battlefield.

Second Lieutenant Noel Crawford Hamilton, Old Olavian, and past school captain commanded a company of the 6th Northamptonshire Regiment, part of 54 Brigade, 18 Division. They had been in action since the 1st July attack on Beaumont Hamel, where they had advanced in support of the 7th Bedfords, sustaining the inevitable casualties.

Noel had been wounded in the first advance along with fellow officers, Captain Frank Neville and Lieutenant George Shankster. As a supporting regiment, their casualties were fairly light – 29 killed, 123 wounded.

On the 14h July, at 02.30 hours, the 6th Northamptons were selected again to support and clear up, after the main attack by the men of the 12th Middlesex, their brigade stable mates. Both regiments had made their way to the 'Sunken' road near La Briqueterie, but as the Middlesex had only one company in position at Zero hour, the two regiments roles were reversed, with Noel Hamilton's company leading the night advance into Trones Wood. Strong resistance was met from 'Central trench' running along the east of the Wood, but it was rushed and taken at 06.00 hours. After three hours the Wood was taken, by breaking the strong point at 'Maltz Horn Trench' and the railway.

According to the war diary for the 6th Northamptons, only three unwounded officers remained, from a starting line up of seventeen; 247 ranks remained, from 550 that advanced. Lieutenant Newberry, their medical officer had been killed whilst treating the wounded between Trones and Bernafay Wood. Despite their weakened strength, they were not relieved as expected, and were ordered to stay in position at Maltz Horn. Four other officers had been killed in the action – Major Clark and Second Lieutenant Lys of C Company, Second Lieutenant Farrell of D Company and Second Lieutenant Hamilton of B Company. In addition, Noel's captain had been badly wounded, and his immediate colleague, Greenwood.

Noel's life had been one of great promise. Son of the Reverend Frederick and Mrs Jane Hamilton, and younger brother to Claud, he had been born in West Kensington on Christmas day 1892. He won a scholarship to St Olave's from the Grocer's School in Hackney in 1905 and worked his way to the top of the School in his seven years of attendance. In his final year, his reputation in the School at its height, he was made classical captain opposite the brilliant Leslie Sanders as science captain. His Masters were impressed by his 'rapid mind, excellent memory and his keen literary perception'.

His school and army friends spoke of his 'modest retiring nature, his sublime sense of duty, his nobility, charm and love of all things Irish'.

Despite a delicate physique, he became school cricket captain, and continued this prowess at Jesus College, Cambridge where he had won a £60 scholarship to study Classics. In 1912, he became a 'Marshall Exhibitioner' and came first in the open entrance examination for the 'Rustat Scholarship'. A year later, he won the University 'Bell Scholarship'.

The War interrupted his academic promotion, as it did with so many others of high ability. He took an immediate commission, was in France by July 1915 and was twenty-three at his untimely death. A death that profoundly affected his friend Leslie Sanders, who himself was to die less than a year later. "Never was he more an Olavian than in the hour of his death. He had won his colours in the sternest game of all: the purple, the black and the white". The 'Irish gentleman' was the first of the eight to fall.

Walter Doughton was a merry and cheerful boy with a great love of fun. Born in Rotherhithe, the only son of Walter and Maria Doughton, on the 10th February 1892, he attended Monmow Road School near the Bricklayers Arms Goods Depot in Page's Walk and Southwark Park. He spent just two years at St Olave's on a short L.C.C. scholarship, and at fourteen, joined as an apprentice clerk in the General Steam Navigation Company. After he had learnt his trade, by 1911, he moved to a shipping agency 'Messr's Tozier, Fisher and Co.' Much of his spare time was taken up in activities with the Rotherhithe Church Hall.

On the outbreak of war, the twenty-two year old shipper, chose to enlist as a private in the 8th Royal Fusiliers (City of London) Regiment, no. STK/958, signifying men recruited mainly from the Stock Exchange and the London clearing banks. The battalion was despatched by train, first to Colchester in Essex and later to Salisbury Plain for the next year, eventually arriving in Belgium in July 1915 in preparation for the Loo's campaigns in the autumn. On his arrival, Walter was transferred to the 10th battalion, which formed part of the 111th Brigade, 34th Division (111 Corps). 34 Division received orders to move south to the Somme Valley shortly after spring 1916. 111th Brigade's first involvement in the Somme campaign had arrived on the eighth day of battle when they were ordered to move forward in support of 19 Division between La Boisselle and Contalmaison.

Exactly a week later, through morning mist and a summer temperature reaching 72 degrees fahrenheit, Walter, with the

10th Royal Fusiliers, became deeply involved in the fight for Delville Wood. After a prolonged bombardment of the Wood, the Division attacked the town of Pozieres at 09.20 hours from the direction of Contalmaison. The 8th East Lancashires advanced first, over an open terrain of 1,300 yards. Nearly at Pozieres, with a mere 300 yards to go, most of the battalion were suddenly mown down by successive waves of enfilade machine gun fire emanating from the Wood. By early evening, after another hour of artillery bombardment, the 10th Royal Fusiliers went forward on the same target, this time with more caution, and succeeded in gaining some ground and consolidating it.

During this last advance, Private Doughton was struck in the body by rapid machine gun fire and badly wounded. He lay in No Man's Land until the end of the engagement, and was later recovered by stretcher-bearers and taken to an advanced dressing station. From here, with his wounds only crudely and temporarily seen to, he was moved over the next three long and painful days to a casualty clearing station, where it was decided that the severity of his wounds were reason enough to send him by hospital truck to Rouen. Clearly, four days of travelling with inadequate medical care, did not help a recovery. He passed away after two days in hospital on the 21st July. He was twenty-four and was buried in the cemetery of St Sever, in Rouen.

Just over three weeks passed until yet another Olavian was killed. On the 15th August, in the B2 Sector at Bailleul at the junction of the Armentieres and Lille Roads, an exhausted officer of the 7th Battalion, the Bedfordshires, sat in his 'dug out' to scrawl in pencil the day's events in the war diary provided. The 7th had taken over this part of the trench line nine days earlier on the 6th. The officer wrote that "day quiet. At 10pm, a dummy raid was carried out. Our artillery and mortars bombarded a section of enemy trench for 30 minutes and then simulated a lift. At the same time, we shoved pole targets above our parapets and sent over smoke. Enemy manned his parapet and opened fire with machine Guns and rifles. A very heavy fire was then opened by our 18 pounders and Stokes Mortars, and it is thought that the enemy suffered severe losses. The artillery reply was feeble. Our losses were Second Lieutenant Roeber and three other ranks killed, two other ranks wounded".

Just another day in the trenches, but the end of the short life of David Arnold Roeber, son of Mr and Mrs A.O. Roeber of Forest Hill. He had just turned eighteen years and was severely wounded with three others, when an enemy shell exploded in their traverse. His body was retrieved and buried at Ration Farm Cemetery, in La Chapelle d'Armentieres.

David was a bright boy, born on the 6th June 1898 to one brother. He spent three years at St Olave's on a short scholarship, leaving aged twelve, to attend Forest Hill School in 1910. In 1912, he went with his parents to Germany where he continued his education and just completed it, in the spring of 1914. As he was under seventeen years of age, when war broke out, he was allowed by the German authorities to return to England, which he reached at Christmas. Initially, he did not enlist, probably believing that the War would soon be over. With his unusual perspective of seeing both of the combatants ways of life, he had opted to join a large city firm as a bilingual translator. However, he changed his mind within a couple of months, and enlisted in February, probably at the behest and encouragement of his brother. They were both subsequently gazetted as second lieutenants in the Bedfords.

His battalion travelled from their training camp at Codford, to Southampton and embarked for Boulogne arriving on July 13th 1915. 31 officers and 820 men marched first to Talmas, then Ribemont and Becordil. In September, they moved into the Belgian line at Fricourt and Meaulte. Following the troop movements of much of the Allied divisions in early 1916, the Bedfords moved down through France to Carnoy and Bray. In mid April they were involved in major raids on the enemy line, before moving into the Front line on the Somme in late June.

David Roeber's 7th Bedfords were in the thick of the fighting on the first day. As part of 54 Brigade, 18 Division, they attacked Pommier

Redoubt with men of the Fusiliers and the Essex. The attack was one of the few complete successes of the day. Trench after trench was taken – Maple Trench, Montauban, Beetle Allies and White Trench. At the end of the day, even the third objective of Caterpillar Valley looked promising. Counter-attacks were beaten off and the position consolidated. Noel Hamilton's 6th Northamptons were in support at Beetle Alley. Despite the successes, one captain in the Bedfords wrote bitterly at the time, that the mine that exploded at Kasino Point, had been responsible for the death of many advancing Bedford troops.

Two weeks later, Roeber survived the capture of Trones Wood, where Noel Hamilton had fallen, and carried on into august, where he was killed unexpectedly on a day of little fighting. The 'German student', with such an untypical Olavian upbringing, was followed a few days later by a man, considered outstanding, by even his most brilliant colleagues. The name Keesey stands out in the Olavian history of this period along with others like Harvard, Hamilton, Sanders and Norris.

Howard Keesey, from a young age, had a 'maturity of manner and thought'. He was the eldest of three including Walton and Edward, who each attended the School. He was born on the 19th June 1886 to the Reverend George Walton Keesey, a Congregationalist minister and his wife Annie, and had started his schooling at the Caterham Congregational School, before winning his scholarship to St Olave's at fourteen. He spent five years at the School, becoming one of the two school captains in his final year, alongside Sydney Grose. As a scholar at Downing College, Cambridge, Howard gained a first class pass in the natural science tripos and decided to teach.

After a first posting to Kendal Grammar School in Cumbria, he married in August 1913, Violet Marian Swinglehurst, and subsequently took up a post as science master at Wellington College in Berkshire in 1911. Whilst he was at Wellington, Marian bore a son, John Howard, their only child, who was later killed himself in action, at Arnhem in 1944 whilst serving as a section officer, 16th Parachute Field Ambulance RAMC, attached 3rd Parachute Battalion; John died of wounds received after being shot by a German sentry when trying to escape from an ambulance train at Apeldoorn. He was 28 years old and also left a widow, Susette.

Howard had enlisted in October 1914 and as a result of his degree and his status, was immediately commissioned as a lieutenant in the 8th Battalion, the Rifle Brigade. After several months of training, his battalion reached the Belgian Front in May 1915. As an officer, he quickly gained respect for his common sense approach, his humour and his sporting ability. As an academic, he appeared to be 'the intellectual', clearly a man of culture, well read and well spoken, but this rarely prevented his strong interaction with his men. Such respect earned him quick promotion to captain after being wounded in June 1915 and being 'mentioned in despatches' the same year, before the 8th arrived in France in late spring 1916.

The 8th Rifle Brigade formed part of the 41st Brigade, 14 Division, fighting alongside two battalions of the Kings Royal Rifle Corps. Delville Wood in August 1916, was their first involvement on the Somme. The six week campaign that had started with Walter Doughton's Fusiliers advance, back on the 15th July, was coming to an end.

The 14th Division was given the task of clearing the Wood. The 8th Rifle Brigade were to support the lead battalions – the King's Royal Rifle Corps, the 5th King's Shropshire Light Infantry and the 5th Oxfordshire and Buckinghamshire Light Infantry. They advanced under a creeping barrage, and by the 27th, the entire Wood was in British hands. Howard Keesey was killed on the first of these three days of 'clearance'. His parents were informed by his colleagues, that he had taken his company up into the line at Delville Wood, to carry out a small operation, which was countermanded at the last minute. He was suddenly killed by a direct hit from an enemy shell, that also killed his orderly. Both bodies were found by the 7th Rifle Brigade who relieved the 8th, lying next to each other. The regimental war diary confirms that 'D company came up to the

Front line to make strong points in the left flank of 61st Brigade. Captain G.E.H. Keesey killed, Second Lieutenant HR Adair wounded, Lieutenant CHT Thompson and Second Lieutenant DH Beves still alive (shell shock)'.

Howard Keesey was thirty years old and was buried at Serre Road Cemetery no.2, in the Somme Valley. Marian Keesey returned to live in Kendal with their small son.

The grave of Austin George Rule lies in the Aubigny Communal Cemetery Extension, number I.E 20. The Cemetery is near the village of Aubigny-en-Artois, 15 kilometres north –west of Arras in France. His grave is unusual, only in so far as it doesn't state his age at his death on the 7th September 1916. It does say he served as rifleman in the 2nd Battalion, 15th London Regiment (Prince of Wales Own) Civil Service Rifles, no. 2986.

Austin was born in East London on the 13th November 1898, making him two months short of full age, when he was killed in France. He was one of four children, which included a brother, John. His father, John Rule was a Welshman from Glamorgan and worked as an examiner for HM Customs and Excise. Austin started his education at the Down Hall School in Ilford, Essex, and won a four year scholarship to St Olave's, starting in 1911. When war broke out, although adamant that he wanted to leave school immediately to fight, he was dissuaded until his sixteenth birthday in November 1914.

He enlisted as a sixteen year old just before Christmas, and was sent to Dublin with the 2nd Battalion in 1915 to quell the Sinn Fein riots, whilst the 1st Battalion, went straight into the line at Givenchy in Belgium. He remained in Ireland until the Easter Rising in 1916. Earlier in the year, he was selected for special training as a 'bomb thrower' and soon had become an expert, wearing the prestigious 'grenade' badge on his sleeve.

Attached to the 1st Battalion, and sent to France as a replacement, he was based at Camblan Ricquoart in the Lorette trenches in late May. Within days, he moved up with the battalion first to Hersin, where the 'Fosse 10' mine shaft had been located, and then to Boyeffles at the end of June, where the 15th relieved the 21st Londons in 'Souchez 1' sub section. In reserve on 1st July, they stayed in reserve throughout the month, moving to Ablain St Nazaire and in August to Drucat and Franvillers. On the 7th September, Austin, 'the boy bomber', still based near Franvillers, was wounded in the head by an enemy sniper with a shrapnel bullet. According to his battalion's reports, he died later that day from wounds that could not be adequately treated in the field. Austin was the second of seven Olavian rankers to serve and be killed with the Civil Service Rifles during the war. Frank Howett, Alf Page, Henry Deem, Henry Shepherd, John Sutherland and Frank Trotman all wore the cap badge with motto 'Ich Dien' under its crown with plumes.

'Bay' Ryley was the younger of the two sons of Harold Ryley, Master at St Olaves. His father's tragic story is briefly recounted in the Palestinian campaign in late1917, as is his brother Don's at Loo's in Belgium in early 1917. Bay himself was also killed in action, completing the trio of family deaths all in the space of fourteen months, all in different foreign theatres of war.

'Bay' or 'Harold' was born in June 1896 attending the School for five years from 1906 to 1911, when he left to move to Emanuel School, where his father had moved as headmaster. Three years later, and just before war broke out, he returned for a final term at St Olave's, again when his father returned to the School.

An excellent swimmer, rugby footballer and all round athlete, he developed a reputation for fearlessness and stoicism. He broke his collar bone on one occasion at the start of a rugby match, and carried on playing through to the end. He was commissioned as a second lieutenant just before Christmas 1914, and after training in the Channel Islands with his new regiment, the 4th Battalion, North Staffordshire Regiment, he embarked for the French ports in May 1915. On his arrival, a number of events changed his fortunes. He was immediately, temporarily attached to 1st Battalion in the Front line, which had recently been formed into the 72nd Brigade,

24th Division. Within a few weeks of this, he was appointed brigade bombing officer, and put in charge of a brigade grenade school of 115 men. He was given four weeks to train them, before they all returned to the Front.

By November 1915, the 4th North Staffs were in trenches near Reninghelst in Belgium. Two months later, they were in the midst of major shelling at the sensitive location of Hooge, at Railway Wood. February saw them at Zillebeke Lake for some rest and recreation, followed by moves to Poperinghe on the Vlamertinghe Road. To that time, all of their focus had been on the protection of the line at Ypres.

With the arrival of spring 1916, they moved south, first to Mericourt L'Abbaye in July and finally to Guillemont and Montauban in August. On the 10th of the month, 'Bay' moved his company – 'B' up to the forward line for a initial attack. Three officers were killed with 22 other ranks. On the 30th, at Delville Wood, 19 officers became casualties, two were killed. Again 'Bay' Ryley was in the vanguard, but emerged unhurt. A week later, the North Staffs engaged the enemy at Guillemont, from their position between the Flers Road and Ale Alley. Two days later on the night of the 5th September, they were relieved by the men of 166 Brigade.

What happened next and cost 'Bay' Ryley his life, is best explained by the regiment's war diary for the 5th September:

> "Relief immediately upset by attack made by 7 Division on our right of which we were not informed until too late. Second Lieutenant Ryley with two platoons 'B' Company, had moved up to Devil's trench...and was asked to co-operate with the 7 Division attack by an officer of 2nd Queens. This he most gallantly did, although 7 Division had been warned that we could give them no assistance. Immediately Second Lieutenant Ryley attacked the enemy, with machine gun fire on him and his men, about half of whom, fell. Ryley was immediately killed, and though a few men reached the German parapet, nobody

got into the trench. There does not appear to have been any co-operation by the 2nd Queens, whose attack also failed. When the enemy barrage had died down, the relief continued".

Bay's body was not retrieved. He is commemorated on the Thiepval Memorial. He had just turned twenty. His death set off a sad chain of events in his family.

Another name on the great architectural memorial to the missing, left St Olave's the same term that eleven year old 'Bay' Ryley was joining, in 1907. Edward Frederick Falby, a bright, cheery boy, the eldest child with three brothers and two sisters, was born in Lee, South London in November 1890 to Frederick Falby, a corn grain agent and his wife Mary Ann.

The younger 'Bay' Ryley would doubtless have heard of the reputation and successes on the rugby field of the elder Falby, as both were keen on the sport. Eddie attended the school for three years, leaving at seventeen, to work in the city. Like many of his colleagues, he enlisted, once it was clear that the War would drift into 1915. His younger brother, Fred, had joined up early with the 16th Londons and was already in France by 1st November 1914. Although wounded and later commissioned, he survived the War. Eddie joined the Artists Rifles, the 28th London Territorials as a Private no. 4728. The 28th, more than most regiments, proving a breeding ground for educated London men of the commercial classes, most of whom, within a year, would be commissioned officers in other line regiments.

Eddie Falby was no exception, becoming a second lieutenant in the 4th Battalion, the Loyal North Lancashire Regiment. His transfer to the 1/4th Battalion in France in mid 1916, placed him in charge of a company, which formed part of the 164th Brigade, men from West Lancashire (55 Division).

Early September found Second Lieutenant Falby's battalion coming up from reserve to a position in the line near Guillemont at Wood Lane and Tea Trench, where they had to immediately defend enemy counter attacks with a small number of Lewis Guns. On the 9th, the battle of Delville Wood began with 164 Brigade ordered to secure Hop Alley and Ale Alley east of the Wood on the road to Ginchy. This having failed, they instigated a frontal infantry attack down 'Pilsen Lane', another route into the town, but this too was repulsed by shelling and machine gun fire. One of the larger shells hit Edward Falby, killing him instantly. It was a costly attack with 24 killed, 125 wounded and 79 men missing. Eddie's body was never found. He was twenty-five, a gallant and charming man just embarking on a life full of potential.

Two months of localised fighting along a line of, no longer than a mile and a half, had produced thousands of casualties, but without significant success. Field Marshal Haig began to attract increasing criticism. What he needed above all was a reversal in fortune, and a victory to restore the confidence of the politicians at home. Talk of the capture of 'Ginchy' was shortly to be replaced by rumours of success at Flers-Courcelette, six days later.

CHAPTER 10

The Somme:
Flers Courcelette, Morval, Transloy Ridge and the Ancre Heights

By the middle of September, General Haig reluctantly agreed to try the new 'secret' weapon in battle for the first time. Nearly fifty tanks had been shipped to France in August. He was 'clutching at straws' and looking for ways to break the deadlock that continued to cause the casualty figures to rise and rise, without any strategic military gain, or rationale.

The main line between the two opposing armies, where the majority of the artillery and infantry activity was in evidence, ran from the banks of the River Ancre in the west through the French towns of Thiepval, Flers and Courcelette, along the north of Delville Wood to Guedecourt, Morval and Le Transloy. The fighting took place on ground that had been gained in August. Allied forces had managed to push the line a few thousand yards forward since 1st July.

During the campaigns that followed, though September and October, effectively helping to draw the long Somme campaign to a slow, painful and wet close, ten more Old Olavians gave their lives. The first, at Delville Wood, Herbert Blackman, through to the last, on the 29th October, at the Schwaben Redoubt, just north of Thiepval, Fred Goenner.

"I am waiting to proceed to the Front tonight. I do pray God will help you to leave the matter in his hands. He has indeed given me a calm and thankful heart. I am prepared to go cheerfully. How I long to be there". Herbert William Blackman was an intensely religious man who died on the first day of the battle of Flers Courcelette, a few hours after writing these words to his parents. He was twenty-six years old.

The Blackmans all went to St Olave's. Alfred, Herbert and their two cousins. Herb was born locally in Bermondsey on the 3rd June 1890, a son of Alfred Blackman, a law clerk and his wife Mary of New Cross Gate. He spent five years at the School, leaving in 1905 to join a provisions firm as a shipping and general clerk, where he remained for the next eight years learning the rules of a commercial life by day, whilst fulfilling a role as assistant secretary of Lynton Road Baptist Church, in the evenings. The outbreak of war in 1914, created a dilemma for Herb, as his employer couldn't now run the business without him. He therefore agreed to remain at home for a while.

As a single, fit man of twenty-five, he felt increasing pressure to enlist, and in February 1916, he duly became Rifleman no. S/15952 in the 8th Battalion, the Rifle Brigade. Unlike in 1914, the period of training was very brief, and mostly confined to understanding how to march, and obey orders. Firing rifles was only a secondary consideration. Arriving in France in early August, the battalion route marched to the Somme Valley, where they were to form part of 41 Brigade, 14th (Light) Division.

Herbert Blackman's first signs of action came on the 18th August at the town of Longueval, west of Delville Wood. Fortunately the battalion were in reserve and sustained only minor casualties. At 02.45 hours, after a 36 hour constant Allied bombardment of the wood, the 6th Somerset's had advanced and taken their objective. The southern section of 'Beer trench' was found nearly obliterated. On Herbert's left, the 7th Rifle Brigade advanced well, but were enfiladed with machine gun fire on their left, and only a small section of Wood Lane was secured. The next day, the 9th Rifle Brigade set up posts alongside 'Beer trench' and pushed out a sap from the end of Prince's Street. By the 25th August, the 9th were clearing the ground and two days later, the wood was, at last, in British hands. Herbert Blackman had so far survived this 'baptism of fire'.

Six days later, their time in support at an end, the 8th were ordered to move up to the new Front line, and advance over the open terrain of the ruins of Longueval and Delville Wood to the rear of the 32 tanks chosen to go in the vanguard. There is no doubt that the immediate effect of the appearance of the tanks was startlingly effective. The enemy turned and ran, and major ground was taken by the supporting infantry. However, tanks were still unreliable, they got bogged down in shell and mud holes and were gradually immobilised by enemy shells. Typically, the Allies weren't ready to capitalise on their success, which was to some extent a surprise to them.

The 8th Rifle Brigade suffered losses from machine gun fire from 'Pint trench' and 'Tea support' and at one stage, ran into their own barrage, but progressed to take 'Switch line' by 07.00 hours. An hour later, they captured their second objective, 'Gap trench'. During this last effort, Rilfleman Blackman was struck by machine gun bullets, wounding him severely, whilst moving forward, pack on his back, bayonet fixed to his rifle. His body was later recovered by his comrades and he was taken to the closest casualty clearing station, where he died. He was buried in Delville Wood Cemetery close to where he fell.

War affected different men in different ways. Herbert Blackman was a realist, and placed his faith in God to decide what was to happen to him. Percy Brittain, four years his junior, met the same fate, also writing his feelings a week before he died. "I have just come off guard and am having a brief respite. We are in a rather warm position, and last night had an exciting time. I'm smothered head to foot in mud. Its a bit quieter now, Fritz is still wasting his ammunition as I write".

Percy seemed far more boyish, naïve in some ways, with an enthusiasm for what he was going through, with little thought that he would be killed. He had been born in December 1894 to Frank Brittain, a builder's foreman from Bedford and his wife Sarah and attended Upper Kennington Lane School in Lambeth. From here, he was bright enough to be awarded a five year L.C.C. Scholarship to St Olave's. A quiet, persistent youth, he developed academically and was remembered for his courtesy, his steadfastness and consistency. In 1911, he joined 'Henry Bull & Sons' a shipping company, as a clerk, and, in his spare time, became involved in local social work through the Wesleyan Church. He moved to a better position a year later, at a competitor, 'P.Speek & Sons' a German shipping company. When war broke out, a year after that, the manager and two of the senior clerks, being German, were interned. Percy, therefore, was left to run the firm, and could not enlist with his friends.

He eventually did join up in 1915 as a Private no. 5286 in the 1st Battalion, the 24th London Regiment (The Queens), which saw action at Givenchy and Loo's in the autumn, and at Vimy Ridge and High Wood on the Somme in mid summer 1916.

On the 15th September, Percy's battalion, the 1/24th, received their orders near Flers. They were to attack the 'Starfish line' in the afternoon, following up on the advance of the 7th and 15th Londons towards the 'Switch line' east of High Wood. Of the four tanks that had moved forward with this advance, two had to change direction due to terrain, one lost direction and ditched in the British Front line after which it commenced firing on its own men, and the fourth provided good support having crossed the enemy line.

At 17.30 hours, two hours after they started advancing, Percy's platoon, passed Delville Wood, but were stopped just short of their objective, where they remained for the night. The division had no organised Front line. The 16th was a much hotter, sunnier day and slight progress was made by battalions in the 47 Division. Little activity followed on the Sunday, but on the 18th, with a steady pouring of rain all day, the 1/24th advanced to reinforce 'Starfish' once again. Enemy bombers pushed the Londoners back during the evening. Two days later the enemy had retreated from this section of line. Percy Brittain was shot by machine gun fire as he was moving forward to have another attempt at securing Flers for the British.

His body was recovered and he was buried in the 'London Cemetery' at Longueval. Percy was twenty-one. On the same day that the 'merchant' died, the 18th September, two of his fellow Olavians were also struck down, both in the same advance and with the same regiment. Percy Henry Riminton, born on the 24th September 1896 in South Norwood to William and Jessie Riminton spent three years on a short term scholarship to St Olaves from January 1909 until his departure, aged fifteen, at Christmas 1911. Henry Shepard Rowe was four years his senior, born in August 1892 in Brixton, spending six years at the school leaving aged sixteen in 1908, just before Percy's arrival.

On leaving school, both men had learnt their profession in the City of London, Percy working for the famous Prudential Association and Henry earning a reputation as a financier. In the years immediately preceding the war, Henry Rowe worked for a British bank in the Canary Islands. Percy Riminton, worked in his spare time supporting his local church in south London, staying in better contact with the School.

Percy Riminton was a shy, quiet individual, brought up to trust in God and to show loyalty to friends, family and country, and to observe a strong sense of duty to school, church and the Empire. With such an education, he, like all the others, enlisted. Henry Rowe, put aside the wonderful climate, the promotional prospects and returned by ship to Portsmouth at the earliest opportunity. Both men became riflemen in the 16th (County of London) Battalion (Queens Westminster Rifles) arriving in France in early 1916 as part of 169 Brigade, 56th (1/1st London) Division Territorial Force.

They shared the brigade with other London regiments, the Fusiliers, the Rifle Brigade and the Victoria's. On the 1st July, both men had survived when advancing in support at Gommecourt, and had continued through the summer months with average casualties, until the 8th September, when they relieved the line near Leuze Wood and Combles trench, south east of Guillemont and Ginchy. They faced the experienced 65th Regiment, part of the

208th (German) Division defending the town of Combles from a well entrenched position. Both men soon found themselves with orders to bomb down the trench system from the wood, and this was carried out with some success for a time, until a fierce counter attack forced withdrawal.

A week later, after some territorial gains, the Westminsters opened the battle of Flers Courcelette with an advance from Leuze Wood to take 'Loop trench' and 'the Quadrilateral', two key targets. They kept in touch with the French Army near the railway, and received strong support from a single tank. Combles trench was taken , but heavy machine gun fire from 'Loop trench', continued, despite constant repeated infantry attacks, and five hours of machine gun fire from the tank which had been routed in the mud. The attack, which had started at 06.20 hours, finished at 23.00 hours, with most of the Londoners still 80 yards from their final objective – the Sunken Road.

For the next two days, Percy and Henry's duties were light. The division, on the far right of the line, were briefed to protect with artillery fire. The weather was fine and sunny, 66 degrees fahrenheit. On the evening of the Sunday, the 17th September, the lieutenant-colonel of the Westminsters received orders to attack the next morning and finally capture the Sunken 'Combles' Road. With the daily weather on the Somme considerably affecting one's chances of living and dying, the 18th was not a good day to attack. Although still warm, it rained constantly all day with 13mm of water falling overall. Poor visibility, slow trudging through trench mud and a 'shell disrupted' landscape, were considerable obstacles for the two Olavians.

The regimental war diary for the day, states 'At 5.50am, the two attacking companies went over the top and both nearly reached the objective, when they came under heavy machine gun fire and were unable to get into the enemy trench. The remainder of the two companies – 3 officers and 90 other ranks, withdrew to the assembly trench, into which Second Lieutenant Thurston had moved up the supporting company, and in which he had been stopped by Captain Green, who saw the uselessness of throwing away more men into the attack'.

Rifleman Riminton no. 4815, the 'Queens Rifleman', was struck by exploding shellfire, and rifle bullets. Rifleman Rowe, no. 4189, was mown down by machine gun fire. Both were approaching the enemy trench parapets. Three of their officers died by their sides. Percy was six days short of his twentieth birthday. Henry Rowe had just celebrated his twenty-fourth.

Meanwhile, the 1/15th Londons with Olavian Frank Trotman, men of the Civil Service, were holding the line with the 47th London Division, at the town of Eaucourt L,Abbaye and the Butte de Warlencourt, a wood just north west of Flers. The once pretty little town and wood were to be the main point of attack for one of the last great battles during the Somme campaign – Transloy Ridge. The battle was to run for eighteen long days from the first initiative on Sunday 1st October. Three Allied corps were involved, 'XV', '111' and the Canadians.

The 17th, 19th and 20th Londons had advanced with tank protection, to capture the town on the 1st of the month. The men of Poplar, Stepney, St Pancras, Blackheath and Woolwich, joined with the New Zealanders, to sweep through the objective. Two days later, it was discovered that an enemy withdrawal had been forced. On the 7th, a fine but windy day, 140 Brigade, with the 15th, came up to hold the Front and relieve others. They were given attack objectives, but wave after wave of men from the Post Office Rifles (8th Londons) and the Civil Service Rifles (15th Londons) were almost immediately cut down by machine gun fire. All that was achieved were some posts near the Le Barque Road in touch with 41st Division.

Private Frank Trotman no. 532108 was believed killed in that action. He had been part of a body of fifty men, who had been tasked with clearing up some newly won trenches, when he was killed by a single bullet. He was thirty-two. The regimental war diary records that "the attack on the Warlencourt Line by 140 Brigade at 1.30pm was unsuccessful. The Battalion was badly cut up. Remnants under Captain Bazes dig in, in advanced position on right of Brigade in front astride the Eaucourt L'Abbaye- La Barque Road. Casualties: officers- killed 1, wounded 4, missing 1; other ranks – killed 22, wounded 257, missing 65".

Frank was born on the 16th September 1884 to three sisters and a brother, Walter of George Trotman, a grocer and wife Margaret, who lived in Camberwell. He attended the school for seven years from 1897 mixing with colleagues, Alwynne Fairlie, the 'sailor', and Ernest Clarke, the 'preceptor', leaving to join the London County Council offices as a junior clerk. Within a few years he had successfully acquired a Bachelor of Science degree in Economics. When the War arrived, he dutifully enlisted as a private, although a commission would have been easily possible with his degree. His reputation, earned both at school and at work, as a hard working, tenacious 'sticker' and 'trier', developed more strongly once in the Army. He was looked up to as the 'older man of experience' by scared young boys in the ranks by his side. His death, as always with such men of inspiration to others, was a severe loss to his comrades.

John Russell Carrier had become a skilled bayonet fighter in hand to hand combat. He was a quite remarkable boy and man. A company sergeant major at twenty-one, a full time soldier, who had enlisted in 1912 and latterly, a commissioned officer serving on the Somme. Another unusual feature of John Carrier's military service was the fact that he had enlisted as a rifleman and worked through all the non commissioned ranks, before becoming a second lieutenant, and remaining all the while in his regiment of choice – the L.R.B. – the London Rifle Brigade, the 5th Londons.

John had been reported missing, presumed killed at Les Boeufs on the 8th October 1916. He was twenty-three years old, and was one of the eighty L.R.B. officers lost during the Great War. Active on the 1st July 1916, John had lost eight fellow officers in just three hours at Gommecourt. Three months later, on another day of 'suicidal' activity for the 5th, John was killed, along with six more officer colleagues – all from one battalion. At first glance, it would appear that on every major advance, the L.R.B. lost most of their officers. It is therefore curious to imagine second lieutenant Carrier's frame of mind as to his likely chances of survival on the eve of such events.

John Russell Carrier was born in August 1893 in London, to one younger brother, Seymour, attending St Olave's for three years from 1906 to 1908. His father having died when the boys were very young, his mother remarried one John Comley, a law clerk which produced a step-brother, Dennis Comley in 1899. John's school years crossed closely with Percy Brittain and 'Muscles' Procter who both fell on the Somme. After a three years apprenticeship in the Ocean Insurance and Commercial Union, John tired of the mundane routine of administration and joined the infantry as a rifleman. At the School, his Masters always remembered his enthusiasms for athletics, sport, competitions and shooting. In the pre war army, soon to become the 'Old Contemptibles' of the Expeditionary Force, Lance Corporal Carrier, regularly won marathons, sharp shooting awards, and excelled at combat with just a knife.

In the first year of the war, as battalion N.C.O., he played a significant role in training new citizen volunteers, some of whom were recruited from the St Olave's Cadet Corps. It is doubtful, if old school loyalties had much sway on the parade grounds of the home counties in early 1915. After an officer's course in late 1915, he arrived in France in spring 1916, headed for the Somme valley and the 'Big Push'. Surviving the same battle initiations as Riminton and Rowe of 169 Brigade, John Carrier found himself dug in on Sunday 8th October in trenches due south of the town of Les Boeufs, south of Le Transloy. The previous day had been the first day of the battle of the Transloy Ridges. It would last until the 20th.

At 15.30 hours, the L.R.B attacked 'Hazy Trench' as other battalions had done the day before; the war diary takes up the story, "Companies almost reached their objectives, and after dusk, after the reserve companies had been put up, dug in. Both flanks being exposed, battalions had to return to original trenches, having suffered very severe casualties from machine guns on left flank. Battalion captured one enemy gun and 17 prisoners. Attack was not successful owing to gun pits on our left flanks not having been dealt with, and these were occupied in force with machine guns which fired in our rear and flank".

The resulting casualty report attached to the diary confirms 196 newly trained recruits and 8 officers joined the Battalion during the month of October 1916. This figure excludes returning wounded and sick. Casualties from two engagements on the 4th and 8th of the month, totalled 318 other ranks, 55 of whom were killed and 97 missing; and 20 officers, 7 of whom were killed.

Let us consider the impact of the loss of young leaders just in that brief period of attack at Les Boeufs in early October 1916 of so many young subalterns, young and intelligent, products of Harrow, Whitgifts, St Paul's, Haileybury and Goldsmiths, many of whom had already been wounded in previous battles; Lieutenant Harold Beard, Second Lieutenant's Charles Cole, Horace Smith and George Taylor, killed outright; Lieutenant M.J.Maynard and Second Lieutenant's James Dewar and Norman Baldwin were missing, wounded and presumed dead; Captain's Richard Charles and EC Wills were wounded as were Lieutenant Arthur Read, and Second Lieutenant's SAF Alford, Clement Hall, Frank Machin, Alex Thomson, John Lindsay and Wilfred Von Berg; and invalided out were Second Lieutenants Percy Dyer, G St John Martin and Alfred Newling. Their fellow comrade and officer, Second Lieutenant John Russell Carrier is commemorated on the Thiepval Memorial to the missing of the Somme.

Rifleman Albert Dawes no. 4775 of the 1st Battalion, L.R.B also has his name commemorated literally inches away from John Carrier's at Thiepval, due to alphabetical order, a fact that doesn't do justice to their strong link as Old Olavians of the same age in the same battalion, and giving their lives in the same action. Albert and

John joined the School in the same year, 1906, with Albert staying on until 1911, after John had left. A multi-talented boy, Albert Dawes was a superb violinist with strong academic capabilities in the newly emerging industry of electrical engineering and still with sufficient time to devote himself to St Lukes Church, the Bermondsey settlement, run by John Lidgett's father and the Church Lads Brigade. At seventeen, he took an apprenticeship, before working in a management position in his father's firm in Bermondsey.

The arrival of war in 1914, led him to enlist as a rifleman and endure monotonous route marching for months on end, at Fovant Camp in Wiltshire. Albert Dawes sailed for Le Havre just five weeks before his death, landing on August 28th. He was destined to be one of the new recruits that perished in a matter of days. Talent obliterated without thought. On the 9th October, the day after Carrier fell, the war diary, describes the scene. "Heavily shelled most of the day, and much sniping. Battalion relieved in the evening by the 1st Royal Warwicks and returned to the trenches between Bernafay and Trones Wood". During this long day, Albert was killed. He was twenty-two.

'The dentist' died just three days later, much further north towards Beaumont Hamel, the scene of some of the worst devastation on the first day of the Somme. He had only just managed to obtain his 'Certificate of Operative Dental Surgery' in time, before the War changed his direction. A man of cheery good nature, cool under pressure, Wilf Hollands was born in February 1893 to Alfred Christy and Chrissie Hollands of Southwark. He attended St Olave's, as did his younger brother Harold, leaving after seven full years in 1909 to enter Guy's Hospital as a student.

A mature, responsible individual, Wilfred applied for a commission and was gazetted as a second lieutenant to the 7th Royal Fusiliers. He was perceived as conscientious and dutiful and was soon sent to France as regimental bombing officer and attached to the 4th Battalion going into action on the Somme. By early October, 9 Brigade, 3 Division were defending the line opposite Serre, and preparing their trenches and supplies ready for a final push before the winter weather made it too difficult. The battle of the Ancre was to start in early November to this end.

During a relatively quiet period in the line, Wilf was killed by an exploding shell, whilst a fellow officer called Howe was shell shocked. It was the 12th October, there were no other casualties and the battalion was about to be relieved by the 1st Northumberland Fusiliers so they could move for some rest and recreation in the village of Mailly Maillet. His grieving parents were to be further devastated when they received news of his younger brother's death two years later in Jerusalem with the 21st Londons.

Supporting the 3rd Division at Serre was the 1st Battalion of the Honourable Artillery Company, based nearby on the Redan Ridge, just to the south of the town. Arthur Daniel Garrett was a Private no.5145 with the 1st Honourable Artillery Company. Born in July 1879 to William and Ann Garrett, he was one of the older men on the Somme at thirty-seven. His only contemporaries amongst 'the Fallen' include Ernest Curtis, the publisher, and Fred Bennett, the artillery major. Arriving at St Olave's from Coleman Street Ward School in 1891, he stayed for six years, leaving to work in the City. In his spare time he helped at the Duke Street Mission School and was remembered with affection by his masters at St Olave's. 'Arthur Garrett was popular, genial, good-natured and vivacious, with untiring patience, unflagging zeal, an unobtrusive manner and very strong convictions'.

Sunday 15th October was an overcast day with slight rain and a temperature of 57 degrees. Rumours were passed up the line northwards, to the Redan Ridge that the previous evening, the men of the Black Watch, the Cambridgeshires and the Kings Royal Rifles had finally captured the stronghold of 'Schwaben Redoubt', near Beaumont Hamel. Amidst further activity to repulse counter attacks, the enemy bombarded Serre and Redan. During one of these shelling attacks, Arthur Garrett was hit by flying shrapnel and killed.

The capture of the Redoubt that had brought such encouragement to the troops along the line, had been achieved through nine hours of courageous advance and engagement. Two of the men present who survived the attack were Riflemen Frederick and Augustus Goenner of 'B' company, 17th Battalion, King's Royal Rifle Corps. Twin brothers from Forest Hill in London, sons of Frederick and Annie Goenner, they had enlisted together in February 1916 in the London Regiment, later transferring to the K.R.R.C.

On the 15th October, 39 Division, of which they were a part, defended admirably against three enemy counter attacks, withstanding trench mortar attacks, shrapnel, gas, machine guns and even the recent introduction of 'flame throwers'. The 'Schwaben Redoubt' was of vital importance strategically, for a good safe view of the whole line.

On the next day, the various battalions of the 39th started to occupy all of the Front line positions, north of the River Ancre. By the 21st, they were ready for a further advance, this time their objective was the capture of 'Stuff Trench', a long line running east of the Redoubt. Before they could commence the attack, enemy troops once again attacked the Redoubt at 5am on a fine but very cold morning. The Goenner brothers and the 17th King's, drove them out with bombs. Augustus was wounded by a rifle bullet, but well enough to embrace his brother, after the attack, before walking to the rear to have his wound seen to, at one of the clearing stations. By the end of the day, both 'Stuff Trench' and the 'Pope's Nose' had been taken.

The next morning, Fred Goenner was defending the trench line, when an unexpected poison gas attack engulfed the trench, causing much distress. After some time, he was taken to the rear, wheezing and with temporary blindness. Despite treatment in hospital at Wimereux, he did not sufficiently recover and died a week later on the 29th. He was twenty. Augustus survived the war.

Both were Old Olavians. Fred, the elder son, was born in July 1896, a boy of 'quiet humour, great care and quite unobtrusive'.

THE SOMME

Both boys attended St Olave's, Fred for three years leaving in 1911 aged fifteen to apprentice as a clerk in a city firm, until he was sufficiently qualified to join his father's firm. A popular and vigorous rugby player, Fred Goenner was a contemporary of Percy Riminton, the 'queen's rifleman' and George Shears, the 'munitions man'. As the Somme campaign drew to a wintry close, stopped simply due to bad weather, the School lost another of its 'sons', buried at Wimereux Communal Cemetery, in the Pas de Calais, another victim of gas.

Haig had been recorded, stating the following words in that summer of madness, "In the stage of the wearing-out struggle, losses will necessarily be heavy on both sides, for in it the price of victory is paid".

The snow in November 1916 fell on the French battlefield, and when it thawed, caused a deep 'quagmire'. Some thought this to be hell, but went on to serve in even worse conditions during the Passchendaele campaign in summer 1917, further north in Belgium.

Telegram informing Joe Oake of the accidental death of his son Dug in 1918.

CYRIL AND DOUGLAS OAKE.

Leslie Edgley's Casualty form showing the uncertainty of his fate.

Flying Corps Mechanic colleagues of George Castell, loading gun magazines for their pilot's machines

Ralph Akerman *Percy Grist*

George Knight's Royal Aero Club record card.

George Knight (right)

One of four known memorial's to Howard Keesey:
*OO Memorial
*Sandwich Memorial
*Natland Memorial
*Serre No 2 Cemetery.

Oliver Wade

CHAPTER 11

The Arras Campaign: Vimy Ridge, Scarpe and Arleux

The French town of Arras stands on the River Scarpe, the capital of the department, Pas de Calais, and previously, of the area called 'Artois'. Much of the architectural and historical beauty of this town, known for its tapestry, was destroyed by the intense and ferocious armed conflict that came to visit between 1914 and 1918. Arras and the Scarpe, formed the southern end of the northern sector of the Western Front. To the north were the plains of Flanders, protected by the British, to prevent the enemy making contact with the channel ports, and to the south was the valley of the River Somme, again, mostly defended by British Empire, as opposed to French troops, where the 'Big Push' occurred in summer 1916.

Whilst the battle of the Somme was raging further south, preparations were being laid for specific Infantry advances in and around Arras. In all, seventeen Old Olavian soldiers were either killed in action or died of their various wounds between May 1916 and May 1917 in these campaigns.

To better understand the military strategy, it is important to know something of the terrain around Arras. In the north lay the Vimy Ridge, with the village of Givenchy at its western foot, the Ridge was held by the Germans from the early part of the War thereby denying the Allies a view over the entire plain of Douai below, where the German army lay. Literally thousands of French troops had died trying to take the Ridge. Towards Arras, the village of Neuville St Vaast housed the Canadian bases, with the village of Mont St Eloi on the edge of Arleux Wood, a scene of fierce fighting in spring 1917.

Arras itself had been occupied by the Germans in September 1914, but they had been driven out by the French in 1915. By this time, the city was in ruins and the French infantry were living in its miles of tunnels and caverns. The Allies continued through 1916 and 1917 to maintain their vulnerable position on the fairly small, Arras Salient. South of the town, the plains dropped away down to Bapaume, Thiepval and the Somme River. The villages south of Arras which became 'flashpoints' in the struggle of 1917, appear, someone once said, like stops on a suburban railway line – Monchy Le Preux, Hebuterne, Heninel and Croisilles.

On the 9th April 1917, the battles of Arras commenced from Givenchy in the north to Croisilles in the south. These campaigns stand out in memory for two key reasons; the fantastic success of the Canadians in taking the strategic Vimy Ridge through tunnels built by the Royal Engineers; and the organised mass aerial campaign carried out by the Royal Flying Corps, no longer focused solely on reconnaissance, but now heavily on armed combat.

Five Olavians had served with the London Territorial Regiments with another, an officer in the Wiltshires, in the proximity of Vimy Ridge throughout 1915 and early 1916, with hopes of storming the heavily fortified enemy defences. Company Sergeant Major Frank Howett and Private Richard Walsh of the 1/15th Londons (Civil Service Rifles) south of Lens, Sergeant Sid Hill of the 20th Londons (Blackheath & Woolwich) at Arras, Second Lieutenant 'Ginger' Wilson of the London Scottish, the 14th Londons, at Aubigny, Private Edward Thompson of the 13th Londons (the Kensingtons) at Mont St Eloi, and Second Lieutenant Walter 'Didi' Maybrook of the 1st Battalion, the Wiltshire Regiment, based at Neuville St Vaast near Mont St Eloi.

In terms of brigade and divisional structure, the 20th formed part of 142nd Brigade, 47th London Division, the 13th and 14th were together in the 168th Brigade, 56th London Division, and the 15th joined the 20th in sister Brigade, the 140th, again in 47 Division. The 1st Wiltshires formed part of the 7th Brigade, 25 Division.

In those earlier stages, long before the detailed planning of the Arras campaign in 1917, each man had his own story in the midst of battle.

Company Sergeant Major Frank Howett had been badly wounded in the thigh on the 21st May 1916. He was last seen lying in a shell hole between the lines, where his men had placed him, before continuing their advance, in the hope that he could be brought in during the night. He was, however, killed in a subsequent bombardment. He was thirty-four. One of seven brothers, he was a son of John and Alice Howett from Peckham, and born in December 1880. A good tempered, sturdy and independent boy, Frank impressed his school masters with his 'instilled confidence' and his general ability. He left St Olaves after only three years in 1896, aged sixteen, and became a boy copyist by day, attending evening classes to improve himself.

By 1898, he had worked his way to a second class clerk in Lord Salisbury's War Office, from where he was transferred to South Africa on the commencement of the Boer War a year later. He remained working in the Paymaster General's Office in Cape Town until the war finished in 1902. During the remaining years before the Great War, he first worked for the General Post Office in London, and then for the India Office. All the while, he maintained his part time role in the Territorial Volunteers. Quite simply, Frank Howett was a man of great experience, one of those, vitally needed in the summer of 1914. On his untimely death, he was variously described as a 'magnificent soldier', as a 'man with a marvellous power of organisation', and 'cool under pressure'.

Sergeant Sidney Hill no. 2963 received a direct hit by a bomb fired from an enemy trench mortar, having successfully repulsed an attack with his platoon, on the slopes of Vimy Ridge on the 24th May 1916. His death was instantaneous. He was thirty years old. Born in February 1886 in Peckham, he attended St Olave's for three years leaving in 1900 to take an apprenticeship. He later changed direction, enrolling at King's College in the Strand, to study his greatest love – physics. His success should be measured by his selection to continue studying at the Sir John Cass Technical Institute, which provided him with a BSc (London). By 1914, he was science master at Stillness Road School in Brockley, the location of his enlistment.

His maturity and teaching experience marked him out for quick promotion, and his continued rise from N.C.O to officer should have been assured, but for his untimely death. Sid's early enlistment ensured that he was in Belgium by August 1915, together with another Old Olavian, Reginald Glenn, just one year out of school. Glenn was killed in July 1915, whilst the older Sergeant Hill later survived the attack to capture the enemy guns at Loos in September. The 'physicist' is commemorated on the Arras Memorial in Faubourg D'Amiens Cemetery in the west of the town.

Five weeks later, on the 2nd July, Edward Thompson met exactly the same fate, during an enemy bombardment by trench mortars, Edward, together with four colleagues were all killed by the explosion, once again, on the slopes of Vimy Ridge. Edward William Murray Thompson was a man of steady purpose and shy reserve. Born on the 1st June 1896, a son of William and Helena Thompson of Upper Tooting, he was ten years the junior of Sid Hill. He spent three years as an Olavian, leaving to join the Civil Service as a clerk in the Superintendent Engineer's Office of the Postal Telegraph, based at Wandsworth. He only worked there for two years, and enlisted as a Private no. 3018 in the summer of 1914. After a long period at home, he eventually embarked for active service overseas in spring 1916, with the 2/13th Londons. The suddenness of his death, prompted his comrades to write to his parents with descriptions of his cheerfulness in adverse conditions, and his value as a good and loyal friend. The 'postal engineer' was buried at Mont St Eloi, he had recently celebrated his twentieth birthday.

'Ginger' Wilson had excelled, with his brother Arthur, at all Sports at St Olave's. When war broke out, he was a successful twenty-eight year old administration manager for a mercantile firm, pursuing his twin loves of cricket and rugby in his spare time. Born Albert Cecil Wilson in May 1886, the first born son, to William Sherry Wilson, a printer's manager from Walworth and his wife Mary Ann, he attended the school from 1898 to 1903. His masters remember his idealism, his brightness and enthusiasm. Needless to say, a keen sense of humour went hand in hand with his shock of ginger hair.

Having enlisted in 1914 as a rifleman in the Territorials, he could scarcely have expected to find himself within a year as an N.C.O and musketry instructor, based at the shooting range at Bisley in Surrey. Shortly after, 'Ginger' was commissioned as a second lieutenant with the London Scottish and arrived in France on 22nd June 1916. Exactly two weeks later, he was shot by a sniper, whilst on duty in the trenches at Mont St Eloi – one of sixty-five officers of the 14th Londons, who would die during the conflict. He struggled on for some hours that day, and was treated at a clearing station, but to no avail. He was buried a few miles behind the front line at the village of Aubigny-en-Artois. His younger brother, Arthur Henry Wilson survived the war and embarked on a career in banking.

Fellow Olavian, Eddie Burn who was present at the aid post when Ginger was brought in, had this to say:

> *"At that time, my company was in reserve my abode was next to the first aid post. Until that afternoon, I had regarded this as some sort of sport on a grand scale; after the arrival of those stretchers, my outlook changed. On one of them lay poor Wilson, fatally wounded by a trench mortar or an aerial torpedo".*

The 'fisherman' was a shy, retiring boy, but very well liked. He came to St Olave's from the St George the Martyr school in Southwark, accompanied by a superb soprano and latterly alto, singing voice which was put to good use in the Choir of St Laurence Jewry for nearly nine years. Richard William Walsh was one of three sons of Richard Walsh of Kennington, an inspector in the Engineering Department of GPG and his wife Rosina, born a few days before Christmas in 1895, making him a shade older than Edward Thompson. Whereas Hill and Wilson had been contemporaries, the same was true of Thompson and Walsh.

On leaving School, Richard became assistant clerk at the Board of Agriculture and Fisheries and was in the process of been promoted, when war commenced. Despite continuing in his new post for another year, he eventually decided that, as a single man, he must enlist. In November 1915, he became Private no. 4553 in the 15th Londons, training at Richmond Park, then Barnes and later at Winchester. In March 1916, he arrived in France and was in the Arras sector within weeks. On one occasion, he had literally just swapped places with another infantryman, when the latter was shelled, badly burnt and died. Weeks later, he had left his rifle for a few seconds, only to return and find it blown to bits by shrapnel. On the final occasion, on the 15th September at Vimy Ridge, he was struck in the head by a bullet during an advance. As his body could not be recovered for burial, he is commemorated on the Thiepval Memorial to the Missing.

Walter Richard Maybrook, together with Fred Norris, followed Noel Hamilton and Leslie Sanders as captains of St Olaves in 1912. 'Didi' as he was affectionately known by his friends, was a boy of 'earnest, determined' temperament, a youth of 'exuberant vitality and enthusiasm' and a man of 'gallant and courageous' action. Born in March 1894 the only son amongst three daughters of Walter Maybrook, London County Council teacher of Inchmery Road, Catford and wife Alice, he moved to St Olave's in 1908 with a probationers scholarship from Brownhill Elementary School. He left the school six years later to go up to university to follow his main love of archaeology, combined with art and literature. The early promise of his name on the St Olave's Honour List, was not borne out.

In 1914, he enlisted, first of all in the 28th Londons, the Artists, as Private no. 2543. During training in the home counties with the 28th, a fertile ground of cadet officers, 'Didi' went to France in January 1915, applied for a commission and was gazetted and transferred to the Wiltshires in July, arriving in Belgium a month later. 25 Division took part in the fighting at Loos and Hulluch; Second Lieutenant

Maybrook was put in charge of a bombing platoon, who specialised in day and night bombing runs, up enemy held trenches.

As the Loos campaign drew to a close in November, and the autumn weather turned to winter, the Wiltshires stayed in the sector between Lens and Arras. On Easter Monday, in 1916, a mine was exploded by the Germans on their left. 'Didi' was given orders to lead an advanced party of Grenadiers to bomb their way to the new front line that was beginning to form. From here, he was to direct operations until reserves could reach them. Having achieved the first objective, and whilst carrying out the second, he was shot cleanly in the neck by a sniper, whilst standing on the lip of a crater, preparing to order further bomb attacks. He was twenty-two. The previous Christmas, he had been informed of the death of his great, great friend, Jack Gill, and had written to Headmaster Rushbrooke about Gill that, 'he has left more sorrowing hearts than he ever dreamed of. It is difficult to speak of him save with a certain awe and reverence. He was such a complete man, and so lovable'. Sentiments that many of Didi's own friends later said of him.

For several more months, there were brief attacks, counter-attacks and skirmishes on the Vimy Ridge; mostly these were to distract the secure enemy from what was going on beneath the Ridge, where the Engineers were excavating the existing mine shafts to make enormous tunnels that could carry thousands of men. This excavation would take over six months to complete.

General Sir Edmund Allenby moved the focal point of the fighting by the spring of 1917, south of Arras to the Croisilles area where, in the days after the great surprise tunnel attack at Vimy, a further ten Old Olavians would fall on the battlefield in the three battles of the River Scarpe – Monchy Le Preux, Gavrelle-Guemappe and Fresnoy.

In April, six of these men died in the first two engagements, three were officers – Captain Fred Sprang of the 6th Dorsets at Wancourt, Second Lieutenant Leslie Hay of the Highland Light Infantry at Etrun, and lastly, Second Lieutenant Miles Wardley of the 22nd Royal Fusiliers at Oppy. The others were 'rankers' – Gunner Archie

Murray of the Field Artillery based at Ervillers, Private Harry Baker and Private Wallace Gray both of the 20th Royal Fusiliers at Heninel.

On the night of the 12th April, the captain of 'D' Company, 6th Dorsets received orders to attack the village of Monchy Le Preux. Following his orders to the letter, he lead his men in darkness into the well fortified ramparts of the village and was wounded in action by enfilade machine gun fire, whilst trying to get through thickets of uncut wire. During the night that followed, whilst British troops captured Fresnoy-Le-Petit and stormed Hermies and Boursies, 'Freddy' Sprang died. He was twenty-five.

Born in March 1892 to Frederick and Catherine Sprang of New Farm, Westmoreland Road, Bromley, 'Freddy' spent eight years at the St Olave's, only leaving to finish his education at a Cambridge Wesleyan School called 'Leys'. He won a reputation at the School for 'high character' and was respected for his 'winning disposition'. Enlisting in 1914 as a commissioned officer, Lieutenant Sprang first went to France on 12th July 1915, surviving many 'hairbreadth escapes'. His last trip home was in June 1916, from where he returned to the southern banks of the Scarpe at the village of Wancourt.

Three days later, at a gun emplacement in a suburb of Arras, a young lieutenant of 291st Brigade, Royal Field Artillery sat down in his poorly protected dugout to write a letter to the parents of yet another man lost in battle. Lieutenant Cave had known Gunner Archie Murray of 'C' Battery for over a year, since the twenty year old had been sent to the R.F.A training camp as a new recruit. That night he wrote to foreman packer, Archibald Murray senior and his wife Sarah, at 27 Pennel Place, Queen's Road, Peckham, that, 'Gunner Murray was directly under me the whole time he was in 'C' Battery, from the day when he joined us at Woodbridge. He was my senior Gunner, and always reliable and painstaking in anything he was put on, to do. His death is a great loss to me personally and to his battery as a whole. The last words that he is known to have said, before he was carried to the dressing station were, "I don't want to leave the battery".

Archie Murray had been manning his gun with the crew at a location near the village of Mory, between Arras and Bapaume, when an aerial attack on their position by shells, shrapnel and 'whizz-bangs' had caused severe casualties; All of the batteries officers – second lieutenants, had also been killed. Archie had been wounded by shrapnel blast, but succumbed to his wounds later, while being treated.

He had left St Olave's just four years earlier, a quiet, retiring boy of poor physique, but strong morals. Armed with a L.C.C scholarship from Bellenden Road School in Peckham, he had entered Tooley Street where he spent four years, leaving in 1913 to briefly join a commercial business house. Born in September 1896 to two sisters, Kate and Lily, Archibald Albert Murray became a man 'unmindful of himself' a characteristic that was demonstrated daily in his artillery battery.

A contemporary of Archie's at St Olave's from 1910 to 1913 was the slightly younger Harry Baker, born on the 30th December 1898, only son, with two sisters, of a booksellers manager, William Baker and wife Emily from Wallington. Harry served in the same battalion of the Royal Fusiliers as another older Olavian, Wallace Gray, eight years his senior, and at the school for five years from 1901 to 1906.

Just one day after Gunner Murray's death, on the 16th April, the 20th Royal Fusiliers were involved in furious combat at the front, between Heninel and Croisilles. With some tank support, the Fusiliers and many other battalions, had been fighting for several days to penetrate the new 'Hindenburg Line' of trenches, despite heavy casualties from enemy machine gun pits on the high ground around Heninel. By April 14th, the Allies had captured 14,000 prisoners and 194 guns, with tanks encouraging enemy retreat.

The Allied line gradually pushed seven miles south east of Arras with men from Northumberland capturing the high ground of Wancourt Tower. The 15th April saw desperate German counter attacks almost all repulsed. Private Harry Baker no. PS/10635, was involved in all of these infantry actions at the tender age of eighteen. On the 16th, he was advancing with his friend, Jimmy Wilde, a Welsh school master, and their officer, Lieutenant C.E. Powell, when all three men were cut down in one sweep of an enemy machine gun from the high ground. The three men were buried alongside each other by an officer of the Kings (Liverpool) Regiment, who later found them, after their brigade had pushed the reinforcing troops forward. The 'clean white' stones of these brave men sit in the sunshine at the Heninel-Croisilles Road Cemetery, on a road that crosses a plateau south west of Arras.

Harold William Baker excelled at cricket and rugby and was an N.C.O in the School Cadet Corps. He is mentioned frequently in the Olavian magazine between the years 1910 and 1915. In his spare time, not content with his strong religious beliefs, he had become an unofficial street preacher, taking the word of God into the slum areas – an often thankless task. His best school friend was Harold Grose, a fellow rugby player, with whom he enlisted in the Fusiliers. Grose, who survived the conflict, would retain affectionate memories of the 'preacher'.

Private Wallace Gray no. G/53109 was also killed in the Heninel/Croisilles action. Possibly the two men knew each other or had sought each other out, despite not having been at the School during the same years. It is likely that Harry may have sought the comradeship of the lately married, Wally. Three months earlier, Wally at twenty-six years, had married, whilst on leave in New Cross, at St Catherine's Church, to his fiance, Florence Portsch.

Born in the summer of 1890, the elder of two brothers, he attended St Olave's for six years leaving aged sixteen to apprentice as a clerk with 'Messrs C.B. Southwell & Co', in Dockhead, Bermondsey. With the arrival of war, his brother Sidney joined the infantry and served in India, whilst Wally became a sergeant in the Army Pay Corps, where he acted as 'paymaster'. By the end of 1916, itching to get to the front, he engineered his transfer to the Fusiliers. Within three months, he had left another young widow. One wonders at his young wife's misgivings about his choice to transfer to more dangerous conditions.

With the spate of bad weather on the Arras front lifting by the 23rd April, St George's day 1917, took on a new meaning. Field Marshal Haig issued orders to General Allenby to attack along a wide front, the enemy line at the towns of Gavrelle and Guemappe, thus starting the second battle of Scarpe River.

Second Lieutenant Arthur Leslie Hay was a twenty-two year old officer in the 10/11th Highland Light Infantry. This battalion was part of the 46th Brigade, with the 10th Scottish Rifles, the 7/8th Kings Own Scottish Borderers and the 12th H.L.I. Together they were the 15th (Scottish) Division of the British Army, based near Etrun.

Arthur Leslie known as 'Leslie', was born on the 4th March 1895, the son of Arthur and Fanny Hay of New Cross. He studied at Tooley Street for three years from 1908 to 1910, leaving to join the South Metropolitan Gas Company in the Old Kent Road, at the age of fifteen. At the outbreak of war, his first instinct was to become a cavalryman, and to that end, he enlisted as a 'Westminster Dragoon'. He was trained as an efficient horseman at Feltham, and was then transferred to Egypt on 3rd July 1915. His lofty ambition to become a 'charging cavalryman' was thwarted, when he was sent as relief transport, with his horse to the beaches of Gallipoli to help deliver supplies, whilst under the terrible risk of sniper fire the whole time.

This he endured with some little good fortune for a period of six weeks without injury. At the end of this time, he caught enteric fever, and was evacuated by hospital ship, but unlike Olavian Neil Wells, was given medical treatment in good time. Early in 1916, having recovered, he was transferred with the Dragoons, to Ireland to help quell the 'Easter Rising'. Shortly after, he applied successfully for an officer's training course in Scotland, and whilst there, was persuaded to join the famous 'Kilties', the Highlanders, feared by the German infantry and dubbed by them 'the Storm Troops'.

He arrived in France in late November 1916 as a newly gazetted second lieutenant, with his new battalion, the 10/11th Highland Light Infantry. Although he had considerable cavalry experience and had been exposed to quashing rebellion, his knowledge, like many young recently appointed officers, of life in the trenches with all manner of ever present danger, was inadequate. Within a few weeks, he had witnessed, more death, destruction and mayhem than he could have imagined even in Gallipoli. He became pessimistic of his chances of survival with fellow officers being killed daily, and subsequently made arrangements for any letters home advising of his death, be sent to his father's business address, to spare his mother from finding out before his father could break the news more gently. Such care for others, when your own life is under threat, is courageous in itself. Leslie Hay was wounded on the 24th April in the great effort to capture Gavrelle. The town was taken and over 3,000 prisoners captured, all counter attacks were repulsed. He was twenty-two and is buried in the Duisans British Cemetery in Etrun.

The village of Oppy lies just north of Gavrelle, a town in Allied hands by 1917. It had been turned into a German fortress to protect the top of the Hindenburg Switch system at Drocourt and all the southern side of the Lens Salient. The key to capturing Oppy was the wood beside the village, occupied by enemy machine guns protected by concrete rocks and felled trees. Further guns were positioned twenty feet up the trees accessed by well protected ladders. Enemy reinforcements were arriving by omnibus and rail and filtering into both the wood and the village's houses.

General Horne bombarded the village heavily, and the amassed British battalions took turns to advance into the deadly wood. Second Lieutenant Miles Wardley of the 22nd Battalion, the Royal Fusiliers was a typical officer encouraging his riflemen to attack against tremendous odds, never questioning the strategy of attack. He was shot by machine gun in Oppy Wood on the 29th April, his body could not be recovered. Despite his youth, he was twenty-seven at his death, he was 'battle hardened', having survived three years at the front, firstly as a Private no. 1258 in the Civil Service Rifles (15th Londons) at Bethune, Givenchy, Loo's and Festubert in 1915, and latterly in the Arras/Vimy sector. He had been commended by his C.O. for carrying out his work in 'trying and dangerous circumstances' at the battle of Irles, and had been badly wounded at Loo's.

Whilst convalescing in England, he took the opportunity to transfer from the Territorials and took a short term position as a musketry instructor at the Harley Down Camp, before taking his commission. Miles Edward Wardley was born on the 24th July 1889, second son of Joe Wardley, a machine ruler from Walworth and wife Elizabeth. His elder brother Joe Junior was fourteen years old when he was born. After Surrey Square school, he won a L.C.C. scholarship and attended St Olave's for six years with 'Fallen' colleagues, Walter Berrow, the 'yeoman', Cecil Talbot, the 'scout' and Sid Weatherston, the 'signaller'.

His masters talked of him as a 'merry and alert boy, with a sense of the mischievous, a boy of tremendous energy and kind heart'. At eighteen, he left to train as a probationer and pupil teacher in Bangor. His first appointment in 1910, was as assistant master at the Westmoreland Road School, at which point he also joined the London Territorials in his spare time. Come the war, he was well placed to be a soldier and potential officer.

In May 1917, the remaining five Olavians, fighting in the Arras sector, died as a result of the push to advance into well defended German territory. The battles of the Scarpe proved a significant turning point in the long war. Bob Dennis, the special constable and ex Buckinghamshire hussar, served with the 2nd Londons at Guemappe; George Wallace, ex medic and 'Kiltie' with the London Scottish, was based near the village of Fins, near Cambrai; Edmund Butler, the 'templar' occupied trenches at Cojeul near Vimy with the Queens Victoria Rifles; Malcolm Sutcliffe of the Post Office Rifles defended the line near Arras, whilst Bill Athow, with the 8th Royal Fusiliers, wounded on Easter Day, was now in hospital at Etaples, fighting in vain for his life with his wife at his side.

Robert Charles Dennis was born in Islington on the 16th November 1895 to Herbert and Annie Dennis. His father ran his own business, later moving to the village of Melton Constable in Norfolk. After seven years at St Olaves, Bob left to join the family business in a managerial capacity. In his spare time, he performed the duties of a special constable in London and was an assistant scout master. As he was instrumental in his father's business he could not enlist in the Army in 1914, his father making him wait until finally, he couldn't stop him leaving. His enlistment with the hussars was short lived as he was not considered tall enough.

Eventually, in spring 1916, he enlisted in Bermondsey as a Private no.232878 in the 2nd Londons and volunteered as a stretcher-bearer during the Somme. He was badly wounded and spent 12 weeks in a field hospital. It may have been his wound that dictated his next transfer, to the machine gun section of his battalion. Once again, in the April attacks, he was slightly wounded but stayed at his post. On 3rd May, the 2nd Londons had received orders to go over the top and take 'Cavalry Farm', but those not wounded, almost immediately had to retire, due to severe enemy fire, leaving Bob and many others, cut off in No Mans Land and badly wounded. No stretcher-bearers could be sent out until night time, by which time, there was no trace of many of them. Although regarded as 'missing in action', it is unlikely that they could have survived. Bob was twenty-one and is commemorated on the Arras Memorial.

George Wallace was a 'thinker' with 'considerable mental power', unusual much in the same way as Leslie Sanders, his contemporary. These two boys spent time not only thinking about the concepts of duty and sacrifice, but also voicing and writing their views. This was rare for boys of such youth. George was only twenty at his death. On his enlistment in early 1915 as a private in the London Scottish, he wrote that 'No thought of sacrifice enters our heads- we are merely stirred by an inner feeling to do what we have done, and we have not been able to help ourselves'.

One of three sons, including Charles and Arthur, of Sub Inspector W.F. Wallace of City of London Police, George joined St Olave's from Southwark Park School, bringing with him a character of 'unusual determination, optimism and positive thought coupled with a great athletic ability'. He joined the Port of London Authority, when he left in 1913, and just a year later, joined the Royal Army Medical Corps. By 27th March 1915, he had joined the London Scottish, a regiment that he greatly admired after their stand at Messines, to get closer to the action at Ypres. His intellect marked him out for fast promotion and by the end of the year he was a second lieutenant transferred to the 20h Middlesex. From July to October 1916, he endured and survived some severe actions on the Somme, with most of his fellow officers dropping at his side. Such was this depletion, that he was promoted straight to the rank of acting captain.

It was particularly galling to him that he was then demoted back to lieutenant, after the arrival of some "Pukka" captains from home. On the 22nd May 1917, Lieutenant Wallace had followed orders to take some objectives on a night raid with his company. Whilst advancing, the men came under rifle fire from an enemy post. George was the first to go down, as he was leading from the front, with a wound to his left side – he was fifty feet from the objective. He was attended by stretcher-bearers but was dead within fifteen minutes.

By May 20th, the British had advanced between Fontaine and Bullecourt south of Arras, and had occupied the first Hindenburg Line.

Corporal Edmund Butler no. 391910 of the 2/9th Londons had earned a reputation as a bit of a crazy man for his platoon visits, via No Mans Land in daylight, to remove the wounded. He had enlisted at Southwark where he had worked as a stationer, whilst dividing his own time between the Borough Road Baptist Chapel and the International Order of Good Templars. Born in October 1886 in Southwark to John Butler, vellum bookbinder of St George's Road, he attended St Olave's from 1897 until 1904, a contemporary of Hill and Wilson. He arrived at Arras in February 1917 with his battalion, and on the 24th May, whilst carrying one end of a stretcher through his own trench, he was hit directly by a 'Whizz Bang' and killed. All the time he spent in broad daylight over the top, he had not picked up a scratch.

THE ARRAS CAMPAIGN

Mrs Diana Sutcliffe of Nightingale Lane, Balham, widow of the late Doctor J. Sutcliffe, was justifiably proud of her three boys – Major Richard Douglas Sutcliffe had served in France since January 1915 and managed to survive the war; Lieutenant S.C. 'Percy' Sutcliffe, an Army dental surgeon also made it through. Second Lieutenant F.M. 'Malcolm' Sutcliffe serving in France with the 8th Londons, had recently become engaged to Marjorie Page of Torquay. Her pride undiminished, her grief at the loss of Malcolm during the Arras campaign, must have caused much pain.

Malcolm was the son who 'persevered'. He had poor health, but battled to overcome this, and to balance his studies and his keenness for sport. Born in 1885, he spent seven years at the School, leaving in 1900. William Dale-James and Frank Howett were his contemporaries, with Grantley Le Chavetois, a year below him. He trained as a lawyer in the Inns of Court, and had a spell as an insurance inspector of Fine Art. He took a commission with his elder brothers and was attached to the London Territorials, the Post Office Rifles, the 8th Battalion, where he commanded 'A' Company at the battles of Festubert and Loos' in 1915, Flers Courcelette in 1916 and Arras in 1917. His death at thirty-one, on the 29th May, made him one of the forty-six second lieutenants of the 8th Londons, killed during the conflict.

Bill Athow was one of the handful of Olavian 'Fallen', well into their thirties at the time of their demise. Bill had been at the School from 1890 for ten years. He was only junior to Beaumont Fletcher, Edwin Robinson and Harry Oxford. Born in September 1882 one of three boys including Alfred and Frank, of a hatter's manager from Borough High Street, Bermondsey, little is recorded of his non military career, his death, in fact, was only reported to the school in early 1918 after years without contact.

William Joseph Athow enlisted at Merton on the 1st June 1916 as a Private no. 50762 in the 8th Battalion, Royal Fusiliers in London. He was residing at Tooting with his wife. He was sent to a training camp in Edinburgh for three months, and then to France at the end of the year. Bill was wounded in April and sent to hospital at Etaples near Wimereux, where he survived for eight weeks, the last three of which he was nursed by his wife, who had travelled at her own cost to France. His body was buried in Wimereux Communal Cemetery, near Boulogne.

His widow, though far from fortunate, was at least able to have some contact and some sense of 'finality' in her husband's passing, unlike the millions of relatives who continued to cling to the vain hope that their 'missing' sons would somehow return.

The Arras campaign was over. Further north, Passchendaele was about to commence.

CHAPTER 12
The Royal Engineers

'Sappers', they were called, not privates or riflemen, as they performed a different function on the battlefields of the Western Front. Once the mobile warfare of Mons and the Marne were over, and both the Allied infantry and their enemy had sensed the approach of deadlock around the Flemish town of Ypres in November 1914, both opposing forces began to create, what to the modern world, was to be a unique military situation.

From Nieuport, the Belgian coastal town close to the North Sea, right down through central Europe, to Belfort, the French Garrison town of Alsace, on the Swiss border, was 'the Front', the dividing line, the balance of power between the aggressor and the defenders. At no point in the line, once established, did either party push further than ten miles through. This Front was characterised by a deep and intricate trench system unlike anything seen before. Front line trenches were supported further back by second line trenches, and served by a system of support and communication trenches, from whence troops and equipment moved to and from the battlefields.

The logistics of keeping several million uniformed soldiers in France and Flanders for four years, required a profound understanding of the need for special 'non-military' skills – transportation, food, drink and clothing distribution, sanitation, billeting and recreation, reconnaissance, telecommunications, medical services and particularly, engineering.

St Olave's lost four of its Old Boys during the Great War, serving with the Royal Engineers. Pioneer Charles Brown, served with 'B' company, Royal Engineers, based near 'Fosse No.10', in the Pas De Calais sector; Sergeant Frank Dixson worked with the Corps at 'No 4 Workshop' near Villers Bretonneaux, near Amiens; Corporal

Ernest Hoare, was with 186 'Special' Company near Cambrin, Arras; and Second Lieutenant Leslie Sanders was attached to a Royal Engineers 'Field Survey Company' from the Royal Garrison Artillery, and based near Pommieres.

1914 had seen the archaic communication methods of visual signalling and limited telegraphy virtually eliminated by artillery shelling, army sizes and the beginning of aerial reconnaissance. The problem wasn't really fully solved by the time of the armistice, with thousands of infantrymen dying on the Somme and at Passchendaele, in particular, as a result of poor communication at divisional and corps level, causing offensive strategic disasters. It was the sappers and their officers in the 'Corps of Royal Engineers' who began to make a difference to the lives of the infantryman. Use of flags, flares, shutters, lamps, carrier pigeons and dogs to aid communication, began to be replaced from early 1916 with wireless telegraphy, with wiring being laid in high risk areas by engineers.

Infantry units still found the wireless cumbersome, as it took several men to carry one version (the British field trench set) and its more portable counterpart (the loop set) was short range and unreliable. Although used for all communication in the 'hinterland' of the front, officers of battalions in action, preferred 'line telegraphy' and the field telephone, to wireless, as the latter was too time-consuming in its ciphering. The problem with the former, was that 'lines' even though wrapped in brass, steel or lead at a depth of six feet under the floor of the trench, were still regularly damaged during heavy artillery bombardments, and a 'nightmare' to locate and repair, in the muddy wet climate. A final difficulty for the engineers, was moving the cabling forward into newly captured territory often under shelling. It was in this challenging environment, that Leslie Sanders, one of the most intellectually gifted Olavians of his generation, found himself seconded. His degrees in both chemistry and physics had been spotted and he was drafted to work on 'secret work' that remains unknown, at Pommieres in 1917.

THE ROYAL ENGINEERS

Another aspect of the Sapper's work, was the supervision of trench construction, with infantry battalions, often digging their own trenches. Such was the demand for this activity that new volunteer 'pioneer' battalions were trained and shipped to the front, specifically to dig and fortify. Soil composition, together with the use, where available of concrete with soft compounded earth or sandbags, provided the defence from enemy sniper's machine gun fire. The science of building strong fortifications had advanced considerably with the mid nineteenth century engineering practices of a soldier called Brialmont, responsible for developing the Belgian defences around Antwerp, Liege and Namur. His lessons were followed by the French at Verdun, a city that the Germans never captured. Frank Dixson, with his special skills as a draughtman, worked at divisional headquarters in R.E. workshops, designing the methodology for the construction of trenches and communications.

A third, specialist, and developing skill required of the Royal Engineers, was that of 'mining and counter-mining'. As adjacent trench systems flourished, often no more than a few hundred yards apart, officers, led by the persevering Lieutenant-Colonel John Norton-Griffiths, began proposing the use of 'tunnellers' to mine out into No Mans Land to lay explosives, to either destroy enemy tunnellers doing exactly the same thing, or to damage the well defended almost impregnable concrete dug outs that German engineers had excavated. Tunneller's companies were created as part of the Royal Engineers. The Sapper's were chosen for their specialist knowledge of pre-war work on the London Underground or in the Welsh and Northern mining industry. They were called 'Clay kickers' as they lay on their backs and dug with their feet. Ernest Hoare and Charles Brown were amongst their number, in a world of rats, canaries, claustrophobia, mud, cold, darkness, noise, and occasional subterranean combat.

Ernest Austin Hoare was born on 25th August 1887 to John and Martha Hoare of Lansdowne Road, Clapham. He spent just four years at St Olaves, where he was reported to be a boy of 'straightforward character with a sense of duty'. At fifteen, he joined the Albany Engineering Works as an apprentice, rising quickly to 'assistant' to Dr Fyleman, a London based analytical chemist. By the time he was twenty-five, he had his degree in chemistry from Borough Polytechnic and an 'exhibition'. The outbreak of war prompted him to move with Fyleman to the Osram Lamp Factory, as a works chemist. In 1915, he won a scholarship at the Imperial College of Science, which, after having the place held open for him, he enlisted in the Royal Engineers. He was in France by late August, having been promoted to the rank of Corporal no. 106558.

After witnessing the frenzied, dangerous environment of the battlefield where he was based between the towns of Cambrin, Vermelles and Loo's, Ernest wrote home, in what turned out to be his last letter, 'If I am killed, please do not worry, but think of me as having done my duty to those at home, and gone to rest. Do not wear any mourning, as I think it looks miserable and I do not want you to be sad'.

Leslie Yorath Sanders, born five years after Ernest, to a brother, Reginald Yorath and sister, Winifred Marjorie, won a scholarship to St Olave's from George Green school.

Their father, Charles Sanders, originally from Devonport, lived for a time in the East India Dock Road in Poplar with wife Agnes, where he worked as the Superintendent of wrecks and loss of life at sea, part of the Civil Service and later for the Board of Trade and the Ministry of Shipping. In his spare time, he also carried out social work amongst the poor in the dock areas of the East End.

Leslie commenced his remarkable academic career in 1906, leaving in 1912 as one of two captains of the School, the other being Noel Hamilton. He went up to Trinity, Cambridge to read Natural Sciences, winning prize after prize. Headmaster Rushbrooke, not known for his outbursts of praise for pupils, was recorded as saying, 'Leslie's career was one unbroken advance in intellectual power and in personal influence. I have known no boy so slightly equipped to all appearance with physical strength, whose moral force was more penetrating and irresistible'.

He enlisted with his brother in 1914, aged twenty one, as a Private no. 3062 in the 9th (County of London) Battalion, the London Regiment (Queen Victoria Rifles). He spent the spring of 1915 in the front line around Ypres and was wounded in the now famous attempt to recapture Hill 60, a strategic point adjoining the Messines Ridge on 20th to 21st April. A fellow officer, Lieutenant Geoffrey Woolley, became the first territorial battalion winner of the Victoria Cross on the same day, for holding the trench on the hill, resisting all attacks, motivating his men and continuing to throw bombs, whilst being heavily shelled. Woolley was a year older than Sanders at twenty-three, and as both were officers in the 9th Londons, would undoubtedly have fought side by side. Whilst these men fought on the surface, it is worth remembering that Hill 60 in 1915, was also one of first sites of extensive mining, and underground fighting by 173rd Tunnelling Company, Royal Engineers.

Leslie was fortunate that his bullet wounds were not mortal, and he was sent home to England to convalesce. His state of mind in these first few months of 1915 in Belgium can be guessed at, by a letter that he sent to his parents. His philosophical approach, and down to earth realism clearly revealed his depth of thought.

> *"I estimate my chance of getting wounded at one in four, of getting killed or totally disabled at one in ten; these are pretty heavy averages, and I should be foolish to go out not prepared for the worst. In a sense, therefore, I count myself already dead. Wear no mourning for me if I am killed. If I die, I die gladly. I have lived longer than many, and life has been very good. Pleasures innumerable, sweet, high and pure, have surrounded me all my days. And if not death, but something worse should fall, well, I am prepared. The only thing I fear at all, is the loss of both hands or total blindness. Both of these are improbable contingencies. If a bullet goes anywhere near your eyes, it usually goes into your brain, still, it does happen sometimes.*

There have been so far, twenty-two cases of men blinded in the B.E.F. Well, that risk had to be faced before I enlisted."

After convalesence and promotion to second lieutenant, he was transferred, first to the Royal Garrison Artillery as an instructor based at Woolwich and Borstal Heath, and afterwards, back to France attached to the Royal Engineers, as member of a Field Survey Company, carrying out 'special scientific work'.

Charles Henry Goullee Brown was from Huguenot stock, baptised in August 1897, to an elder brother, William. His father, also William, at one time a second hand bookseller and street trader from Battersea, was also a minister of the Wellington College Mission Church, and arranged his confirmation there. Four years the junior of Leslie Sanders, Charles spent seven years at St Olave's, having gained entry through a L.C.C. scholarship from All Saints School, East Street, Bermondsey. The twelve year old joined in 1909, leaving in 1916 with an Intermediate Batchelor of Science.

Taking leave of his studies, he enlisted immediately, aged nineteen in a battalion of the London Regiment. His arrival in the army at this point in time coincided with the urgent need for new 'Pioneer' battalions, likely to be attractive to those with religious reasons for adopting non-combatant roles. It is unclear if this was so with Charles Brown, but his transfer to the Pioneers proceeded, and by the winter of 1916, he was in France based at the village of 'Sains en Gohelle'.

Frank Dixson was a few months older than Leslie Sanders, but started at St Olave's at the end of 1905, whereas Leslie arrived in 1907. Again, unlike Sanders who progressed towards university, Frank left at sixteen in 1909 to take an apprenticeship as a draughtsman in a local engineering firm. Frank was described by his contemporaries as cheerful, thoughtful and brotherly, whilst excelling at rugby and developing his faith as a Wesleyan sunday school teacher. Much of his compassion and understanding may have come from his relationship with a disabled brother. Similarly to Ernest Hoare, he enlisted in 1914, as a sapper in the Royal Engineers, without previous training in an infantry regiment. He was twenty-one and equipped with excellent technical drawing skills, in high demand for both trench construction and telegraphy route planning. By late 1915, he was based at divisional headquarters and had been promoted twice to sergeant.

Of the four men, all operating in different areas of the Royal Engineers, Ernest Hoare was the first to die. He was killed instantly by a trench mortar on the 21st December 1915, and was buried by his comrades in 186 Company, in the churchyard at Cambrin, a village, 24 kilometres north of Arras, east of Bethune, on the road to La Bassee. The whole area had been a centre of combat activity since the end of 1914, with Bethune, a forward base for allied forces, and Vermelles and Loo's the scene of bloody fighting and the early use of gas by both sides in mid 1915. He had been involved most of that year with the tunnelling programmes in that area, especially at Cambrin. From April 1915, tunnelling was used increasingly regularly to fire mines near the German Front Line, either as a diversion or offensive attack. It is unclear whether Corporal Hoare was killed whilst supervising 'clay-kicking' underground, or on the surface, whilst in respite. He was just eighteen.

The next was Second Lieutenant Leslie Sanders, Royal Garrison Artillery who had been attached to the Royal Engineers. In March 1917, he was billeted comfortably near the Front line at Pommieres, reputedly with time to sleep at night, working on a special secret brief, but still within heavy shelling range. Pommieres was a small village, near Warlencort and more specifically the town of Bapaume, held by the enemy until that March.

The mass well planned and unprompted retreat of the enemy to a better defensive position known as the 'Hindenburg' or 'Siegfried' Line, left behind it, hundreds of booby traps in and around Bapaume. The sappers of the Royal Engineers had to deal with these threats, leading to many casualties. Heavy artillery shelling continued as the British forces moved forward cautiously into General Von

Falkenhayn's trap. One such shell landed on Leslie's room, killing him outright on the 10th March. He had been recently engaged to be married, and was twenty-four.

Pioneer Charles Brown of B Special Company died five months later on the 19th August. His body was recovered and was buried at Fosse Number 10 communal cemetery extension in Sains en Gohelle, a village close to Mazingarbe and Loo's. He had been involved with a tunnelling company in controlling and keeping open the 'Fosse' mine shaft system in the Bethune/Lens area. Since early 1915, these mine shafts had been used for the comings and goings of enemy spies, and for the employment of listening devices in the hope of overhearing enemy conversation. Many pioneers were employed in unblocking Fosse shafts that had been deliberately blocked with enemy debris. Charles had been killed instantly by an exploding shell.

Frank Dixson made it through three years of warfare to the 'Kaisers Offensive' of March 1918. As a draughtsman he worked for General Grant in the engineering workshops at Villers Bretonneaux. In March 1918, this was not a good place to be. Within a few days, following a five hour bombardment by over 6,000 guns, one million enemy troops advanced through the town, pushing Gough's Fifth Army back with it. Sergeant Dixson was shot whilst by his major's side, by the advancing enemy on the 29th March – Good Friday, a day of significance for him. His major, who somehow survived, was clearly mortified by his death. He was seen as a man of great spirit and enthusiasm. He had celebrated his twenty-fifth birthday the week before.

'The chemist', 'the realist', 'the huguenot' and 'the draughtsman' had added their skills to ensuring some future victory.

CHAPTER 13
Third Ypres:
Messines, Pilckem Ridge and Langemarck

Three key factors created the circumstances for the third offensive at Ypres on the Belgian front in summer 1917. Firstly, the failure of the 'frontal infantry assault' concept on the Somme the previous summer had not convinced Douglas Haig to alter his approach. If anything, he had become more intransigent, and blamed the Somme failure on other factors. More than anything, he felt the need to prove his concept on a different field of battle with favourable conditions. His succession to Sir John French, had brought the political spot light directly on him, and he gradually came to the conclusion that to repair his reputation, so regularly under attack by Prime Minister Lloyd George, he would have to engineer a complete break through and armistice himself, without French or American army support.

Secondly, with several divisions of French infantry having openly mutinied, General Petain, who had replaced Nivelle after Verdun, desperately needed Haig to operate without French support in the short term, to allow him time to resume military control. Furthermore, Petain urged Haig to launch an offensive in the north to shift German attention away from the south. The final factor, was the American declaration of war on Germany in April 1917. Within a few months the Western Front would be swarming with novice American soldiers, removing Haig's last chance for 'truly British glory'.

The battle had commenced on the 7th June and continued unabated until the winter weather forced its cessation the following November. The British infantry and artillery were to lose over quarter of a million men, in return for the allied occupation of various strategic ridges around the British strong point of Ypres. The campaign, which can be sub-divided into six main battles – Messines, Pilckem, Langemarck, Menin Road, Poelcapelle and Passchendaele – claimed the lives of fifteen Old Olavians, of which those that perished in the first three battles between the 7th June and the 24th August are chronicled in this chapter.

Haig promised the War Cabinet that the campaign would be 'limited' in terms of the estimated casualties that Lloyd George was so concerned about. So intent was the commander in chief on getting his way, that, in order to gain support for his favoured location – the Ypres Salient, he claimed untruthfully, that one major objective would be Belgian based, U-Boat bases, that were doing so much damage to the Royal Navy. These were in fact based in Germany. Finally, Haig's promise that six more months at the current intensity would break the Germans and end the War, clinched the Cabinet's reluctant support.

Messines and Wytchaete were the starting point. A Belgian village at the southern end of the Salient, under enemy control, the objective was to secure a foothold, as a prelude to further advance. From these villages, German machine gunners could enfilade the entire British Front line, such was the strategic advantage. For many months, running up to the planned launch on 7th June, the Royal Engineers, at General Plumer's command, had been mining and tunnelling on a scale only previously carried out at Vimy. They had been briefed to dig under the ridge in a ten mile arc and prepare to lay powerful land mines capable of creating enormous damage in cratering on the surface. In the days leading up to 7th June, tunnellers risked tunnel collapse, explosion, asphyxiation and other deadlier perils, to lay over a million pounds of high explosive in 19 locations from Hill 60 in the north down through Messines to Ploegsteert Wood in the south. After the success of a similar venture by the Canadians at Vimy in April, the lesson had been learnt regarding the need for detailed preparation and

THIRD YPRES

good communication at company level. For the first time, British 'Tommies' had limited and precise objectives to attain.

At 03.10 hours the mines exploded after fourteen days of continuous bombardment of the ridge by over 2,000 guns. A captain in the Royal Engineers, wrote that "the earth seemed to open and rise up to the sky. It was all shot with flame. The dust and smoke was terrific. And all this debris falling back". Three Old Olavians were killed in action during the days fighting to secure the ridge, before the urgent telegraph had been received at G.H.Q. the next morning, "Messines Ridge captured. Attack on nine mile front. Brilliant British success. Over 5,000 prisoners".

Private Harry Hunt no. S/31329 was serving with the 3rd Battalion, the Rifle Brigade; Captain Fred Norris commanded 'C' Company, 23rd Battalion, the Middlesex Regiment; and Corporal Henry Shepherd no. 530639 was in charge of a platoon of the 15th Londons, the Civil Service Rifles. During the first wave of infantry attacks, varying reports were coming back. The 21st Kings Royal Rifle Corps met hardly any resistance and took many dazed German prisoners; however the 8th Royal Irish Rifles who advanced early towards a late exploding mine, suffered many casualties in No Mans Land.

Harry Hunt, as part of 24 Division, went over in the second wave of attack, being struck by a piece of flying shrapnel as he advanced. He was twenty-four. Fred Norris, with 41 Division, was shot by a sniper whilst leading his company in a 'victorious engagement' whereby a first line of enemy trenches had been taken. He was twenty-three. Henry Shepherd and the 47th (London) Division had moved forward and Henry had been killed by exploding shell fire. All three men are commemorated on the Menin Gate Memorial in the centre of Ypres town, as their bodies could not be recovered.

Harold Hunt was an unusually talented boy, coming, as he did, from a family of slender means, with three other brothers, Edward, James and George and two sisters. Born on the 18th November 1892, to William Hunt, a vellum binder come stationer and wife Annie, of

143 Fort Road, Bermondsey, he won a United Charities scholarship allowing him to attend his local grammar school for a period of four years. He spent his scholarship years at St Olave's wisely, aware of his good fortune. He had a tremendous aptitude for languages, and he was an enthusiastic, attentive and steady student. In 1909, he left to learn the business of commerce, moving regularly between positions and commercial houses. Three years later, he managed to secure a good posting to Valdivia in Chile, where he played rugby, learned to ride and developed a love for indian ethnic culture. In 1914, he was informed by letter, that two of his brothers had enlisted, but he chose to remain in Chile, until news arrived of one brother's wounding on the Somme. He returned to England and enlisted in January 1917. With only two week's formal training, he was sent to the Front.

Frederick Norris was one of the nine captains of School that St Olave's lost during the conflict. He shared his year in office with 'Didi' Maybrook, and followed those other high achievers, Noel Hamilton and Leslie Sanders. He was born on the 27th January 1894, with siblings, Harry, Victor and Rosa, son of Walter Norris, an oven builder's labourer and wife Annie, of Brook Street, Kennington. He spent his early years at local West Square School, where when he was eleven, he won a L.C.C. scholarship to Tooley Street. Clearly he was a student of exceptional ability – a first class debater with 'intellectual gifts', great 'strength of character and genuine goodness'. Fred Norris drew plenty of accolades, ending his school career on the honour list in 1913. He went up to Corpus Christi College at Oxford and won the 'Hertford prize' in his second year, becoming a 'very sound classical scholar'.

As a man, Fred Norris was mature for his age, apparently fearless, earnest, reliable and conscientious, with a strong sense of duty – everything desirable in a leader of men, and an officer in the British Army. With war approaching, Fred put his degree on hold, and took an officer's training course. By May 1916, he was in France as a second lieutenant, and within a couple of months, the

23rd Middlesex were in the thick of it, at the capture of Flers, the start of many campaigns from Arras to Vimy and on to Messines.

Henry Alick Shepherd, the son of Alick Shepherd, a compositor from Westminster, was born in Newington to an older sister, Kate, on the 14th December 1887. Armed with a L.C.C. scholarship of three years duration, Henry entered the school in 1901, the same intake as Ralph Akerman, Charlie Ruggles and Stephen Bishopp. He remained for just three years, leaving to take an apprenticeship in the Civil Service. By the end of 1910, he was a 2nd division clerk, and living in Newington with his father who had remarried. In 1914, aged twenty-seven, he enlisted at Somerset House, as a rifleman with other local government colleagues. After six months of training camps, the 15th Londons were sent to France arriving on the 17th March 1915. Also in the 15th, he either renewed, or made the acquaintance of several Olavians destined to fall in the years that followed – Henry Deem, who survived until September 1918, Company Sergeant Major Frank Howett who died just before the Somme, Arthur Junkison, a week before the Armistice, Alf Page at Flers in September 1916, John Sutherland, and Frank Trotman on the Somme in October 1916.

Alick's baptism of fire came in May 1915 at Festubert, then three months later at Loos. In 1916, he fought through Flers, Morval and Le Transloy. Few ranking soldiers were exposed to such levels of fighting over such a long period of time, without being killed. Promoted to corporal in 1916, Alick Shepherd went without wounds for over two years in some of the toughest fighting men had ever seen.

At the end of the 7th June, three Olavians had been killed along with many others – especially the Ulstermen of 39th Division, the Irishmen of 16th Division and the Anzacs.

However, the complete domination by the Allies of Messines was highly motivating to all involved. The tanks had been effective and the Flying Corps had held superiority in the air. What followed is close to inexplicable – instead of a massive follow up blow, once again, the British Forces were ordered to hold their ground – for what turned out to be six weeks, thereby losing the initiative, allowing the enemy to re-fortify and losing the fine weather. Various excuses were given – artillery had to be moved, no easy matter, reserves had to be assembled etc. Maybe the Messines mines had been purely a one day diversion to help Petain ? The battle was not to resume until the 22nd July with the quest for the Pilckem Ridge.

In the meantime, one more Olavian, John Sutherland, also serving with the 15th Londons and with Alick Shepherd, was killed on the 3rd July. The 15th had been moved north along the line after Messines Ridge was taken, to commence bombing runs along enemy trenches at the village of Wormezeele near St Eloi. Private Sutherland no.533432 was killed in action by a shell. He was nineteen. Just weeks earlier, he had had a near miss with another shell, and wrote home "It didn't do me much harm, knocked me out for a few minutes, grazed my face and broke a tooth, but I feel pretty well except for the shaking up".

John was born on the 18th October 1897, the third of five children, in Walworth, the son of William Sutherland, a Metropolitan Police constable from Aberdeen and his wife Elizabeth, from Aldershot. Of his two brothers, William served and Gordon was too young. John went to the local elementary school, Westmoreland Road School until 1909, when he won a scholarship to St Olave's. After six years at the school, alongside colleagues, Frank Dubery, Reginald Glenn and Percy Riminton, he left to join the staff of the Northern Telegraph Company, where he became fluent in Danish, which he used daily in his business. Enlisting in 1915, he went to the front in 1916 and was present at Flers.

Nine days of preliminary bombardment began on the 22nd July, followed by an advance by eleven British divisions on an extremely wide eleven mile front in torrential rain. The concentrated shelling had destroyed the 'water table', preventing the heavy rain from draining. A sergeant in the Somersets recorded that "It seems madness on the part of higher authority to expect any advance over this indescribable morasse". Progress on foot was painfully slow, with many men and horses sinking in the mud if they missed the duck boards laid by the pioneers. On the left of the salient, the Guards Division had discovered the new German defensive plans; that they had moved back from their Front line to the deep concrete defences with pillboxes, a 1,000 yards back. The Guards on the eve of the advance had taken the trench thereby securing their first objective before the battle began. As well as better defences against bombardment, the Germans had also secretly prepared to introduce mustard gas to the front.

Lieutenant Ken Harvard was in command of a platoon of the 2nd Battalion, Grenadier Guards at Pilckem on the 31st July. His battalion were in support of the 1st Battalion. With French troops on their left and the 38th Welsh Division on their right, but at least an hour behind them, they advanced with success through Pilckem village right to the Steenbeek River, near to Langemarck. Up to this time, unlike other battalions, the Guards had suffered little loss. Digging in, Ken returned to battalion headquarters in the rear to report and receive new orders. On hearing of a possible enemy counter attack, he rejoined his men, and was shortly shot just beneath the heart by a sniper. With the counter attack, there was no time, to evacuate him to a dressing station until dark. Early the next morning, he had bled to death. He was twenty years old and was buried in Artillery Wood cemetery at Boezinghe.

Kenneth O'Gorman Harvard, younger brother of Lionel De Jersey and John De Jersey Harvard, was the son of Thomas Mawson Harvard of Forest Hill, manager of the Indian Rubber Company and his wife Maud, born in Southport, Lancashire. Ken was born on the 4th June 1897 and spent five years at St Olave's, leaving at fourteen to attend a boarding school at Rhyl where he matriculated. Coming from the famous Harvard family, he remained in the limelight of the press attention towards his older brother, Lionel, who studied for a while at the American University bearing their name. In 1914, Ken joined the School of Engineering at South Kensington and passed his Intermediate Bachelor of Science degree in 1915. Meanwhile he had joined the London University Officer Training Corps and was commissioned in August 1915.

He was gazetted as a lieutenant in the Yorkshire Regiment, but in February 1916, transferred to the Grenadier Guards, where Lionel, a captain, was serving. Ken went to France with the 2nd Battalion on New Year's Eve 1916, and was moved up to Ypres ready for the battles of the summer. On the 31st July, the Guards were in the main advance to Pilckem Ridge.

Also on the 31st, the 18th Division commenced their advance from Hooge, south west of Polygon Wood. 53rd Brigade led the advance to take Glencorse Wood, with 54th and 55th Brigades in reserve. Over the next few days, the men off 55 Brigade, especially the 7th Battalion, the East Kents (the Buffs) tried to consolidate their position. On Friday 3rd August, a day of equable weather, a temperature of 59 degrees fahrenheit with 10mm of rainfall, the 18th relieved the 30th Division at Sanctuary Wood.

Lance Corporal Frank Clifton no. G/7332 was in charge of a platoon that day, when heavy shelling through the torrential rains, caused many casualties. It rained without stopping for four days and nights from the start of the month. Trenches turned into rivers, shell holes into swamps, full of the dead. The engineers worked at repairing communications, and the artillery requested waterproof maps. During the day, Frank Clifton was killed by an exploding shell. His body was lost in the mud of Flanders. He was twenty-four and is commemorated on the Menin Gate memorial in Ypres.

Frank Osenton Clifton was born in Brockley on the 12th March 1893 to Herne Hill restauranteur, Frank Clifton and wife Annie. A younger brother born in 1901, Alan Newell Clifton was too young to serve. Frank has no apparent biography or eulogies in the Olavian magazine; He appears with photograph in the three volume, red honour books, does not appear on the printed honour roll kept by the School Foundation, but does appear on the memorial in the School hall. He attended the school for three years from May 1905 until July 1908. Philip Burwood, Harry Hunt, Herbert Harris and Frank Dixson were his contemporaries. Above all else, he was an Olavian and a leader of men, the equal of any man in these pages.

The death of Frank Clifton marked the end of the battle for Pilckem Ridge. Two weeks passed before the next major confrontation of what became known as 'Third Ypres'. The battle of Langemarck took place over three days from the 16th to the 18th August 1917. The line of battle was drawn to the west of St Julien down to Glencorse Wood, where the 36th, 16th, 8th and 56th Divisions formed the Front line. William Elijah Holman, a Private no. 245019 of the 1/2nd Londons, Royal Fusiliers had moved forward as part of 169 Brigade, 56 Division. They advanced from 'Clapham Junction' the confluence of the trench system, with the 5th Londons, the Rifle Brigade. Moving to the right because of marshland, they entered the wood, under fire from an entrenched line of enemy concrete pill boxes. The first men into the wood, managed to get through it and pressed on, to Polygon Wood, but subsequent waves of men, were forced to stop under heavy fire. With support from the 9th Londons, the vanguard tried to protect their advanced positions, but were driven out of Glencorse later in the day, by strong German counter-attacks.

Private Holman had been killed by a single shot to the head, during the initial advance into No Mans Land. As the remainder of the battalion had to retire quickly, the dead and wounded were left where they lay. His body was not recovered. He was nineteen, and is commemorated on the Menin Gate in Ypres.

William Holman was born on the 25th February 1898 in Walworth, to a brother, Herbert, and sister, Ellen, son of Elijah Holman, dust inspector for Southwark Borough Council and his wife Ellen. After a spell at John Ruskin School, he spent four years at St Olave's from 1909 until 1913 alongside Private Glenn and Lance-Sergeant Oliver, both of the 20th Londons . He was remembered as a slow developer, but a fearless and independent boy. After school, he took an apprenticeship in a local firm which was interrupted within a couple of years by the onset of war. His sister, four years older, taught pianoforte. William enlisted in London in 1916 as a Signaller no. 5726, in the 12th London Regiment, the Rangers, and reached France in April 1917. Once there, he was transferred to the 2nd (City of London) Battalion (Royal Fusiliers) as a private. In this capacity, he became a 'runner' and was often ordered to take orders or vital information from the front to neighbouring battalions, or to Brigade Headquarters behind the lines. It was extremely dangerous work, with most runners, becoming obvious targets of enemy snipers.

'Ginger' Jones passed away in an ambulance car taking him from the Front to the first available dressing station, which proved to be 3rd Canadian Casualty Clearing Station. He had received a direct shell hit and was mortally wounded. His brother, standing with him at the time, had also been hit by the same shell and was badly wounded. The twenty year old, who had been hit in the head, and had additional gunshot wounds to the thigh, was carried away from the battlefield, somewhat unusually, under the protection of a white flag, which the enemy machine gunners had honoured. The place was Hooge, the date, 24th August, the temperature, 68 degrees fahrenheit, 50% cloud cover, and no rainfall.

James Thomas Jones was the seventh Olavian school captain to perish in the Great War. A boy of unique talent, he appeared to be a contradiction, at once shy and timid, then whimsical and playful. He was at times, diffident with 'half-awkward silences', but on other occasions, 'mirthful, obstinate with firm purpose'. Born on the 28th October 1896 in Aberayron, Cardiganshire, he was one of two sons of David Rees Jones and wife Mary, who had moved to Amersham Grove, New Cross while he was a small boy. He attended Brockley Secondary School, where he made a life long friendship with G.E. Mann, with whom he moved to Tooley Street on a L.C.C. scholarship. Both boys were gifted scholars, with 'Jimmy' winning a 'Demyship' of £800 to go up to Magdelen College, Oxford in 1915. He came top in the entrance exam, and had his name placed on the STOGS honour list.

THIRD YPRES

Jimmy or 'Ginger' as he was fondly known, was an 'all rounder'. Academic excellence the equal of Leslie Sanders, and athleticism the quality of the Ryley and Harvard brothers, ensured his position as captain of school from 1914 to 1915, alongside Olly Wade. In September 1915, he went straight from classroom to recruiting office, and joined the Inns of Court Officer Training Corps. Armed with his commission, he became Second Lieutenant Jones in July 1916, and was attached to the 20th Londons (the Blackheath and Woolwich Rifles) where Bob Hearn was also an officer. He went to France on the 21st September 1917. It is probable that the nineteen year old officer came into contact with some Old Olavians in the ranks, specifically Lance Sergeant Oliver, a few years his senior, who had been 'mentioned in despatches'. His life, so full of promise, was regrettably cut short; he is buried in the Lijssenhoek military cemetery west of Ypres.

The end of August, created a much needed lull in the fighting. Langemarck had gradually ceased and the new offensive to take the Menin Road ridge was not planned to commence until the 20th September, with thousands of new reserves being brought in to relieve the survivors of Messines, Pilckem and Langemarck. St Olave's had lost eight more boys, amongst them two school captains and three fine officers.

CHAPTER 14
The Artillery

Whilst the infantry are remembered for their courage and endurance in slogging slowly across the mud of 'No Mans Land' only to be cut down with little mercy by concealed machine guns, the artillery played a significant part in unwittingly creating the conditions whereby this could happen. The continuous, and often inaccurate, firing of shells, from positions behind the Front line trenches, usually used as a prelude to planned infantry advances, resulted in, not only exposing Allied troops to uncut barbed wire defences and enemy weaponry that could withstand severe bombardment, but also to a muddy, terrain of craters, holes and ditches through which the plentiful rainfall was unable to drain.

Communication between the battalions waiting to go 'over the top' and the artillery batteries was poor at the best of times, but disastrous when the lines laid by the engineers were damaged by the more accurate enemy shelling. Far too often, during the Ypres and Somme campaigns of 1915 and 1916, woods were shelled by Allied artillery, when occupied by Allied troops. One analysis suggests that 58% of all wounds in the Great War were caused by artillery shelling, as opposed to 39% from rifles and machine gun fire.

At other times, as with the Loos campaign in 1915, the shortage of shells, further crippled the infantry advance, leading to political infighting at home. British gunners, who had operated in Africa and India in the closing years of the nineteenth century, found it hard to adapt their skills, gunnery strategy and technology to the static warfare of the Western Front. In 1914, with aerial reconnaissance still in an embryonic state, accurate map references were nearly impossible. Gunners didn't understand the need to adapt range equations when faced with poor weather, to allow for differences in shell trajectory.

THE ARTILLERY

Mobilisation of the British Expeditionary Force in the summer of 1914, saw the utilisation of twenty brigades of the Royal Field Artillery, split four to each of the five divisions of infantry. Each was also assigned a heavy battery of the Royal Garrison Artillery, along with a squadron of Hussars and two field companies of Royal Engineers. Four batteries of the Royal Horse Artillery (C,T,K &L) were also drafted and shipped to France ready for Mons.

On the 23rd August at Obourg, 23,30,40, and 42 Brigades R.F.A.with 48 Heavy Battery RGA supporting 3 Division, made the first contact of the war with Von Kluck's rapidly advancing army. British retreat was unavoidable on this occasion.

Evi Feben, a thirty-four year old artillery corporal and Old Olavian, experienced that first sighting and clash with an impressive enemy. He was born on the 7th September 1880 in Walworth to two brothers and a sister, all children of Harry Feben, a bricklayer and his wife, Sarah. As Gunner no. 25401, the young Feben had enlisted prior to the national emergency in 1898. He trained in England and later embarked by troopship for South Africa, where he saw action. He attended St Olave's on a L.C.C. scholarship for just three years from 1892 to 1894 and was a contemporary of Fred Bennett, another Olavian later to choose the artillery. Leaving at fifteen, he apprenticed to a local Bermondsey business, but took the opportunity for an army career on his eighteenth birthday.

Following the end of the Boer War, he spent some time with his brigade at home in England and in various colonial locations. By 1914, he had been transferred to the 40th Brigade, R.F.A. as corporal. He arrived in Le Havre on the 19th August, 1914, only a week after the first infantry battalions had arrived. Travelling mostly by very slow trains, his mobile artillery unit, arrived at Mons after three days. The retreat caused much confusion for Smith-Dorrien's '11 Corps'. Three days later, Evi's brigade was caught again at Le Cateau losing 38 guns in the enemy attack. Through September and October, he witnessed the first stages of trench warfare at the battles of the Marne and the Aisne, culminating in the first mass

German attacks around the Belgian city of Ypres. Based near La Bassee, 40th Brigade were involved in heavy shelling at Gheluvelt and Messines. Corporal Feben survived and spent Christmas in France, transferring to the 6th Brigade early in the New Year. His luck ran out in early March 1915. During a relatively quiet period on the Front, leading up to the battle of Neuve Chapelle, he was killed in a manner unknown, and is buried at Bailleul, a French town ten miles south west of Ypres.

Evi Feben was joined by ten other 'Olavian Fallen', in giving service to the artillery during the Great War. With Feben in the various brigades of the Field Artillery, were four men: Gunner's Frank Dubery of 'A' Battery, 236 Brigade and Ernest Halliwell of 'D' Battery, 232 Brigade, Captain Douglas Oake M.C. of 92 Trench Mortar Battery and Major Fred Bennett of 'C' Battery, 84 Army Brigade.

Three others had taken commissions with the Royal Garrison Artillery. Captain Claude Hamilton was assigned to 287 Siege Battery; Lieutenant John Hood MID, commanded 39 Siege Battery, and Second Lieutenant Fred Husk MID, MM, with 301 Siege Battery.

Another officer, Second Lieutenant Ralph Lunn, had been gazetted to the Royal Horse Artillery with the 6th Battery, and the remaining two, served with the Honourable Artillery Company, both as privates. George Shears, a munitions expert, had joined the 1st Battalion and Harry Ebsworth, the 2nd Battalion.

As 1915 wore on and improved engineering on both sides developed stronger fortifications and deeper, better protected trench systems, artillery requirements began to change. The quick firing, mobile, field guns of Le Cateau were replaced with static more powerful guns, called Howitzers which could fire shells at a high trajectory into enemy areas, previously protected by breastworks and parapets. High explosive rounds started to be used, to destroy barbed wire defences, and bombardments grew in duration and intensity, removing any possibility of surprise attack. Needless to say, the increasing immobility of artillery, prevented it from taking

THE ARTILLERY

advantage of quick infantry advances. Many such small territory gains were lost hours later, due to lack of artillery support from the new position.

It wasn't until late in 1916, that real improvements in artillery practice began to happen. Vastly better reports from aerial reconnaissance, with good quality photography allowed targeting of enemy batteries. 'Predicted fire' was enabled due to the innovative ability to 'calibrate' the muzzle velocity and barrel wear of guns. Detailed maps could be created from topographical surveys. 'flash-spotting' and 'sound-ranging' provided the locations of enemy batteries. The '106 percussion fuse' enabled wire to be destroyed without the creation of devastating cratering. All of these developments brought back artillery as a surprise. The 'rolling' or 'creeping' barrage allowing infantry advance behind it, had been perfected by spring 1917. With the Passchendaele campaign, Allied gunnery had 'come of age'.

The Honourable Artillery Company was part of the territorial infantry, along with the London Regiments. It had served in the South Africa campaigns as a volunteer battalion. Harold Charles Ebsworth had enlisted in summer 1914 whilst just sixteen. He was the only son and child of Frederick Ebsworth, a chartered accountant in a city life insurance firm and his wife Alice Amelia, born on the 9th December 1897. When he was nine, he entered St Olave's, where he was to spend the next eight years of his education. Of the Olavian gunners, he is most likely to have known Frank Dubery well. He is remembered as a 'big, diffident boy with genial smile and a stoop'. His masters remarked that his fast physical development was followed by a slower mental one, but his perseverance paid off in his studies. Leaving in January 1914, aged seventeen, he had intended to find work in the City, but with war on the horizon, he decided to enlist as Private, no. 5061, in the 2nd Battalion, H.A.C.

With the 1st Battalion going off to Belgium in early 1915 to fight at Ypres, the 2nd stayed in England, training. They eventually received news of their posting, in summer 1916. By October, they were engaged in front line combat on the battlefields of the Somme. Harold's first involvement in a major action was at the battle of the Ancre Heights on the 1st October, lasting several weeks. In this attack, the H.A.C. supported 25 Division, men from the north-west, and several Canadian brigades to push their line north of Flers Courcelette to take the 'Regina trench' and 'Schwaben Redoubt', two enemy strong points. On the 13th November, Harold also took part in the five day battle of the Ancre, whereby the enemy were pushed back, east of the town of Beaumont Hamel by the combined strength of 19th (Western) Division, 39 Division and 63 (Royal Naval) Division. The Somme campaign of 1916 closed on the last day of the Ancre action, mostly due to the poor weather conditions. The thawing snow had turned the battlefield into a 'wilderness of mud'. Just over two weeks later, Harold was killed in action. He had been part of a party of men occupying an outpost position, when he was shot in the head by a snipers bullet. A companion carried his unconscious body along fifteen yards of mud filled trench under severe fire, getting shot in the process. Both men died. He was two days short of his nineteenth birthday, and is buried in the Ancre British Cemetery, just south of Beaumont Hamel. The 'big man' had perished.

Meanwhile, George Shears was in the process of enlisting, having spent Christmas of 1916 at home in England with his parents, Willie and Louisa Shears in Eltham. His job with the new 'Ministry of Munitions' prohibited him for joining many of his school friends on the Western Front, as he was involved in what the Government called 'essential services'. But towards the end of 1916, his insistence to be allowed to enlist, had finally changed the minds of his employers.

He was nineteen at this time, born a few months earlier than Harold Ebsworth on the 29th June 1897, to a sister Edith, and another father who was a schoolmaster. He only attended the School for three years on a scholarship, leaving in 1911 aged just fourteen years, to apprentice as a mechanic and electrician. His

THE ARTILLERY

skills over the next few years were to lead him to become extremely technically competent in the manufacture and use of explosives and artillery shells.

In January 1917 then, he enlisted as Private no.10060, in the 1st Battalion, H.A.C. and left for France on April 13th. He arrived at the front at Gavrelle, east of Arras in France, just a few days later, to find the major campaign had commenced. British and French troops, that had clung for so long to the Arras Salient, launched its attack on April 9th. General Haig, trying to draw enemy troops away from Nivelle's planned attack in the Aisne sector, bombarded the enemy for five days prior to the 9th, with 2,800 guns and gas. George found himself working as part of an artillery team, at all three battles of the Scarpe, sometimes referred to as 'Monchy Le Preux', 'Gavrelle/Guemappe', and 'Fresnoy'. It is possible that he witnessed the gallantry of an H.A.C. officer, who had been awarded the Victoria Cross at Gavrelle on the 29th April. The man, of course, Alfred Pollard, a fellow Olavian only four years, George's senior.

The two day action at Arleux led to a more drawn out conflict at Bullecourt starting on the 3rd May and lasting for two weeks. Arras proved fruitless as it was checked by the enemy with relative ease at a cost to both sides of 150,000 casualties. George, like many others, had survived the major 'push' only to be killed during the interminable lulls in activity. He had been on a rations party on the 22nd May, and went missing. A few shells had landed a little distance from the party, but no-one had been thought to be hit. His disappearance was never explained. He is commemorated on the Arras Memorial to the missing at Faubourg-d'Amiens Cemetery in west Arras. His company sergeant-major spoke of him in the highest terms.

The death of the 'Munitions expert' was followed shortly after, by that of Gunner Dubery near Ypres on the 7th June 1917, the day famous for the opening of Plumer's successful attack on the German held 'Messines Ridge'.

Frank Arthur Dubery, was the same age as Harry and George of the H.A.C. Born in August 1897 in Stockwell to brothers, Alf and

Robert, sister, Adeline and much younger adopted brother, Sam Kirby, his father, Alf Dubery, was a labourer from Croydon and his mother, Emma from Portsmouth. Frank attended the School with his brothers. Spending six years there, he left in July 1914, just before his seventeenth birthday, with every intention to take up a position in the City. After three months as a trainee clerk, he joined up.

He was despatched as Gunner no. 956236, Royal Field Artillery, to a training camp where he remained until his brigade went to France in autumn 1915. Once there, he was assigned to 'A Battery' 236 Brigade, as part of a six man gunnery team with 9.2 inch howitzers. These guns had a range of between 10,000 and 12,700 yards depending on the shells used. Most shells weighed 290 pounds. Men were kept occupied digging 'gun-pits' to house the howitzers, and creating camouflage to shield it from enemy aeroplanes. Usually the unit was commanded by a non-commissioned officer, who gave and received the orders. Another man acted as a 'layer' responsible for checking for alignment and elevation. The 'gunner', as with Frank, opened and closed the breech, a dangerous occupation, with shell-cases being ejected from the breech automatically after firing. Three further men were employed to handle the heavy shells and set the fuses.

Throughout 1916, Frank Dubery fired shells at the enemy in France at Beaumont Hamel, Thiepval, Delville Wood and so forth. He took his leave in December and came home to England to see his family, now living at Herne Hill. In early 1917, his battery and many others, featured in Haig and Plumer's plans to break German control of the Messines Ridge, from where they could enfilade long lengths of the Allied Front line.

Meticulously planned, nineteen mines had been planted by the tunnellers in a ten mile arc from Hill 60 via Spanbroekmolen to Ploegsteert Wood. Four miles of tunnels and over a million pounds of explosives provide testament to the work and investment applied to this attack. For once, infantry success was possible, as time had been allowed to brief right down to company level, with limited

THE ARTILLERY

and precise objectives. When the mines exploded at 03.10 in the morning of the 7th June, two whole weeks of Allied bombardment came to a close, and British 'X Corps' with Anzac 'II Corps' rushed the Ridge supported by 72 tanks, and the Royal Flying Corps dominant in the air. J.W. Naylor, a Royal Field Artillery officer present, wrote later that 'the earth seemed to tear apart... it was an extraordinary sight... it was like a huge mushroom. It had a tremendous moral effect'.

At 11.05, General Headquarters received a telegraph – 'We have everywhere captured our first objectives. Messines Ridge captured. Attack on nine mile front. Brilliant British success. Over 5,000 prisoners'. But Gunner Dubery had been killed at some point during the morning, presumably by German shelling in counter-attack. His body was recovered and buried at Bedford House situated between Ypres and Armentieres. He was also nineteen. His brothers survived the war.

The first of the officers to give his life, came ten days later back in the south, at Arras.

Ralph Lunn was a second lieutenant with the Royal Horse Artillery, whose brigade had been involved in the 'famous' cutting of the wire at Mametz Wood on the 3rd July 1916. He himself had been an infantry rifleman at the time, with the 16th Londons (Queen's Westminster Rifles) present at the capture of Combles on the 26th September 1916. His battalion had been trying to push the enemy out of Leuze Wood since the 10th with little success. Early in the morning of the 26th, 169 Brigade advanced down the Combles trench system, combining with French troops, to take the town.

Ralph had been a quiet unassuming boy, born in February 1891 with one brother Percy, sons of William Henry Harvey Lunn, a surveyor and architect from Kennington and his wife Ruth. From the start, they were involved in the family business of building. William Lunn owned his own building yard and encouraged Ralph to learn his sciences, prior to training as an associate in the Surveyor's Institute. Ralph attended St Olave's for five years, leaving at seventeen. He is remembered for his modesty, his 'straightness' of personality, a willing, cheerful but determined boy. By 1911, Ralph was employed as a qualified quantity surveyor, living in the family home in Balham with older sister Grace and articled accounts clerk, Percy. His talents as a builder would probably have suited him better for a life with the Royal Engineers, but he obviously thought differently, enlisting as an ordinary soldier on the outbreak of hostilities. In 1915, he had been promoted to lance corporal, and after Combles, had been sent to England to train for a commission. It was during this time that he took the opportunity to marry his fiance, Daisy. When he was assigned to the Royal Horse Artillery and returned to France, she went to live with his parents who had by this time moved away from London to Southampton.

Ralph arrived at the front in April 1917, in time for the opening attacks on the 9th. He had been attached to 15 Brigade, RHA, and was in command of 'B' battery, based at Monchy au bois, a small village west of Arras. He was heavily involved in bombardments for the first battle of the Scarpe river at Monchy Le Preux and other subsequent actions. He was killed in action at 'Infantry Hill' near Monchy on 17th June. Standing near the trench which hid the battery, in discussion with his immediate superior officer, a major, and another second lieutenant, a shell exploded near to them, killing the major outright. Ralph was taken to hospital with all speed, arriving within hours, but to little advantage. His wounds were severe, and he passed away later in the day.

Both artillery officers were buried at Faubourg-d'Amiens Cemetery, in a funeral with full military honours. Their coffins proceeded through the centre of Arras on an 18 pounder artillery gun, followed by the entire battery as a mark of respect. Bearing in mind, the fact that the city was under siege, this was a considerably unusual step.

Ralph William Lunn, son and husband, was twenty-six years old. His brigade commanding officer was reported at the time, as saying, "It is daily becoming harder to find men of his calibre, who by their courage and example, both from a moral and physical standpoint, can encourage and inspire their men, to rise to any occasion, and do their duty manfully and well, in the face of tremendous odds".

Another such man was Harry Trotman. At the outbreak of war, he resided with his wife Lilian, near the Elephant and Castle and close to his parents, Henry Trotman, a local draper and shirt-cutter and wife Elsiena, at 40 Tanner Street, Bermondsey. Born in April 1890, Harry, and his younger brothers Edward and Eric, were the third generation of Trotmans to attend St Olave's. Previous Trotmans had been educated at the 'English School', once attached to the School Foundation but since discontinued. Harry spent four years at the School, joining from the Boucher School and leaving in 1905 aged fifteen to go into business. In 1915, he enlisted as Driver no. 2635 with 'D' Battery, 236th Brigade, Royal Field Artillery and although significantly older than Frank Dubery, may have come across him in Belgium.

Harry spent over two years on the Somme and at Ypres with only one leave, to return to see his wife, but he handled himself with fortitude and adopted a 'no nonsense' pragmatic view to his orders. On one occasion, he was 'mentioned in despatches', when, having volunteered to go out into No Mans Land at night and under heavy shell fire, to re-erect some aiming posts in an old cemetery, which a previous man had seemingly failed to do, he found the man stricken with terror, caused by the fact that the bombardment had literally blown the dead out of their graves under a full moon. Harry completed the job, and persuaded the man to retire to safety.

Henry Morriss, ex Mayor of Bermondsey, in his book, 'Bermondsey's 'Bit' in the Great War', suggests that this was an 'example of manliness from one no more than a boy himself. An exercise in coolness and courage'. Towards the end of the Passchendaele campaign, Harry, deputising as a gunner, due to severe losses and lack of new recruits, was killed by a bomb blast, on the 12th September 1917. He was twenty-seven and his remains were buried at the Bailleul Communal Cemetery Extension, south west of Ypres.

In July 1917, further north in Belgium, around the Ypres Salient, a new Allied offensive was underway. It would last for over three months, eventually taking the Passchendaele Ridge at the cost of over 300,000 British lives. An eye-witness involved wrote that 'rain has turned everything into a quagmire. The shell holes are full of water. The debris of war is lying about. But very few human bodies, for they have been swallowed up in the mud and water. It seems madness on the part of Higher Authority to expect any advance over this indescribable morass'. Gunner Ernest Halliwell was there, trying to cope with the conditions. He was part of 'D Battery' 232 Brigade, R.F.A. based to the east of Ypres, supporting British and Anzac divisions in pushing the enemy back across the muddy bogland of the Zonnebeke to Poelcapelle and Passchendaele.

Ernest was the older brother by just a year of William, of the Rifle Brigade, who had won a Military Cross as a company sergeant-major at the first battle of Ypres and was later killed in action at Pilckem Ridge. Ernest was immensely proud of his brother's achievements. They were two of the six sons of Thomas Bennett Halliwell, secretary of the Licensed Victualler's Society and wife Martha Elizabeth known as Lucy, from Rotherhithe. Ernest was born on the 25th August 1884, the third son, younger than Archie and Albert, but older than William, Harold and Sidney. He joined St Olave's at the age of thirteen in 1897 and remained there for three years on a scholarship. On leaving, he joined a local Bermondsey firm, James Budgett & Co. He worked loyally for this employer for the next eighteen years, unable to enlist in 1914, as Budgett's were manufacturing materials which were 'important to the War effort'. As the war developed, and the supplies of young single men were exhausted, the older married men were gradually called upon to enlist. Such was the case with Ernest. A steadily resolute man, he was strong, and unselfish, with a simple straightforward ideology, but had been told of his younger brother's death at the Front. He had married Grace, and they resided with their children at 242

THE ARTILLERY

Ivydale Road, Nunhead in South London, but he was unsettled and felt his duty was to join the Army.

At the start of 1917, at the age of thirty-three, the Government had released him to enlist. He joined the Royal Field Artillery and was sent to France in the summer. With the turmoil that surrounded the third battle of Ypres, Ernest didn't last for very long. Although the full circumstances of his death are not known, he died on the 12th October, a cold rainy day – the day of the first battle of Passchendaele, the final action of the Ypres campaign. Like the many thousands that also perished, he is buried at 'Tyne Cot' Cemetery, north east of Ypres town. This, however, was not the end to the grieving for the Halliwell family. Having lost William in July 1915, then Ernest in October 1917, a third son, Harold, serving with the 12th Northumberland Fusiliers was lost during the German Offensive on 28th March 1918.

Operating on the same Belgian Front during the Passchendaele attacks, was the Royal Garrison Artillery. One of their siege batteries was commanded by a young twenty-seven year old newly promoted captain. His name was Claude William Hamilton. He was an Old Olavian.

Claude was the elder brother of Second Lieutenant Noel Hamilton of the Northamptonshires who had been killed in 1916 in the attack on Trones Wood during the Somme campaign. Born in August 1890 in High Barnet, Hertfordshire, fourth child of seven of the anglican clergyman from Ireland, the Right Reverend Frederick John Hamilton and his wife Jane from Haggerston, he and Noel later moved to West Kensington, travelling daily to St Olave's in Bermondsey. Claude attended the School for just a year and a half leaving in the summer of 1906 to take a course of study in practical engineering at the Sandiacre works in Nottinghamshire. After several years of experience in engineering, in 1914, he took his Inter B.Sc. in London, enlisting just two months later, on hearing of the opening of hostilities. As a young boy, he was described as honourable and conscientious, character traits that he bore well in his training as a rifleman with the 28th Londons, the Artists Rifles.

He arrived in Boulogne by troopship in early January 1915, taking part in the first battle of Ypres, and then spending a period at General Headquarters. When an opportunity arose to return to England and take an officers training course, he jumped at it, and was soon gazetted as a second lieutenant and posted to the King's Royal Rifle Corps later in the year, on the 27th November. The following February, he joined his new regiment on the move from the French town of Armentieres to the Ypres Salient. In early June, he escaped death by a whisker, when a shell exploded on the roof of his dug-out, killing all of the fellow officers that he had previously been conversing with. He did sustain some injuries to his shoulder and to his eye, which meant two months of recuperation and some opportunity to see his family, sisters, Lilian, Ursula, Amy and Elsie, and eldest brother, Fred. Having missed Loos though his officer training, he also missed the start of the Somme, as, shortly after he was transferred to field hospital, the K.R.R.C. received orders to move to the Somme valley ready for the 'Big Push'.

Claude returned in late August, only to be more seriously wounded this time, at the same location of his younger brother, Noel's demise a few weeks earlier – at Trones Wood. He was hit by flying shrapnel whilst trying to supply an ammunition depot. The severity of this wound returned him to 'Blighty' for a while. One may suspect that his endurance and confidence were at a low ebb, and maybe a thought that he might not be so lucky on the third occasion. From all reports of men who served with and under him, an impression develops quite quickly of Claude Hamilton. A religious man, cheerful, a strong devotion to duty, with a remarkable, quiet courage and a strong affection for his men.

When the garrison artillery started recruiting for experienced and qualified mathematicians and scientists to train with them to become subalterns responsible for the improved organisation and logistics of transport and supplies, Claude volunteered, leaving hospital to go back to school. Typically he came first in the

THE ARTILLERY

examinations and was placed second in command of the officer intake. In April 1917, he went with his artillery battery – 287th Siege Battery, back to the Front. He was promoted to captain, and was present on the 7th June, the day of Gunner Dubery's death, when the Messines Ridge was captured. Fighting right through the dreary, muddy, wet, hell of the third battle of Ypres, Claude was injured for the final time on a Tuesday, November 6th, in the last few days of the Passchendaele campaign.

The day was overcast with showers, with 5 Division, the men of Devon and Cornwall attacking Polderhoek Chateau. At eight in the morning the enemy opened with a very heavy barrage lasting for two hours. The rest of the day saw small withdrawals of infantry. Claud Hamilton's battery was destroyed bit by bit, until he was the last officer left in command. At some stage he was hit by shrapnel, and mortally wounded. He died soon after, in the field ambulance on the way to the advanced dressing station. His body was buried in the Menin Road South Military Cemetery, in the east of Ypres. He was the last Olavian claimed by the terror of Passchendaele.

Several months went by before more serious damage was done to the British Artillery and to more Olavian soldiers. The battle of Cambrai in November led to no Olavian artillery casualties. It was not until what has become known as the 'Kaisers Offensive' of March 1918, that another was claimed.

Fred Husk was an officer who had worked his way through all of the ranks, staying all the while in the garrison artillery. During this journey, he was 'mentioned in despatches' and was awarded the Military Medal for gallantry. As a signalling sergeant in 1916, he had taken part in the 'Givenchy Raid' staying out all night alone in No Man's Land, under fire, repairing the telecommunications lines which enabled his battery to communicate with General Headquarters. His despatch for a commission was incited by General Julian Byng personally.

Frederick John Husk was born in October 1891, the only son with one sister Edith, of John Husk, a sugar manufacturer from Jersey in the Channel Islands and his wife, Eliza. Fred spent four years at St Olaves, leaving in 1907 to join a solicitors office where he worked until 1911. To busy himself in his spare time, he acted as secretary of both the Old Olavian rugby football club and the Rotherhithe cricket club. Tiring of the boredom of the legal life, he yearned to follow his true love, as an antiquarian. He set up in business with a friend, buying and selling antiques from a small modest shop in High Wycombe.

In early 1915, he and his partner put the business on hold, and enlisted, Fred in the Royal Garrison Artillery. He went to France on the 9th October 1916 during the Somme campaign, winning the Military Medal for gallantry as Sergeant no.71131 and later, whilst in England taking his commission in 1917, he married his fiance, Florence. Two months later, on the 18th August, he returned to France as Second Lieutenant Husk M.M. Within a matter of weeks, his courage was 'mentioned' at Cambrai, for the way in which he had kept the artillery informed during the engagement at 'Tunnel Trench'. In March 1918, like many others, he was just in the wrong place on a bad day. The 21st March 1918, was the day when the German High Command decided to bombard the area south of Arras for five solid hours with shells from over 6,000 guns. Shortly after, a million enemy soldiers advanced on a fifty mile Front. Husk's 301st Siege Battery was based at the village of Croisilles, between Arras and Bapaume, right on the Front line, where the 2nd German Army took on the British 3rd Army. In the south, Gough's 5th Army was pushed back over forty miles, but at Croisilles, the line was only withdrawn a few hundred yards – a tribute to the coolness of the defence.

Fred had been wounded either by a shell casing or a bullet, whilst trying to command his section. He had exposed himself without regard to danger on the top of a railway bank in the best position to control and direct his howitzers, shouting orders, and encouraging his men at the guns below. As the advancing enemy infantry got to very close quarters, he was hit, but carried on directing his batteries withdrawal. He survived long enough to learn that his men removed

THE ARTILLERY

themselves unscathed, at least on this occasion. He was twenty-six years old and due to the success of the enemy advance, his body was left and not recovered. He is commemorated on the Pozieres Memorial, north east of Albert on the Somme.

Douglas and Cyril Oake were born in Bermondsey, sons of Councillor Joseph William Oake. Joe Oake Senior served as a Governor of St Olave's School, was himself an Old Olavian and was also elected Mayor of Bermondsey in 1911. This was on top of his real job as publican of the Bunch of Grapes at 39 Tooley Street. Both of his sons won the Military Cross for gallantry, Cyril Oake as a four times wounded, captain in the East Yorkshires, who had led his company in a daylight attack on Gavrelle taking 31 prisoners and 6 guns. Cyril survived the conflict to return to sister Gladys and his widowed father.

'Dug', the younger brother, born in September 1891 spent seven full years at the school, and is remembered as a boy and man of jubilant spirit, an organiser, a competitor with a plain honesty. At fifteen, he started work as a shipping clerk in the City for a lighterage firm. After a few years, he joined his father by becoming one of the Court of Governors of the School. Much of his activity was influenced by his brother Cyril. They enlisted together in the public schools 'special corps', were trained as officer cadets at Pockington, Ripon and Salisbury, and both gazetted as second lieutenants with the 11th Battalion, the East Yorkshires, stationed at Kingston-upon-Hull.

When the battalion was made operational, they sailed for Alexandria in Egypt just before Christmas on the 23rd December 1915. Attached to the 92nd Brigade of 31 Division, the brothers spent several months in the early protection of the Suez Canal and the Sinai Peninsula, before returning to Beaumont Hamel on the Western Front for the battle of the Somme. Dug was, at this point, split from his brother and attached to a a trench mortar battery, no. 92 TMB, which served the 92nd Infantry Brigade. On the 16th July, after two weeks of furious fighting, Dug was promoted to the rank of captain, and earning his Military Cross for gallantry at Serre on July 1st.

His award was published in the supplement to the London Gazette on the 1st January 1917:

> "Temp. Lt. Douglas Oake, Gen. List, attd. T.M. By".

> "The attack had gone off at 07.20. According to the War Office, Lieutenant Oake had been wounded seven times up to this point in the War. Fellow officers said of him that 'he was always 'first'. As a commander of his battery, he was 'always on the spot', never missing a tour of duty in the trenches. During the lull in the fighting, when the brigade was resting, he formed 'the Tonics' concert party to keep the men amused. When his brother was not wounded and away recuperating, he used to go down the trench line and wait to see Cyril when he came back from a raid".

After the retreat to the Hindenburg line in March 1918, Cyril Oake was removed to England and sent as an instructor in tactics to newly qualified American officers, as part of the British Military Mission to the U.S.A. This probably saved his life, as he was only to return to France in late October for the final advance. Dug meanwhile, met an untimely end on August 8th, killed accidentally, whilst demonstrating an experimental new type of mortar shell with a different fuse. It burst prematurely, killing many of his own men, the Royal Engineers present and himself. The brigade's general in attendance, survived. Another unnecessary waste of a talented, strong, courageous Olavian. He was twenty-seven and is buried in Le Grand Hasard Cemetery on the outskirts of Hazebrouck, west of Ypres. Tributes poured in, amongst which he was described as 'game to the last', and 'one of 'the whitest men I have ever met'. Many local Bermondsey people, remembered the brothers when they used to entertain at the town hall with music and ragtime songs.

THE ARTILLERY

Frederick Barberry Bennett almost made it through. He had been in France since the start of 1915, and by October of 1918, he was still there, having recovered from bullet wounds in Flanders at the third battle of Ypres. By 1918, he was a married man of thirty-eight and a full Major – the most senior ranking officer within the 'Olavian Fallen' of the Great War. Fred was one of four brothers, including Charles, George and Arthur, and a sister Lilian. All of the boys attended St Olave's in the 1890's. Fred was born on the 24th June 1890 to a father working as a clerk for the Thames Conservancy Board, spending four years at the School from 1892 to 1895, when he left at sixteen to join the London Stock Exchange. He later married, Ethel and they lived at Purley in Surrey. In 1911, they had a daughter.

When war came in 1914, Fred joined the Inns of Court O.T.C. as Private no. 1618 and was soon commissioned as a second lieutenant in the Royal Field Artillery Territorial Force on 1st March 1915. He went to France with his brigade on 16th October 1917, having been promoted first to lieutenant and then captain; and whilst he was recuperating from wounds in a French field hospital late in the year, he learnt of the birth of his son at home. Returning to the Front, in early 1918, he was promoted to major and commanded 'C' Battery, 84th Army Brigade, based around 'Bray-Sur-Somme', a strategically important town on the north bank of the winding river, south east of Albert. Major Fred Bennett took part in the defence of his line against poisonous gas attacks from the enemy, being badly gassed himself in the process, succumbing to his injuries just a few weeks before the Armistice. He was buried at Bronfay Farm at Bray-Sur-Somme and is commemorated on the Stock Exchange Memorial in London.

Nine Olavians had served and died in the artillery. Men of finance, science, surveying, engineering, antiques; men of duty, courage, fortitude. Products of St Olave's.

London Rifle Brigade in late Summer 1914 – John Carrier and Albert Baker's chosen Territorial Regiment. Both went to France with the BEF in the Autumn being awarded the 1914 Star.

Frank Clifton's Medal Index Card showing his entitlement to the Victory Medal and the British War Medal, as well as his rank, regiment and number.

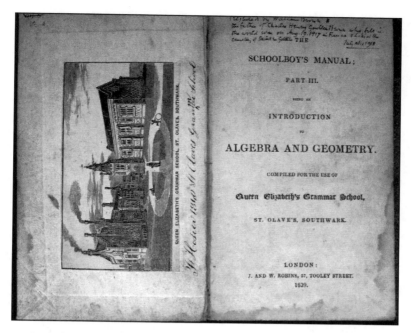

Book donated to the School in memory of Charles Henry Goullee Brown by his Father.

Reg Stubbs

Cecil Gaskain

Stanley Mann

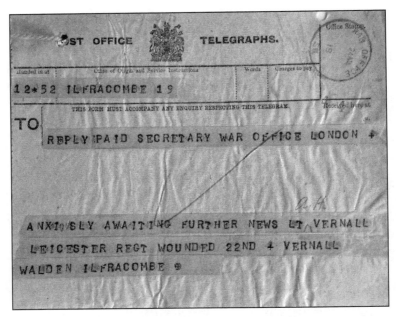

Telegram from Arthur Vernalls parents in Devon asking after him.

Jack Gill

The Goenner Twins

ORIGINAL.

ATTESTATION PAPER.   No. 106216

CANADIAN OVER-SEAS EXPEDITIONARY FORCE. Folio 106205

QUESTIONS TO BE PUT BEFORE ATTESTATION.
(ANSWERS).

1. What is your name? — John Durant
2. In what Town, Township or Parish, and in what Country were you born? — London England
3. What is the name of your next-of-kin? — Mrs Lewis Maud Durant
4. What is the address of your next-of-kin? — 54 Remington Rd, New Cross London England
5. What is the date of your birth? — May 26th 1883
6. What is your Trade or Calling? — Farmer
7. Are you married? — No
8. Are you willing to be vaccinated or re-vaccinated? — Yes
9. Do you now belong to the Active Militia? — No
10. Have you ever served in any Military Force? If so, state particulars of former Service. — No
11. Do you understand the nature and terms of your engagement? — Yes
12. Are you willing to be attested to serve in the CANADIAN OVER-SEAS EXPEDITIONARY FORCE? — Yes

_____ J. Durant _____ (Signature of Man).
_____ W. K. Pearson _____ (Signature of Witness).

DECLARATION TO BE MADE BY MAN ON ATTESTATION.

I, John Durant, do solemnly declare that the above answers made by me to the above questions are true, and that I am willing to fulfil the engagements by me now made, and I hereby engage and agree to serve in the Canadian Over-Seas Expeditionary Force, and to be attached to any arm of the service therein, for the term of one year, or during the war now existing between Great Britain and Germany should that war last longer than one year, and for six months after the termination of that war provided His Majesty should so long require my services, or until legally discharged.

Date 23rd Dec. 1914.   J. Durant (Signature of Recruit)
                         C. Donegan (Signature of Witness)

OATH TO BE TAKEN BY MAN ON ATTESTATION.

I, John Durant, do make Oath, that I will be faithful and bear true Allegiance to His Majesty King George the Fifth, His Heirs and Successors, and that I will as in duty bound honestly and faithfully defend His Majesty, His Heirs and Successors, in Person, Crown and Dignity, against all enemies, and will observe and obey all orders of His Majesty, His Heirs and Successors, and of all the Generals and Officers set over me. So help me God.

Date December 23 1914.   J. Durant (Signature of Recruit)
                           W. Geo Barker (Signature of Witness)

CERTIFICATE OF MAGISTRATE.

The Recruit above-named was cautioned by me that if he made any false answer to any of the above questions he would be liable to be punished as provided in the Army Act.
The above questions were then read to the Recruit in my presence.
I have taken care that he understands each question, and that his answer to each question has been duly entered as replied to, and the said Recruit has made and signed the declaration and taken the oath before me, at Brandon this 23 day of December 1914.

_____ A. R. Fryery P.M. _____ (Signature of Justice).

I certify that the above is a true copy of the Attestation of the above-named Recruit.

_____ (Approving Officer)

John Stride Durant's Military Attestation Papers signed just before Christmas in Canada.

CHAPTER 15

The Machine Gun and the Tank Corps

The British Army in France were late in accepting the military significance of many of the recent technologies appearing on the battlefields. Mostly trained in cavalry regiments in the colonies, the military leadership was slow to promote the use of machine guns in volume, over single shot rifles, despite their use for decades in the Mexican and Russo-Japanese wars; they were slow to protect their men against the use of mustard and other gases permeating their way across No Mans Land, and they were slow to invest in the concept of 'armoured vehicles' in all theatres of war, especially the Western Front.

Clearly, a more open minded view on the use of new materials and techniques, as well as a government willing to invest in the mass production of such weaponry, could have saved the lives of many conscript infantrymen, daily being asked to climb out of their shelters and walk to their deaths.

The enemy had two distinct advantages in the use of new technology; firstly, for at least a generation, their youth had been educated in technical schools and had provided a consequent rise to power of a strong economy built on coal and iron ore production, engineering and so forth: and secondly, as the aggressor, their build up to war allowed them time to test and plan the use of various new weaponry.

Heavy machine guns on low mounts were used by both sides from 1914. Mostly using ammunition supplied on a woven fabric belt, these guns were capable of firing 250 rounds before reloading was necessary. The French believed one well positioned machine gun to be comparable to over 100 trained riflemen. Often able to dispense over 600 rounds per minute, the gun crew had to cope with many problems. Air or water had to be available to reduce the heat of the barrel, the equipment had to be kept clean, protective armour was removed to reduce the weight of the gun for transportation. As the war progressed, lighter more mobile guns were developed, operable by one trained soldier.

The Olavians supplied many riflemen with cadet corps experience and sporting awards for shooting, but four of the 'Fallen' single themselves out for inclusion in the early history of the development of the army's Machine Gun Corps. All of them London men, three had originally enlisted as privates in the London regiments and one in the East Surreys.

Albert Baker, born on the 11th July 1896, was the only son with three younger sisters of George and Margaret Baker from Rotherhithe. He was a student at St Olave's from 1909 until late in 1912, when he left, aged sixteen years to train as a bank clerk at the River Plate Bank in the City. Within three years, he was head of department, but left to enlist, when many of his school colleagues started to volunteer. He had maintained his connections with the cadet corps at St Olave's, and was accepted as Private no. 9927, in the 5th London Regiment, the London Rifle Brigade.

At school at the same time as Albert Baker, was Alf Page, also an only son with three sisters, of Harry Page, a policeman of Trinity Square, Southwark. Born on the 25th November 1895, Alfred spent four years at St Olave's, leaving in 1911 to become a law clerk for the London County Council, based at Spring Gardens in Bermondsey. Somewhat curiously, he enlisted as a private in the 15th London Regiment, the (Prince of Wales Own) Civil Service Rifles, just after Christmas 1913, some eight months prior to the opening of hostilities. He was at a training camp in southern England when war broke out. Volunteering for foreign service immediately, he was one of the first of the London Territorials in France in March 1915.

Ernest Howell Clarke was somewhat the other boys senior. He was born in July 1885, the younger of two brothers of the Reverend

Elijah and Clara Clarke of Rotherhithe. Reverend Elijah was from Birmingham where he was part of the Baptist movement. After studying for six years at the school, Ernest left in 1903 aged eighteen and trained as a schoolmaster. Following in his fathers religious footsteps, he became the 'Licentiate of the College of Preceptors' and of the 'London College of Music'. He taught and played the organ at the Seaman's Chapel in Rotherhithe and was choirmaster at the Baptist church in Greenwich. As a patient and religious man, he didn't enlist immediately, but waited to see how the war would develop. In February 1916, he joined the Royal Sussex Regiment as an infantryman, transferring, after training, to the East Surrey's.

Conrad Lorey was the fourth man to be drawn to the machine gun. He was born in May 1895 as Conrad Clifford Smith to a family in Alresford in Essex, but was later adopted by Mary Lorey and her husband residing in Camberwell. Mary had lost three of her four birth children , her remaining daughter marrying and giving her a grandson, Henry Ashley, born in 1905 and mercifully too young for the war. After six years at St Olave's as a junior L.C.C. scholar, Conrad matriculated and joined a silk merchants office, before moving to become a chartered secretary at the Savoy Hotel. He enlisted in London immediately war was announced, and joined the 7th City of London Regiment. During his training in late 1914 and 1915, Conrad excelled in all regimental exams and consistently won all rifle shooting competitions, going to France with a reputation as his battalion's highest scorer.

By mid 1915, the heavier Vickers belt-fed guns, were being replaced by the Lewis gun for the British, and the 'Muskete' and 'Bergmann' for the Germans. The Lewis, by way of comparison weighed only 25 pounds, three times less than the Vickers Mark 1, and it employed a drum magazine, capable of quick fire of 600 rounds per minute.

By 1915, the British Army's 'Field Regulations of 1909' were being questioned by junior officers, in terms of how machine guns were deployed. In the early campaigns from Mons to Loo's, it appeared that

Akerman, Ralph Portland, 2Lt, 11th Londons

Almond, James Edgar, Pte, 9th Royal Fusiliers

Athow, William, Pte, 8th Royal Fusiliers

Baker, Albert George, Pte, 5th Londons

Baker, Harold William, Pte, 20th Royal Fusiliers

Barton, Ernest, Lt, Royal Field Artillery

Beecraft, William Henry, Pte, 16th Middlesex

Belcher, Douglas Charles, L/Cpl, 102nd Sanitary Section, Royal Army Medical Corps

Bendixen, Leonard, Caporal, French Army

Bennett, Frederick Barberry, Major, C Battery, 84th Army Bde, Royal Field Artillery

Benson, George Enoch, Rfn, 2nd Bn, The Rifle Brigade

Berrow, Lewis Walter, Pte, Yorkshire Dragoons

Berrow, William Rushbury, Pte, E Bn, Tank Corps

Bishopp, Stephen M.M. Pte, 17th Royal Fusiliers

Blackman, Herbert William, Pte, 8th Rifle Brigade

Blencowe, Charles Edward, 2Lt, Royal Sussex att'd 1st Wiltshires

Bliss, Harold Edgar, Pte, 7th Norfolks

Boone, John William Donald, L/Cpl, 22nd Rifle Brigade

Brittain, Percy James, Pte, 1/24th Londons

Brown, Charles Henry Goullee, Pte, B Coy, Royal Engineers

Budd, Victor John, Flight Sub Lt, Royal Naval Air Service

Burn, Edmund Alfred Henry, Pte, 2/14th Londons

Burwood, Philip, Pte, 2/23rd Londons

Butler, Edmund Hearn, Cpl, 2/9th Londons

Carrier, John Russell, 2Lt, 1/5th Londons

Castell, George Charles, 1st Air Mechanic, 12 Sqdn, Royal Flying Corps

Castle, Ewart William King, Rfn, 1/16th Londons

Chapman, Robert Stanley, Rfn, 2/5th Londons

Chester, Harold Thomas, Pte, 1st Royal Guernsey Light Infantry

Child, Albert George, Pte, 3/5th Londons

Chubb, John Lethbridge, Pte, 19th Canadian Infantry (Central Ontario Regt)

Churcher, Edgar, Lt, 32 Sqdn, Royal Flying Corps

Clarke, Ernest Howell, P 95th Coy, Machine Gun C

Clifton, Frank Osenton, L/Cpl, 7th East Kents

Cock, Edward Millar, Pte, 28th Londons att'd 9th Suffolks

Cook, Alleyne James, Rfn, 18th Londons

Cook, William Edwin, Lt, 1/2nd att'd 4th Yorkshires

Curtis, Ernest John, 2Lt, 5th att'd 7th Royal West Kents

Dale-James, William Rushbrooke, Royal Naval Wireless Service

Dawes, Albert Ernest, Rfn, 1/5th Londons

Deem, Henry Theodore Samuel, Pte, 15th Londons

Defries, Frederick, Cpt MID, 5th att'd 3rd Middlesex

Dell, Claude Stanley, L/Cpl, 5th Yorkshires

Dennis, Robert Charles, Pte, 1/2nd Royal Fusiliers

Dixson, Frank, Sgt, No.4 Workshop, Royal Engineers

Dodkins, Lionel Claud, Flying Officer, 25th Londons + 31 Sqdn, Royal Air Force

Dodson, William Albert, 2nd Air Mechanic, Royal Naval Air Service

Doughton, Walter George, Pte, 10th Royal Fusiliers

Doyle, Gilbert, Army Blankets Inspector, Ministry of Munitions

Dubery, Frank Arthur, Gnr, A Battery, 236 Bde, Royal Field Artillery

Dunkley, William Henry, 7th Londons

Durant, John Stride, 1st Canadian Mounted Rifles (Saskatchewan Regt)

Ebsworth, Harold Charles, 2nd Honourable Artillery Company

Edgley, Leslie Seymour, Trooper, Royal Horse Guards

Edmunds, Cecil Harry, Lt, 21st Londons

Edwards, Albert Frederick, Rfn, 12th Londons

Ellis, Charles Albert William, Rfn, 1st Monmouthshires att'd 10th South Wales Borderers

Evans, Leonard Austin, 2Lt, 15th Bn, Tank Corps

Fairlie, John Alwyne, Able Seaman, Royal Naval Volunteer Reserve

Falby, Edward Frederick, 2Lt, 1/4th Loyal North Lancashires

Falkner, Clarence Beach, Cpt, 2/2nd Londons

Feben, Evi, Cpl, 6th Battery, Royal Field Artillery

Finnimore, Henry James, 2Lt, 7th Royal Sussex att'd Royal Flying Corps

Fitzgerald, Robert, L/Cpl, 1/24th Londons

Fletcher, Beaumont, L/Cpl, 13th Royal Sussex

Foreman, Roland John, 2nd Waiter, Royal Navy

Gale, Percy James, L/Sgt, 1/24th Londons

Gant, Harold Holden, 2Lt, 2nd Royal Fusiliers

Garrett, Arthur Daniel, Pte, Honourable Artillery Com

Gaskain, Cecil Stanley, Lt, 29 Sqdn, Royal Flying Corps + RFA

Gill, Jack Woodward, 2Lt, 6th KOYLI

Glenn, Reginald James, Pt 20th Londons

Goatcher, Fred, Lt, 9th Suffolks

Goenner, Frederick Charles, Rfn, 17th Kings Royal Rifle Corps

Grant, Harold Allan, 2Lt, 4th S.Staffs att'd 7th N.Staffs

Grant, Philip Thomas Wilson, 2Lt, 8th att'd 5th Wiltshires

Gray, Wallace James, Pte, 20th Royal Fusiliers

Grist, Percival Charles Hugh, Lt, 25th Londons

Halliday, Eric, Pte, 2/4th Royal West Surreys

Halliwell, Ernest, Gnr, D Battery, 232 Bde, Royal Field Artillery

Halliwell, William Co Sgt Major, M.C., 1st Rifle Brigade

Hamilton, Claud William, Cpt, 287th Siege Battery, Royal Garrison Artillery

Hamilton, Noel Crawford, 2Lt, 6th Northamptonshires

Harris, Herbert Cecil, Cpt, 6th Royal West Kents

Harvard, Kenneth O'Gorman, Lt, 2nd Grenadier Guards

Harvard, Lionel De Jersey, Cpt, 1st Grenadier Guards

Haseldine, Newton Woollcor, Rfn, 1/5th Londons

Hay, Arthur Leslie, 2Lt, 4th att'd 10/11th Highland Light Infantry

Hearn, Robert Cecil, Cpt, M.C., 2/20th Londons

Heron, Joseph Solomon, Rfn, 1/21st Londons

Hill, Sidney Ernest, Sgt, 1/20th Londons

Hoare, Ernest Austin, Cpl, 186th Special Coy, Royal Engineers

Hocking, Leslie Harold, Pte, 2/1st London Field Ambulance, RAMC

Hollands, Harold Evan, Cpl, 2/21st Londons

Hollands, Wilfred George, 2Lt, 7th att'd 4th Royal Fusiliers

Holman, William Elijah, Pte, 1/2nd Royal Fusiliers

Hood, John William, Lt, MID, 39th Siege Battery, Royal Garrison Artillery

Howett, Frank, Co Sgt Major, Londons (Civil Service Rifles)

Howett, Robert Plunkett, Sgt, 1/5th Notts and Derby

Hunt, Harold, Rfn, 3rd Rifle Brigade

Husk, Frederick John, 2Lt, M.M., Royal Garrison Artillery

Jones, James Thomas, 2Lt, 20th Londons

Jones, Norman Aldham, Pte, East Kent Regiment

Jones, Thomas Idwal, Lt, M.M., 18th Londons

Junkison, Arthur Charles, 15th Londons

Keesey, George Ernest Howard, Cpt, 8th Rifle Brigade

Kenyon, Harry Thomas James, Pte, Royal Army Medical Corps

Kiddle, Robert Henry, Pte, Liverpool Regt

Kidney, Leonard Edwin, Sgt, 9th Royal Fusiliers

King, Stanley Edward, Rfn, 5th Londons

Knifton, James McKinlay, 2Lt, 3rd att'd 2nd Royal Sussex

Knight, George Bertram, 2Lt, 54 Sqdn, Royal Air Force

Knox, John Lawrence, 2Lt, 7th Royal Sussex

Lansdale, William Morris, Cpt, Adj, Royal Army Medical Corps

Laurie, Arthur Wyndham, Sgt, 8th Canadian Infantry

Le Chavetois, Grantley Adolphe, Cpt, 22nd Londons

Levy, Godfrey, Rfn, 9th Londons

Lidgett, John Cuthbert, Lt, South Lancashire Regt

Lorey, Conrad Clifford, Sgt, 7th Londons att'd Machine Gun Corps

Lovekin, Vyvyan Ivor, Gnr, Canadian Artillery

Lunn, Ralph William, 2Lt, Royal Field and Horse Artillery

Mann, Stanley Walter, 2Lt, 9 Sqdn, Royal Flying Corps

Marner, George Lionel Stuart, Cpt, 10th Leicesters

Marriott, Herbert Percy Gordon, Rfn, 5th Londons

Mason, William John, Cpt, 8th Gloucesters

Maybrook, Walter Richard, 2Lt, 1st Wiltshires

Miles, Frank David, Pte, 28th Londons

Murray, Archibald Albert, Gnr, Royal Field Artillery

Norris, Frederick, Cpt, 23rd Middlesex

Oake, Douglas, Cpt, M.C., East Yorkshires att'd 92nd Trench Mortar Battery

Oliver, William Henry Rudland, Pte, 20th Londons

Oxford, Harry Arthur, Pte, Royal Army Supply Corps

, Alfred, Pte, 15th Londons tt'd Machine Gun Corps

Pearson, Eugene Arthur, Sub Lt, Surgeon, Royal Navy

Perkins, Douglas, Rfn, 12th Londons

Phare, Dudley Gershom, Lt, 7th Kings Shropshire Light Infantry

Plowman, Oswald Cheyney, Pte, Kings Royal Rifle Corps

Procter, Alexander Duncan Guthrie, 2Lt, 8th Royal Fusiliers

Prout, Arthur Stanley, Pte, 12th Londons

Quixley, Arthur Newman Charles, Pte, 24th Londons

Richardson, James Bert, Pte, 12th Rifle Brigade

Riminton, Percy Henry, Rfn, 16th Londons

Rings, Fritz Ludwig, Pte, Royal Sussex Regiment

Roberts, James Roderic Trethowan, 2Lt, 2nd Suff

Robinson, Edwin Hall, Rfn, Kings Royal Rifle Corps

Roeber David Arnold, 2Lt, Bedfordshire Regiment

Rowe, Henry Shepard, Rfn, 16th Londons

Royal, George Dudley, Pte, Royal Army Supply Corps

Ruggles, Charles George, Pte, Australian Contingent

Rule, Austin George, Pte, 15th Londons

Ryder, Gordon William, Pte, 14th Londons

Ryley, Donald Arthur George Buchanan, Lt, N.Staffordshires

Ryley, Harold Buchanan Snr, Lt, 1/5th Suffolks

Ryley, Harold Buchanan Jnr, 2Lt, 4th att'd 1st North Staffordshires

Sanders, Leslie Yorath, 2Lt, Royal Garrison Artillery att Royal Engineers Survey Co

Schooling, Geoffrey Holt, Pte, 16th Londons

Schulz, Harry Albert, Cpl, 12th Londons

Shears, Edmund George, Pte, Honourable Artillery Company

Shepherd, Henry Alick, Pte, 15th Londons

Shore, James Harold, Pte, 14th Warwickshires

Smith, George William, 2Lt, Royal Lancaster Regime

Spencer-Smith, Herbert, Pte, Princess Patricia's, 49th Canadians

Sprang, Frederick William, Cpt, 6th Dorsets

Stables, Leonard Theodore Drury, Lt, 6th Bedfordshires

Stockins, William James, 2Lt, 28th Londons att'd 27 Sqdn, Royal Flying Corps

Stubbs, Reginald Arthur, 2Lt, 32 Sqdn, Royal Flying Corps

Sutcliffe, Frederick Malcolm, 2Lt, 8th Londons

Sutherland, John, Pte, 15th Londons

Taffs, Charles Reginald, Lt, 1st Royal Berkshires

Tait, Leonard Sidney, Pte, 16th Londons

Talbot, Cecil Melliar, 2Lt, 14th att'd 4th Middlesex Regiment

Talbot, Ernest, Sgt, Royal Fusiliers

Taylor, William Frederick, L 3rd East Kents

Terry, Sidney Frederick, Cpt, M.C., 1st Wiltshires

Thompson, Edward William Murray, Pte, 2/13th Londons

Trotman, Frank William, Pte, 15th Londons

Trotman, Henry John, Dvr, Royal Field Artillery

Veale-Williams, John Marcus, Rfn, 3/5th Londons

Vernall, Arthur Humphrey, 2Lt, M.C., 6th Leicesters

Wade, Oliver John, 2Lt, Royal West Kents att'd 45 Sqdn, Royal Flying Corps

Walker, Sidney Herbert, Pte, 6th Seaforth

Walker, William Richard, Pte, 14th Londons

Wallace, George Frederick, 2Lt, 24th Middlesex

Walsh, Richard William, Pte, 15th Londons

Wardley, Miles Edward, 2Lt, 22nd Royal

Weatherston, John Frederick, Able Seaman, Royal Naval Volunteer Reserve

Weatherston, Sidney Bowler, Pte, 14th Londons

Wells, Neil, Pte, 6th Australian Imperial Force

Wensley, Harold William, 2Lt, 1st Lincolnshires

West, Harold Douglas, 2Lt, 1st Kings Royal Rifle Corps

Wilson, Albert Cecil, 2Lt, 14th Londons

Young, Henry George, Pte, 4th Essex

THE MACHINE GUN AND THE TANK CORPS

the enemy had a far greater number of machine guns; what became apparent as time went on, was that the German military organisation structure was more flexible in its use of machine guns. In a nutshell, the enemy realised first, that 'concentration of machine guns' as separate units to infantry, was more successful, than deploying 2 machine guns per battalion, as the British were doing.

The Machine Gun Corps, with its structure of companies, and its training school at St Omer, in France, was born. The year was 1916, a few months before the battle of the Somme. Field Marshal Haig's note in a minute to the War Council on the 14th April 1915, 'The machine-gun is a much over-rated weapon and two per battalion is more than sufficient', was rapidly being revised.

Finally, in 1917, thanks in large measure to the Canadian Forces based at Vimy Ridge, the machine gun companies started to be seen as an 'offensive' not 'defensive' force. Planned fire attacks on the Ridge and at Messines, proved successful in attacking the German fortifications. The men that were selected from infantry battalions to fulfil the role of machine gun specialists had certain skills – technical knowledge, physical fitness, speed of action and co-ordination, courage and commitment.

Albert Baker and Alf Page died on the Somme within the first three weeks of the campaign. They were too early to be formed into special machine gun companies, and they still were the men responsible in their respective battalions, for Haigs' 'two guns'.

Albert had seen early action with the L.R.B., part of 169 Brigade, 56 Division, at the first battle of Ypres in Belgium in November 1914. He had been sent home to convalesce from wounds received the following January at Ploegteert Woods. By June 1915, he was in the Front line again at St Eloi and Dickebusch. Such was his skill with gun, grenade and rifle, that he was offered the opportunity to undergo special training at the new machine gun school at St Omer from autumn 1915 to spring 1916. On his return to his battalion, he was attached to the 169th Brigade Machine Gun Company and promoted to the rank of lance corporal.

In July, his section, attacked with the brigade at Gommecourt, and Albert was one of a small group to survive the first day. Two months of continuous fighting followed at Fricourt, Hardecourt, Maurepas and Combles. Whilst manning his gun on the 16th September, he was shot in the lungs and moved to casualty clearing station behind the lines. His wounds were severe, and he died three days later in hospital. He was just twenty, and is buried at Corbie, near Amiens.

Alf Page, with the 15th Londons, went to France in March 1915, as part of the 140th Brigade, 47th Division. In September, the 47th attacked on the extreme right, as one of six divisions in the line at the Battle of Loo's. Their objective was to sweep south of Loo's and take the 'Double Crassier' area. Alf, at this stage, still a rifleman, took part in this advance and survived well enough to request a transfer to the machine gun Section of the 15th in October. St Omer trained him and returned him as part of the 140th Brigade's gun section. On the 16th September, Alf was hit by shell whilst with his gun during the battle of Flers Courcelette. He was reported missing, and his body was never found. His section had held the line east of Bazentin Le Petit, and attacked the 18th Bavarians at 'Crest Trench', their objective to take 'Cough Drop trench' and 'Prue trench'. Alf, like Albert, became a casualty on the same day, and at the same age – twenty. He was killed outright and is commemorated on the Thiepval Memorial to the missing of the Somme.

Meanwhile, Private Clarke, Machine Gun Section, 1st East Surrey Regiment, also fought his way through the drudgery, noise, danger and daily casualties of the long Somme campaign. When it finally ended in November 1916, his regiment moved to the Italian Front just prior to Christmas. Here he remained, enduring light skirmishes but missing any major battles like Isonzo River and Caporetto, until he returned to France in April 1917.

Back in Flanders, he was transferred to the 95th Company of the new Machine Gun Corps and stationed in the Ypres sector, where preparations were taking place for the Passchendaele campaign. Ernest made it through the whole of the carnage of 1917, and remained in Ypres, at Ploegsteert into 1918. In the opening months of that year, he had written a letter home, which was to turn out to be his last. In it, he clearly upheld his optimism, 'Each day I go forward with a restful mind – patiently. There is nothing that will perturb me. I have quiet confidence and trust'. For such a man to write this, in the cold, disease, mud, and waste of 1918 Belgium is extraordinary. His faith in God must have been unshakeable.

When compared to the words written by a young Lieutenant Owen at around the same time, 'Bent double, like old beggars under sacks, knock kneed, coughing like hags, we cursed through sludge', and of another officer, Sassoon, 'In winter trenches, cowed and glum, with crumps and lice and lack of rum, he put a bullet through his brain, and no one spoke of him again', one can imagine that religious fortitude helped some men get through.

Unfortunately, like Owen, survival was not for Ernest Clarke. He was killed in action on the 13th April 1918, a few weeks into the Kaisers Offensive. The world had never seen the scale of artillery bombardment that the enemy threw at the British Army across Belgium and France. Ernest was killed by one of the millions of shells, and is commemorated on the Ploegsteert Memorial to the missing. 'The preceptor' was thirty-three years old.

Conrad Lorey, now a sergeant, almost made it. He had been badly gassed at Thiepval during the Somme campaign of 1916 and had spent some months in England allowing his lungs to recover sufficiently to enable him to return to the Front. His injuries were such that he was really unfit to return to his battalion engaged in Flanders. Owing to his skills and experience as a member of the 7th Londons Machine Gun unit, he was offered a home based job as a gun instructor at the training camp at Clipstone in Nottinghamshire. He stayed here throughout 1917, sending many young gunners in the new corps, out to fight at Passchendaele.

Finally, despite, breathing problems, and a constitution weakened to all colds and influenza, he found a way, to get sent out to the Front yet again, in March 1918, as a lance corporal in the 2nd Battalion, M.G.C. Having survived the last big German offensive of March and April, he was promoted to sergeant in July; On August 15th, he was severely wounded by a shell, and expected to die that day. Somewhat surprisingly, Conrad made it to hospital at Wimereux, where he hung on for three weeks, being cared for by his fiance, who had been contacted to come to Boulogne with urgency. He died on the 9th September, eight weeks before the Armistice, aged twenty-three years.

'Armoured warfare' most obviously depicted by the arrival of the tank, ' Little Willie', was in use from 1914, based on the early designs of Lieutenant-Colonel Swinton and of an Australian called Mole, but had encountered a number of insurmountable problems on the Western Front – the poor weather, the sodden mud of Belgian and French farmland, the development of complex trench lines and the impact on the terrain, of shell bombardments, all combined to make the initial military advantages of tanks seemingly worthless. By 1916 on the Somme, with further developments by Lieutenant Wilson and Bill Tritton, the managing director of Fosters, the main Government supplier, tanks were first tried in battle. It was a disaster, many broke down, others became wedged in trenches or craters, and the successful ones were halted by shells. The tank was reserved for use in Mesopotamia, Palestine and Africa.

Operating in these early tanks was a difficult task, assigned to the 'Heavy Branch' of the Machine Gun Corps. As it was mainly an attacking weapon, in retreat, it was a problem. Inside the tank, the crew had to withstand awful ventilation, terrifying heat, the release of gases from the heating of previously soldered, joints, and ammunition that regularly exploded. Many vomited, were burnt and had bouts of delirium. Such was the world of Olavians, Private William Berrow, and Second Lieutenant Leonard Evans, both recently transferred to the fledgling Tank Corps in 1917.

William was the older of the two men, born the eldest of three brothers and six children, of William Lewis Berrow from Worcester, Registrar at the Foreign Office, on the 24th April 1889 in London. With

THE MACHINE GUN AND THE TANK CORPS

one of their children dying in infancy, William and wife, Henrietta Adeline had two daughters remaining, Frances and Henrietta and the three older boys, William Junior, Lewis and Philip. Lewis served with the Yorkshire Dragoons and also became a war casualty. After five years at St Olave's, William Rushbury Berrow joined the Bank of England in 1907, at eighteen years. In his spare time, he joined the 1st City of London Yeomanry, otherwise known as 'the Rough Riders' and mobilised with them on the outbreak of war.

He fought at Gallipoli for the entire duration of the campaign and must have been one of the few to receive no wounds by the time of the evacuation. By 1916, he was a 'time-expired' man, due to his pre-war service, but was subsequently recalled to the Colours at the end of the year. At this point, his interest in the newly emerging use of tank warfare, enabled him to get a transfer. He left for France after training in July 1917.

Leonard Austin Evans was born in August 1894, the youngest of four children born to Charles Evans of Clapham, a tracer for the General Post Office, and his Bermondsey born wife, Matilda. Leonard had earned an L.C.C. scholarship to St Olave's. Of above average academic ability, he excelled in the sciences, before leaving to become an assistant auditor for Norwich Union in 1913, aged 19. After the first big rush to enlist, he decided to join the Honourable Artillery Company in early 1915.

A year later, Leonard came first in the inaugural War Office monthly examinations, and received his commission, being transferred immediately to the new Tank Corps owing to his scientific ability and his technical work in the H.A.C. Much of his time in late 1916 and early 1917 was employed in special tank development work in Leeds, with his eventual move to the Front in November, ready for the big tank attack at 'Cambrai'.

So both men played a part in the Cambrai tank attack – only the second attack on the Western Front to show a real success (the other being the Canadian attack on Vimy in 1917) in the three long years of war.

Private no. 91863 Berrow was part of 'E' Battalion, Tank Corps on the 20th November 1917 having convinced his commanding officer to let him go up with the others, thereby dropping his clerical role, held since July. Surviving diaries held at the Tank Museum at Bovington describe the situation that day:

'The Hindenburg line was a truly formidable obstacle... We crashed upon the other side, splitting open my section commanders head, and petrol cans and ammunition boxes scattered all over the place ...the Hun were bravely standing on the fire step of their reserve trench, fully exposed, and giving us a rather warm time with machine gun and rifle fire ...tanks were all over the place; some with noses up, some afire, but all motionless...we received a direct hit which left a gaping hole in the side of the tank, and wounded everyone except the driver and myself....the carburettor was pierced by a splinter, a fire started on top of the tank amongst the spare ammunition, we evacuated...overall all troops seemed very pleased with the tanks, many were the drinks we had on the way back – its astonishing how much whisky the British Army carries into battle'.

On the day of the attack, he went up in the tank of his company commander, but it got into difficulties and did not return. On evacuating, some of the crew were taken prisoner. Their reports claim that William was struck by a shell that had hit the side of their tank, and in the confusion, none could recollect if he had made it out. He was posted as missing, presumed dead on the 23rd November. He was twenty-three years old and is commemorated on the Cambrai Memorial to the missing at Louverval.

Meanwhile, Lieutenant Evans of the 15th Battalion, Tank Corps, a man of technical intelligence, quiet demeanour, and unassuming courage, was at Cambrai, witnessing and to some extent responsible, for the successes of the attack. 378 Mark IV tanks had moved to the

Front, with another 54 in reserve. Each tank had huge 'fascines' or rigid planks that could get tanks over wide trenches; some had wire cutting capabilities, others were used as mobile wireless stations, receiving reconnaissance from the Flying Corps, and for carrying supplies.

At Christmas, Leonard Evans returned to England on leave. Returning in February to the Front, he was struck down by shells, and severely wounded. He was moved quickly from the clearing station to hospital near Abbeville, but died in the ambulance train. The date was the 27th March 1918, six days into the 'Kaisers offensive' in the Arras and Amiens sector, and two weeks ,before Haig's famous dictum, 'With our backs to the wall, and believing in the justice of our cause each one of us must fight on to the end'.

Leonard Evans was also twenty-three years old and was laid to rest at the Abbeville Communal Cemetery.

CHAPTER 16

Third Ypres:
Menin Road, Passchendaele and Poelcapelle

With the heavy rains continuing throughout August and early September, the Front in the Ypres sector of Belgium, witnessed the influx of many fresh Allied divisions to support the wearied and depleted Fifth Army under General Gough. Langemarck, on the 16th August had been an expensive defeat, morale was getting lower and lower, partly because of the conditions, but mainly because of the decisions from senior officers to launch tactical offensives with the sole objective of strengthening the line before the next main attack. These were seen to all present as producing very little. A well executed German counter-attack, in the midst of this, to wrest the 'Inverness Copse' area, prompted Haig to seek an offensive plan from Plumer with Second Army. Plumer's subsequent initiative was to herald a series of 'bite and hold' attacks to take the Gheluvelt plateau and the Broodseinde and Passchendaele ridges, north-east and east of Ypres.

With three weeks to plan, brief, rehearse and launch, time was tight. Infantry practised hard and were well informed; artillery prepared sufficient shells for a creeping barrage which would protect the infantry advance, and three subsequent standard barrages which would help them consolidate. The best new idea was to ensure that the advance was well within the capability of the attacking troops, and therefore limited in its objectives. The 20th September was launch date, with the Menin Road Ridge the objective.

Two Old Olavians serving at the Front on the 20th September, died as a result of the battle that day. Rifleman Herbert Marriott no. 303416 was based with 'C' company, the 2/5th Londons, the London Rifle Brigade, at Ypres. Rifleman Stan Chapman no. 302410, seven years older than Herbert also served in 'C' company, 2/5th Londons, having been transferred from the 25th Londons, the Cyclists. Both men had written home about meeting each other and their realisation of the School connection. In their company, they also drew great support from the presence of four other Old Olavian's who survived the conflict, H.Monte Richardson, the two Tracy-Richardson brothers and one of the Maitlands.

Herbert Percy Gordon Marriott had one very illustrious military predecessor. His grandfather, Nathaniel Marriott had served under Colin Campbell in Hodson's Horse at the 1857 Indian Mutiny, and on his survival, returned to Tooley Street in Bermondsey and spawned nine children. Coming from a traditional family, as Grandfather Marriott had sent his boys to the English School attached to the St Olave's Grammar School Foundation, Herbert, in time found himself also heading for the School along with his younger brothers, Charles and Leonard.

Born on the 24th January 1898 in Bermondsey, to Herbert James Marriott, superintendent of a sack and bag warehouse and his wife, Alice Naomi, Herbert Junior spent some time at Hither Green School, before joining St Olave's in 1909. A contemporary of Ewart Castle and Charles Brown, he proved a boy of 'independent thought and great intensity of feeling, a talented linguist'. On leaving school in summer 1915, he initially secured a position at a merchant bank owned by the Sassoon family, but later resolved to enlist after Christmas, as a result of the recruiting drive for Kitchener's new citizen army.

He enlisted at Catford in the London Rifle Brigade, the 5th City of London Regiment on his eighteenth birthday, and was in Belgium by the summer. H.Monte Richardson remembered a conversation in the trenches shortly before the Menin Road attack, when Herbert said "Yes, I thought about taking a commission, but I thought it better that I should come out here first and see what things are really like. I wanted to know what it really feels like to have the shells shrieking overhead and bursting all around. Perhaps I shall be able to take up a commission later on?" Herbert Marriott was killed by an exploding shell as the London Rifle Brigade advanced on the 20th September. He was nineteen, and is commemorated on the Menin Gate.

Alongside him stood, Robert Stanley Chapman, a man who had given him such confidence and helped him wrestle with his fears. Stanley Chapman, had he lived, would have shortly become an ordained minister of the Church. In 1910, when he was eighteen, he had gone up to King's College, Oxford to read theology, after a brilliant Olavian career. He was born in Hornsey in north London the eldest of three, with two sisters, June and Gladys, to Robert and Ursula Chapman of Stoke Newington, on the 20th September 1891. As a boy, he had a retiring disposition, appearing nervous, unassuming and with a bad stammer. However, Stanley was also a boy of strong beliefs and of ability and independence. He first entered St Olave's in 1904 along with contemporaries Don Ryley, Leslie Hocking and Ollie Wade. His excellence at History led to an entrance scholarship in May 1911 from King's College to Pembroke College and a bursary of £60.

As a rifleman with the 5th Londons, he went to France on the 24th January 1917 seeing action in the early summer at Bullecourt and Gravenstafel. As the months drifted by, he experienced continual trench service in awful weather conditions and was involved in the heavy labour of road building for a while. His main job was as a stretcher-bearer and general medicine man to his platoon, personally requested on religious grounds. On the night of the 20th September, whilst he was attending to wounded, he was badly injured by a shell fragment to the head. It was his twenty-sixth birthday. He continued to attend to at least five or six other wounded men, before going to the dressing station to be treated himself. Once treated, he proved unwilling to leave the line, and seemed quite happy and confident of his short term recovery, as the pain was slight. However, the shrapnel had penetrated his brain, and having returned to the Front, he later collapsed and was taken to the Mendinghem Military Hospital where he passed away two days later on the 22nd. His body was buried there, between Ypres and Poperinghe.

For four more days and nights, the British fought to take the Menin Road Ridge. On the twenty-sixth, Plumer put into action his second targeted offensive on the line from Zonnebeke down to Gheluvelt, the objective being Polygon Wood. The day of the attack was unusual in its absence of rain. Again seven days of fighting brought forth more allied success, with enemy fortifications being captured and counter attacks repulsed. Plumer's tactics were working, much to the concerns of Ludendorff. The narrow front of attack, and strong reserves had originally been his idea, and it was now being used against the German Army with considerable success. In the days leading up to the end of the battle of Polygon Wood on the 3rd October, the Germans launched massive infantry counter-attacks as their only answer to Plumer's gains. These attacks were contained effectively by British artillery, now far more accurate, and machine guns, which were, at last, more plentiful in their supply.

On the 4th October, Plumer launched the third attack, at Broodseinde. The Allied bombardment hit the enemy at one of the strongest parts of their defensive line – at 'Flandern 1', but at a time, when they just were not expecting it. Most were out in the open preparing to counter attack. Masses of infantry were shelled, and the position was totally overcome. The battle of Broodseinde lasted just a day. Such was Haig's confidence in Plumer's results, that he called the cavalry forward, an indication that he thought a breakthrough to be imminent. Plumer and Gough both insisted this to be premature, and that more focussed assaults to gain key ridges of high ground to be necessary. Once again the wet weather drastically affected British plans.

The battle of Poelcapelle on the 9th October, although still of some success, was limited because of the sodden ground over which infantry could only move very slowly, and also major improvements in the quality of German wire defences. The first battle of Passchendaele commenced three days later, with the usual Allied bombardment which made the job of the infantry far worse. The Canadian Corps was brought forward to try to support the herculean effort of the infantry to take the Passchendaele-Staden ridge, but to no avail. Very little ground was taken.

This proved to be the last real opportunity of the campaign; the need for reinforcements at Caporetto on the Italian front led Haig to, reluctantly, send five of his divisions and his top man – Plumer, south to help. Without the master tactician, and adequate fresh troops, the second battle of Passchendaele proved to be a 'mopping up' operation, conducted in terrible conditions. It began on the 26th October, and eventually secured parts of the Ridge, but not all. By November 10th, Haig finally accepted that the weather had beaten them, and that further initiatives would have to wait until the following year.

Edwin Hall Robinson was a Rifleman no. R/31386 serving with the 13th Battalion, the King's Royal Rifle Corps at the foot of the Passchendaele ridge in October 1917. As part of 111th Brigade, 37 Division, Edwin had been involved on the 4th at Broodseinde, attacking at dawn, alongside the Royal Fusiliers. They had come under severe fire from a blockhouse and from Lewis Farm, both of which had been missed by the bombardment. Their objective of the deep enemy dug-outs in the north of Gheluvelt Wood, proved impossible because of this obstruction. Their success in taking 'Tower trench' was short lived, as enfilade fire from the farm forced them to withdraw.

After Broodseinde, the battalion remained in the line until the 14th October, when it had suffered badly from an enemy counter attack. On the following day, they were relieved, and sent to brigade headquarters. Edwin, a qualified signaller, was killed whilst defending the headquarters from an enemy air attack just ten days later. He was reportedly hit by the explosion of an enemy aeroplane shell which had landed near to him. He was thirty-six years old, and was buried in the White House cemetery, north east of Ypres.

Edwin was the son of Thomas Robinson, an oil and colour man from Aldgate and his wife Mary Ann, and was born on the 25th February 1881. Of the ten children born to the Robinson's, three had died young, of the five boys out of the remaining seven, three were over age for the war, and only Edwin and his younger brother, Harry fought.

He had started his career at Tooley Street in 1888, entering the school as a young boy of just seven. Eight years later, in 1896, he walked out, a youth of fifteen, to attend the Borough Polytechnic and continue his love of languages. He was soon to win a Bronze Medal from the Royal Society of Arts for his command of French. His contemporaries amongst 'the Fallen' were few, the older men, like Monty Fletcher, Harry Oxford and Bill Athow. By 1899, he had become a technical sales representative for a Scottish oils and colours firm, following his father's occupation. After a few years learning the business, he left to set up a firm of his own. It had just started to become successful, when the war arrived.

Within a day of the death of Edwin Robinson, his fellow Olavian, Clarence Falkner was also killed by a shell at Poelcapelle. Clarence, although only twenty-two at the time of his death, was already a captain, in the 2/2nd London Regiment, Royal Fusiliers. On the 25th, he had been in command of a platoon who had been taping out an assembly area, when a rogue shell exploded killing him instantly. He is commemorated on the Tyne Cot Memorial.

Clarence Beach Falkner was the second child of five, born on the 13th March 1895 to Alfred Beach Falkner, who ran his own building firm, and his wife, Annie. He spent five years at the School studying with contemporaries, the Walker brothers, Bay Ryley, Lionel Dodkins and Fritz Rings. A superb athlete, Clarence excelled as a swimmer, and as a goalkeeper, both with St Olave's and later, as secretary of the Old Boys football club. In 1911, aged sixteen, he left to join his father, training to be an architect and surveyor. A younger brother, Alfred Cecil born in 1904 was too young for the hostilities.

In the summer of 1914, he enlisted as a Private no.1980 in the 18th Londons, the London Irish Rifles, and was at the Front in the November, thereby qualifying for the Mons or 1914 Star. By March 1915, he was in Flanders, and saw action at Neuve Chapelle, surviving a severe bullet wound thanks to the presence of a thick bible in his haversack. At Aubers Ridge, he lost many of his comrades, and having made it through, decided to apply for a commission, probably to get back to 'Blighty' for a while. In October 1916 he was gazetted as a second lieutenant, and found himself as brigade intelligence officer in Ypres by May 1917. On July 1st, he was promoted to lieutenant and later in the same month, made adjutant and captain. His fiance at home, Miss Norah Miles was immensely proud, specifically because he had achieved such recognition and respect, whilst constantly battling bouts of dysentery and fairly indifferent health. Had he not succumbed, he may well have become a major, and most likely a post war architect of note.

Fritz Ludwig Rings, as previously mentioned, was a school colleague of Clarence Falkner. He was born on the 21st July 1897 in Camberwell, with one younger brother, Franz Wilhelm, (later a spectacle maker with the Freedom of the City of London), to Fritz Hubert Appollinarius Rings, a German-born architect who ran an engineering business and his wife, Elisabeth. Fritz spent five years at St Olave's from 1907 until 1911, where he went, following time spent at Hazelbank Road School in Lewisham. He left, aged fourteen, because of an illness which required convalescence at the coast, where he could have plenty of sea air. When better, he joined the London County Council School of Architecture, and was later engaged by several engineering firms, as a draughtsman, with a view to taking up a full partnership in his father's firm. It is possible that their combined love of architecture could have linked Fritz

Rings and Clarence Falkner in some way, besides their coincidental death on the fields of Belgium.

By 1914, Fritz had changed his first name to 'Frederick' and attested for the army on the 16th November 1915. It is not known if his parents were interned during the hostilities. Private no. 3104 Rings was sent to the Army Reserve. On the 4th August 1916, he was mobilised but then stood down again. A week later, he was re-mobilised and sent as Private no. 266686 to the 1/6th Cyclists Battalion, the Royal Sussex Regiment, but still remained on the home front, until he requested a discharge from the Army to re-enlist as an Able Seaman no. R/3299 in the Nelson Battalion of the Royal Naval Division Reserve on the 17th June 1917. Shortly after this, he embarked for France for the first time and was based north east of Ypres at Passchendaele, not as a sailor, rather as a sea soldier.

The second battle there commenced on the 26th October and raged for fifteen days. On the second day, the 27th October, his Nelson Battalion were in support as part of the 63rd (Naval) Division of II Corps, attacking the line at Varlet's Farm, an enemy machine gun strongpoint at Poelcapelle. Fritz Rings was shot two yards from reaching a German pill-box. He was twenty and his body was not recovered. His father, had also earlier anglicised his name to 'Frederick' Rings, and his brother, later to 'Francis William' Rings, living until he was 80.

On the last day of October 1917, Halloween, though most could not remember celebrating the last peaceful event, a fine lieutenant with the 9th Suffolk Regiment, based in the southern part of the line towards Bethune, was shot by an enemy sniper. He was twenty-nine years old and died of his wounds after a brief struggle, at the casualty clearing station. His body was buried at Noeux-Les-Mines communal cemetery. This lieutenant had arrived in France on the 25th September 1916, surviving as a sub-altern for over a year.

Fred Goatcher was his name. He had made the St Olave's Honours list. He held the School's athletic distinction for shooting. whilst he was at the school from 1903 to 1908. The only better shot in memory was Leonard Bendixen, who had joined the French Foreign Legion as a 'Caporal'. Fred had won an entrance scholarship worth £30 to read natural science at Selwyn College, Cambridge in 1908. A year later, he took the second class Inter-Collegiate examination and in 1910, the third class. By 1911, he had a Diploma in agriculture and had secured a position as assistant manager, of the Hevea Rubber Plantation in Johore, in the southern Malay states, north of Singapore.

Fred Goatcher was born on the 30th December 1888 in Boxgrove, near Chichester in Sussex, one of four brothers and a sister, Ada. Despite his younger brother Herbert being gassed, Fred was the only brother to fall in the conflict. William and Arthur also survived. Their parents, Arthur and Mary Goatcher, had run the Boxgrove School which Fred and his siblings had attended whilst young, before Arthur moved, to work as an elementary teacher for the London County Council, residing in Lambeth then Clapham. After attending the Higher Grade School at Crawford Street, Camberwell, Fred moved to St Olave's where he was described by master's as a boy of 'grit and determination', with many sterling qualities; as 'firm, unselfish, and straightforward', whilst also holding a reputation for his hatred of 'cruelty and oppression'. Working as a farmer in Malaya, he had continued his leisure pursuit of shooting, by joining the Malay States Rifle Volunteers. Four years later, he had returned to England to take a commission at the Cambridge University Officer's Training Corps.

Shortly after this final death, the campaign known as 'Third Ypres' drew to a close. It is fitting to finish with a quotation from Cyril Falls, in his 'History of the Royal Irish Rifles', "The battle will always remain one of the most extraordinary monuments to the courage and endurance of the British Soldier. Those hard-used words are indeed inadequate to describe his virtues. If mortal men could have pulled down reinforced concrete with their naked hands, these men would have done it".

CHAPTER 17
The Royal Flying Corps

In his job trying to keep the B.E.2's of 12 Squadron, Royal Flying Corps in the air, Air Mechanic (1st class) George Castell, an Olavian, had known an Australian pilot called Francis Penny, who on his maiden flight across the channel to join 12 Squadron in 1916, had encountered a returning pilot from the same unit, whilst refuelling at Boulogne. On hearing of Penny's destination, he had remarked that he'd "just come from there, and in the last month, we've lost twenty pilots and observers, either killed or taken prisoner". The fellow pilot maintained that Penny, would "last about six weeks."

Raoul Lufbery, the famous Franco-American pilot, had warned on another occasion that "there won't be any 'after the war' for a fighter pilot". Cecil Lewis, author of 'Sagittarius Rising', and flying colleague of Olavian, Stanley Mann at 9 Squadron, later wrote that, the life of a pilot might be more comfortable than that of the men in the trenches, but it was no less dangerous, with a life expectancy of three weeks, and in an era before parachutes, a disabled plane could take five minutes to plunge 10,000 feet to earth.

This, then was the view of three remarkable survivors of the conflict, who had seen most of their colleagues either, explode, crash, burn, go missing or be taken prisoner behind the lines.

The formation of the Royal Air Force on April 1st, 1918 proudly demonstrated an organisation of a quarter of a million men and over 20,000 aircraft. Just a decade earlier, the force did not exist. Although there was significant interest in using air machines, not just for reconnaissance, it was not until the formation of the air battalion of the Royal Engineers focusing on both airships and aeroplanes, and a Royal Navy school of flying in 1911, that the force started to emerge. Secretary Haldane's Imperial Defence Committee recommended that Great Britain have a national air service, formed through the army, with a naval wing, a flying school, and a research and experimental centre.

In 1912, the Royal Flying Corps was instituted by Royal Warrant, under the command of Major Fred Sykes (and later General Sir David Henderson), absorbing the engineers battalion. By 1914, the Admiralty, maintaining the separateness of the naval wing, had formed the Royal Naval Air Service. At the outbreak of war, the R.F.C. had a strength of six squadrons (60 air machines, 120 pilots); the R.N.A.S. had 128 officers, 700 other ranks and over 70 air machines and 7 airships.

Nine of the Old Olavian 'Fallen' served in the Royal Flying Corps – eight as pilot officers, and one, George Castell, as a mechanic. Most had transferred from infantry battalions between 1914 and 1916.

Reginald Arthur Stubbs, a second lieutenant in the 4th Battalion, the Royal Munster Fusiliers, had joined 20 and then 33 Squadron after receiving his pilot's certificate on the 5th December 1915, and 32 Squadron on receipt of his wings on March 27th 1916. He had enlisted on the outbreak of war as a private in the Royal Fusiliers (Public Schools Battalion) and during action in Belgium throughout 1915, he was promoted to corporal and later sent to England to take an officer's training course. He had taken his aviator's Certificate at the Military School in Shoreham, Sussex, flying a Maurice Farman bi-plane. Reginald was born the middle child of five on 27th October 1891 in Balham with one elder brother, Stanley, and sisters, Doris, Gladys and Constance, of parents, George Blaseland Stubbs, a staff clerk in the Civil Service and wife Annie Louisa.

Unusually, he had decided whilst a young boy, to enter the Ministry, but on leaving St Olave's after seven years of study in 1907 aged sixteen, he opted to take a business course before a spell at the London and South-West Bank as a clerk. Two years later, he reverted to his original plan, and went up to Keble College, Oxford, where he studied theology with the objective of taking Holy Orders. Like many other religious men of his age, one can only imagine his sense of inner conflict attempting to balance

THE ROYAL FLYING CORPS

his feelings with regard to patriotism, aggression, pacifism, and religion. Some became medical orderlies, others, stretcher-bearers to avoid having to kill. Redge Stubbs fought in the trenches of Neuve Chapelle, Ypres and Hill 60. His selection to become an officer, may have saved him from further bloodshed at the front, and his attachment to the Royal Munsters was very temporary. He may have seen the option to become a pilot as a way of detaching himself from the hand to hand fighting; alternatively, he may have expected to be more involved in observation and long range reconnaissance activities.

The day after receiving his wings in March 1916, he flew with 32 Squadron to their new base in France. They were equipped with DH2 single seat fighters, manufactured by the Aircraft Manufacturing Co. Ltd of Hendon, and designed by Captain Geoffrey De Havilland (hence the 'DH'). The machines, also known as 'Airco's' and 'Bi-plane (Pushers)' were not specifically designed for fighting purposes, but what they lacked in synchronised machine guns, they made up for in high speed performance.

Redge Stubbs served alongside Second Lieutenant's W.E. Nixon and O.V. Thomas, Captain S.G. Gilmour, Second Lieutenant's J. Godlee and E.Lewis, and of course, the Squadron Commander, Major Lionel W.B. Rees.

Gwilym Lewis, the youngest pilot of 32 Squadron, a survivor, remembered well the first few weeks of 32's baptism in the weeks leading up to the battle of the Somme. He was convinced that his commanding officer, Rees, a pugnacious Welshman, was mad. How scared he was at the thought of attacking an enemy machine; of his admiration of the FE's (the Bombers) of 25 Squadron, who 32 had to escort; and of how he sometimes hoped for a small wound to rescue him, and how he was strangely addicted to the war, despite the freezing temperatures of the open cockpits of the DH2's.

Within seven weeks, Stubbs was killed in action, the first airman lost to 32 Squadron in action, Nixon, Gilmour, Rees and Lewis had been wounded, with Godlee dying of wounds. Only Thomas had survived being shot up and crash landing. Rees, the 'madman' had won a V.C. on the infamous 1st July.

Redge Stubbs had been carrying out a combat patrol in the early hours of the morning of the 8th June 1916 over the area above Souchez and near the village of Frevin Capelle in his DH2 Solo. Having taken off at 3.15am, shortly after 4am, his machine was hit by an artillery shell, he is presumed to have fainted, with his machine crash landing. Having been wounded by the shell exploding, he died of injuries incurred in the crash. Another contemporary report, claims that he came down apparently intending to land. But when he was 100 feet up, he stopped his engine and dived into the ground. His death was instantaneous. Major Rees report into the event confirmed "the pilot lost consciousness and dived into the ground (seen by two gunners). Machine completely wrecked". Redge had lasted just eleven days, and was twenty-four. His body was recovered and is buried at Quatre Vents military cemetery, near Estree Cauchy, north west of Arras. 'The theologian' never returned to take 'Holy Orders'.

Second Lieutenant Stubbs of 32 Squadron was the first Olavian pilot to be killed in action. Oliver John Wade, four years his academic junior, joined St Olave's in 1904 and remained there for nearly eleven years leaving in 1915 aged eighteen years, after a fully committed school career.

Born on 1st May 1896, Oliver Wade was the only son of John Wade, a chemist at Guy's Hospital who had died in a motorcycle accident in 1912. John from Deptford was a Doctor of Science, an investigator and lecturer and resided with wife Clara at Hunstanton Lodge, in the village of Downe in Kent. Olly's masters spoke of his 'distinct and original' personality, of his precision in speech, of his detached individualism, his good humour and easy courtesy. He became junior shooting champion and classical school captain.

In his final year at School, he made two surprising decisions – clearly brilliant at sciences, he sat an entrance exam winning a scholarship to King's College to study classics. His literary compositions were based on scientific notions and often grotesque. Shortly after, he left School, four months early, to enlist in the army.

As a second lieutenant in the Royal West Kent Regiment, he sailed for Egypt in late 1914, and took part in the Egyptian campaign from January 1915. Returning to England later in the year, he trained to fly. He passed his certificate on the 24th July 1916 at Thetford, also in a Farman Biplane. He arrived in France, at Candas on the Somme, with the rest of 45 Squadron on 15th of October under commanding officer, Willie Read with 12 air machines. 41 Squadron had arrived at the same time, flying FE8 single-seat 'pusher' fighters, whilst Oliver had Sobwith Strutters with the new Scarff-Dibovsky interruptor gear, allowing forward fire through the propeller, and Scarff ring-mountings for the rear machine gun.

Read was concerned to find no shelter arranged for his men, and no rations, despite being met by 'Boom' Trenchard, from R.F.C. Headquarters. Later, Hugh Dowding, another senior influential officer, ordered Read to put his machines, and not his men, in the hangars. As Ralph Barker reports in his book on the R.F.C. "It was normal for a new squadron to be given at least a week, in which to get acquainted with conditions before venturing over enemy territory, but 45 was ordered off at once by Dowding".

Wade served alongside Captain, the Hon. E.F.P. Lubbock, Second Lieutenant E.B. Samuels, Captain L. Porter, Second Lieutenant W.J. Thuell, Sergeant P. Snowden, Second Lieutenants W.F.H. Fullerton and HH Griffiths and Lieutenant F.Surgey. On the day of his death, the 22nd October, just seven days after his squadron arrived, 45 had the misfortune to encounter 'the finest enemy fighter squadron on the Western Front – Jadgstaffel 2'. 45's crews were paying the price for being rushed into battle so quickly. On the 22nd alone, Snowden, Fullerton, Thuell, Samuels and Wade were killed; Porter died of wounds as a prisoner, Surgey was wounded – only Griffith, the latter's co-pilot returned safely.

Olly had been on an offensive patrol of four Strutters over the Bapaume-Peronne sector, on a day described as 'fine with deadly and determined air fighting'. His co-pilot was Thuell. They had left the aerodrome at 10.15 in the morning, and were claimed to have been shot down by a Jagdstaffel 2 pilot and later, an ace, called Leutnant Erwin Bohme, over Les Boeufs at 10.50am. Both pilots were killed in action. He was twenty years old, and had spent even less time flying than Stubbs. His body was not recovered. He is commemorated on the Arras Flying Services Memorial. He was one of the nine school captains to fall in the war. A typed report written within hours of the patrol stated 'German message dropped in our lines states "Lt Oliver John Wade – Born at Purley on 1/5/96. Pilot's certificate numbered 3343. He and his observer are dead".

Willie Read, was quoted as saying after the disastrous 22nd October, "On our first patrol of three machines, only one came back, and I lost my best flight commander, one Porter by name". Within a month 45 was sent away to recoup. Dowding blamed Read for inefficiencies. 45 later became one of the highest scoring Sopwith Strutter squadrons.

While Oliver Wade, 'the scientist' was beginning to fly over Bapaume, Stanley Walter Mann, a few months older, with a crossover of three school years, was based further north with 9 Squadron around Guillemont and Beaumont Hamel, an area of intense infantry and artillery activity during the opening weeks of the Somme campaign in the summer of 1916.

Cecil Lewis, also in 9 Squadron, wrote of the first day of the Somme, "At Boisselle the earth heaved and flashed, a tremendous and magnificent column rose up into the sky. There was an ear-splitting roar, drowning all the guns, flinging the machine sideways in the repercussing air".

Stanley Mann had arrived in France a couple of weeks earlier, and should have been operational by July 1st. Stanley, born in January 1895, to two younger sisters was the son of Walter Mann, a market gardener from Brentford and wife May, of Erncroft, Twickenham, Middlesex. A boy of retiring disposition, he is said to have developed into a man of 'intellectual vigour' and 'moral

THE ROYAL FLYING CORPS

strength' always grasping the essentials in a quiet and unassuming way. He was an unusual boy and moved in a strikingly different direction to his school colleagues. By the age of twenty-one, he had become assistant producer at the London Film Company based near his home at St Margarets. For several years he had been both writing and illustrating stories and plays. He had only spent three years at St Olave's, leaving at seventeen as a senior Oxford scholar.

Stanley, apparently, waited until 1915, before deciding to offer his services to the British Army. He took an officer's course and was gazetted as a second lieutenant in the Northumberland Fusiliers. He commenced his flying career at the Hall Flying School, Hendon, getting his aviators certificate on 16th January 1916. After receiving his commission in the R.F.C. on March 6th, he was stationed for a few weeks at Northolt until being posted to 9 Squadron and flew to France on the 14th June of the same year.

Stan was now in the Royal Flying Corps, flying Bristol BE2c's. Lewis's comments on this machine are by now famous, "2c's...that meant artillery observation, dawdling up and down the lines while 'Archie' took pot shots at you; that meant photography; that meant beastly long reconnaissances, with Fokkers buzzing about on your tail. Friends, Mess companions would go out on patrol and never come back. As the months went by, it seemed only a matter of time until your turn came. You sat down to dinner faced by the empty chairs of men you had laughed and joked with at lunch. They were gone".

The BE2e, built by the Royal Aircraft Establishment, and again designed by De Havilland, had a 100hp engine, with space for the passenger to sit to the front and pilot to the rear. Stanley Mann, 'the movie man', well versed in mobile photography, was a good catch for the reconnaissance work of 9 Squadron, recently converted from 'the wireless flight' under the command of Hugh Dowding. Later it became the Home Wireless Squadron before returning to France. Stanley shared the squadron at this time, with pilots, Second Lieutenants E.A. Wynn and T.E.G. Scaife, Lieutenant B.T.

Coller, Lieutenant M.G.Begg, Second Lieutenants E.R.H. Pollack, C.P. Creighton, A.L. Macdonald, S.M. Smith, A. Gray, Lieutenant C.W. Hyde, J.V. Barry, Second Lieutenant J.T. Hanning and Lieutenant V.A. Strauss.

Seven were killed in action between July and November. Air records record 32 aerial incidents over nine months.

Tom Scaife's activities which have been written about, illustrate life at this time for Stanley. Scaife used his Lewis guns to attack German machine gun nests. They communicated with the ground by klaxon horn that could be heard above the battle noise and urged ground troops to indicate their position by signal. Achievement of an infantry objective was often associated to the R.F.C.'s visibility at low level in extremely dangerous circumstances. Scaife was killed in action weeks before Mann.

On September 3rd, Stanley was aerial photographer in a machine flown by Lieutenant Begg; it was a contact patrol, according to casualty reports, over Beaumont Hamel. Their BE2e serial no. 5817 was shot through by enemy ground fire, and they were forced to land, both men were reported as OK.

Less than two months later, with the squadron in constant action, Stanley, again flew as observer/photographer, this time with Second Lieutenant Wynn. Their brief was to photograph the German trench system, to provide G.H.Q. with information for further ground attack. They were engaged in combat with four enemy air machines over the village of Rocquigny. After a forty minute flight at 2.30 in the afternoon, they were shot from the rear, sending their BE2e into a spin. They were spotted going down behind enemy lines, being chased down by three enemy machines. (They may have accounted for one). They were presumed to have crashed, 90 minutes after leaving their aerodrome. Back at 9 HQ, they were marked MIA – missing in action, presumed dead.

German 'Anschluss' records claim that a BE2e was shot down by Jagdstaffel pilot, Oberleutnant S.Kirmaier over Le Sars. Stanley is presumed to have been struck by machine gun fire and died in his cockpit, as it was later revealed that Wynn had landed the plane, and succumbed to his wounds a few days later at an enemy dressing station.

Twenty-one year old Stanley Mann is commemorated at Arras, on the Flying Services Memorial. Dowding, himself, described, Stanley as "one of our finest and most brilliant pilots".

29 Squadron, veterans of the Somme campaign, under the command of Eric Conran, had been used to flying DH2's in their role as a single-seater scout squadron. Jimmy McCudden, joined 29 in August 1916 as a flight-sergeant pilot and mechanic of two years standing. Still involved in escort work, and flying obsolete machines, the 29 pilots fought hard to survive. He made his first 'kill' on September 6th. 56 other 'kills' were to follow before his own demise. On 9th November 1916, 29 lost four machines during the biggest allied aerial attack of the war so far, on the German ammunition dump at Vraumont. Other losses occurred in the DH2, until the squadron moved to Nieuport 17 'Destroyers' in March 1917. These single-seat bi-plane fighters (Baby Peugeot's), were quicker and more manoeuvrable with the gun mounting on the top plane.

On 25th March, Second Lieutenant Gilbert of 29 became the first pilot to be shot down in the new Nieuports by none other than Oberleutnant Manfred Von Richthofen, 'the Red Baron'. It was into these surroundings that twenty-four year old Lieutenant Cecil Gaskain made his entrance. Cecil Stanley Gaskain was the son of Denis Hinton Gaskain from Buckinghamshire, owner of a local hop and sud factory and his wife, Hannah. He was born on 5th May 1892, the third of four children, attending St Olave's for just three years between 1902 and 1905, when he left prematurely, aged sixteen to attend Eastbourne College. He was close in age to his sister Irene, with two much older brothers, Albert and William, who would both have been in their mid thirties when the war began. Whilst at home in Grove Park, he worked for a small oil company and indulged his love of cricket, as secretary of Grove Park cricket club, having represented St Olave's at the game in the first X1.

On the outbreak of war, he enlisted as a gunner in the 1st Battalion of the Honourable Artillery Company, and is very likely to have served alongside Alfred Pollard, the only Olavian to win the coveted V.C, as the latter was less than a year younger, and also in the H.A.C. Cecil Gaskain found himself in France earlier than most, disembarking from the ship at Havre on the 18th September 1914. Surviving the second battle of Ypres in April 1915, he returned to England, to take a commission in a Howitzer brigade of the Royal Field Artillery which he was gazetted for on the 12th July. In June 1916, he returned to the front as a Lieutenant attached to the 9th Londons in preparation for the Somme. In the autumn, he requested a transfer to the Royal Flying Corps and returned home to learn to fly at the Ruffy-Baumann School in Hendon. On 10th November he was awarded his aviator's certificate at Hendon and assigned to 65 Squadron at home. He remained with them until receiving his wings in early March 1917. A month later, on the 18th April, he joined 29 Squadron as a new pilot based around Arras.

When he arrived, he joined Conran's pilots – McCudden, Rogers, Pascoe, Birks, Gilbert, Muir, Owen, Scott-Foxwell, Sadler, Morgan, Elderton, Atkinson, Watts, Humble, Milling, Shepherd, Sloan, Dunn and Sutherland – nineteen men, of whom three were missing, seven killed and three wounded before April and May were out.

By May 1917, the R.F.C. had commenced its 'round the clock' tactical strikes on the German Jasta 2 base, run by the Von Richthofen brothers – Manfred and Lothar, with support from Kurt Wolff, another Jasta ace. This target was given special treatment because of the recent havoc caused to allied air machines by roving groups of Jasta Albatrosses.

On May 7th, 29, 40 and 56 Squadrons were all in action wandering regularly behind enemy lines to prevent planned Jasta attacks and in the case of 40, to attack kite balloons. 40 Squadron attacked in the morning in their Nieuports. The occasion is marked by the first kill for their new pilot, Lieutenant E.M. (Mick) Mannock, future great British ace. Later in the day, eleven SE5's of 56 Squadron engaged the Jasta pilots over the village of Annoueullin. Four machines were shot up, with two pilots wounded, and two reported missing presumed dead. Chaworth-Musters and Ball VC were gone. Captain Albert Ball V.C., having been shot down by Lothar Von Richthofen at 7.30 in the evening.

Four hours earlier, at 3.45pm, a group of Nieuport Scouts of 29 Squadron had left their aerodrome on a combat patrol, with Lieutenant Gaskain in A6609. They engaged enemy air machines an hour or so later, over the town of Fresnes. Cecil was reportedly last seen spinning down out of control with three enemy Albatross's on his tail, having been hit by enemy heavy artillery. Lothar Von Richthofen claimed the kill later that day, having despatched Ball. He was listed as missing, but after several months of hoping he was a prisoner, he was presumed killed. He had just turned twenty-five two days earlier, and much like his fellow Olavians, had survived but a short time in action – twenty days. His total flying time totalled 51 hours and 45 minutes.

Edgar Churcher had enlisted in 1914 as a Private no. 466 in the 5th Londons, the London Rifle Brigade. He was twenty-two years old, an Old Olavian, a qualified teacher, and a poet. He was born, one of three boys in 1892, son of Herbert Churcher, a bookbinder from Bromley and Isabella Harnot from South Lambeth. He attended St Olave's on a probationer's scholarship for four years, arriving aged 14 in 1907, shortly before his younger brother, Athelstan. Another seemingly unique boy, Edgar's masters wrote of his many virtues. Specifically, he possessed a great sense of humour, marked out by all, as a boy of merriment, mischief and gaiety. Sensitive while strong, he appeared always alert, devoted and ardent in spirit, with a love of the poems of Robert Browning.

He crossed years at St Olave's with both Finnimore and Stockins, his fellow pilots, although four years their senior. After teacher's training at Islington, he took a post as an assistant master under the London County Council in a local school. With the death of his mother, he and Athelstan and their widowed father moved into elder brother, Alfred's spacious house in Stockwell.

August 1914 changed everything. He was very early to enlist, and after training, was in France by the 24th January 1915. He fought with the London Rifle Brigade at St Julien and at Frezenberg, before returning to England to take a commission, which he received on 18th September. He was gazetted as a second lieutenant in the Rifle Brigade and set sail for Macedonia shortly after. He remained there for the first half of 1916, took a pilots course and became attached to the Royal Flying Corps, as an army officer by May. He remained an officer in the Rifle Brigade, even his aerial activities are not held by R.A.F. records. On his regiment's recall to France, he was sent as a flying instructor to Egypt.

Having survived, considerably against the odds so far, largely thanks to his 'indomitable courage', a little luck had saved him from likely death on the battlefields of Albert, Delville Wood and Guillemont that July. In early 1917, Edgar, now a lieutenant, returned to England, as a test pilot on new machines with 14 and 65 Squadrons. He was twenty-four. During one particular flight, he tore all the tendons in his shoulder, and was hospitalised for a short while. Once recovered, he was posted to 32 Squadron, R.F.C. in France, Redge Stubbs old squadron, based near Lijssenhoek, west of Ypres.

Despite his experiences in Greece, and his obvious bravery in test flights, his combat experience was very limited, only 22 hours flying time at his death. July 1917 in France witnessed the final preparations for the third battle of Ypres. Air combat was ferocious, on the 7th July alone, fifteen British pilots were killed in a few hours. The Fifth Army had use of 'V Brigade' R.F.C., which included 32, flying DH5's. The German High Command had doubled its number of machines, and the new fighter wing, the Jagdgeschwader 1, manned by various aces, was used as a 'concentrated attack force'. Edgar Churcher lost his life on his first flight over enemy lines on the 14th July 1917. He was returning from a offensive combat patrol, when his DH5 was seen to nose dive. The report stated "pilot crashed in stall-dive about 50 feet and was killed".

Less than a month later George Castell, the twenty-six year old air mechanic of 12 Squadron died in a road accident. He was returning from a machine gun training course for air mechanics on new air machines, when the truck that he was in, ran down the side of a railway embankment at night and overturned. He was killed and was buried in the Avesnes-Le-Comte communal cemetery, twenty kilometres west of Arras.

George Charles Castell, only son of George Castell, a docker at the Surrey Commercial docks in Rotherhithe and his wife Emily, was born in March 1891, of the same generation of schoolboys as Stubbs, Wade and Knight. He had won a scholarship from St Mary's Rotherhithe to St Olave's and spent four years there leaving aged sixteen, in 1907, and was remembered as a vigorous rugby player. He apprenticed as an engineer mechanic for a further three years and then decided to train as a draughtsman for another three years. In May 1914, he took a position with an architect's practice in Chancery Lane. Three months into the job, he left and enlisted as a Private no. 2764 in the 20th Londons, 'the Queens Own'. After basic military training, he embarked for Flanders and arrived on March 7th 1915. The month of May saw the baptism of the 20th at Festubert, Givenchy and in September the battle of Loo's. By the end of the year, lucky to be alive, he managed to use his engineering experience to obtain a transfer to the fast developing Royal Flying Corps.

In June 1916, George became Air Mechanic, 2nd Class, no. 39594 and was posted to 12 Squadron flying BE2's around St Quentin and Aubigny. Initially, George was involved in aircraft repair and maintenance. 12 had been in France since late 1915. June 1916 found a squadron of pilots that included Lieutenants C.J. Van Nostrand, LA Wingfield, and Philpott; Captain E.G. Tyson and Second Lieutenant R.M. Wilson-Browne. By September, they had moved to Bapaume and Marcoing. Bombing raids were carried out on Queant in late October, on Vraumont ammunition dump in November and even some photographic patrols in December. With many pilots gone by the spring of 1917, the squadron was rebuilt with new blood and new machines, the RE8's, the reason for George's re-training. 12 had a new commanding officer, Major C.S. Burnett, who indulging his love of both whisky and milk, insisted his men find and purchase a squadron cow.

Like many men from the ranks in the R.F.C., George tired of seeing young inexperienced pilots fly off to die, and opted to train as a pilot and as an officer himself. In June 1917, he went to England on leave, and stayed to take a commission and a pilot and gunnery course. He was already a crack shot with a rifle. He was back in France on August 8th ready to attend the RE8 course. Such is the great tragedy of war, 'the mechanic', on the threshold of becoming a pilot officer, died by accident.

A squadron of Bristol Fighters (F2B's) reached France in time for 'Bloody April' 1917. This newly blooded group was 48 Squadron. Ralph Barker writes that "The 'Brisfit' was a sizable machine for its time, 26 feet long with a 40 feet wing span. The two crew sat back to back, the pilot with a synchronised Vickers, the observer with a Lewis mounted on a scarff ring with a swivel seat, firing on the flanks and to the rear".

With Leefe Robinson V.C. in charge, six machines left their base on the 5th April in search of Von Richthofen's Jasta near Douai. Disaster struck, four of the six F2B's were destroyed, and Robinson was taken prisoner after landing.

The Bristol F2B's reputation was in tatters. It was into this situation that a fresh pilot officer, Second Lieutenant Harry Finnimore arrived at 48 Squadron on attachment from the 7th Battalion, the Royal Sussex Regiment. Third of seven children of James Finnimore, a grocer, originally from St Pancras, who later had a leg amputated, and his wife, Jane from Southwark. Harry had been born in December 1896, with two younger brothers, Bernard and John, both too young for the war; he won a L.C.C. scholarship to St Olave's and studied there for four years until leaving in 1912 to join the Civil Service based at Somerset House in London.

At School, Harry excelled as an outstanding swimmer, and in competition was seen both to lead and lose well. With an alert mind and generous heart, he progressed from Somerset House and became a secretary to Colonel Fenwick at the London Hospital. This appointment precluded him from immediate enlistment in September 1914, but a year later, he joined the 28th Londons, the Artists Rifles, as Private no.760885, going to France on the 21st April 1916. The 28th was the main territorial battalion from where officers were recruited, as many of the rankers were educated middle class men. Towards the end of the Somme campaign, Harry was selected for officer training and sent to England. He was commissioned in March 1917 as a second lieutenant and was due to be posted to the 7th Royal Sussex but had opted instead for pilot training; he wasn't actually sent to the front until the 20th February 1918, when he turned up at 48 headquarters.

With Robinson a prisoner of war, the squadron was run firmly by his superior, 'Zulu' Bettington, with three of the best flight commanders in the R.F.C. – Keith Park, Brian Baker and Sam Sibley plus his unique observer, 'Puggy' Shone. By March 1918, 48 was based as an Army squadron at Flez, when the 'Kaisers Offensive' began on the 21st. Plans had been laid to disrupt the R.F.C.'s reconnaissance work, and the surprise element gave the enemy control of the air. In the proceeding six days of constant air combat, 48 Squadron fought well, with ten significant actions by squadron pilots. Seven pilots were wounded, C4707 crew, Captain Wells and Corporal Beales scored several victories. Harry Finnimore was the first solo pilot to be killed in action during the brief but intense campaign, on the 27th. In a surviving casualty report, he was said to have been flying a F2B and to have died of wounds received. He was twenty-one and is buried at St Pierre Cemetery in Amiens. Harry had been with his squadron for 35 days.

Ten days after Harry Finnimore of 48 Squadron had given his life, Second Lieutenant Bert Knight of 54 Squadron flying Sobwith Camels, succumbed to his injuries in hospital at Rouen. His machine had been seen to come down in flames, and his fellow pilots returned to base, reporting him missing in action presumed dead. He was actually picked up unconscious by British infantry and transported to hospital. Although he stayed alive for over two weeks, he didn't regain consciousness, and passed away on the 7th April.

Bert had been assigned to 54 Squadron under the command of George Maxwell in late 1917. He flew under nineteen year old flight commander, Ewart Stock and Francis Kitto, and alongside Know, Richardson and Drysdale. Born George Bertram Knight in May 1889, he, brother Norris, and sister Elsie, were the three surviving children of Bertram Knight, a schoolmaster at St Olaves who specialised in metalwork and engineering, and his wife, Georgiana. Bert attended the school for six years leaving in 1907, travelling from home in Ilford. He would have known Castell, Gaskain and Stubbs as contemporaries. At eighteen, he joined the London and County Bank, and took his Institute of Banking exams. Offered a transfer to the Bank of British North America, based in Calgary, Canada, he jumped at the chance. Exploiting his new lifestyle to the maximum, he took regular fishing and shooting holidays into the Rockies. On the outbreak of war, he enlisted in Canada, in the engineer's battalion of the Canadian Ordnance Corps.

During training, he so impressed his superior officers that on his arrival by ship in England in early 1915, he was promoted to quarter master sergeant. Another aspect of his skills, involved him in technical development work for the Canadian Army in what became known later as the 'Ross Rifle'. The resulting rifle, part designed by Bert Knight, which was manufactured in volume at the start of 1916, became the 'Ross Mark 111B' with a .303inch calibre, 5 rounds magazine capacity, 50.5 inches in length, weighing 9 pounds and 12 ounces and a muzzle velocity of 2060 (fps). Its maximum effective range was 2,000 yards. Many Canadian infantrymen used this rifle throughout the war.

Throughout 1916, in his role as engineer, designer and QMS, he remained far from the front, but like many, was persuaded

THE ROYAL FLYING CORPS

that, as he was a single man, that he should offer his services in a more dangerous environment, to prevent a married man having to go instead. He and Norris both decided to take commissions and volunteer for duty as pilots in the R.F.C. They trained at the London and Provincial School in Edgware on bi-planes and took the opportunity to visit the school. Bert and Norris received their aviators certificates on the 23rd September 1917, having both been commissioned in August. Bert was in France with 53 then 54 Squadron by 16th March 1918. Within six days he had been wounded and he succumbed on 7th April in hospital in Rouen. He was twenty-eight.

In June 1919, St Olave's produced Volume XX111 No.5 issue of the Olavian. In the 'Pro Patria Mortui' list, under the heading – 'William James Stockins', the editor lamented, 'Our last word from his home is that hope is not abandoned, and we cannot but sympathise with the love that still clings to an almost hopeless hope'.

William Stockins was the last of the 'flying Olavians' to perish in the conflict. He was at St Olave's at the same time as Edgar Churcher, Harry Finnimore and Oliver Wade. Born in January 1896 the eldest of five boys of Bill Stockins, a house decorator and wife Minnie of Bermondsey, he spent five years at St Olave's leaving aged fifteen to apprentice as a clerk in the City. War broke out in his eighteenth summer, and he enlisted immediately, like so many others. He became a private in the 28th Londons, the Artists Rifles, and was quickly selected for a commission (similarly to Harry Finnimore). In May 1917 he was commissioned as an officer in 2/2nd Londons, and later took a pilot's course and was transferred to the R.F.C., arriving in a 'Martinsydes Elephant' mono plane at 27 (Bomber) Squadron on the 18th April 1918 in the Arras sector of France.

According to recently transferred fellow pilot, Stuart Campbell, 27's role was 'long distance daylight bombing', and it was without question, an absolute death trap when up against fast moving Albatross scouts'. As 1918 wore on, 27 Squadron eventually had the slow cumbersome Martinsydes replaced with a new 'day bomber' the DH4 from Aircraft Manufacturing. This machine had better speed, climb and armaments than previously, and raised 27's pilot's chances against enemy technology. The advances in aircraft technology from the early days of summer 1916, when Redge Stubbs had been killed in his DH2, was gigantic.

William served alongside pilots like G.E. French, F.Y. McLaughlan (both killed in a flying accident 23rd May), F.J. Bull, C.B. Law (both taken prisoner 18th May) Captain G.B.S. McBain D.S.C., M.C., W.Spencer (both killed 10th May) W.H. Gibson (wounded 10th May). As air activity increased towards the end of the war, more and more pilots died.

Early in the morning of the 6th June, at 08.20 hours, several DH4's from 27 Squadron took off from their base near Arras. William was co-piloting serial no B2080 with Lieutenant M.F. Cunningham. They had bombing objectives and had all left the aerodrome in format, however on the return, their aircraft was seen leaving the formation east of the lines, but in control over the town of Chaulnes. This was the last sighting of B2080. They had two Lewis Guns and a Vickers on board, plus two bomb racks and an oxygen set. Meanwhile, another DH4 carrying Second Lieutenant D.B. Robertson was shot up, wounding the solo pilot, and a third DH4 piloted by Major G.D. Hill and Second Lieutenant C.Nesbit was also shot up, causing wounds to Nesbit. Returning to base, the surviving pilots reported both men missing and held out hope that they may have landed safely and been taken prisoner.

German Abschusse records show that around this time and location, two Jagde pilots put in separate claims to have shot down a DH4. Firstly, over Assainvillers by Leutnant O.Von B-Marconnay of Jagdstaffel 15; and secondly, over Ferrieres by Leutnant G.Von Hantelmann of Jagdstaffel 15 at 10.40 hours.

William was twenty-two and is commemorated on the Arras Flying Services Memorial.

THE ROYAL FLYING CORPS

'I took my leave of the earth and men,
And soared aloft to the lonely sky,
Thro' the gathering dark, to the silent stars,
And the whisper of Angels passing by'.

(Molly Corbally)

CHAPTER 18

Loos, Cambrai and Ypres

From the end of 1915, the village of Loos-en-Gohelle had become a strategic 'flash point', situated, as it was, just north of the German fortified town of Lens. As late as August 1917, British and Canadian Forces were launching major assaults from the north west. The Germans held Lens until the last days of October 1918; Lens was to the Germans, what Ypres proved to be, to the Allies. The Belgian town, further north, was under continual attack throughout the four years of fighting, totally destroyed by bombardment; south of Lens, in the Arras sector, the French town of Cambrai had become another German stronghold, the headquarters of Crown Prince Rupprecht of Bavaria. In late 1917, the advancing Allies came close to seizing the town in the famous tank battle that ensued. The Germans finally withdrew a year later, but not before mining the outskirts.

Many thousands of British soldiers died in between the main campaigns which have become infamous in their recollection. This chapter describes the story of the nine Old Olavians who lost their lives in Loos between February and May 1917, in the battle of Cambrai in November and early December 1917, and at Ypres between January and May 1918. Four were commissioned officers, the most senior of which was Lieutenant Don Ryley, older brother of 'Bay' and son of Harold Senior, both of whom fell in the War. Donald served with the North Staffordshire Regiment at Loos. Three second lieutenants followed him as next in rank – John Knox of the 7th Royal Sussex based at Louverval near Cambrai, Charles Blencowe, also of the Royal Sussex, but attached to the 1st Wiltshires, based just outside Ypres, and Ernest Curtis of the 7th Queens Own (Royal West Kent) Regiment stationed at Boezinghe.

Five ranking soldiers made up the total. Teddy Cock, a private with the 28th Londons attached to the 9th Suffolks, was based at

Mazingarbe near to Loos, Doug Perkins, a Private with the 12th Londons, also at Loos; Godfrey Levy was a rifleman with the Queen's Victoria Rifles, the 9th Londons at Roclincort near Cambrai, Len Kidney, an N.C.O. with the 9th Royal Fusiliers of 12 Division at Louverval, and finally, young Bobbie Kiddle was a private in the 1/10th Kings (Liverpool) Regiment at Lapugnoy near Bethune.

January 1917, witnessed a variety of localised Allied raids on the German lines at Vermelles, Loos, Hulluch, Le Transloy and on the Ancre. During the first few days of the following month, British Forces had made major advances, capturing Sailly Hill, Serre Hill and Grandcourt. Lieutenant Donald Ryley, who had been promoted on 28th July 1916 and attached to the North Staffordshires from the Manchester Regiment, was in charge of a platoon in trenches at Hulluch in February 1917, as part of 72 Brigade, 24 Division. On the morning of the 11th, he was leading his platoon in an attack, when they were held up by barbed wire entanglements. During the delay, he was picked out by a sniper and shot. He was twenty-three. His body could not be retrieved and he was initially reported as 'missing believed killed'. No further news of his burial promoted his later commemoration on the Loos Memorial at Duds Corner.

Don was born in July 1893, the eldest son of Harold Ryley, Old Olavian and master. Starting his schooling at Sir Roger Manwood's School in Sandwich, where his father was headmaster, he transferred to St Olave's in 1904 aged 11, where he spent the next eight years, leaving in 1912 to go up to St John's College, Cambridge. Seen as a shy, sensitive youth but with a great inner strength and sense of self reliance, Don was a superb athlete and a keen rower, becoming captain of the 'Lady Margaret Boat' whilst at Cambridge. Another side to his personality, recognised in his last years at the School, was his fearlessness and general reckless behaviour, which came to the fore in many dangerous episodes at the Front.

When war came, he immediately took a commission, being posted on 26th August 1914 to the 8th (Ardwick) Battalion of the Manchester Regiment as a second lieutenant, and sent as reinforcements to Gallipoli a year later in October1915. In early 1916, his regiment moved to the Western Front via Marseilles. After a year of some of the bloodiest fighting there, when informed of the death of his younger brother 'Bay' and his father's consequent return to England from America to enlist, a different side to Don Ryley became known.

In a letter to friends at home, he wrote, "to tell the truth, I 'funk' life after the war. I really believe that it will be less hard for some to live on here, than to change this life for the unknown. There are so many dear friends on the other side, and the struggle here is so hard at times that I have almost yielded to despair before now, and I do not believe that I am so very morbid. The more I go on living, the more do I love".

Just over two weeks after the shooting of Lieutenant Ryley at Hulluch, his Olavian colleague Private Doug Perkins no. 1/43968 of the Royal Irish Rifles was killed in action whilst in the trenches at Loos. He was thirty-two, married to retired Olavian Master, Joe Pearce' s daughter, Beatrice and a father of three young children. Douglas was born on the 10th September 1884 to George Perkins, a corn dealer from Southwark and his wife, Mary. He was the youngest of twelve children, with five brothers, of which only Stephen and Wilfred were young enough to serve. All of the boys were schooled at Tooley Street, with some becoming schoolmasters themselves. Douglas, spent three years of a L.C.C scholarship and left in 1901 aged seventeen. He enlisted in 1914 first as a Rifleman no. 6186 in the 12th Londons (The Rangers) later being transferred as Rifleman no. 1/43968 in the Royal Irish Rifles, serving in France.

Edward Millar Cock was just eighteen when he walked into the Deptford recruiting office in January 1916. Known to his friends as 'Teddy', he shortly became Private Cock no. 761351 in the 28th Battalion, the London Regiment, better known as the 'Artist's Rifles'. He spent the following months in camp in France and was eventually transferred into the 'Colonel's Class' where his school friends Leslie Galloway and Micky Lowe had previously moved. He completed an intensive course of bayonet training, physical drill and lectures on gas, trench construction, enteric and sanitation. In the middle of May 1917, the 28th moved up to the Front at Vermelles, between La Bassee and Lens. He survived less than a week in action, dying aged just twenty years on the 26th May. He was buried in the Philosophe British Cemetery in Mazingarbe. His death provoked great sadness from his many friends.

Edward Millar Cock was born on the 1st February 1897, the eldest son and child, with two younger sisters, of Edward Cock, a lighterman and waterman on the river, and his wife Alice of Evelyn Street in Deptford. He moved from Deptford Park Elementary School to St Olave's, where he spent eight years from 1908 to 1915. In his last year he was made captain of school, succeeding Jimmy Jones and prior to Vic Budd, both also to lose their lives in the conflict. Teddy is remembered by masters as a 'remarkably attractive' boy, with a 'vivacious and charming' temperament. At once, both 'intelligent and mercurial', he excelled in the sciences and spent much of his extra curricular time in the School Cadet Corps, and learning to appreciate art and literature with his friends, contemporary, Leslie Sanders and the more senior, Howard Keesey, both of whom he had come to know through the Old Olavians, whilst he was still at the School. On leaving, his intention had been to further his scientific studies at the Royal College of Science in South Kensington, but by late 1915, he was under significant pressure to enlist and 'do his bit' for his country.

Six months elapsed on the battlefields of France and Flanders before the death of John Lawrence Knox. Throughout the summer of the year, the British Army had focused its attention on the Ypres sector, where the third battle, in as many years, took place between July and November. The campaign, induced by the capture of the Messines Ridge and the need to push on, to take the Passchendaele Ridge, was renowned for its heavy shelling bombardments and inclement weather, reducing the ground to a virtual swamp of mud, where many soldiers simply disappeared without trace.

After sixteen weeks, the objective was finally secured, at a cost of over 300,000 Allied lives. Two separate chapters chronicle the involvement of the Olavian 'Fallen' during the third battle of Ypres.

Just ten days after the end of the fighting at Ypres, the British Third Army launched a surprise attack on the enemy at Cambrai, employing over four hundred tanks – the first mass use of tanks in battle. The idea had been that of Colonel Fuller, with General Byng's approval to use the Third Army. Haig, however, had made them wait while he completed the Ypres campaign. The tanks proved themselves by piercing a six mile wide hole in the Hindenburg Line. As usual, the infantry follow up was insufficient and far too slow. Despite the planning, the level of success had been considerably underestimated.

The infantry forces employed came from '111 Corps' which included the 6th, 12th, 20th and 29th Divisions plus two tank brigades; and 'IV Corps' including the 36th (Ulster) Division, 51st (Highland) Division and 62nd (West Riding) Division, with the 1st Cavalry Division and another tank brigade. The aim was to break the line between the Escaut Canal and the Canal du Nord; to take Cambrai and Bourlon Wood and to move towards Valenciennes.

Second Lieutenant Larry Knox of the 7th Royal Sussex was in the 'jumping off' trenches at Louverval on the day of attack, the 20th November 1917. As part of 36 Brigade, 12th Division, his platoon was in the vanguard of the attack. At 06.20 hours, British guns opened fire and Brigadier General Hugh Elles moved his tanks forward into No Mans Land, followed by the infantry. The enemy turned and ran as the tanks moved across the wooden 'fascines' laid to allow progress over the enemy trench lines.

The 7th Royal Sussex helped achieve all of '111 Corps' objectives that day. The line was breached between Crevecoeur and Bonavis and troops moved up to the St Quentin Canal. Larry was killed in action by machine gun fire whilst advancing ahead of his platoon. He died on the field and his body was not recovered. He was thirty-one years old and married with a four year old son. He is commemorated on the Cambrai Memorial at Louverval.

John Lawrence Knox had been born on the 18th January 1886, to John Knox, a stockbrokers clerk from Birkenhead and wife Mary Jane from Shropshire. He was one of seven surviving children, with three brothers, Andrew, Clifford and Harold. A boy of 'bright, sunny disposition' he became a keen sportsman and a 'universal favourite', attending the School for three years from 1899 to 1901, when he departed at fifteen, to join the London and Brazilian Bank in the City. Douglas Perkins and Percy Grist were his main contemporaries amongst the 'Fallen'. As he worked his way through the administrative grades of the bank, he began courting Miss Jenny Feaver, who he married in 1912. A year later, their first son, John was born, and it was not until late 1915, that he felt the moral need to leave the bank and offer his services to the war effort. Single men were running out, and the Government had started to ask for married volunteers (especially officer material, who were in short supply). He joined the Inns of Court Officer Training Corps and was commissioned in 1916 in the Sussex Regiment. He went to France on 6th January 1917.

On the same day, 20th November 1917, Sergeant Len Kidney no. 1136 of the 9th Battalion, the Royal Fusiliers was mown down by enemy machine gun fire whilst leading a platoon of men in an advance. He was twenty-three years old and his body could not be recovered. He is commemorated on the Cambrai Memorial.

Leonard Kidney was born in Rotherhithe on the 22nd January 1894, son of Edwin Kidney, an insurance agent and wife Eliza, and was one of the first London boys to win the new L.C.C. scholarship. He first entered St Olave's in 1905 and stayed for six years. His younger brother, John also attended. He excelled in mathematics and was seen as a tenacious and talented student. In his leisure time, he followed his family's strong religious beliefs, by becoming a sunday school teacher at fifteen and an active worker with the Southwark Park Wesleyan Chapel attended by his parents and much younger sisters, Doris and Maud.

He enlisted on the 26th August 1914, being promoted to corporal the following February, whilst still in training in England. The 9th

Royal Fusiliers sailed for France on the 1st June 1915 and saw action at Loos in the autumn. After Christmas, he was promoted again to lance-sergeant. His leave in September 1916, proved to be his last.

The break in the line was not exploited because of poor communication between the brigades and headquarters; and the cavalry had been stationed too far to the rear. General Haig, who had only reluctantly agreed to Byng's lobbying, allowed 48 hours for the attack. Most of his forces were still at Ypres or had been shipped to the Italian Front. He decided however, to continue to press the attack, but had allowed the German Divisions sufficient 'breathing space' to regroup and launch bloody counter attacks particularly at Bourlon Wood. Von Hutier's 'stormtrooper' tactics were used, to bypass Allied centres of resistance, coupled with heavy use of both artillery and aircraft. By the 14th December, the British had retreated to where they started and had been ordered to take a 'defensive posture'. 40,000 lives had been wasted.

Rifleman Godfrey Levy no. 415193, serving with the 9th London Regiment, was one of those that died, in his case just three days before Christmas. Part of 140th Brigade, 47th (London) Division, they had been brought into the Cambrai area as reserves, to help fortify against enemy counter attacks. On the 22nd December, two days after the battalion had been relieved by the 1st Londons, they had been ordered to spend the day repairing the trench fortifications and wiring; Godfrey had been wounded by sniper rifle fire and had been taken to the rear by comrades. From here, he was being stretchered to the advanced dressing station, when he and those carrying him, were hit by a shell. He was killed by a fragment of the shell casing. He was twenty-six and is buried in the Roclincourt Military Cemetery between Arras and Lens.

Godfrey Levy was born in April 1896 in Deptford, the eldest of seven children of Samuel Levy, a tailor from the Russian area of Poland, who had taken British nationality, and his English wife, Esther. He had two brothers, Israel, four years junior and Abraham, eleven year junior, and four sisters. Godfrey and Israel attended St

Olave's for a very brief time, just a year, 1910, on a L.C.C. scholarship from the City of London School, before the family moved to Brockley and Godfrey commenced work as an office clerk at a wharfinger's. Despite the temporary nature of his life at Tooley Street, Godfrey retained fond memories for the School and wrote letters to the headmaster, from the front. A cheerful boy, he is remembered as a tough competitor on the athletics track, and a man who expressed regret at leaving his education at such an early age.

One memory of Godfrey which made him stand out amongst many of his contemporaries in the War, was his warning or plea, in his last letter home received just two days before his death. He wrote that the masters should,

> "Teach the boys the horror, not the Glory, of war. To those that have been in it, its frightful realities are known. Let Olavians resolve that when this war is over, they will do their part to save the world from another. Our lives are being laid down now by the thousand, that this salvation may be wrought out. Don't let our lives be sacrificed in vain".

Exactly a month after Godfrey Levy was killed, on 22nd January 1918, an officer of the Royal West Kent's was hit repeatedly by machine gun fire at Langemarck, later dying of the many wounds he received. He was a thirty-eight year old husband, and father of a fourteen year old son. Ernest John Curtis was born the eldest of three in Bromley, Kent on the 14th August 1880, the son of Ernest Curtis, a foreman in a corn grain and feed warehouse in Bermondsey and wife, Lizzie from Gravesend. His younger brother Bertie would also serve. Ernest attended St Olave's for four years leaving in July 1894 to apprentice as a journalist with a military publication, entitled 'The Regiment'. A quiet reserved young man, his only direct contemporary amongst the 'Fallen', was Arthur Garrett, who died at Redan in October 1916. He is remembered chiefly by masters as 'a good friend' to all around him.

As his career developed, he chose to marry whilst quite young, at twenty-one, in 1902, to the older, Florence Gibson, who was 29. They had their only son, Ernest Arthur the following year and lived at 96 Caledon Road in East Ham where Ernest commuted to his work as a photographic publisher's clerk. When war came, Ernest stayed in publishing, seeing an obvious role for military reporting. It was not until quite late in 1916, after the casualty statistics of the Somme campaign were understood at home, that he felt the compulsion to follow the young English bachelors to the front. He initially enlisted in the Royal Garrison Artillery as a ranking gunner, later transferring as a private to the Kings Own (Royal Lancaster) Regiment, where he saw action on the Somme in late January 1917; in March he was plucked out for officer training, from where, on 31st July, he was gazetted, and was transferred to a line infantry regiment, the 5th Royal West Kents, reaching France in October, where he transferred again to the 7th Battalion who were in the line at Langemarck. Second Lieutenant Curtis is buried at Boezinghe in 'Artillery Wood' Cemetery.

'Bobbie' Kiddle was one of the youngest Olavians to fall during the conflict. As a Private no. 358315 in 'Y Company', the 1/10th Kings (Liverpool) Regiment, he was badly wounded by machine gun and shell fire on the 15th March 1918, a week before the 'Kaiser's Offensive'. He had been stretchered to the casualty clearing station with severe wounds to his head, arm, thigh and abdomen. He appeared 'quite sensible, sent his love to all and died very quietly at about 7.15pm'. A few weeks earlier, he had turned twenty. He was buried in the Lapugnoy Military Cemetery, west of Bethune. His death prompted a poem from an anonymous school friend,

> 'In France he lay, in battle bruised and broken –
> His heart was in the land that gave him birth,
> For dear ones there, his words of love were spoken,
> His last on earth.

Without complaint he bore the grievous burden,
War lays on youth, took what stern fortune gave,
Did his appointed task, and won as guerdon,
A Soldier's grave'.

Robert Henry Kiddle was born, the younger son, by two years of John Henry and Elizabeth Parker Kiddle of Forest Hill on the 5th February 1898. His father was employed by H.M. Customs and Excise as a surveyor. The family were proud of their Scottish heritage, even though John was born in Leicestershire, with 'Bobbie' and elder brother Thomas Walker Kiddle donning kilts on special occasions. Bobbie attended St Olave's for seven years from 1910 until 1916. He is remembered as a 'remote' and 'uncommonly thoughtful' boy whose brother's untimely death in early 1913 aged just 17, had a profound effect on his subsequent development. A fine debater, he was also the editor, for a time, of the Olavian magazine.

When war broke out in August 1914, he was only just sixteen, and was forced to wait until he was eighteen, by his parents, who one can imagine were extremely anxious about losing their other son. Despite enlisting as Private no. 358315 in the King's Liverpools in February 1916, he remained in training camps in England throughout most of 1916 and 1917, only arriving in Havre in the late autumn at the time of Cambrai. Sadly he survived for only four months. His mother's parting words to him being, 'May God take care of you, my boy'.

The spring of 1918 witnessed further fighting on the Somme and at Arras, with the Germans almost breaking through in the 'Kaisers Offensive' at St Quentin, Pargny and Bapaume. The 1st Battalion, the Wiltshire Regiment were based, at that time, with the rest of 7 Brigade, 25 Division, north east of Ypres, near Zonnebeke. Charles Blencowe was a second lieutenant, recently attached to them from the Royal Sussex Regiment.

Blencowe was in good company, as the 1st Wiltshires had other Olavians in their officer ranks – namely 'Didi' Maybrook who fell in spring 1916 at Neuville St Vaast, and Sid Terry who was killed in March 1918 at Arras.

Charles had arrived in France on April 22nd as an experienced colonial soldier, but novice officer. He went into the firing line almost immediately, lasting less than two weeks. He was killed instantly, in action on 3rd May by a enemy shell. He was twenty-nine years old and is commemorated on the Tyne Cot Memorial.

Charles Edward Blencowe was born, the youngest of six, with two elder brothers, Herbert and Frederick, on the 12th April 1889 in London, son of John Blencowe, a accountants clerk for a printers from Peckham and his wife Isabella from Camberwell. He attended Tooley Street for five years leaving in 1907 to move to Canada. His contemporaries amongst the Fallen are several – Norman Jones, Herbert Spencer-Smith – sixteen boys in all, starting with him, later died on the battlefield. An 'all round excellent athlete', Charles yearned to be a 'frontiersman'. With the intention of buying some land in the west of Canada, he spent three years travelling in the Rockies and living part of the time in San Francisco. In 1911, he returned to England at his father's request to help run a small farm between Bognor and Billingshurst.

Back in England, he renewed his relationship with sisters, Alice, Nellie and Elsie, with St Olave's and became active in local Sussex rugby and cricket. With the possibility of war in 1913, he enlisted in the Sussex Yeomanry as a private, and was called up in August 1914. The decision to hold back the yeomanry from embarking for France with the British Expeditionary Force, led to nine months of square-bashing and basic training at Canterbury in Kent. In March 1915, Charles, fed up with this inactivity, requested a transfer to a line regiment of the Royal Fusiliers – the 25th, appropriately named for Charles, 'the Legion of Frontiersman'.

Within a few weeks he was aboard ship from Southampton bound for Eastern Africa, where he remained for two years, seeing action in the battles of Kilimanjaro in March 1916, and Beho Beho in January 1917, before returning to England on leave in April

1917. Whilst on leave, he enrolled on an officer's course passing all examinations with great credit. Shortly after Christmas, he was gazetted and posted to the Royal Sussex Regiment as a second lieutenant, and went to France in the April, never returning home.

Between February 1917 and May 1918, eight more talented Olavians had lost their lives – a superlative rower, a mercurial 'captain of school', a fine teacher, a 'Brazilian banker', a 'free spirit', a 'jewish philosopher', a mathematician, a 'publisher' and a 'Scottish debater'.

Ken Harvard   *Lionel Harvard*

Don Boone's adventures in Serbia with Mrs Stobart's Mission in 1914-15

Newton Haseldine

Joe Heron

CHAPTER 19
The Canadian Contingent

On the 9th April 1917, Field Marshal Ludendorff's 52nd birthday, the Allied 'First Army' successfully stormed the Vimy Ridge, the strongest enemy defensive position in northern France. The assault was meticulously planned and rehearsed, with many miles of underground tunnels used, to bring the Allied troops closer to the enemy lines. German casualties numbered over twenty thousand with a further eleven thousand taken prisoner and 166 guns requisitioned. Four Victoria Cross awards were made for gallantry during the capture of the Ridge and Hill 145. Haig's forces had succeeded in deflecting the enemy away from Nivelle's offensive on the Aisne.

A hole had finally been punched in the German line – 12 to 15 kilometres deep and 6 kilometres wide. This was one of the first major strategic and tactical successes experienced by the Allies in over two years of warfare. Who was responsible?

General Julian Byng's Canadian Corps was given the job by General Henry Horne. Vimy Ridge subsequently proved to be the Canadians finest moment, a stage on which to demonstrate their skill, commitment, loyalty and training, to decisive effect. Byng proved to be one of the few Western Front leaders to be praised and ennobled for his war services. He chose the title 'Baron Byng of Vimy'. His successor at the Front from June 1917 was Arthur Currie, the first Canadian to rise from the rank of part time militia man to the lofty rank of lieutenant-general.

Both English, and to a lesser extent, French Canadians, who had so readily enlisted in the first days of the conflict almost all found themselves on the Western Front for the duration of their military service. Certainly they had leave, like the British troops, but they had to be satisfied with spending a few days in London, far from

THE CANADIAN CONTINGENT

their friends and family, who only heard of their whereabouts intermittently.

Despite its autonomy from Great Britain, Canada's Dominion status, in place since 1867, kept it extremely close in terms of politics and economics. Wilfred Laurier and his successor as Prime Minister in 1911, Robert Borden, were both firm supporters of British imperial interests, in tune with the Governor General, the Duke of Connaught.

By 1916, Canada's contribution to the war effort had been made clear. Not only were they providing healthy, well trained infantry men for the front, but also nearly half of all the shrapnel and shells for the British artillery, as well as massive quantities of food for the war effort. Their expertise in forestry and railway construction, led them to build all the light rail and half of the standard gauge rail to the Front line.

When war broke out in summer 1914, five Old Olavians, who were to give their lives during the conflict, joined up in Canada. All were English born, but transplanted to Canada, because of its opportunities for land purchase, adventure, freedom and travel. The eldest at thirty-one, was John Stride Durant, working as a farmer in Saskatchewan. A fine horseman, he decided to enlist as a Private no.106205 in the 1st Canadian Mounted Rifles (better known as the Saskatchewan Light Horse). John had been born in Camberwell on the 26th May 1883 to six sisters – Charlotte, Emma, Grace, Marie, May and Olive, the son of Luke Leo Durant, a hardware merchant and his wife Charlotte Marietta. He won a L.C.C. scholarship to St Olave's in 1896 and spent four years at the school, leaving aged sixteen to move to Canada to be a farmer.

Five years younger was Arthur Wyndham Laurie, born on the 21st October 1887 in Karachi, then part of India, to a father most likely working in the Indian civil service. His family had returned to London shortly after his birth, following his father's untimely death. The year 1901 found the family living at 'Belmont', Holland Road in Hove, Sussex, where the widowed Marion Laurie at 32, was living on her own means and supplementing her income by taking in boarders. Arthur was the eldest, next was sister, Hilda, two years younger born in Weston Super Mare in Somerset, and finally, another sister, Phillis, born at Milford in Hampshire. He won a scholarship to St Olave's in 1903 aged fourteen and spent just a year there leaving in January 1904 to apprentice to a London firm. In 1907, he left for Canada and bought land in Saskatchewan and later Alberta. The war saw him, a twenty-six year old farmer, enlist as a Private no. 466252 in the 8th Canadian Infantry (the Manitoba Rangers) on July 7th 1915.

On the 2nd May 1892, twins, Ernest and Herbert 'Bertie' Spencer-Smith were born in London. They both attended St Olave's for six years from 1903 to 1908, leaving aged sixteen. At some point, their father had died, and their widowed mother remarried and lived at Winchester. In 1911, both Bertie and Ernest were boarding at 13 Cathcart Hill, Islington with Headmaster Rushbrooke, one working as an insurance clerk and the other as a merchant's clerk. Also boarding in the house were two students at St Olave's, John Chubb and Lawrence Neal, both 15.

Bertie took an opportunity the following year, in 1912, to work as a farmer in Canada, and within two years owned some acreage including a lake, an island and some livestock. He was only twenty-two, when he put his dream on hold to enlist. He became a Private no. 433039, a stretcher-bearer, in the 49th Battalion, Canadian Infantry –the Alberta Regiment. Perhaps better known to most as, the 'Princess Patricia's' or 'Pat's Pals', named after the governor general's daughter. The 49th had been raised with private funding from Hamilton Gault of Montreal who served as a major, and most of the men who enlisted were ex-British soldiers resident in Canada. Initially the 49th served as part of the British 27th Division, later transferring to the 3rd Canadian Division in December 1915.

Alfred and Florence Lovekin of 395 Devon Flats, Tower Bridge could throw a stone at St Olave's they lived so close to it. Their son, Vyvyan Ivor, born on St Valentine's day, 1895 in Finchley, spent six years at the school, along with his two older brothers, Bernard and Cyril, leaving in 1911 aged sixteen to travel to Canada. In 1914, he enlisted as a Gunner no. 42523 in the 9th Battery, 3rd Brigade, Canadian Field Artillery. He was nineteen.

Younger still was the previously mentioned, Jack Lethbridge Chubb, also just nineteen in the infamous summer of 1914. Born on the 23rd July 1895 in Hampstead, he attended prep school from 1904 in Walmer on the Kent coast, later going to Keswick Grammar School and St Georges (mixed) school in Harpenden, Hertfordshire. In January 1911, aged fifteen, he spent his final two years of schooling at St Olave's. Like the others, Jack found his way to a farming life in Canada, but in his case with different motives. His disinterest in academic pursuits was of significant concern to his parents, Thomas, the secretary of an ironworks and wife Anne, who arranged for his despatch to Ontario to spend time working in agriculture to teach him the 'harsh facts of life'. His arrival in 1913 didn't allow him much time to achieve his parents hopes, and in late 1915, he enlisted as a Private no. 158050 in the 19th Canadian Infantry or Central Ontario Regiment. His remaining siblings, Edith, his elder sister, and younger brothers, Thomas and Richard, remained at home.

Before the War, the Canadian military mostly comprised part time militia-men aged between eighteen and sixty with average health. The 'permanent' militia totalled 3,110 men in 1914, whose idea of active service was the protection of Halifax and Nova Scotia harbours. They received three weeks training per year. Partly due to this situation, Minister of Militia and defence, Sam Hughes, decided to send a Canadian Expeditionary Force to Europe instead of mobilising existing units. The C.E.F. called for new volunteers, that were formed into numbered battalions each with eight companies. Four battalions made a Canadian brigade. Hughes spared no expense, collecting over 32,000 men at a massive camp at Valcartier in Quebec province, where organisation, clothing, fitness, training and transit arrangements were made. As the war progressed, the original area militia's developed their own battalions, so that by 1917, over 260 different areas were represented. Only two battalions were outside the C.E.F., the Patricia's and the Royal Canadians.

The 1st Canadian Division was the first to arrive in Great Britain and also the first to arrive at the Front in February 1915. The 2nd Division arrived in time for the battle of Loos in September at which point the Canadian Army Corps was formed. By the start of the Somme campaign in July 1916, two other divisions had been added. During the war, 595,000 Canadians enlisted, of whom 418,000 C.E.F. soldiers saw service overseas. 14,500 reservists returned to Canada to re enlist. Over 20,000 Canadians served outside the C.E.F., mostly with the Royal Flying Corps and the Royal Naval Air Service. The introduction of conscription at the end of 1917, had little effect, as most had volunteered anyway. By the Armistice, Canada has sustained over 200,000 casualties. With 56,500 soldiers dead, a very high casualty rate of 48%.

Gunner Vyvyan Lovekin, kitted out with 1903 service uniform with detachable red shoulder straps, and bronze C.E.F. badge, comprising Maple Leaf, Crown and the word 'Canada', arrived in Belgium in early 1915, with the 1st Canadian Division. His battery was based at the Pilckem Ridge, north east of the town of Ypres as artillery support to the 3rd Brigade. On 22nd April, the Germans had pounded the Ridge all morning with heavy artillery. The day was sunny and very warm with little breeze, the latter being what the enemy needed, before releasing its first major poison gas attack. The chosen destination of the deadly 'fog' being the Canadians and French Algerians defending Pilckem.

The panic retreat of the Algerians on connection with the gas, exposed a devastating hole in the line, opening the way to Ypres. The cool control exhibited by Brigadier General Turner's Canadians saved the day. Despite no respiratory protection from the mustard gas, and the obvious fear, pain, blinding and asphyxiation, the Canadian infantrymen stood their ground. Curiously, this lack of physical movement lessened the effect and it was later found that those that stood up on the fire step had a better chance of survival than those at the bottom of the trench, as the gas would stay there.

Vyvyan, sadly, was one of the casualties. Gassed in the initial attacks on the afternoon of the 22nd, he was moved to a casualty clearing station in the rear, where the lack of facilities and medical understanding of the effects of gas was acute. It is difficult to imagine the gunner's last hours. He was buried behind the lines on the 23rd at Poperinghe Old Military Cemetery. He was a mere twenty years old. Two days later, the Germans released more gas on the poor Canadians at Keerselare, but Ypres was held. A doctor in the Royal Army Medical Corps was quoted as saying 'It was most dramatic, long, long, lines of Canadian soldiers, single file, each man with his hand on the shoulder of the man in front. There would be a man in front who could see – all these other chaps couldn't; hundreds and hundreds of these chaps stumbling along, single file'.

'Sanctuary Wood' lies just south of the villages of Bellewaarde and Hooge, south of the Menin Road and east of Ypres. The wood today, owned by a French businessman, is kept as it was found in November 1918, with preserved trenches, rusting metal, live but buried ammunition, barbed wire, mud, water and dead tree stumps. It is one of the few places in modern Belgium where there is still a hint of the desolation of the Front in 1916. Sanctuary Wood was on the Front line after the second battle of Ypres. No Mans Land ran through the wood, and both sides observed each others defences and snipers through the trees. Private John Durant of the Saskatchewan Light Horse was based here in 1916.

On Friday, the 2nd June, the Germans initiated a new barrage on the line at Hooge. The Ypres-Roulers railway was one target. The British 2nd Army covering this sector sustained heavy casualties from shell and shrapnel wounds. The Allied trench line was broken by the artillery bombardment and a 700 yard deep 'bulge', 3000 yards in length was created. The three divisions of the Canadian Corps, of which John Durant was a part, together with the British

20 Division, suffered very badly. Major-General Malcolm Mercer was killed at Mount Sorrel and General Williams was wounded and taken prisoner. The next day the Canadians counter-attacked to recover the lost trenches. Three days later, the Germans realised new territory gains at Hooge, by which time, John Durant had been killed by an exploding shell. He was reported missing on the 5th and as his body was never found, he was commemorated on the Menin Gate Memorial in Ypres. A week later, the remaining tenacious Canadian troops recaptured Zillebeke-Sanctuary Wood. Private Durant's Light Horsemen went on to endure the battles of Arras in April 1917, Hill 70, Third Ypres, Amiens, the Hindenburg Line and finished the war in the pursuit to Mons. The 'horseman' was thirty-three years old.

Bertie Spencer-Smith became known by the name 'Prahn' at school. He was one of two sons of Percy Ledger Smith, a doctor of medicine, and his wife Helena. Sadly, Percy had died in 1899 quite young leaving Helena to bring up the boys. Bertie was a boy of great community spirit, starting up the boy scout troop associated with St Peter's Church on Dartmouth Hill Road in Blackheath. With his twin brother, Ernie, he trained as a sunday school teacher and worked by day as a warehouseman at Messr's Spicer's in Upper Thames Street. Prahn was remembered clearly by both school masters and army colleagues alike. A man 'devoted to duty, charming and full of goodness and an advocate of splendid isolation'. His officers in the famous 49th, the Patricia's, described him as 'supremely the man to be a stretcher-bearer, for in him there were depths of compassion, strength, and tenderness to which pain and suffering made an irresistible appeal'.

Prahn arrived in England with the 49th in late 1914, where he undertook basic training, before embarking from Southampton for the front. After Vyvyan Lovekin was gassed at Pilckem in April 1915, Prahn defended with the infantry at Frezenberg, north east of Ypres. The Germans bombarded the British 'V Corps' on the 8th May – the Patricia's were reported for the gallantry of their combined stand. The 84th Brigade of some 3,000 men was almost entirely wiped out, but only 1,000 yards of land was ceded.

THE CANADIAN CONTINGENT

The battle continued for five days. On 24th May, the Patricia's were again in action at Bellewaarde, this time equipped with some basic, British issue, flannel bag gas masks, which came into use when the Germans released a gas cloud over a five mile front at 3am the following morning. The ending of the Ypres campaign a few days later, gave some much needed rest. The Patricia's were next involved in a major action the following June at Mount Sorrel, the scene of Mercer and Durant's demise.

By this time, Prahn had seen terrible things, and his religious beliefs were all that sustained his spirit and kept him going. 'Without other strength than my own, I could not play the man in the face of danger, though I walk through the valley of the shadow of death, I will feel no evil, for thou art with me – that is the key to my strength'. For nine days, Prahn went into No Mans Land in the mud and shell holes of Zillebeke and Sanctuary Wood, amidst heavy shelling, and came through without injury. Over the next few weeks, the Patricia's moved south to the Somme Valley ready for the 'Push'. They were spared early involvement in July, and were next engaged in the tank attack at Flers Courcelette on 15th September.

From 06.20 hours, after waiting patiently in trenches for the obligatory forty minute Allied shelling to finish, Prahn and two Canadian divisions joined twelve other divisions in advancing on foot following the new 'creeping' barrage tactic. 32 of the first 49 tanks were also employed as an experiment. The six mile Front progressed 3,000 yards, successfully taking Flers, Martinpuich, Courcelette and High Wood within five hours. Other British advances on Les Boeufs and French advances on Santerre were markedly less successful and lack of fresh reserves limited the early success. On the following day, the British repulsed a counter-attack near Courcelette but five new German divisions were deployed to avoid further damage.

Prahn was killed in action by shelling in the thick of the action, helping wounded to get back to the line. The stretcher-bearer was reported missing and his body was not recovered. He is commemorated on the Vimy Memorial, as an adopted Canadian. He was twenty-four.

Meanwhile, armed with his Ross rifle, (part designed by an Olavian contemporary) and wearing his leather 'tump-line' strapping for carrying equipment, Private Arthur Laurie of the 8th Battalion, fought his way through the Mount Sorrel campaign in the south of Sanctuary Wood, and then moved south to Flers Courcelette in preparation for the battle of Thiepval Ridge and Combles, due to commence two weeks later. He had proven to be the best marksman in the 14th platoon of 'D' company, and was recommended for a commission. His refusal was based on the fact that he had heard that Canadian officers were not being sent to the front. Instead he endured the worst of battle conditions and regularly volunteered to go out into No Mans Land as a stretcher-bearer to rescue the wounded.

In the midst of all the devastation to the French terrain, Arthur, a keen naturalist, took every opportunity to pick and press available cornflowers and send them with his letters home. In possibly his last letter before his death, he wrote 'It is curious how one grows accustomed even to this ghastly work, and you forget the danger to yourself when you are getting some poor beggars into safety. I am enclosing some cornflowers I picked as I was sitting in a trench. It seemed queer in this awful place to see the dear little flowers; they carried me back to the prairie with its countless blossoms. Please God, I shall soon be back there'.

Tuesday 26th September was a day of fine weather on the Somme with a temperature of 75 degrees fahrenheit. The 56 Division of Londoners advanced from their trenches to capture the town of Combles, the 11th and 18th Divisions pushed east of Thiepval to fight for Mouquet Farm, and the 1st and 2nd Canadian Divisions of '111 Corps' moved on the German trench system around Flers and Courcelette.

Arthur Laurie's 8th Battalion crossed the 400 yards to Sudbury Trench and occupied it. A subsequent advance succeeded in taking

THE CANADIAN CONTINGENT

the eastern end of Kenora Trench, where German bombing attacks were repulsed. In the evening, the 8th were enfiladed with machine gun fire from the left, but still took Zollern Trench and then pushed on to a further objective. On one of these occasions, according to his officer, Lieutenant Maund, Arthur was hit by several machine gun bullets as he climbed onto the parapet with his stretcher in hand. He died instantly and fell back into the trench. He was carried to the rear and was later buried at the Courcelette British Cemetery. The 'naturalist' was twenty-seven. The 8th Canadians, comprising the men of Manitoba, went on to fight in 1917 at Arras, and in 1918 at Amiens, the Hindenburg Line and in the pursuit to Mons.

Jack Chubb, the Ontario farmer, had enlisted in the 81st Battalion, the Canadian Force in late 1915 and was transferred to the 19th Battalion before boarding HMS Olympic to make the crossing to England in May 1916. He arrived in France in September, but his unit did not go into action until the Arras campaign of March and April 1917. During this series of engagements, he was badly wounded by snipers and was sent home to England by hospital ship. His recuperation took four months and he didn't return to his unit until August, thereby missing his comrade's glorious success in the tunnels of Vimy. His return was unfortunately timed.

Within weeks, he was embroiled briefly in the muddy hell of the battles of Passchendaele where he was slightly wounded, remaining in the casualty clearing station for three more weeks. Making it through to the spring of 1918, his battalion and the rest of the Canadian Army Corps were swiftly and secretly moved south to Amiens, ready for the Allied advance through Picardy. The Germans, although expecting an attack, thought it would come further south, and when it started with a great artillery bombardment on the 8th August, they believed it to be a diversionary attack. It was however the real thing and was conducted in heavy fog, which had been accurately forecast by Allied meteorologists.

The attack was a success with many German reserves captured in the melee, and one Australian battalion advancing nine miles with only three casualties. Retreating enemy troops blocked the roads to Peronne where they had to deal with active Royal Flying Corps Bombers. Chaos reigned. The Canadians crossed the River Lure and marched eight miles into enemy territory. This was clearly a turning point in the long stalemate war. Jack Chubb, who had climbed out of his trench to push further forward, was cut down by machine gun fire and died instantly. The farmer had just turned twenty-three and had learned his parents 'facts of life'. He was buried at Crucifix Corner Cemetery in the town of Villers-Bretonneaux east of Amiens, close to where he fell.

The Canadian Army brought much to the Western Front, their baseball practice, their unquenchable optimism, their bawdy humour, their higher rates of pay, their will to win and their ex-patriot Englishmen, none more typical than the five 'Olavian Fallen'.

CHAPTER 20
The Kaiser's Offensive

After their inability to capitalise on the success of the tank breakthrough during the battle of Cambrai just prior to Christmas 1917, the British Army began to turn their attention to better fortifying the entire Front line of defence from Ypres in the north, to St Quentin in the south. A fresh line structure was developed, so that a forward zone was protected by well constructed defensive redoubts, with the intention of engaging and delaying the oncoming enemy. These redoubts would only be manned with a small number of infantry, equipped with occasional machine guns. Three thousand yards to the rear of the forward lines lay larger, deeper dug redoubts holding the mass of troops. It was thought that an increasingly tired advancing enemy, once engaged by the forward line, would then have to move on over a large battle zone area, before meeting the main defence. A third line, known as the 'green Line' had also been approved, an indication of Haig's acceptance that discretionary retreat could be necessary, and was set four miles behind the battle zone. In reality, this line was given scant attention and consisted of no more, in some places, than a belt of barbed wire.

By late 1917, the German High Command under Ludendorff had regained the initiative, after the surprise dominance of the use of tanks by the Allies the previous year. They had recognised that the British had weakened their defences in the Arras/St Quentin sector, to pour reserves into the Passchendaele campaign in Flanders – 46 divisions compared to the 14 under General Gough in Arras. Furthermore, it was clear to Ludendorff that Haig's primary concern was not the provision of more and more support to the French commander, Foch, in the south, but to ensure that the enemy never got through Ypres to the channel ports. The German Field Marshal was also aided by a new tactical fighting theory tried and tested on the Eastern front, Geyer's tactically employed 'Storm Troopers', a sudden and great replenishment of troops available for the Western Front, due to the cessation of hostilities with both Russia and Romania, and finally, a new approach to intensive artillery bombardment, as practised in Italy by General Oscar Von Hutier and his Chief Gunner, Bruchmuller.

The build up in troops, guns, and rehearsal took place throughout January and February 1918, so that by the night of the 20th March, the Germans had moved up sufficient infantry to the lines opposite the new Allied 'forward line redoubts' in the Arras/St Quentin sector to outnumber their opponents by at least four to one. Over a million German soldiers would soon advance behind a creeping barrage along a fifty mile line, to test Haig's new battle zone areas and 'green line'. Bruchmuller had positioned over 6,000 big guns, with specific targets to bombard the Allies in six stages over a period of five hours before the late evening attack commenced.

The British officers and soldiers of the third, fourth and fifth armies were not prepared, detailed intelligence had not revealed the scale of the attack, even though General Gough had advised the location to Haig repeatedly and to no avail. Along the front, it was obvious to senior Allied officers that the British divisions were spread too thinly on too broad a front, and that men were short in number both for fighting and for preparing fortifications. The intensity of the forthcoming attack caused many thousands of Allied casualties amongst whom fifteen Old Olavians were destined to fall. Eight of the men were officers, all in different line regiments; Two held the rank of captain and were contemporary at School – Sid Terry served with the 1st Battalion, the Wiltshire Regiment near Bapaume; Lionel Harvard, a captain in the 1st Battalion, the Grenadier Guards, based at Boisleux-au-Mont, on the outskirts of Arras, knew Captain Terry well, from their years at the School, from 1905 to 1910, when Lionel left to attend Harvard, the American University, (bearing the same name as his illustrious ancestor). A little later Sid moved on himself, to Oxford.

THE KAISER'S OFFENSIVE

The three lieutenants ranged in age from twenty-eight to thirty-two; One had latterly been a master at St Olave's – Cecil Edmunds from 1911 to 1915, and had run the cadet corps with a fellow master, Grantley Le Chavetois; the other two were old boys whose years had just missed ; Jack Lidgett, son of the renowned London social reformer, Doctor Scott Lidgett, was based at Muille Villette, near Peronne, to the south of the line; the younger Dudley Phare, son of George Phare, Chairman of the Bible Crusade, served with the 7th Battalion, the King's Shropshire Light Infantry at Henin-sur-Cogeuil, south east of Arras.

Completing the Olavian officers were three second lieutenants; the eldest, Harry West, serving as adjutant to General Watson, was based at Beaucourt L'Abbaye near Arras with the 1st Battalion, the King's Royal Rifle Corps; 'Wee Willie' Cook, of the 4th Yorkshires and George Smith of the 8th Royal Lancaster Regiment were 'dug in' near Wancourt, in the Arras section of the line.

Of the ranking soldiers, there were seven Olavians; The eldest man, in fact, eldest of all Olavians to fall, (with the exception of the ex Olavian pupil and master, Harold Ryley Senior), was Lance Corporal Beaumont Fletcher of the 13th Battalion, Royal Sussex Regiment at Tincourt, near Peronne. Rifleman Charles Ellis of the 10th South Wales Borderers, nearly ten years younger, was part of a 'bombing team' near Pozieres; Private Stephen Bishopp of the 17th Londons, recently awarded the Military Medal for gallantry at Cambrai, occupied trenches at La Vacquerie, and Private James Shore of the 14th Royal Warwickshires, who had only recently transferred to Flanders from the Italian Expeditionary Force, found himself in unpleasant circumstances in the north at Ploegsteert on the outskirts of Ypres. Private Harry Chester of the 1st Royal Guernsey Light Infantry, also at Ploegsteert, continued the parade of Olavian youth present in spring 1918. At nineteen, Harry was only three weeks older than his school friend, Marcus Veale-Williams serving as a rifleman with the 28th Londons (Artist's Rifles) at Neuville Bourjonval near Cambrai. The list is completed by Private Oswald

Plowman of the 17th King's Royal Rifle Corps serving at Templena near Pozieres.

The early morning hours of the 21st March 1918 stood out in the memory of the Allied survivors of the campaign. At exactly 04.40 hours, a terrific noise began, upstaging the Somme bombardments of 1916 by a considerable margin. 6,473 guns and 3,532 trench mortars started firing on the Allied, front and secondary lines. After five hours, with the British lines of communication virtually destroyed, the German infantry assault began with Geyer's 'storm troopers' prodding, testing and piercing the new British defences at various points, covered by, not only a creeping barrage, but also by a thick and convenient fog and mist. Poison gas shells had been fired long range at Allied artillery targets with great accuracy, nullifying their effectiveness. The British forward line redoubts were quickly overrun, with many prisoners taken. Other manned redoubts, unable to see the approaching enemy, were also unable to provide covering fire in support to their comrades. Breakthrough was particularly fast in the area of the greatest Allied weakness, where the British and French troops met, near the Crozat Canal, between Peronne and St Quentin.

By the end of the 21st, the British had endured over 38,000 casualties with a further 21,000 troops taken prisoner. By the 23rd, after a further deterioration, the Fifth Army had been pushed back over 12 miles. German long range guns began bombarding Paris.

Captain Edmunds of the First Surrey Rifles, an experienced man of modest and unassuming character, was the first Olavian to be reported 'killed in action' on the 23rd, whilst his battalion tried to hold the line near Fins, just north of the German thrust towards the Crozat Canal. Cecil was the youngest son and fifth child of eight of Alfred Edmunds, a draper, grocer, coal and flour merchant originally from Sussex and living in Soham, Cambridgeshire with wife, Marion. He had two older brothers, Alfred and John, two older sisters, Evelyn and Annie, and three younger brothers, Reginald, Claude and Guy. Later he was also to be husband to Ada with a baby son, born just weeks before his death. Cecil was buried in Fins New British Cemetery. He was twenty-eight.

Cecil Harry Edmunds, born on 21st February 1890 in Soham Cambridgeshire, became an Olavian, not as a pupil, but as a young, enthusiastic master of chemistry, replacing his predecessor, Freeman in 1911. A twenty-one year old science graduate from Downing College, Cambridge, Cecil became renowned for his extra-curricular activities with his great friend, 'Chavvy', Grantley Le Chavetois. In 1914, after an impromptu officer training course at Cambridge, both men returned to Tooley Street to form the School Cadet Corps and build on Mr Weaver's previous training work. Cecil Edmunds took no little responsibility for equipping jingoistic, but naïve and immature schoolboys with a sense of the realities of army life – the unpleasantness of the work, the discipline and above all, the danger.

Many of the Olavians who survived the conflict, owed much to their experiences in the School Cadet Corps. After the first Camp at Bitton, he was appointed corps adjutant, then promptly passed his job to another and took a commission in the corps affiliated Territorial Regiment, the 21st Londons (First Surrey Rifles). By late 1916, he was still in England, as his superiors had realised his significant abilities by making him an instructor at the training camp at Winchester. A year later, he finally arrived at the Front, only just surviving the battle of Messines Ridge. The 'Kaisers Offensive' found him in the wrong place at the wrong time. Casualties in his battalion were heavy. Another brilliant scholar, with such potential, had been lost.

Captain Sidney Frederick Terry of the 1st Wiltshires, had meanwhile, been given orders by his colonel, whilst under heavy shelling, to collect all the men he could muster and to hold the advancing enemy at all costs. A neat, orderly man of great inner strength and conviction, he remained in the thick of battle, until he was, quite simply, the last of his rearguard group remaining, at which point he too was shot, whilst carrying out his orders. He was awarded a posthumous Military Cross with a citation that read:

> "For the most conspicuous and constant good service and consistent devotion to duty from September 22nd 1917 to March 24th 1918. This Officer has maintained the very highest standard of courage, energy and efficiency as Adjutant in the Battalion. On all occasions when there has been heavy shelling or when danger is more than usually imminent, this Officer has, at once, on his own initiative, been on the spot, organising, directing and supervising, in a manner beyond all praise. His great coolness under the most trying circumstances, his foresight and indefatigable energy, have on many occasions proved themselves invaluable to the Battalion".

His M.C. award was announced in the supplement to the London Gazette on the 3rd June 1918:

> "T.Lt (A/Capt.) Sidney Frederick Terry. Wilts. R.".

Sidney Frederick Terry was the second youngest of five children, born on the 7th June 1894 to Tom Terry, secretary of a timber company and his wife, Florence, both from London. Along with his brothers, Thomas and Ernest, he attended St Olave's, spending nine full years there, leaving to go up to Oxford with fellow schoolboys, Jack Gill, Olly Wade, 'Didi' Maybrook and 'Chavvy' Le Chavetois. He was perceived, whilst at the School, as a youth of 'quiet, good nature', with a 'shy reluctance for the limelight'. His subsequent years at Oxford, followed by his short army career, marked him out as a 'conscientious, helpful' officer, always 'cheerful, courageous and unselfish'. Although he had originally enlisted as Private no. 2579 in the Artists, the 28th Londons, he was quickly commissioned and later acted as adjutant to Major Sholto Ogilvie, who on hearing of his death, wrote to the School, that:

THE KAISER'S OFFENSIVE

"For the three years of the heaviest fighting on the Western Front – calling for the utmost endurance that anyone is capable of – he served with my Battalion. No job was too hard for him. No work too much for him. He was of invaluable assistance. No better soldier could be found along the front. His charm of manner and character brought him innumerable friends and never an enemy. Personally, I am most proud to have been associated with him".

Following the deaths of these two fine officers, came a young rifleman of the Artists, Marcus Veale-Williams, the enthusiastic son of Bermondsey Alderman John Veale Williams of Vanbrugh Park, Blackheath, a well known local official. Born in November 1898, Marcus had studied at St Olave's for five years leaving in summer 1914 at fifteen, to take up fruit farming in Kent. In early 1916, he tried to enlist in the Inns of Court Officer Training Corps, and then the Honourable Artillery Company, both to no avail due to his age. In 1917, he eventually joined the 5th Londons, the London Rifle Brigade, as a Private no.305327 in the 3rd Battalion, home based. For one so keen to fight the 'Hun', he endured months of square bashing first at Dawlish, and later at Farnborough, only getting to France in early March 1918. Within a week, he was transferred to the Artists and was in the Front line near Cambrai.

On the night of the 20th March, the Artists had just been relieved and had marched for some rest at Havrincourt, when their orders were countermanded and they had to return to the front to defend against the enemy offensive. They had been roused from just two hours sleep and were dead on their feet. By the 23rd, they had evacuated their base at Neuville and had moved back to Ytres. Whilst at a temporary halt, a shell burst close by, killing two and injuring more, Marcus being wounded in the leg. As another retreat was ordered, based on new field intelligence, a comrade and a Red Cross man did their best to tie several tourniquets around his wound to stem the bleeding, expecting him to be taken prisoner quite quickly. It was later revealed that the advancing enemy did not arrive at that point for another eight hours, by which time, Marcus had bled to death. A final comment on this tragic episode, taken from Herbert Morriss's book, *Bermondsey's 'Bit' in the Greatest War*, suggests that "it was the blowing up by our own men of our own dumps, and that young Veale-Williams was killed by one of our own shells. More's the pity of it". He was reported missing in action and is commemorated on the Arras Memorial.

The death of Jack Lidgett was a considerable loss to civic and social life in Bermondsey. The thirty-two year old son of Doctor Scott Lidgett, Warden of the 'Bermondsey Settlement' and his wife Emmeline from Monmouthshire, Jack was an Old Olavian, leader of the Bermondsey Boy's Brigade, honarary legal adviser to the fledgling National Society for the Prevention of Cruelty to Children, and secretary of the Insurance Society with over 4,000 members. He had taken a classical tripos at Emmanuel College, Cambridge as an Exhibitioner, followed by a law tripos and LL.B. He came second in the Law Society intermediate examinations in 1910.

John Cuthbert Lidgett, born in August 1885 in Wolverhampton, Staffordshire with one sister two years his junior, Lettice, is remembered as a man of 'social conscience' sympathetic and shy, but with a great resolve, passed down to him by his father's example. He stands high in the list of young men whose future promise was tragically cut short by the War. He had spent nine full years at St Olave's, leaving in 1904, aged nineteen. His indispensable work at the Bermondsey Settlement, delayed his immediate inclination to enlist in the summer of 1914. Late the following year, with the war still raging, he decided to enlist and joined the 28th Londons as a Private no.7353, later taking a commission as a Lieutenant in the 11th Battalion, the South Lancashire Regiment. By Arras in 1917, he was second in command in his company. Based at Muille-Villette, near Ham in the southern section of the line, he was killed instantly, on Palm Sunday, the 24th March, by a sniper's bullet, whilst covering the retreat of his company. His major wrote of his bravery, nobility of spirit, his modesty and his care for others.

THE KAISER'S OFFENSIVE

Also on the 24th, Second Lieutenant Harold Douglas West of the 1st Kings Royal Rifle Corps was shot by a series of machine gun bullets in his lower spine at Eaucourt L'Abbaye. He was wounded at a critical point in an enemy counter attack. West's company formed the rearguard, which was in the process of falling back to another position, with the overpowering enemy advancing around their right flank. Harry was thirty-five years old, and clung to life for a day, dying of his wounds in a temporary shelter, with no formal medical help available, such was the nature of the 'Kaisers Offensive'. General Watson wrote of his 'magnificent work as acting adjutant to me in all the Cambrai fighting'. His Colonel referred to 'an absolutely invaluable officer who has done splendid work during those most trying days of retirement where his cheerfulness and disregard of danger were a great example to his men'.

Harry was born on the 22nd April 1882, with a younger brother, Cyril, both sons of John West, a tea dealer and grocer of Forest Hill and his wife, Ellen. He spent only three years at the School, joining at the same time at Jack Lidgett, Fred Defries and John Durant. By 1899, he had begun work as a bank clerk for the London City and Midland Bank, where he stayed for four years. He then moved to the Mercantile Bank of India and within a further three years, in 1907 was married, to Edith from Kennington. His decision to leave the bank, aged thirty-two and a married man, to enlist in the late summer of 1914, was prevented by his employers. This led him to volunteer as a special constable with sergeant rank. He also joined the London Territorials, where he learnt how to handle a rifle. By early 1916, after he had fully trained another to take his place in the bank, he left to join the Inns of Court Officer Training Corps based at Berkhampstead. Within weeks, such was the impression he made, he was offered a permanent position there as sergeant instructor, which he turned down, to become a commissioned officer in the King's Royal Rifle Corps. He was at the Front in France by March of 1917. Harry West lasted longer than many junior officers, but not long enough to see his only daughter born just two weeks after her father's death.

Beaumont 'Montie' Fletcher was forty-two when he died; he had spent four years of his youth at St Olave's where he was a contemporary and lifelong friend of H.G.Abel, the headmaster who would replace Rushbrooke shortly after the War. His father, Alfred Fletcher, the editor of the Daily Chronicle, originally from Lincolnshire, lived first at Camberwell then later at Ealing, from where Montie travelled each day to the School in Bermondsey. He was the third of nine children born to mother, Rebecca, from Redhill, with four younger brothers, Ruskin, Alfred, Cavendish and Wilfred.

Having taken a degree in English literature at St Andrews, he took a junior position as a journalist in Fleet Street in 1897, working for his father's paper and the Manchester Despatch. Within ten years, he was the London Editor and Parliamentary Correspondent of the Northern Mail and the Chronicle, lecturing on Art in his spare time for the London County Council, and devising artwork for 'Greater London' a new publication. By the outbreak of war, he had succeeded in having a monograph on Richard Wilson published. His wife, Florence, whom he had married in 1907, at home in Streatham, wasn't keen for him to enlist, and tried to persuade him to allow younger single men to go. His step-son, Percy Armitage was 16 when war broke out and they had a very young son of their own, Alfred Vincent Fletcher who was just 5. Nevertheless, Montie decided to enlist in the Army for home defence as many thought that invasion was likely. When he found that this was not the case, he transferred to the 13th Royal Sussex Regiment and went to France in 1917.

Having survived the Cambrai offensive, his battalion moved to Peronne in the spring of 1918. Four days into the 'Kaisers offensive', on the 25th March, Lance Corporal Fletcher no. TF/290298 was fighting a rearguard action at the village of Tincourt, when he was struck by machine gun fire. His battalion had been badly decimated,

THE KAISER'S OFFENSIVE

and it was not possible to recover his body. Initially he was posted as missing, before an eye witness to his death, came forward. He was later commemorated on the Pozieres Memorial.

The circumstances of the death of 'Wee' Cook are still shrouded in mystery. According to the School magazine, as a second lieutenant in the 4th Yorkshires, the Green Howards, he was reported missing presumed killed on the 28th March 1918. As all of his fellow officers were also killed on that day, no report exists of his actions. However, the War Graves Commission locate his grave in the St Roch Communal Cemetery in Valenciennes, a French town, very much behind the lines in March 1918, to the north east of Cambrai. Elsewhere in the magazine, it is suggested that he was taken prisoner and died in Germany. If this is the case, it is likely that he was wounded in the first few days of battle and was forced to surrender.

William Edwin Cook, born on the 21st February 1894 in Dulwich, was the son of William Cook, a wine presser from Brompton near Kensington and his wife Eliza from Buckinghamshire. He spent four years at the School, arriving with a London County Council scholarship from Bellenden Road (Higher Grade) School. His masters remembered him as quiet, manly for his age and extremely keen on natural history – butterflies in particular. In Denmark Hill, he was secretary of the local Boy's club and a local sunday school teacher. He had one older sister, Mary and a younger brother, Sidney.

His athletic prowess afforded him a position in the 8th Yorkshires as sergeant instructor of gymnastics, at least until he took on the role of regimental quarter master stores in France in August 1915. Two years later, he was commissioned with the Howards, preparing to defend the line at Cambrai. Right up to the first shells of the offensive, 'Wee' Cook was sending letters of hope home to his friends and family, with pressed butterflies in the pages. After he was declared missing, his butterfly net was sent home with his kit, showing signs of recent use.

By the 28th, the vast successes in breakthrough by the German infantry was slowing down. Advancing and often drunken, they were looting Allied supplies to supplement their half rations and poor quality clothing. The further they advanced, the more troop congestion occurred, allowing rich pickings for the increasingly powerful pilots of the Royal Flying Corps. The elite storm troopers had suffered heavy casualties and were hard to replace. German motorised vehicles and tanks were unreliable after years of blockade. Ludendorff had simply not expected such a breakthrough, and proved unable to strike the final blow.

Oswald Cheyney Plowman also went missing on the 28th March 1918. He was a rifleman in the 17th King's Royal Rifle Corps, part of 39 Division, Fifth Army, based in the southern part of the line near Pargny. His battalion were giving ground, when they came under fierce fire. Oswald was shot and killed at Templena. His sergeant described him as 'brave careful and good – the light of his battalion, and its peacemaker'. He was twenty-four years old and the only child born to Bermondsey draper, Bert Plowman and wife Ada, who had moved from Hampshire and Suffolk villages to settle in Southwark Park Road. Oswald had spent five years at St Olave's leaving in 1910 to train as a banker with the Union of London and Smiths Bank. Described as a boy with 'zest and a glad confidence', he did not have a strong constitution: He was rejected from early enlistment several times due to his poor eyesight, until, with hundreds of thousands already slain, the recruitment offices had become less particular. Arriving in France in July 1917, he endured trench fever, a septic hand and gas poisoning, all before his final demise less than a year later.

George Smith was the 'quiet hero' of the 8th Royal Lancaster Regiment at Arras. Although reported as missing on the 28th March, a fellow officer writing to his father held out little hope. "Your son and myself were in charge of the Front line trenches with eighty men. We were surrounded, but were still holding out five hours after our headquarters in the rear had been captured. The Front on our right was broken, and we were forced to retire, but we came very heavily under machine gun fire and only eight in all escaped being casualties, and they were made prisoners. Your son went down under a fusillade and did not rise again. I could not get to him, and do not know that he is actually dead, but I dare not now hold out any hope".

George William Smith was born on the 17th August 1898, to sister Marguerite and brother Charles, children of George Smith, a Rotherhithe provisions dealer and wife, Emma, earning a council place from Silwood Street School to Tooley Street in 1910. Amongst his contemporaries were Marcus Veale-Williams and Harry Chester. He remained at the School with his reputation for 'confidence', and 'cheerful bearing' until late in 1915, when he left aged seventeen, to enlist. By this stage of the War, the Army was happy to give commissions to under aged schoolboys with zero training, but the right type of education. By 1918, they were the 'fresh blood'. Fortunately, George was a young man of exceptional character – 'there was always a rush of volunteers to go out on patrol with Second Lieutenant Smith'.

At twenty-four, Dudley Phare was a partner in the accounting firm of Woodman Cox & Co, in Basinghall Street in the City. He was also a fervent evangelist touring the local Bermondsey lodging houses looking for converts. As the only son, with one sister Beatrice, of George Phare, commercial clerk, F.A.A., and the Chairman of the Bible Crusade, he had a comfortable life ahead of him. Even as a commissioned officer in the Army, he was protected by his skills from getting too close to the Front line danger.

Lieutenant Dudley Gershom Phare became a senior accountant for the Royal Army Supply Corps in late 1914 but, like many others, sought battle experience without prior knowledge of what it really meant. He was attached to the 7th Kings Shropshire Light Infantry in 1917 and based near Arras late in the year. On the 28th March 1918, as the German advance was slowing, and the Allied Forces were starting to dig in a new front line, Dudley was struck in the head by a sniper's bullet early in the morning whilst striding along a hastily made and poorly defended, Front line trench at the village of Henin-Sur-Cogeuil. He was killed instantly. Rapid retreat again meant that his body had to be left for the Germans to find and bury. Consequently, the location of his remains are unknown and he is commemorated on the Arras Memorial.

Towards the end of the month of March, Ludendorff changed his tactics, recognising his communication limitations and advised his divisional commanders to seize Amiens. This decision formed the basis of much of the British infantry defence until the middle of April. On the 30th March, Lionel De Jersey Harvard was killed in action. A captain in 1st Battalion, the Grenadier Guards, he joined his brother Kenneth in the many graves of France and Flanders. Needless to say, the famous Harvard family and to some extent the American media, were shocked by the loss of these two fine young men from such a famous family, and the personal tragedy of the loss of their two remaining boys of three, following the infant death of brother John in 1892.

Lionel was the elder of the two surviving brothers, born on the 3rd June 1893 in London to Thomas Mawson Harvard, manager of the India Rubber Company and his wife Maud de Jersey. He attended St Olave's for seven years entering in 1904 at the same time as such characters as Bob Chapman, Don Ryley and Olly Wade. Howard Keesey was captain of school, when young eleven year old Lionel first walked through the imposing gates of Tooley Street.

He is remembered as a boy of 'unusual charm and simplicity' who made 'steady progress' academically, but who really shone on the athletics field, winning the junior athletics championship. His ancestor, the Reverend John Harvard, a Wesleyan Minister from Plymouth, had been a brother of the founder of Harvard University in Massachusetts, USA. Shortly after leaving St Olave's, he had been offered a place at the University until his graduation early in 1915. As a direct descendant of the founder, he and his new wife, Edith, were subjected to a high level of attention and scrutiny from the American press, which he handled with dignity.

THE KAISER'S OFFENSIVE

He returned to London by boat in late 1915 to enlist in the British Army. His name and standing were responsible for his immediate place on an Inns of Court Officer Training Corps course and his subsequent transfer as a second lieutenant, to the primary battalion of the premier line regiment, the Grenadier Guards. His younger brother, Ken, followed him into the 2nd Battalion. He was in France and Flanders by February 1916. His first major battle was at Ginchy in September, followed quickly by Flers Courcelette and Morval. In 1917, he endured the later months of the Ypres campaign, followed by Cambrai in November.

Whilst advancing with revolver and baton in hand at Ginchy on the Somme in 1916, he had been wounded in the chest by machine gun fire, just a week after hearing of the birth of his son. His recuperation allowed him time at home, and he only returned to his battalion in June 1917 as a newly promoted lieutenant. He was not present at the Guards advance to the Pilckem Ridge where his brother was killed in action, as he had been seconded for 'special duties' with the Royal Engineers.

He returned to France as a captain to command a mixed battalion of reinforcements from the Guard's depot, after leave in late February 1918, leaving his family to grieve the loss of Kenneth. Within two weeks, they were based at the village of Boisleux-au-Mont near Arras.

The Guards regimental war diary for the day of the 30th March, records that at 8am, the enemy 'put down a very heavy bombardment on our front line trenches....strongly supported by minenwerfer'. An hour later, the bombardment is described as becoming 'intense', and at 10.20 am, was accompanied by 'machine gun fire in the back areas which swept down the valley'. At 10.45 am the barrage lifted and was replaced by 'heavy machine gun fire which swept the parapets from the flank in enfilade...assistance was rendered by 14 hostile aeroplanes which fired at the trenches...and also dropped bombs'. The enemy infantry then started to advance up the Sunken Road, believing the Guards to have been either destroyed or demoralised.

The Guards had succeeded in cutting off the advance with enfilade Lewis gun and rifle fire, followed by a strong counter attack. The battalion lost two officers in the advance down the Sunken Road trench – Captain Harvard and Second Lieutenant Mays. The defence was seen as a major success with congratulatory messages from Brigade Headquarters. The enemy, the 452nd and 453rd Regiments, had been prevented from breaking through, at high cost in lives.

Captain Lionel Harvard, twenty-four, husband and father, had been hit by a 'minenwerfer' and killed instantly. He was laid to rest in a civilian cemetery at Boisleux.

Harry Chester and James Shore were both declared 'missing in action' at Ploegsteert near Ypres, in the north of the line between the 13th and the 14th April. Harry was just a day older than James, born on fireworks night, 1898, the second son of John Chester, a railway engine driver and his wife Kate of New Cross. His elder brother, Charles, was seven years his senior. Harry attended the local Alverton Street School. James was the eldest of three sons, including Benjamin and Charles, and a sister, Rebecca, born to Jim Shore of Stepney, a brewer's storekeeper and his wife, Amelia.

Harry was the first to enter Tooley Street in 1910 for six years, with James, following a year later and staying for just four years, leaving in 1914. Harry was remembered by his masters as a steady, persistent and unassuming boy, whilst James is described as a boy with 'cheerful outlook, affectionate nature, and a simple steadfastness'. Harold Thomas Chester became an examiner for the Port of London Authority, and James Harold Shore, after a spell as clerk in the Topical Press, and as an accountant, became clerk to the Surveyor of Taxes at Coventry.

The War changed their lives and their fate. Harry enlisted as a Private no. 1758 in the 1st Battalion, the Royal Guernsey Light Infantry, embarking for Belgium in late 1917 having refused a commission to remain with his comrades; James became a Private no. 25343 in the 14th Battalion, the Warwickshire Regiment, reaching the Italian front as part of the expeditionary force during

THE KAISER'S OFFENSIVE

a similar period. By April 1918, both men found themselves in Ploegsteert Wood in Belgium, James having arrived on the 9th, straight from Italy. The Wood, known by the tommies as 'Plug Street', provided a degree of shelter for vast numbers of men, as many as a million, throughout the war. A 'labyrinth of paths and drives', it was returned to British hands in summer 1917.

On the 10th April, the battle of Messines, just north of the Wood, began, as part of the second great German offensive, code named 'Georgette'. The bombardment and infantry attacks focused on the line from Wytschaete to Givenchy and Armentieres. Ludendorff had moved Von Quast's Sixth Army and Von Arnim's Fourth Army to the Front. The objective was Hazebrouck, the strategic railway centre. Haig's forces were stronger in this sector than they had been further south, but reserves were in short supply; the advancing Germans were 'trench divisions' and not 'attacking storm-troopers' which limited enemy success. Nevertheless, the heavy shelling led to an easy break through the Allied Portuguese Line at Neuve Chapelle, followed by the German capture of Messines Village and Ridge, and the British evacuation of Armentieres. Within two days, the Germans were five miles from their objective, and Haig was desperately attempting to have Foch urge the reluctant Petain to release French reserves to provide support in Flanders.

It was on the 11th April, that Haig issued one of his more famous 'Orders of the day', saying that 'There is no course open to us but to fight it out. Every position must be held to the last man: there must be no retirement. With our backs to the wall, and believing in the justice of our cause, each one of us must fight on until the end'. The situation was eventually saved by the timely arrival of the British 5th and 33rd Divisions and the Australian 1st Division. James Shore arrived with the Warwicks as part of 5 Division. In the final struggle to contain the German Armies and refuse them access to Hazebrouck, two Olavians went missing. They were not repatriated as prisoners the following year. They were both in the part of the line most obliterated by shell and gun fire.

Private Stephen Bishopp M.M. of the Poplar and Stepney Rifles had been wounded and captured by the Germans towards the end of the first 'Kaisers Offensive' code named 'Mihiel'. Having slogged his way through Ypres, Bourlon Wood and Cambrai in 1917, he had found himself at La Vacquerie, Le Mesnil and Bray Sur Somme in the opening months of the following year. He is the only fallen Old Olavian to be buried in Germany. His grave is in the Berlin South Western Cemetery in the village of Stahnsdorf between Berlin and Potsdam. Severely wounded and untreated, on his capture, he was taken on a series of long uncomfortable journeys to a German hospital in Burg in Germany. Within days of treatment, blood-poisoning developed, and he passed away, aged twenty-eight.

Stephen Bishopp was born in Woking in Surrey on the 15th September 1889, the second of four children, including a brother, Leslie, born to Stephen Bishopp Senior, a building manager and his wife Ada. A boy of quiet retiring nature, unassuming and with integrity, he started his Olavian career in 1901 alongside Ralph Akerman and Herbert Blackman, friends that he had learnt had died in Gallipoli and at Delville Wood respectively. Quite religious, he helped in his spare time at Lewisham Church, and left Tooley Street at Easter 1905 to take a position, as a shipping clerk in the City, where he remained until 1914. As a qualified administrator, he initially enlisted in the Army Pay Corps as Private no. 3768. With the increasingly urgent call by 1917 for all single men to go to the Front, he arranged to transfer to the 17th Londons as Private no. G/68461. On reaching France, he was attached to the Royal Fusiliers. At the battle of Cambrai in November 1917, he won the Military Medal for 'conspicuous bravery on the field'.

The day after Private Bishopp had died as a prisoner of war, Charles Ellis, three years his senior at St Olave's, was blown up in a trench at Pozieres. The thirty-two year old, a bomber with the 10th South Wales Borderers, had originally enlisted as a rifleman with the First Surrey Rifles, 21st Londons then as no. 263065 with the 1st Battalion, the Monmouthshire Regiment. As he crept along an enemy trench system on a bombing patrol, a fragment of enemy shell hit the un-activated grenades in his own greatcoat pockets, and caused massive explosion, killing him instantly.

Charles Albert William Ellis was born on the 7th November 1885, the son of Albert and Phyllis Ellis of New Church Street, Bermondsey. After a spell at the St Olave's elementary School, he attended the School at Tooley Street for just two years together with colleagues William Halliwell, Gordon Ryder and Sid Hill, leaving in 1899 at fourteen to enter business, owing to his father's premature death. Working his way up the firm, he held a responsible managerial position by the time war broke out. He was remembered by his Masters as a young man of 'cheerful nature without any complaint'. From a Welsh family, it seemed appropriate for Charles to enlist in a home grown battalion. He was in Flanders in 1915 and saw action at Aubers Ridge and Loos before moving south for the 'Big Push' on the Somme and later at Arras.

The British Army, through the trying months of the spring of 1918, had eventually held the line, despite having to evacuate land, hard won in the Somme campaign of 1916. This transpired to be the last German mass attack on the Allies, and had cost the lives of many thousands, amongst which there were fifteen brave young Olavian men.

CHAPTER 21
The Balkans and the Middle Eastern Campaign

It had all begun in the Balkans. Gavrilo Princip's assassination of Archduke Franz Ferdinand of Austro-Hungary took place in the Bosnian city of Sarajevo. The opposing forces were sorted through an elaborate set of treaties, extending back for decades into the nineteenth century. For the Balkans, the key was that Germany pledged support to Austro-Hungary, and Russia, to little Serbia. German overtures to the young rebel nationalists that had overthrown the ailing Ottoman Empire, had succeeded.

With the invasion of Belgium, by German Forces, spearheaded by Von Moltke, Great Britain was seemingly obliged to honour its treaty of support to the former; France mobilised because it was obviously the target of aggressive German ambitions. In London, it became immediately apparent that 'Axis Powers' would endeavour to extend their already massive empire in the south east of Europe, North Africa, Persia and Arabia.

Senior Liberal politicians in Great Britain – from Asquith and Grey to Churchill and Lloyd-George – already realised that the oil reserves in the Arabian deserts had to be protected from enemy gain. Paramount was the need to preserve Imperial territory and to extend British political influence. For this reason, the activities of two men, came to have a conflicting, and long lasting effect, on the region.

Chaim Weizman, was the Manchester chemist who solved the government's munitions crisis, through the invention of a more efficient method of making acetone, the essential ingredient of explosive. Perhaps more importantly, he was the President of the English Zionist Federation and, in return for his help in the War

THE BALKANS AND THE MIDDLE EASTERN CAMPAIGN

effort, he eventually secured the famous commitment from the Foreign Secretary, Arthur Balfour on 2nd November 1917, that 'His Majesty's Government view with favour the establishment in Palestine of a national home for the Jewish people' without prejudice to 'the civil and religious rights of the existing non-Jewish communities'.

Meanwhile, the very same British Government, still with imperialism in mind, supported the creative ideas of another unusual man. Second Lieutenant T.E. Lawrence, an intelligence officer in Cairo and an expert cultural historian of the region, saw the opportunity to work in alliance with the disparate tribes of Arab nationalists to overthrow the Turks both in Mesopotamia and Damascus, Palestine. The results of his work enabled many of General Allenby's successes at Gaza, Megiddo and Baghdad. The end of the war brought political expediency, and both causes could not be supported in equal measure. Emir Feisal, Lawrence's Arab ally, was no longer needed at the Versailles peace conference. However his influence in the Middle East increased in his position as firstly, King of Syria and then of Iraq.

In the opening months of the War, the Austro-Hungarian Army started bombarding Belgrade, and Turkey invaded the Russian Caucasus. As an immediate result, the British annexed Cyprus, declared a protectorate over Egypt and invaded Mesopotamia from the Persian Gulf, taking the city of Basra in late November. The following year, the German supply route to Turkey was stopped, when Romania closed its borders; Bulgaria, hoping to secure Macedonia, joined the 'central powers' having monitored Allied setbacks at Gallipoli. Greece first sought assistance and a Franco-British Force landed in Salonika, then they changed their stance and became neutral. Late in the year, the central powers virtually knocked Serbia and Montenegro out of the war, with survivors being evacuated to Corfu. General Mahon's forces in Salonika, could only prepare defensively for further enemy advance into 'neutral' Greece.

Of the nine Old Olavians who gave their lives on the Turkish and Balkan Fronts, four served with the London Regiment – the 14th, 20th, 21st, 22nd – in Palestine; two as captains and two in the ranks, a corporal and a private. They each became a casualty in the space of six months between October of 1917 and April 1918.

The two captains were Robert Cecil Hearn M.C., and Grantley Adolphe Le Chavetois.

Robert was five years younger than Grantley, born in 1892, attending the school for ten years from 1900 to 1911. He was the youngest of three children, with two sisters, Helen and Florence, of an Old Olavian, Charles Hearn, a commercial traveller for a vinegar making business in Deptford and his wife, Florence. On leaving St Olave's, he went up to St John's College, Cambridge as a classical exhibitioner. His skills as a violinist prompted his membership of the Cambridge University musical club. In June 1914, he graduated with a 3rd class classical tripos. Whilst waiting for a place at the Wells Theological College for ordination, he went for one term as a temporary assistant to the headmaster of Bolton School, during the headmaster's illness. By Christmas, with the war still raging, he decided to enlist in the Inns of Court Officer Training Corps. By the following summer, he was commissioned as a second lieutenant in the 2/20th Londons (Blackheath and Woolwich Rifles).

He embarked at Southampton with his battalion and arrived in France in the autumn, fighting through the actions at Vimy Ridge and returning to England late in 1916 to recuperate from some wounds received. He returned to his battalion in time for their move to Salonika in December 1916. On their arrival he was promoted to the rank of lieutenant and spent several months in fierce action with the Romanians, fighting the German-Bulgarian alliance. By the spring of 1917, the Greeks had at last joined the Allies, and Romania had been overrun by the enemy. The 20th Londons departed for Palestine.

Grantley Le Chavetois, his fellow officer, was born in September 1887 with a sister, Ida, in Southampton to Adolpe Le Chavetois and

THE BALKANS AND THE MIDDLE EASTERN CAMPAIGN

his formidable wife Minnie, who started as a school mistress and later became a London County Council headmistress. He spent ten years at the School from 1895 until 1905, when he left to train as a teacher at King's College, London University. In 1908, he took his degree to his first teaching position at Emmanuel School in Wandsworth, where he taught under his old master at St Olave's, Harold Ryley Senior. After four years, the twenty-five year old 'Chavvy', secured an appointment back at Tooley Street, where he replaced the retiring Mr Hartley, simultaneously being awarded a Master of Arts, for a thesis on roman history. Back at the School, he became a favourite with the boys. He was ubiquitous, secretary of the Elizabethans, pioneer at the summer camps, benefactor of Howard House in Spitalfields, initiator of the School Cadet Corps, organiser of the 'Alliance of Honour' with the older boys, and a special constable in his 'spare' time.

On the outbreak of war, with a view to gaining an early commission, 'Chavvy' joined an Officers Training Corps at Denham in Middlesex with fellow master, Cecil Edmunds. Having taken the course, they were both persuaded to stay as teachers for the time being, and to concentrate their efforts in developing Olavians through a cadet corps. Many of 'the Fallen' moved through its ranks in the war years. Eventually, Grantley was gazetted as an officer and assigned as lieutenant in the 22nd Londons (The Queens). He arrived in Boulogne in August 1916, moving just two months later to Salonika. By spring 1917, the Queens were in Egypt, ready to move into Palestine.

The two ranking soldiers left St Olave's in the same year, 1913. Edmund Burn was sixteen and had only spent three years there on a scholarship; Harry Hollands was a year older at seventeen. Edmund, the engineering apprentice, was born in west London, only son and child of Henry William Burn, a law clerk for the Board of Guardians, originally from Kent and his wife Rose. Harry, with his older brother, Wilf, a regimental bombing officer, were sons of Alfred Christy and Chrissie Hollands, who ran a baker's shop in the

Walworth Road. The boys also had two sisters, Elsie and Winifred.

Harry was the first of the two to enlist in October 1914, as a Rifleman in the 2/21st Londons (the First Surrey Rifles), however it wasn't until June 1916 that he went to France, where he was mostly engaged in salvage duty at the front. In December of that year, he moved to Salonika, then Egypt, where he met up with both Captain Le Chavetois and Lance Sergeant Oliver.

Meanwhile, Private Eddie Burn, who had waited until Christmas 1915 to enlist, joined the London Scottish and was sent with the 2/14th battalion, in Easter 1916, to quell the Sinn Fein uprising in Dublin. Two months later he was in France, ready for the long Somme campaign. He took part in various enemy engagements, with one action where he was the only survivor, his platoon all having been killed by exploding shells. He was posted to Salonika arriving on 1st December 1916 then, like the others, his battalion made the trip to Egypt in the sweltering heat of July 1917 where he took part in the Allied advance into Palestine.

During 1916, Eddie had written to Headmaster Rushbrooke thanking him for his latest copy of the Olavian magazine which he received in France:

> "I opened a parcel from home and found the July 'Olavian'. The receipt of those blue books with the wide margins, has, during the last nine months, given me more pleasure than anything else, and I think that if the compilers realized the joy it affords hundreds of others in a similar position, they would feel amply repaid for their hard work".

Of the remaining five Old Olavians, Captain Fred Defries served with the Middlesex Regiment in Salonika. Second Lieutenant Harold Grant fought with the 7th North Staffordshires in Iran; Captain Lionel Marner led a company of the 10th Leicesters in Iraq; Lieutenant Harold Ryley, the same Ryley that was 'Chavvy's superior at Emmanuel School, saw action with the 1/5th Suffolks at Ramleh

THE BALKANS AND THE MIDDLE EASTERN CAMPAIGN

in Palestine, and finally, Private Harry Young witnessed combat in different theatres with 'B' company, the 1/4th Essex Regiment in Turkey and Palestine.

Operations on the Palestinian and Mesopotamian Fronts in 1916 were governed by two overriding factors. In Palestine, the critical issue was to maintain possession of the Suez Canal, the main reason for British bases in Egypt. An early attempt by Von Kressenstein and Djemal Pasha in March 1915, to capture the Canal through Sinai, was rebuffed with ease, but enhanced British fears of future attacks. Defence of Suez was to drain military resources desperately needed in the Dardanelles. Despite the success of Lawrence's Arab revolt, a further unsuccessful German-Turk attack was launched in August 1916 at Rumani.

In Mesopotamia, the issue was to restore British prestige in the Muslim world (badly lost during the Gallipoli campaign) by taking Baghdad in an advance up the Euphrates and Tigris rivers with fresh Indian troops arriving at Basra in the south. The men chosen to lead this task were Sir John Nixon and his operational commanders, Charles Townshend and George Gorringe. They took the battle to the Turks at 'Nasiriya' on the Euphrates, in summer 1915, followed by the capture of the City of 'Kut-el-Amara' on the Tigris three months later. Nixon, under pressure from London to push on to Baghdad, fought the Turks at 'Ctesiphon' in November and was pushed back to Kut which he held until the following April, at which point, out of supplies, and with no relief expected, he surrendered both the city and his army, in another serious blow to Allied prestige. It was not until the start of 1917 that British Forces returned to the offensive. A new commander arrived in August 1916, and early the following year, plans were in place to advance northwards and attack the Turkish Sixth Army. In February 1917, Maude's Army defeated the Turks at the second battle of Kut. Pushing on, Baghdad at last fell on the 11th March with the campaign to defend its capture continuing until the last day of April.

Lionel Marner had marched with General Maude's Army to capture Baghdad that spring. He was attached to 'B company' the 2nd battalion, the Leicester Regiment, which had arrived in Mesopotamia in late 1915. Born in June 1888 to George William Marner of Bermondsey, brass founder and wife Jane, he was the youngest of three Olavian brothers, Reginald and Sidney being older; Sidney died of pneumonia in Scotland working as an Army motor engineer during the war. Marner Senior was also a St Olave's School Governor, when not manufacturing brass castings to be used in wireless telegraphy and munitions. Moving to St Olave's from Fair Street School in Bermondsey, Lionel spent five years at the School. Of the others in the desert campaign, he is most likely to have known Le Chavetois well. On leaving school, he articled as an architect and surveyor, moving on, to work for the Metropolitan Asylums Board, and acquiring the qualification, 'Professional Associate of the Surveyors Institution'. Having enlisted as a rifleman in the Public Schools Battalion of the Royal Fusiliers, he was soon plucked out for officer training.

By December 1915, he was a lieutenant with the 10th Leicesters. Transferred to the 2nd battalion, already in action on the River Tigris, he embarked for the city of Basra in spring 1916 arriving there in July. His skills as a draughtsman led to a new role as a field sketching specialist to a junior officer's company, numbering 350 men; He was also promoted to captain and made second in command with a platoon of eighty men, in the advance on Baghdad. Surviving the battle of Kut, his last letters home talked of his delight in reaching the ancient city of Baghdad. Captain Lionel Marner was struck by a single rifle bullet at 'Beled Station' on the banks of the Tigris, in the siege of Baghdad. It was Easter Sunday, April 8th

Lionel was taken to a field hospital, where he fought for his life for six days, sadly to no avail. He died on the 15th aged twenty-eight years. He is commemorated on the Basra Memorial with forty thousand other colleagues. His comrade, and chaplain, a man called Thompson, wrote the following poem to commemorate his life.

'The rushing brook, the silken grass,
And pride of poppies burning red, where Marner died,
Unchanged – and in the station still as then,
The water that was bought with blood of men'.

Spring 1917 in the deserts of Egypt, witnessed the removal of Commander Archie Murray after two failed attempts to build on the British hold on Sinai by taking Turkish positions in Gaza and Beersheba, giving entry to Palestine. The new man had a dramatic effect, restructuring the Egyptian Expeditionary Force, and as a cavalryman, deciding to increase the use of his 'Desert Mounted Corps'. On October 31st 1917, Edmund Allenby prepared the bulk of his Army – 'XX' and 'XX1 Corps', to attack Beersheba again, leaving only a small part, to cover Gaza.

The attack was a surprise and a success, especially the employment of the mounted corps on a wide flank movement; the infantry moved rapidly and pushed a hole between the Turks and the Germans, both under the command of Von Kressenstein. The Turks fell back northwards to the coast, at the city of Jaffa, whilst the Germans retreated to Jerusalem. On November 13th the Allies attacked the Turks at 'Junction Station', then moved on Jerusalem, which eventually fell, after fierce fighting on the 9th December.

Captain Bob Hearn of the 2/20th Londons, was awarded the Military Cross for his gallantry in the advance on Sheria, Nabi Samwill and the capture of Beersheba. His citation, published in the Edinburgh Gazette on the 22nd July 1918 reads:

"For conspicuous gallantry and devotion to duty. He led his Company with marked skill and courage in the face of heavy machine-gun and rifle fire, and succeeded in capturing a strong position, together with eighty prisoners including a battalion commander and three other officers".

Private Harry Young of the 1/4th Essex had been stationed on the banks of the Suez Canal in Egypt for nearly a year, after their evacuation from the beaches of Gallipoli. In February 1917, they joined other battalions in the 'desert march' to the Holy Land by the ancient northern caravan route. They reached the city of El Arish on the 22nd March, at which point Harry sent, what was to be his last letter home. The next day, whilst advancing in country with no cover, to attack a ridge manned by the enemy, he was shot in the head by a sniper and died of his wounds three days later. He was twenty-seven years of age and was buried in the war cemetery at Gaza, now in Israel.

Henry George Young was born on the 4th November 1889, the second of five surviving children of George and Eliza Young of Latham Road, East Ham. Three children had died in infancy, leaving two girls, Daisy and Dorothy, and boys, Edward and Frank. Henry and Edward both attended St Olave's and Edward later served as an officer in a trench mortar battery in France. Henry, proved to be a boy of 'steady perseverance' 'well liked and respected' spending six years at the school, a near contemporary of Hearn and Marner, and leaving in 1906 aged sixteen to work for a wholesale woollen manufacturer, and later an Australian shipping merchants. By 1910, he was head shipping clerk. In his leisure time, he was a chorister at St Dunstans, a sunday school teacher at St Pauls, East Ham and assistant secretary of the 'Hospital Saturday Fund'.

In January 1915, Harry Young enlisted as a Private no. 200794 and was assigned to the 1/4th Essex, who within three months were in the Mediterranean preparing for the Suvla Bay landings on the Gallipoli peninsula. On the day of the landings in August, such was the severity of casualties in his battalion, one thousand strong, that the remnants of the men that had got ashore untouched, were designated a 'sick battalion' and relocated to Egypt to re-staff, before further action. It was from here that they started the 'desert march' in spring 1917.

Towards the end of the summer that year, Private Edmund Burn, returning from leave in Cairo, had written home about life in

THE BALKANS AND THE MIDDLE EASTERN CAMPAIGN

Palestine, "We are encamped in a dry water course of great extent, one of the most famous rivers in history. The Chaldeans, Persians, Egyptians, Crusaders, Napoleon, and lastly, ourselves, have fought for it, which, so far as I can see, is strong evidence of recurrent insanity, as there is nothing here but sand, and then more sand". He was advancing on foot with the 2/14th London Scottish and was killed by a Turkish bullet on the outskirts of Beersheba on the 31st October. He was just twenty, and is buried in a rocky glen on the north side of the road from Khilassa to Beersheba.

His last letter home had said, "Next week I will be in the Promised Land".

'Chavvy' of the 22nd Londons and his mentor, Harold Ryley of the Suffolks were also both heavily involved in Allenby's plans that autumn. Now a captain and adjutant, 'Chavvy' went forward, with inspirational leadership style, typical of the man, in an attack on Hill 1070, a key Beersheba defence. The hill was taken in two hours with the award of three Military Medals and three Military Crosses. A week later, orders were given for the Brigade to push on and capture the ridge of 'Tel-el-Sheira'. Unfortunately only 'the Queens' arrived on time without other battalion support to right or left. As a result, they were pinned down by machine guns. 'Chavvy' was on his way with a message from the officer commanding, explaining the situation, and to guide the other battalions in, when he was shot in the head. The battalion held the position until relieved by the rest of the brigade under Colonel Borton, who won a V.C. for this engagement.

After two operations in hospital, Captain Le Chavetois, surprised most, not only by pulling through, but also by returning home to England, to convalesce as a 'walking case' with the bullet that had pierced his brain, in his pocket. Back in London, he was treated at a convalescent hospital, and saw his family and friends, even visiting St Olave's on occasion. But headaches began to blight him more regularly, and doctors could not find the cerebral problem. He sank into a coma on the 21st January 1918 and died at the age of thirty.

The School took the loss of one of its favourites badly. Eulogies spoke of his 'affectionate and unselfish nature', of 'his moral strength and earnest endeavour'; He was praised as a 'hard worker' a 'born leader' 'another Galahad' and a 'true sportsman'. 'Chavvy' 'helped others' with 'utter courtesy', no man in this tribute did more to inspire the boys and men around him to do their duty and serve. Now the School had to let him go.

Forty-nine year old Harold Buchanan Ryley's story is one of even greater sadness for the history of the School, but representative of the suffering caused by the Great War. He was killed in action whilst advancing with his company, on the cities of Ramla and Jaffa, in late December 1917. Having already fought his way though Gaza and Beersheba, the Suffolks played their part in pushing the Turks further north towards Megiddo.

Harold Ryley was one of six children of congregationalist minister, the Reverend George Buchanan Ryley and wife Isabella of Croydon, Surrey. He had been born in July 1868 in Bocking in Essex, attending prep school in London in the early 1870's. In 1880 at the age of twelve, he came to St Olave's, where he spent eight years, culminating in a open classical scholarship at Exeter College, Oxford. Shortly after graduating, he married, Hughiena Fraser from Carshalton and went to live in Colorado Springs in the United States, returning in 1894, with a small son, Donald, to take up a post as master at St Olave's. Two years later, his second son, Harold, known as 'Bay' was born. Six years later, he was offered the post of headmaster at Sandwich Grammar School. During this time, Hughiena began suffering from an extremely debilitating illness which was to cut short her life. She died in September 1919 aged 53 years.

Harold cared for his family, but still found time to move back to London to take a post at the Emmanuel School in Wandsworth in 1906. Both sons were sent to St Olave's leaving in 1911/12. Harold meanwhile, had joined the Officers Training Corps and received a commission as a captain in the 16th Londons (the

Queens Westminster Rifles). In 1913, with both boys out of school, he returned to America from where he championed the Allied cause. Because of the outbreak of war, he decided to stay living in California, using what influence he had to encourage the Americans to join the Allies. Even at the outbreak of war, at the age of forty-six, Harold was not on the active list for service overseas.

A man of powerful character and charm, he had many different sides to his personality. Without doubt talented, he taught, preached, wrote poetry and music and aspired in the role of politician, sportsman, soldier and patriot. In his intellect, his convictions and his feelings, he sometimes clashed with other teachers, and would never 'suffer fools gladly'. Above all he was 'razor-sharp' with rapid verbal discourse and repartee, a 'hammer man' and a 'master of wit'. His life in California was destroyed by news of his youngest son's death on the Somme in September 1916 aged 20. He returned to England to enlist and, shortly before receiving his commission in the Suffolks, learnt that his eldest son, had been killed at Loo's in February 1917. It is difficult to imagine his frame of mind, when arriving to serve with Allenby in Palestine, leaving his disabled wife at home with her grief.

The following are some of the lines of poetry that he wrote as a tribute to his sons:

> 'They have won great promotion, these our dead,
> taken from us so young, so clean, so bright,
> We do not mourn for you, O Loved, O dear,
> More dear, more loved, since you have left our life'.

In 1918, Allenby's plans to push the Turks out of Palestine altogether, were limited by the drain on his resources in favour of the Western Front in France and Belgium. During this 'hiatus', the Arab Forces, backed by teams of British specialists with armoured cars, engineers and artillery capability, scaled up their terrorist harassment of Turkish lines of communication. The Hejaz railway was severed, isolating the Turkish garrison of Medina. The fall of Jerusalem in December 1917, had prompted one more attack on Jericho before the 'hiatus' began. On 19th February, ten battalions of the London Regiment, including the 2/21st's, with Corporal Harold Holland, attacked the Turks and Germans at the walled city. The fighting on the ground was fierce, and on the second day of the three day battle, Harold was struck by a bullet and killed instantly. He was twenty-one and had recently written home saying that, he would do whatever was necessary to 'ensure that England might be free'. The successful storming of Jericho paved the way for the final advance towards Damascus in the far north.

Robert Hearn M.C. died from bullet wounds rising from the involvement of the 20th Londons in the first 'Trans-Jordan raid' in late March and early April 1918. He died on the 30th, which suggests that he had received wounds weeks earlier and had eventually succumbed to them. Having fought for three years in theatres of war from Vimy Ridge and High Wood, through Salonika, Gaza, Beersheba to Jericho, he fell at the precise moment that the War in the Middle East was seen to be almost won. He was twenty-five years old and is buried in the Jerusalem War Cemetery.

Since the entry of the Italians into the conflict on the side of the Allies, additional resources had been available, especially in Albania, to divert the Austrians. A reformed Serbian Army also improved the defence. Unfortunately 'Muckydonia' to the British Forces stationed there, spelt regular bouts of malaria. Allied political machinations ensured the abdication of the pro-German King, and in June 1917, Greece entered the war on the Allied side. With French Army reorganisation and Greek Army integration, the major push was delayed until September 1918. But earlier in the year, with the British line astride the area around Lake Doiran, regular actions arose from Bulgarian and Austrian attacks.

Captain Fred Defries of the Middlesex Regiment was killed in action defending the front at Doiran, Greece on the 6th April 1918. He had taken a company of men to draw enemy fire from a local wood, to divert attention from the main attack force whose objective was a local village. Having opened fire, the Bulgarians responded with enfilade machine gun fire sweeping the area where the platoon were trying to take cover. Artillery shelling from across the lake made retirement necessary, and Defries remained with his sergeant and a private until all his men had retreated. A rapid Bulgarian advance killed the sergeant and took the private, prisoner. On repatriation after the war, the same private claimed that his captain had been both alive and unwounded, when he, the private, was captured. It is possible therefore, that either he was shot subsequent to this or he chose to take his own life rather than face capture. Either way, his body was buried by the enemy.

Frederick Defries was born, the third of six children, on the 19th May 1884 to Albert and Martha Defries of Finchley. He had two brothers, Reginald was older and Gerard younger. He joined St Olave's on a L.C.C. scholarship from Mina Road School in 1896, with Le Chavetois as a fellow schoolboy and Ryley as a master. He left in 1900 to join an ecclesiastical insurance office, where he remained for nine years, until an opportunity to travel arose, when he was twenty-five. He went to Shanghai and worked for the China Mutual Life Insurance Company, moving up to actuary of the China United Assurance Society, three years later, in 1912. Fred Defries had become well known in Masonic circles in Shanghai by this time.

On the outbreak of hostilities, he enlisted in Shanghai and was immediately commissioned as a second lieutenant in the 5th Middlesex, returning by ship to England immediately. He was, in fact, in France, before Christmas 1914, the first Chinese citizen in action at the front. A man of strong personality, and personal magnetism, he had many narrow escapes over the next three years in France, Salonika, and Egypt. He was returned to England to convalesce on at least one occasion. At some point, Captain Defries was 'mentioned in despatches', but his luck ran out in April 1918, and he is commemorated on the Doiran Memorial, near Lake Doiran, on the border of old Yugoslavia and Greece. War Grave records suggest that he had no known grave, but his sister was reported as saying that his grave and that of his sergeant, were found in a wood near the lake, where they had been buried by the Bulgarians.

Five months later, as the long war was starting to draw to a close in the Allied favour, a truly remarkable, thirty-eight year old Olavian collapsed on the British infantry march in North Persia, somewhere between Basra and Baku. In this book, the words 'unusual', 'remarkable' or 'unique' are often used, in an attempt to describe the loss of boys that had been shaped by St Olave's, and then cut down in their prime.

Harold Allan Grant, son of Doctor Alexander Grant M.A (Aberdeen) a General Practitioner of Commercial Road, Mile End and his wife Jessie, was a good example. Born in January 1880 with a younger brother, Alex and and older sister, Jessie, he was taught at home until the age of ten, spending the next nine years at Tooley Street. He made a strong impact on masters at the School, who talked of him as 'capable of holding his own when he chose to exert himself' and 'a very considerable power of declamation and composition'. As an adolescent he had a massive frame, and dwarfed many of his sporting colleagues. He won the champions cup for swimming, and held the 100 yard sprint title for a time. His love of literature, prompted his involvement on the stage and in the choir, singing solo parts in 'the Revenge'.

He would have been taught by Ryley, and may have known Le Chavetois and Defries as much younger boys, while he was at the School. In 1899, aged nineteen, he left to join the Berlitz School to further his talent for languages. After a short period, he decided to travel in both Germany and Russia, eventually, in 1903, taking up a position as English tutor to a Russian nobleman at his country house. Here he had met and courted the nobleman's daughter and married her in 1905. She became Mrs Marie Fanny Charlotte Grant.

After a holiday in England, they settled down in Moscow, where Harold took private pupils and taught in schools. This continued until summer 1914, by which time he had a reputation as one of

THE BALKANS AND THE MIDDLE EASTERN CAMPAIGN

the best and most popular teachers in Moscow. Although life as a teacher was hard and involved long hours, he had an instinctive ability to make his students confident and to get their best effort. In what spare academic time he had, he continued to write articles for English literary magazines, and in 1913, had commenced a translation of the works of Pushkin.

In early 1915, witnessing the worsening situation on the Western Front, his patriotism led him to leave his beloved Russia with his wife, to return to London to enlist. It is extremely unfortunate that those that proposed his drafting as a ranking soldier into the premier line regiment, the Grenadier Guards, did not reflect that his talents might have been more useful to the British Government as an undercover intelligence officer back in Moscow. His network of friends were certainly well placed enough for him to have a deep understanding of the attitudes towards the Tsar, the role of Rasputin and the gradual build up to revolution in the streets. Consider for a moment that Harold and Marie Grant arrived in Moscow in 1905, two years after the formation of the Menshevik and Bolshevik parties, in the year when Tsar Nicholas was persuaded by pro-imperialists to go to war against Japan over the control of Korea, and the very same year when the Tsarist troops slaughtered worker demonstrators as they approached the Winter Palace in St Petersburg.

However, he went to train to be a soldier with the rigid discipline of the Guards, where he may well have come into contact with the Harvard brothers, both Guards officers. In early 1916, he was eventually seen for what he was, a man of strong leadership qualities, and was recommended for an Officers Training Corps course at Lichfield in Staffordshire. By summer, he had been gazetted as a second lieutenant in the 4th Battalion, South Staffordshires. His wife, Marie, stayed in London with her two young sons. He was thirty-six years old.

Just after Christmas 1916, he was sent to the Mesopotamian front, to Basra on the Persian Gulf, where he was attached to the 7th North

Staffordshires. Like Lionel, Marner, Harold Grant marched on Kut and Baghdad in the spring. Grant, however, survived both Marner, and the commander, Maude, who had died of cholera after drinking tainted milk. William Marshall who succeeded Maude, in early 1918, oversaw the consolidation of defensive operations around Baghdad on the one hand, whilst sending other infantry divisions east to Baku on the Caspian Sea to prevent German/Turkish forces taking possession of the oil fields in the Caucasus. These were no longer protected by Russian troops, who had been recalled after Lenin had made peace, to concentrate on the domestic revolution.

Harold Grant set out for Baku, by way of Tehran and Tabriz – a march of 500 miles through the Persian desert. Despite his fitness and athleticism, at some point near to Tehran, he contracted the influenza virus. His tireless willingness to undertake the hardest of jobs, and his popularity with his men, meant he was always occupied. He was taken to a field hospital in Tehran, where he refused to allow himself the rest needed to recover. He collapsed while trying to share in the work and died. He was thirty-eight. He was buried in the city's war cemetery, now in Iran.

Another keen poet, the following words were written by him as the last verse of his poem 'The Choice', when editor of the Olavian in 1898. Written at such a young age of innocence, it is particularly poignant with regard to his early death:

'Such is the easiest life of all,
But hardly seems it to be the best,
To leave our brothers of the fall,
And hide in an abode so blest.
To dwell in an abode so blest,
While thousands groan in mortal pain,
take your paradise of rest,
I go into the world again'.

THE BALKANS AND THE MIDDLE EASTERN CAMPAIGN

Nine men and a desert war. A sketcher, a 'desert trekker', a veteran of the Easter Rising, a classical scholar, a natural leader, a salvage expert, a mason from Shanghai, a violinist and a Muscovite. What might they have achieved if they had lived.

CHAPTER 22
Bapaume and Peronne

Between March and July 1918, the German Army had launched five massive, well planned offensives, at what they perceived as weak points in the Allied Front line – firstly the 'Michael' offensive at Peronne and Amiens, followed by 'Georgette' further north at Hazebrouck and Armentieres on the Franco-Belgian border. Later came the third attack, 'Blucher' way south on the River Aisne between Soissons and Reims. A few miles north west, was the location for the fourth initiative code named 'Gneisenau' at the Canal du Nord at Noyon, and the final campaign, without a name, was focused on the 'Reims-Marneschutz' area.

These attacks had succeeded in pushing the German infantry forty miles into Allied territory, so that they had almost reached Amiens, and were getting closer to Paris by the day. However Ludendorff had carried the campaigns on for too long, and the Allies, through effective rail networks, were able to move thousands of reserves to weak areas of the line, faster than attacking enemy infantry on foot, could penetrate that weakness.

By July, with both sides having a combined casualty loss of nearly half a million men, the tide began to turn in the Allied favour. Ludendorff's inability to break through in any of the five offensives was eroding morale. spanish flu began to spread through tired, poorly fed, German troops and, on the 28th May, the American 1st Division commanded by General Pershing, attacked and captured Cantigny near Montdidier, the tip of the enemy held, Amiens Salient. Initial American inexperience led to many casualties, but with the capture of Belleau Wood and Chateau Thierry, they began to prove that German battle experience could be overcome. Coupled with the arrival of the brilliant Australian Corps Commander, John Monash, in charge of the newly reformed Australian Corps, the Allies fought back and began to push the German army back. New tactics, adopted by Monash, worked effectively at Hamel and Villers Bretonneaux. Infantry were helped forward by all available mechanical technology. All men were briefed in depth. As a result, all objectives were taken in ninety minutes with a dramatic reduction in casualties.

Ludendorff, instead of concentrating on defence, gambled. He still had hopes of breaking through against the B.E.F. in Flanders, and attacked in the south near Reims, in an attempt to draw sufficient allied resources southwards, away from Ypres. The French Army directed by General Charles Mangin, supported by the Americans, advanced six miles in two days. By the 6th August, the German 1st and 3rd armies, having lost 168,000 men and nearly a thousand guns, retreated back over the Aisne river evacuating Soissons. Ludendorff had surrendered the strategic initiative.

Twelve Old Olavians, serving in different Infantry units, were to give their lives as the Allies moved into the final stages of the long war on the Western Front. Nine served with the London Territorial battalions, five were officers, two had been decorated, one with a Military Cross and the other, the Military Medal. The eldest was a Leicester based electrician at thirty-five, and the youngest, an eighteen year old chorister.

Some of the officers had known each other well whilst at St Olave's between 1897 and 1902. Percy Grist, a lieutenant with the 25th Londons (the Cyclists) was a contemporary of both Harold Gant, a second lieutenant in the 2nd Londons (Royal Fusiliers) and Arthur Vernall M.C. a second lieutenant in the 6th Leicesters. James Knifton, another second lieutenant, with the 2nd Royal Sussex, had only left St Olave's after six years, in late 1916, but whilst there, had known Thomas Idwal Jones M.M. now a lieutenant in the London Irish.

Of the rankers, four had been in school together from 1905 – Henry Deem was twenty-five, a private with the Civil Service Rifles; Frank Miles, a couple of years younger, had enlisted as a private with the 'Artists'. Philip Burwood, at twenty-six, was a private in the 2/23rd Londons and finally William Dunkley had joined up as a private with the 7th Londons.

The three remaining Olavians covered the school years 1908 to 1916; Percy Gale, at twenty-one, was the eldest and most senior in rank at lance sergeant, having been promoted twice in a short period; Ewart Castle at nineteen, was a rifleman with the Queens Westminsters, and James Almond at just eighteen, was a private with the 9th Royal Fusiliers.

Second Lieutenant Jimmy Knifton was the first to fall, on the 21st July at the village of Auchy near La Bassee. The second battalion of the Royal Sussex had received orders to take part in an Allied offensive. During the raid, having gone over the top, Jimmy, together with an orderly, had failed to return. His captain took a patrol to the enemy line at great personal risk, but failed to find him. His youth was obvious and he had only just arrived at the front. At first, his company commander, who valued him highly, had not planned to take him over, but he had insisted, saying that he 'wanted to share all of his men's experiences'. He was regarded as 'missing believed dead'. He was nineteen and is commemorated on the Loos Memorial.

James McKinlay Knifton was born, with two brothers, Charles and Alfred, on the 25th January 1899 in Plumstead, to John Knifton, a head teacher with the London School Board, originally from Sunderland, and his Silvertown born wife, Agnes. Jimmy spent six years at Tooley Street, excelling at sports and in his academic studies. He left in July 1916 to become an officer cadet at Sandhurst. Once commissioned in late 1916, he was assigned to the 3rd Battalion of the Royal Sussex, who were on a tour of duty monitoring home defences. Alf, the younger brother had died in 1901 as an infant. The third brother, older by two years, Second Lieutenant Charles William McKinlay Knifton, also in the Royal Sussex Regiment, was killed in action in Belgium on 23rd November 1917. James Knifton took the opportunity to go to France when it arose, and he was transferred to the 2nd Battalion at the Front. The Kniftons had lost all three of their boys.

BAPAUME AND PERONNE

Two weeks after Jimmy Knifton died at Auchy, the battle of Amiens commenced on the 8th August. It was to last for four days and nights. Henry Rawlinson's Fourth Army combined with the French General, Marie-Eugene Debeney's First Army, attacked the enemy east of the city. The Canadian and Australian Corps, now operating as separate 'national' Forces were crucial to the success of the infantry role. Tactically the B.E.F had vastly improved. 'Wireless' was used intensively in the planning stage, the newly formed Royal Air Force prepared for ground attack roles, and false radio traffic in Flanders was initiated to defuse any enemy suspicion of a major attack further south. armoured cars, motorised machine guns, 'Mark V' and 'Whippet' tanks and mortars were provided through the Canadian Independent Force and the Tank Corps. Even Cavalry were prepared for the break through and were to operate 'hand in glove' with the tanks.

At 04.20 hours on the 8th, after Major-General Charles Budworth's 2,070 gun bombardment on the enemy line, the infantry advanced through a thick mist. The colonials advanced between six to eight miles that day, with the men of the British 111 Corps moving forward two miles near Morlancourt, where the line had been made stronger because of a previous Australian raid. 400 Guns were taken, 27,000 Germans were killed at a cost of only 9,000 Allied troops, and over 15,000 prisoners received.

Private James Almond of the 9th Royal Fusiliers had moved up with 36th Brigade, 12 Division on the 8th. Although the nature of his death is unknown, he is thought to have been struck down where the fighting was toughest for the British, around Morlancourt. He was buried at the Beacon Cemetery in the village of Sailly-Laurette, which is just a couple of miles south, on the banks of the River Somme, east of Amiens. He was eighteen.

James Edgar Almond was the second of five children, born on the 10th January 1900 in Bow, East London, to James Almond, a bookbinder from West Ham and wife Florence. He joined St Olave's in the autumn term of 1911 alongside colleagues, Stan King and

Austin Rule. He reached the Matriculation Class in 1916, before leaving to take a position in the City. He is remembered primarily for his work with the School's choir, and as the possessor of an exceptionally beautiful voice. He decided to join the army shortly after he turned eighteen, in February 1918, at Whitehall. His younger brother Leonard was too young to serve and remained at home with sisters, Florence, Margaret and Eva. After three and a half years of war, and the knowledge that many Olavians had been cut down in their prime, one can only imagine, the social and moral pressures placed on him to enlist. Most likely, he felt that the war had to be over soon. What he would certainly not have expected is to have been killed the following summer.

His part time engagement in the 53rd Y.S. Battalion of the Middlesex Regiment, had prepared him for his eventual enlistment in the 9th Royal Fusiliers. He became Private no. 79055. After six months of training, he arrived in France in July, making his way to the Front. The young chorister died on the day, described by Ludendorff in his diary as "the black day of the German Army in the history of this war".

The second day of battle saw the advance slow down. The synchronisation between the tanks and the cavalry was poor, but the reinvigorated B.E.F. were now fighting a demoralised German infantry, where new defences were shoddy and relief infantry were chided by regulars as 'Blacklegs' for prolonging the war. Private no.350959 William Dunkley of the 7th Londons was also at Morlancourt. On the morning of the 9th August, his battalion was advancing under heavy fire. He was manning an observation post, recording the penetration. When his intelligence officer was wounded, he carried him to the rear and took him to the nearest clearing station. Soon after, he disappeared, never returning to his post. He was presumed killed by heavy shelling between the support and Front lines. In October, some of his personal effects were found between Chipelly and Peronne, and it was assumed that his body had been found and buried by passing troops. He has a grave in the Beacon Cemetery at Sailly Laurette not far from James Almond. He was twenty-two.

William Henry Dunkley was born on the 30th September 1895, son of Henry, a carpenter, and his wife Frances. He attended the School for six years from September 1906 to May 1911. By fifteen, his mother widowed, he was living with his building contractor uncle in Tooley Street itself, and left to join Messrs W.J. & H. Thompson, rubber brokers of Mincing Lane, Bermondsey. After a year, he moved into the sales room. As a schoolboy, he was remembered by masters as 'happy and trusting, with a ready smile and of good disposition'. He enthusiastically enlisted at nearby Sun Street on the 2nd October 1914, shortly after his nineteenth Birthday. He chose the 7th (City of London) Battalion, no doubt influenced by his workmates. No other member of the Olavian 'Fallen' served with the "Shiny Seventh".

As Private no. 350959, he was training throughout the winter of 1914 at Burgess Hill and Watford, leaving for France from the south coast in March 1915. It was not until late in 1916 that the battalion endured its first major action, at Flers Courcelette, closely followed by Le Transloy. In 1917, having been promoted to lance corporal, William saw action at Bullecourt, and Messines Ridge. In August, he transferred to the intelligence section and trained as both an observer and a sniper, skills put into practice in the autumn campaigns at Menin Road, Polygon Wood, Passchendaele and Cambrai.

After three years in France and Flanders, with only one short annual period of leave, he was eventually wounded. In June 1918, he was gassed, but recovered sufficiently, to avoid the ship home. A month later he had gone. His C.O wrote "we felt his loss keenly, as he had been with us for so long, and was so splendid and cheerful. Our casualties in August were very heavy, but I felt his loss as much as that of any one, as I had known him so well".

Two weeks went by before news of another Olavian. The success at Amiens had prompted Rawlinson, who had learnt the lessons of the previous long battles of attrition, to persuade Douglas Haig to initiate another fast, but short lived attack further north, to catch the enemy off guard. Haig agreed and on the 21st August, Julian Byng's Third Army attacked in the Somme/Arras sector gaining three miles of front. The following day, the Fourth Army recaptured the town of Albert. Haig then issued a new command, "All ranks to act with the utmost boldness and resolution in order to get full advantage from the present favourable situation".

This message was not received by Second Lieutenant Arthur Vernall M.C. of the 6th Battalion, Leicester Regiment, based in the line at the River Scarpe near the Thiepval Ridge. He had been carrying out a daylight reconnaissance patrol across the river and on the Ridge in preparation for the attack on the 23rd, when he was fatally wounded by a sniper's bullet. He succeeded in transmitting his reconnaissance report, before he died. Earlier in the day, before the patrol, he had taken tea with his brother Edgar, who made it safely over the Thiepval Ridge the next day. He had jokingly complained that recent shelling had destroyed his favourite pipe. Arthur was thirty-five years old and is buried in the Bagneux British Cemetery at Gezaincourt. On the 23rd, the British Third and Fourth Armies attacked along a thirty-three mile front.

Arthur Vernall was born in London on the 21st March 1883, the eldest of four, including Laura, Charles and Edgar, borne to Arthur Vernall Senior, an insurance company superintendent from Hackney and his wife, Sarah from Boxmoor in Hertfordshire. After three years at St Olave's from 1897 to 1899, Arthur left to train as an electrical engineer, later working for the Leicester Co-op Boot Stores. He was one of the first to enlist as a private in Leicester in the 3rd Battalion, Leicester Regiment. By the summer of 1915, he was in France attached to the 6th Battalion as part of 110 Brigade, 21 Division.

He took an officer's course in early 1917 and was commissioned as a Second Lieutenant, returning to the front in July 1917. His brother Charles, a lieutenant in the 11th Manchesters had also been in France since July 1915. Surviving with Edgar, the fierce fighting on the Somme in March 1918, Arthur moved north in April to Flanders, where his bravery won him the Military Cross. The official statement states that:

> "He was left in charge of four platoons and exhibited magnificent courage and coolness, keeping the men well in hand and inspiring them with his example. On April 29th, when after terrible shelling the enemy made three determined attempts to penetrate our line, he moved up and down the line and inspired the men to such efforts that the attacks were beaten off. When some of his men were buried by the shell-fire, and he himself was badly shaken, he organised and led a digging party to get them out under a barrage and heavy machine gun fire. He kept and organised men from several units in his trench. The confidence he inspired in the men of the company undoubtedly saved the trench and enabled the line to be handed over in tact".

The citation published in the supplement to the London Gazette on the 16th September 1918 stated:

> "2nd Lt. Arthur Humphrey Vernall, Leic. R.
>
> For conspicuous gallantry and devotion to duty while holding an advanced post with his platoon. He successfully beat off a strong enemy raiding party which attached under cover of trench mortar barrage. Later, he again repulsed an enemy attack, inflicting heavy casualties. He showed fine courage and leadership".

On the Belgian front further north, just one day later, Philip Burwood, a veteran of four theatres of war in less years, was killed by shelling at the village of Godsterveldt, west of Ypres near Poperinghe. He was twenty-six, one of four children of Philip and Catherine Burwood. Born in March 1892, with two sisters, Catherine and Alice, and a younger brother, Charles, he attended St Olave's from 1905 to 1908 leaving to apprentice to a Stockbrokers firm. Charles meanwhile became a pilot's apprentice. On the outbreak of war, Philip was to be found queuing at the Clapham Junction recruitment office, swept along in the patriotic atmosphere. Within hours, he was Private no. 700714 in the 2nd Battalion, the 23rd Londons.

The speed of his recruitment was followed by a year of training tedium. It was not until June 1916 that he was sent abroad, to France. For six months as part of 142 Brigade, 47 Division, he fought in most of the Somme campaigns. In December, the Londoners swapped the winter cold and shelling for the 'shrubbed' slopes of Salonika, where they fought the Turks at Lake Doiran. In the spring, he transferred to Egypt and thence to the deserts of Palestine where, after enduring intensive and successive periods of fighting at Gaza, El Mughar and Nebi Samwill, he was one of the first to enter Jerusalem, before being reassigned on August 20th 1918, after two weeks leave in England, back to France. Refusing the offer of a commission several times, he was killed four days after his move back to France.

Back in the Arras sector on the 26th August, General Henry Horne's First Army had now moved up east of Arras to support the work of Byng on the 23rd. They attacked along the banks of the Scarpe, forcing gradual enemy withdrawal from Lys, Noyon and Mount Kemmel. Two days into the battle, Rifleman no. 555344 Ewart Castle of the 1/16th Londons, the Queens Westminster Rifles, had advanced from his position in the line at Vis en Artois, west of Cambrai. The battalion had taken up positions to attack a village, when Ewart was hit in the head by machine gun bullets and killed instantly. His body could not be recovered. He was nineteen and is commemorated on the Vis en Artois Memorial.

Ewart William King Castle, born on the 5th March 1899 at Beckenham with one younger sister Muriel, was the son of William

Castle, a builder and decorator from Walworth and wife Emily from Gloucestershire. A keen, cheerful boy, he spent six years at St Olave's from 1909 to 1915 commuting from the family home at Upper Grove, South Norwood, and helping out at his local Wesleyan Church in his spare time. At sixteen, he joined a firm of City based ships brokers. In March 1917, on his eighteenth birthday, he enlisted in the 16th Londons, following in the footsteps of several Olavians – Tait, Schooling, Riminton and Rowe. After training at Redhill and on Wimbledon Common, he was selected for officer training and passed the exams. However, days before his commission, the rules changed so that only men with six months battle experience could be made officers. Consequently, Ewart went to France on March 12th 1918 as a rifleman !

During the 'Kaisers Offensive', he was wounded by rifle fire and spent several weeks in a base hospital, returning to the front in April to fight on the Ancre. The next main action for the Westminster's was the Battle of Amiens on the 8th August, followed by the Battles of Bapaume and Scarpe towards the end of the month. A letter, sent to Mr Castle Senior, from Ewart's lieutenant stated that "immediately after the company left the trench, heavy fire was brought to bear by a 'nest' of German machine guns some distance away on the right, and your son was one of those who fell, killed instantaneously. On the day of his death, his work had been invaluable. He was very popular amongst his comrades, and is greatly missed by officers and men alike".

German retirements along the Scarpe river encouraged further advance. On 31st August, the Australians stormed and captured Mont St Quentin, causing Peronne to fall into Allied hands. The Canadians attacked the Drocourt-Queant line for successive days in early September, the seizure of which finally pressured Ludendorff to signal a wholesale retreat to the Hindenburg Line. Lieutenant Thomas Idwal Jones M.M. of the 18th Londons, the London Irish, was intelligence officer to his Brigade, the 141st, reporting to one of the brigadier generals of 47 Division, based at Combles, near Bapaume.

On 31st August, having found that the enemy were counter attacking the advance line on the left, and hence threatening to cut off access to the brigade, he immediately organised a platoon of reserves and led them to close the gap. He was mown down by enemy machine guns as he led his men forward. His body was recovered and he is buried in the Combles Communal Cemetery. He was twenty-one.

Idwal was born in May 1897 in the Welsh coastal town of Aberystwyth as was his younger brother, Hywel in 1901, both sons of John Thomas Jones, a dairy manager from Cardigan and Amelia his wife from Brecon. Having later moved home to Leyton in East London, the boys attended St Olave's, Idwal for five years leaving in 1912 to go into business. He had rubbed shoulders at Tooley Street with Harry Finnimore, the RFC pilot and Philip Grant who had died at Gallipoli.

He was remembered as a boy with a 'thirst for knowledge', one who was 'keen and interested', who regularly challenged his Masters intellect, especially in the study of hydrostatics, where he succeeded in separating the Magdeburg hemispheres. He enlisted under age in the summer of 1914 and refused a commission, in order to get to France quickly with the 15th Londons, the Civil Service Rifles. In 1915, he earned the Military Medal for gallant action and was promoted quickly through the ranks to sergeant, later deciding to return to England to become an Officer. He was gazetted as a second lieutenant with the 18th Londons on New Year's Eve 1916. As an officer with the 'Irish', he developed a reputation amongst his men, for 'integrity, simplicity of character and above all, courage'.

Just one day later on the 1st September, another Olavian officer in the London's was killed in action. Second Lieutenant Harold Holden Gant of the 2nd (City of London) Battalion, Royal Fusiliers, was shot whilst leading his men into attack near Guillemont on the Somme. He was thirty-two years old and is buried at Sailly-Saillisel British Cemetery near Rancourt.

Born on the 5th February 1886, the second youngest of six children of Arthur Gant, from Kings Lynn, who managed a dressing gown manufacturing business, and his London born wife Catherine.

Harold had an elder brother, Sidney and one younger, Alfred. After four years at St Olave's from 1899 to 1902, he joined the family business in Plumstead. In early 1915, illness struck both boys. Harold caught quinsy, from which he recovered, but Alfred died of an absess on the brain. The aftermath of this family tragedy meant Harold could not be spared from the business where he ran the warehousing and his sister, Louie was forewoman and the youngest, Dorothy also assisted. The third brother Sidney had died as an infant.

Consequently, Harold delayed his enlistment until the summer of 1916, when he opted to join the Honourable Artillery Company as a Gunner no. 7503. By the following October he was on the Somme and was wounded the next spring. After convalescence in England, he took an officers training course and was transferred to the infantry as a new subaltern commissioned on the 26th March. He returned to France on 1st August 1918. A month later he was dead, adding the Gants to the many parents, grieving the loss of their children.

On the 2nd September, as the suburbs of Peronne were cleared by the Allies, Lance Sergeant Percy Gale, a twenty-one year old Olavian serving with the 15th Londons, the Civil Service Rifles, was killed by a hail of machine gun bullets. His captain, at his side, wrote that "he was right in the front on the battle line and only about 20 yards from the gun that killed him. He was respected...throughout the whole battalion".

Two days before his death, the paperwork had been raised, promoting him to full sergeant with a strong recommendation for a commission. Much like the Gant parents, William and Mary Gale, had now lost three sons either in the conflict or in peacetime.

Percy James Gale was a Sussex bricklayer's son with seven siblings, four of which were brothers – Walter, the eldest, then Percy, and Maurice, Walter and Cecil who were all younger. Born after 1901, the younger two avoided military service. Percy was born on the 15th December 1896 and attended St Olave's for six years from 1908 until 1913, meeting contemporaries, Roberts, Beecraft and Wallace along the way. An extremely keen footballer, he also devoted much time to St Gabriel's Church in Newington, where he was described as a "splendid example of a Christian man". On leaving school, Percy took a position as clerk with the head office of the Church of England 'Waifs and Strays' Society. In April 1915, he joined up and went to France that August. In 1916, he was promoted to corporal and used his vocational skills as company clerk.

On the 3rd September 1918, as the B.E.F. continued to push the line further east from the traditional battleground of the Somme valley, an Olavian fell at Mericourt L'Abbe, between Amiens and Albert. He was wounded by gun fire and taken to the nearest casualty clearing station, where he passed away the next day. Harry Deem was twenty-five. The son of Henry William Deem, a billposter from the Channel Island of Jersey now living in Rotherhithe with wife Eleanore from Guernsey, he was born in September 1892 with one younger brother, Willie, and spent just two years at Tooley Street from fourteen to sixteen.

When he left, he took a position as a clerk in the City, and indulged his interest in local politics by joining Bermondsey Borough Council. By 1914, he was in a senior administrative position at Battersea Council. Remembered at School as a boy of 'modest and retiring' nature, Harry was also 'steady, reliable and persevering'. In 1916, he attested under Lord Derby's scheme, which released Civil Servants from their responsibilities, so that they could enlist. He became a signaller with the 15th Londons and embarked from Southampton for Salonika in the December. Within weeks he had been wounded and evacuated back to England to recuperate via a spell in hospital in Malta. After several months in hospital in Huddersfield, he was not back in action until 1918, when he was sent to the Western Front.

The death of Harry Deem marked the end of the remarkably successful third battle of the Somme, the second battle of Arras and the battle of Drocourt-Queant. Just over a week later, the month long battle of the Hindenburg line commenced. Despite low morale in the infantry, the German High Command was deploying tough loyal units to hold key strategic areas at all costs. The infamous Alpine Corps were positioned to defend Epehy and Havrincourt, the last two strongholds, before the Hindenburg Line. During the third week of September, the B.E.F., after an advance of 25 miles along a front of 40 miles, with a casualty loss of 180,000 men, overcame these last fortified defences.

On the 18th September, at the height of the fighting to break Epehy, Lieutenant Percy Grist of the 25th Londons lost his life through a bullet to the head. He was thirty-one. His C.O wrote that: "we have lost a really good comrade, a first rate brother officer". Percy Grist was buried at Epehy Wood Farm Cemetery.

Peter Simkins, in his book entitled 'World War 1', described the situation that faced Grist and many others around Epehy.

"(what followed was) several days of bitter fighting for the Hindenburg Line outposts at Ronssoy, Lempire, the Knoll and Tombois Farm. In the latter series of actions, between 18th and 24th September, its soldiers were exposed to murderous artillery and machine gun fire, and were frequently called upon to engage in savage close-quarter fighting in order to gain any ground".

Weariness was countered by British persistence and endurance in taking the fighting to the enemy and maintaining the pressure for several weeks at a time. This was the quality that finally defeated the German army.

Percival Charles Hugh Grist was a son of Arthur Algernon and Elizabeth Grist of Southwark. His father was employed as a sanitary inspector for Southwark Council. Born, the second of six children with brothers Herbert and Cecil, in November 1886, he spent three years at St Olave's from 1899 to 1901, when he left aged sixteen to article as a surveyor. He had known Knox, Perkins and Gant while at the School and busied himself with various extra curricular activities. He was the leading soloist at St Lawrence Jewry and was selected for the Aylesbury Festival; he was also an amateur member of the London Opera Company. Whilst working as a surveyor, he also trained as a cadet in the cyclists section with the London Territorials and volunteered his services to the King's Royal Rifle Corps during the 1902 Boer emergency in South Africa.

When 1914 arrived, he followed a similar course, re-enlisting as a Private no. 1252 when the 25th Londons, to whom he was attached, were mobilised. During training he was commissioned and was transferred as a lieutenant to the Norfolk Cycling Battalion with responsibility for surveying the east coast defences, a job he was more than qualified to do. He remained on home service until August 1918, when he received orders to move to France, presumably because all reserves were needed in the final advance. During September 1918, Percy Grist was subjected to an intensity of warfare that he was just not prepared for, and in his last letter home remarked repeatedly on his faith in God, and his hope of surviving.

Two days later on the 20th September whilst the fighting raged in France, a badly wounded man in a clean bed in Southwark Military Hospital passed away after struggling for three weeks with severe bullet damage to both neck and spine. The transit from Arras, through dressing stations, to field hospital to ship to port and then to London, had been far from helpful in allowing him rest. In much pain, Frank Miles died with his family around his bed. He was twenty-three.

Born in September 1894 with a sister Jessie to David Miles Senior, a joiner from Old Ford Road in Bow and wife, Jessie, he articled as a confidential clerk after three years of education at Tooley Street, whilst working as a copper engraver with a wallpaper manufacturer. When war arrived in 1914, Frank tried to enlist but was rejected due to a weak heart. As a result, he became involved in 'work of national importance' becoming an inspector at the Woolwich Arsenal, where he was one of the youngest men to manage a staff. With the need for soldiers in volume by 1917, the medical rules were relaxed and Frank became a Private no. 766390 in the 28th Londons, the Artists Rifles.

He arrived in France by troopship on January 31st 1918. In letters home, he claimed to have survived the 'Kaisers Offensive' only because, their captain had very ably 'extricated' the company from the danger soon after it had begun. Through 1918, Frank saw action at Havrincourt Wood, Ypres, Aveluy Wood and Thilloy. His wounds came during the battle of Bapaume. He is buried in Stepney.

Twelve Old Olavians had died amidst the carnage of the Western Front during the summer of 1918; the summer when the Allies finally broke through the last line of German defence. Even the Kaiser was seeking a face-saving peace, now that the final result was becoming obvious. October and November would witness further fighting at Cambrai, Selle River, Valenciennes and Sambre, before the Armistice was finally announced. Six more Olavians were to fall in the last six weeks.

Ernest Halliwell's Grave.

Jimmy Jones

Didi Maybrook

Ginger Wilson London Scottish

Jack Chubb

*Four of the Fallen Officers:
Fred Norris, Bay, Ryley, the Head, Noel Hamilton and Sid Terry.*

CHAPTER 23
Hindenburg Line, Armistice and Aftermath

A modified form of warfare began with the German retreat to the Hindenburg Line. Buildings in all towns discarded, were wired, mined and detonated, causing mass destruction. Many thousands of British soldiers were killed by 'booby trap' devices. The British successes at Havrincourt and Epehy, combined with the American infantry advance on Metz, had further reinvigorated the Allies. The last week of September saw a lull in the overall campaign due to persistent rain on the chalky ground. But as October began, and hot weather dried out the ground, the assault restarted.

In Flanders, on 28th September, with help from a re-formed Belgian Army under the leadership of King Albert, a fresh attack began on Aubers Ridge and Neuve Chapelle. With the enemy line broken at the Menin Road, everything began to fall. Within a day, the B.E.F. were on the Messines Ridge with Menin in sight. The fourth battle of Ypres lasted until the 2nd October and had quickly turned into a pursuit. A few days later, the Canadians, after some initial resistance, pushed into Cambrai, with American Expeditionary Forces crossing the Scheldt river, the St Quentin Canal and the Canal du Nord. For the first time, Allied soldiers pushed over the Hindenburg Line and into countryside completely untouched by war. Beaurevoir and Villers Outreaux were captured, threatening the main German rail connection to the Front. By October 9th, the Germans had retreated to the River Selle.

Rifleman no. 305893 Stan King serving with the London Rifle Brigade, was involved in the pressure to take Cambrai from the south. On October 12th, whilst advancing near the village of Beugny, he was badly wounded by machine gun fire, and died the same evening in a field hospital. He was just nineteen, having only left school in the third year of the war. He was later buried in the Delsaux Farm Cemetery. Stanley Edward King was born the youngest of three sons, Athur, the eldest and Sidney, on the 1st August 1899 to James King, a stationery printer from nearby Walworth. He first entered St Olave's School as an eleven year old boy in September 1911, along with the other younger members of the Fallen – Almond, Burn, Chubb, Rule and Shore. He was remembered by masters for his 'love of literature, a maturity beyond his tender years and his keen sense of humour'. After a short time working in the City during 1916, he decided to enlist the following year, and, following a short period of training, arrived in France in time for the Kaisers offensive on 21st March 1918.

Ten days later, at the village of Quievy, just short of Le Cateau and far beyond the previous line at Cambrai, Lance Sergeant Will Oliver of 'C' Company the 2/20th Londons, the Blackheath and Woolwich, was hit by a sniper's bullet directly through the heart whilst preparing to attack. A comrade wrote to his parents that "he lived a few minutes and I stayed with him. He was loved by all who knew him. His courage was unfailing and an inspiring example to all men. I have indeed lost a fine friend".

Just a year earlier, Will had been mentioned in the despatches of General Milne in Salonika, and had been presented with a Gallantry card by Major General Shea in recognition of his gallant conduct at Shab Salah on December 29th 1917. Having transferred to France early in 1918, he was wounded at Essalt in April and returned after recuperation in July. William Henry Rudland Oliver, fourth of seven children, was born on the 26th November 1897 in Stratford, East London, son of Harry Oliver, a provisions merchant originally from Bayswater and his wife, Leila. William had two elder brothers, Sidney and Norman and two younger, Leslie and Laurence. He spent five years at St Olave's, entering in Class 3 under Mr Pearse, and leaving in 1913. He voluntarily enlisted at Catford on August 8th 1914 and was accepted, when he was only sixteen years of age. As Private no. 630491, he was first sent to France in the spring of 1915, then to Egypt, Salonika, Palestine and back to France. After spending the entire war on active service in several war theatres, he was killed just as the Allies were starting to win, just three weeks before the Armistice that signified an end to hostilities. He was twenty.

Three days passed, and the British Forces continued to move slowly east, through Le Cateau towards the banks of the River Sambre. On the 23rd October, the 1st Battalion the Northamptonshire Regiment were situated at the village of Mazinghien. They were at jumping off stage for an attack, when a young twenty-seven year old lieutenant called Stables was struck on the head by a flying shell splinter. He died within minutes and was buried by his men in the Highland Cemetery at Le Cateau.

Leonard Theodore Drury Stables was born on Firework night 1891, fourth of five children of Doctor Walter Stables, a yorkshireman who lived in Fair Street, Horselydown with his Irish born wife Isabella and worked as a general medical practitioner with the local police and Poor Law committees. His two elder sisters, Jane and Dorothy both worked as teachers, one of physical education and the other of music; his elder brother, Walter worked as a stockbrokers clerk at the Stock Exchange, and the youngest, John, was at school. Len first walked into Tooley Street as a young boy of twelve in 1903, with contemporaries, Eugene Pearson, the surgeon and Lewis Berrow, the cavalryman.

In his first few years at the School, he was often ill, with a weak constitution, but in his last two years, he developed both physically and mentally, to leave in 1910 as a regular member of the First X1 at football. He joined the Civil Service, and moved in early 1914 to the Public Trustee Office. A year later, at twenty-four, he enlisted, first of all, as a Private no.305 in the 25th Londons, the Cyclists. His leadership skills were soon recognised and he was promoted to Lance Corporal no.1570 whilst still on home service. It is possible that he may have crossed paths with two other Old Olavians in the 25th – Bob Chapman and Percy Grist. All three transferred before the 25th were assigned to the Indian North West Frontier.

Len Stables took an officers training course in England and was commissioned on the 23rd November 1916. He went to France as a second lieutenant with the 6th Bedfords and was attached to the 1st Northamptonshires. His school masters remembered him as a boy in possession of the "charm of manner, the grace of courtesy and the love of truth".

Meanwhile, in a remote corner of the world at Kut in present day Iraq, Harry Arthur Oxford was serving in the last days of the conflict, in a motor transport section of the Royal Army Service Corps. Since the capture of Baghdad in 1917, by a combination of British and Indian Forces, the Turks were in retreat and on the defensive. The Germans were more aggressive in their fighting on the northern frontier of Persia and around Baku near the Caspian Sea. By late September 1918, preparations were underway for the last battle against the Turks, along the River Tigris at the City of Sharquat. Motor transport was absolutely crucial to waging a war in the desert, and Harry Oxford, at 38 years old, had enlisted quite late, in May 1917 as a Private no. M/334631, leaving his wife, Ethel, at home in Rustington in Sussex. He was sent that summer by ship to Mesopotamia, and, on arrival, attached to the 815th Motor Transport Company.

What prompted a married, almost middle aged, man to join up halfway through the War, is unknown. He had two brothers, one elder, serving as a school master for the newly formed Royal Air Force at Hoo, and a younger one, who was a volunteer worker on the land. All of the boys had followed their father to St Olave's, where the latter had been a 'Queen Elizabeth boy' from 1854 to 1860. After a year in Mesopotamia, a weakened Harry had picked up a bad viral infection, and like so many others, was treated in the British Hospital at Kut, but could not find the strength to recover. He later died on the 28th September 1918.

Harry Arthur Oxford was born in Bermondsey one of five children, on the 15th April 1880 to Harry Oxford, a hat factory manager from Horselydown and his wife, Anne from Dover. He spent six years at St Olave's, arriving from the Boutcher School. Whilst at Tooley Street, he excelled academically, featuring regularly in the annual prize lists. In his first year, 1889, he won prizes for seven subjects. He left in 1894 aged fourteen to take a seven year apprenticeship in the manufacturing trade. The work and the conditions were unsuitable for his health, and after a few years, he changed direction, training in the relatively new area of modern sanitation methods, later becoming a laundry manager, whilst his sisters Edith and Ethel became school mistresses. By the outbreak of war, Harry was a certified sanitary inspector, both for the countryside and the metropolis.

Curiously, his closest contemporary amongst the Fallen, was Gilbert Doyle, who, similarly had sought an unconventional career, had married and was killed in the last few months before the Armistice. Gilbert was born on December 23rd 1878, attending the School for five years from 1890. Although eighteen months older than Harry Oxford, he entered St Olave's a year later than him. Whereas the trio of Oxford brothers were well known in Olavian circles in the 1890's, the seven Doyle brothers eclipsed them, their school years spanning over two decades, from 1883 to 1903, sons of Joe Doyle, a weighing scale maker from London and his wife Sarah from Watford. Only the younger sons, Vincent and Norman were young enough to see military service overseas.

Gilbert, also a contemporary of Bill Athow and Harold Grant, left the School in 1894 to take an apprenticeship in the drapery trade. His masters spoke of him as a "jovial, generous and kind hearted boy with a keen and enthusiastic temperament". After his apprenticeship, he joined brother Vincent, in a firm based at Tulse Hill, and settled down with his new wife, Grace from Camberwell, and later their only son, born in 1911. When war broke out, Gilbert obtained a post as inspector of Army blankets through his knowledge of drapery. He was initially based at the Woolwich Arsenal and later travelled throughout the north of England, and

Scotland, inspecting clothing and army issued materials at training camps. In 1916, he attested under the 'Lord Derby Scheme', to seek permission to enlist for active service.

At this stage, he was thirty-eight. He was persuaded however, that his talents would be better employed, developing munitions for the Front, and consequently, he worked for Lloyd-George's new Ministry of Munitions, and was based at a factory near Nottingham called the National Filling Factory No. 6 at Chilwell. This factory alone during a two year period filled 19 million shells with high explosives, a volume that represented 50% of the shells used on the Western Front. On July 1st 1918, a munition's malfunction involving 8 tons of TNT caused a volley of explosions inside the factory killing 134 people of whom only 32 were recognisable and injuring a further 250. Gilbert Doyle was one of the casualties and his death was registered in Shardlow in Derbyshire. Lax safety standards in light of ever higher production targets, the instability of TNT compound on a very hot day were seen as the causes as opposed to the originally suspected, sabotage.

Churchill, the Minister of Munitions, sent a telegram:

> "Please accept my sincere sympathy with you all in the misfortune that has overtaken your fine Factory and in the loss of valuable lives, those who have perished have died at their stations on the field of duty and those who have lost their dear ones should fortify themselves with this thought, the courage and spirit shown by all concerned both men and women command our admiration, and the decision to which you have all come to carry on without a break is worthy of the spirit which animates our soldiers in the field. I trust the injured are receiving every care".

Work continued at the factory the very next day and within a month of the disaster, had achieved its highest weekly production target. Such were the needs of war.

The fierce street fighting for control of the city of Valenciennes, spilled over into the opening days of November 1918 in France. With the Canadians moving round the north side, the Germans threw every available resource into the town in a rearguard action. To the south they counter attacked, but were broken by the intensity of the gun fire. Eventually the town was taken by direct assault on November 2nd. The French, to the south, forced a German retreat to Mormal, whilst the Belgians pushed forward north of Tournai. Mauberge was the objective, where the Mauberge-Cologne Railway formed the main German supply and transport route.

Having fought at the battle of the Ancre, Albert and Bapaume, Private Arthur Junkison had never known such fatigue. Poor food, lack of sleep, bad sanitation, extreme cold, the wet, and technological hazards, present every minute of the day and night, produced a life unimaginable for most, even today. Old wounds, many still suffering the effects of having been gassed two years previously, and the onset of viruses and diseases, started to claim as many lives as the bullets and shells. After Bapaume, in early September, Arthur caught influenza, and tried to continue at his post. He was evacuated to a field hospital behind the lines, west of Lille, at Armentieres, where he struggled to recuperate through various fevers throughout October. He lost the fight on the 4th November, a week before the Armistice, his fever changing to pneumonia. He was twenty-nine years old.

Arthur Charles Junkison was born in Peckham on the 18th March 1889 to William Junkison, an insurance broker from Southwark. William had, himself, attended St Olave's in the 1860's, like Harry Oxford. Arthur, who had three sisters, spent only two years at the School from 1903 to 1905, leaving aged sixteen to join the Civil Service as an abstractor. Before the war, he had married his fiancé, Lottie Hall Leeson. He enlisted at New Cross in the summer of 1914, and spent nearly two years with the 15th Londons, the Civil Service Rifles, in England, before embarking for Salonika in 1916. In early 1917, he moved to Egypt and then to Palestine, where he

HINDENBURG LINE, ARMISTICE AND AFTERMATH

was involved at the battles of Gaza, El Mughar, Nebi Samwill and finally, the capture of Jerusalem. In Spring 1918, he took his last leave in England, before returning to France in July. In addition to having to cope with the dramatic change in climates, and battle conditions, Arthur was the victim of a gas attack that August, but was considered fit enough to continue at the Front. Undoubtedly many of these factors made him susceptible to the spanish flu epidemic which had started to hit the armies of both sides.

Arthur Junkison was the last Olavian to die on active military service, before peace was announced at 11am on the 11th November 1918. But the pain, agony, grieving and death did not cease because those in control had decided to end hostilities.

Four days after the Armistice, two more fine Olavians had died. Harry Wensley, a second lieutenant with the 1st Battalion, the Lincolnshire Regiment caught influenza on the day of the Armistice, as he went about his daily duties, based east of Cambrai. Peace had brought with it a need to adapt the skills of the British soldier. Whilst they were no longer firing guns, and dodging shells, there was an unbelievable amount of work to be done, repairing communications, feeding and recording prisoners, moving wounded, and searching for evidence of thousands of men lost in action. Harry, only nineteen, fought the virus for four long days and nights, eventually succumbing on the 15th. His famous father, Chief Constable Frederick Porter Wensley, formerly a detective inspector at New Scotland Yard, had lost a second son, the first, Harry's elder brother, Fred, an officer, also with the Lincolnshire's, was killed in 1916 on the Somme. Harry was buried at Caudry British Cemetery.

Harold William Wensley was born on the 8th February 1899 and attended St Olave's for eight years from 1910 to 1917. He and his good friend, Vic Budd, school captain in 1916-7, were the last Olavians to leave the School, at Easter 1917 and die in the War. The family lived in Dempsey Street, Stepney, with their mother, Laura from Eastbourne and mother-in-law, Jane Wensley originally from Taunton, nurturing the three children – Frederic,

Edith and Harold, the youngest. Harold's teachers remarked on his 'straightforward independence of character, his genial good nature and his explosions of humorous merriment'. To his friends, he was 'G.T.' – good tempered.

He was always involved, a keen athlete, a member of the School Cadet Corps and a good academic. Above all, he was thorough. In 1917, he chose to take a commission in the regular army and not a temporary commission. He entered Sandhurst in May 1917 and won a prize cadetship as his entrance examination mark was so high. He was motivated by brother Fred's service and subsequent death in France, to transfer to Fred's old Regiment, the Lincolns, who were training at Cork in Ireland. Shortly after, he was informed of the loss at sea of his best friend, Vic Budd. In summer 1918 he went to France, writing in a letter home that, 'I looked upon it (my service) in the light of a sacred duty'.

John Hood also caught influenza just before Armistice day, dying also on the 15th November in hospital in Valenciennes. He was twenty-eight years old, a lieutenant with the 39th Siege Battery, Royal Garrison Artillery. John William Hood, son of John Johnson Hood a printer's compositor from Sunderland and wife Jane, was born on the 28th November 1889 with two surviving younger siblings, Laura and Arthur, and joined the School in 1901, remaining there for nine years. John was one of the select group of pupils that took full advantage of what the School had to offer. He excelled academically, reaching the science sixth, from where he won an open entrance scholarship, worth twenty pounds, to Selwyn College, Cambridge in 1909. His success in passing his Natural Sciences degree in 1912, placed his name on the Olavian Honour list.

During the immediate pre-war years, John worked for the General Electric Company on scientific work, but found the commercial life not to his liking. In September 1915, he became science master at Abingdon School. With the continuance of the war, he felt obliged to offer his services in early 1916, taking an officers training course with the Inns Of Court. By November 1916, he was on board ship for France with the artillery. His technical work and his supervisory skills were such that General Haig mentioned him by name in his despatches during the third battle of Ypres. In hospital in Valenciennes, he understood that the war had been won, before he sadly relinquished his grip on life and passed away.

News of the Armistice brought mass celebrations in London, Paris and New York, but just a sense of tired relief at the Front. The Germans had fought on until the final hour, with over 300,000 British soldiers dying in the last three days of the War. Now the process of rebuilding and repatriation commenced. Although British deaths had been very high, the logistics of making provision for the far greater numbers of maimed, limbless, blinded and mentally disturbed troops was complex. Further mistakes would be made in the attempt to place several million men back into a fragile economy and society.

Three Old Olavians had already died during the war, whilst at home, either in training in preparation for going into active service, or whilst on home service. All three had died over a period of nine months from April 1916 to January 1917.

First was Albert Child, a Rifleman no. 3278 in the 3/5rd Battalion of the London Regiment, the London Rifle Brigade, based at Fovant training camp in Wiltshire. He had developed appendicitis after a long route march during training, and although he recovered quite well from the subsequent operation, he relapsed ten days later, passing away on the 29th April 1915. He was nineteen and within weeks of going to France. Albert George Child was born on the 15th October 1896, the youngest of three children of Jim Child, a sawyer from Dorking and wife Martha from Horselydown, now living at Keetons Road in Bermondsey. He had spent four years at the School in Tooley Street, leaving to become an insurer with the new fledgling 'National Health Insurance Office'.

Dudley Royal, Private no. MS/3012 in the Army Service Corps had arrived in France with the B.E.F in the summer of 1914, one of the first 100,000 men to arrive. After two years at the Front, whilst working in the mechanical transport section, he was crushed between two motor lorries on a dark night, resulting in serious injury, particularly to his ears. He was sent home, where he underwent several operations at Cardiff, and was later discharged as partly cured. His insistence on continuing his work as a mechanic with the A.S.C wore him down, as he continued to get persistent headaches. Whilst waiting in camp at Salisbury Plain for his official discharge as 'unfit for further service', he developed an absess on the brain and was rushed to hospital at Fargo Military. He died within a day, on 3rd December. Dudley was 25 years old and was buried in Hither Green Cemetery.

George Dudley Royal was one of five children of William Royal from Dartford, a trained engineer and his Rotherhithe born wife, Elizabeth, born in May 1891. A 'kind and good natured' boy, he attended the school for seven years leaving in 1912 to work in his father's engineering firm as a mechanical engineer on repair contracts, alongside his much older brother Charles, before securing a position with a new motor firm at Brooklands near Weybridge, later the home of motor racing.

The third was Ernest Talbot, a company quarter master sergeant in the 4th Battalion, the London Regiment (Royal Fusiliers). Based on home service at Aldeburgh in Suffolk, protecting the eastern defences from possible sea borne invasion, he had risen rapidly through the ranks from private in less than a year. After several transfers, first to Shoreham in Sussex and then at Seaford, where he ran the Army Post Office, he endured the recurrence of a childhood illness, rheumatic fever, from which he could not recover. The disease claimed his life on the 4th January 1917, leaving his wife Margaret, whom he had married just thirty-one days earlier, a widow. He was buried in Brockley Cemetery.

Ernest, born in Bermondsey in the summer of 1889, was the youngest of five with three brothers, of James Talbot a Bermondsey-born lime and cement builders merchant and his wife Mary from

HINDENBURG LINE, ARMISTICE AND AFTERMATH

Mile End. After five years at St Olave's, Ernest apprenticed as a bank clerk with A.Ruffer and Sons, a local firm, whilst his elder brothers, James, Arthur and John worked as carpenters, building clerks and shipping clerks respectively.

Fever, illness and accidents had robbed post war society of three more young lives, on the threshold of great potential. Both Royal and Child, instrumental in the early developments of both health insurance and motor vehicles, and Talbot, an extremely capable administrator and manager.

Five other Old Olavians, who were to die after the Armistice, as a direct result of their war injuries and experiences, made it home to England, to peace and with a chance to build their lives again with their families. Ernest Barton, a lieutenant with the London Brigade of the Royal Field Artillery, was thirty-one when the armistice was signed; he had been commissioned just before Christmas in 1915, so had seen three full years of active service. He had been sent home suffering from shell shock, and was receiving out-patient treatment at a London hospital. He lived with his wife, Adelaide at 53 Leighton Road in West Ealing. Late in 1918, he had visited St Olave's at Tooley Street as a special guest at the School prize day, and most thought him well enough, despite obvious signs of shell shock. In the Spring of 1919, he became worse and was taken into hospital near Kingston, where he passed away on the 1st April, the result of an absess on the brain.

Ernest Barton was born in London on the 23rd January 1887 with nine younger siblings to Bill Barton, a labourer from Ewell and his wife Dinah. He attended the School from his family home in Battersea for eight years from 1900 to 1907. He was a contemporary of Reginald Stubbs and Dug Oake, the pilots. He served as one of eight Olavian Fallen in the field artillery.

Private no.1352 Billy Beecraft had been a prisoner since May 1917, held in a succession of German camps. He had enlisted after Christmas 1914, joining the 16th Middlesex Regiment, the Public Schools battalion. Throughout 1915 and 1916, he had fought at first at Gallipoli, then on the Somme and at Arras before being captured. During his captivity, he spent most of his time digging, and nursing fellow prisoners with fever. Extraordinarily lucky to escape the influenza epidemic himself in winter 1918, he was eventually repatriated to England on 13th January 1919, four years to the day after his enlistment. Unfortunately, within just a couple of months he had contracted tuberculosis, largely as a result of his long captivity in poor conditions, and harsh treatment. He died at home of phthisis in Tooley Street, Bermondsey, within sight of St Olave's School on the 29th July 1920 aged twenty-three. Billy's body was buried in Abney Park Cemetery.

William Henry Beecraft was born on the 9th September 1896, the son of Joe and Hannah Beecraft who ran a dining rooms business at no. 98 Tooley Street with help from their three children, Gertrude, Clifford and William. William, himself, spent six years at the School from 1908 to 1913. He is remembered as a boy of 'peculiar reticence, with a strong devotion to duty and friendship, a quiet, steady boy'.

Lewis Berrow had lost his brother Bill during the war. He had been killed during the, now famous, Tank Corps advance at Cambrai. Lewis himself had volunteered as a cavalryman, following Bill's original enlistment with the City of London (Rough Riders). Lewis had enlisted at Doncaster as a private in the Yorkshire Dragoons. Owing to early military confidence in the use of cavalry at the Front, Lewis was shipped to Belgium very early in 1915, before the static nature of trench warfare had become obvious. After two years in France and Flanders, he was severely wounded in 1917, when he and his horse were blown up and buried, by enemy shelling. The horse was killed, but after a while, he was dug out and taken to the local dressing station. Recuperating in England, his physical wounds gradually healed, but psychologically, he had deep scars from the terrifying sensation of being buried alive. He returned to France in early 1918, and survived the final months of the war, being demobbed in spring 1919. He resumed his pre-war work in various employment exchanges in the Kent area, living at Faversham with his family. Regular headaches led to a cerebral haemorrhage just after Christmas 1921 and he passed away in a nursing home in Preston, a long way from his home in Kent.

Lewis Walter Berrow was born on the 22nd March 1891, the second of five children of William Berrow, Foreign Office Registrar from Worcestershire and wife Henrietta and attended St Olave's with his elder brother. He spent eight years at the School earning a reputation as a 'bit of a loner, a shy, diffident boy, and a fine mathematician'. His academic studies ensured his inclusion on the School Honour List. He left in 1910 to take a position with the new Ministry of Labour based at Doncaster in Yorkshire, from where he enlisted.

In the summer of 1921, Lionel Claud Dodkins died. Youngest child of four of Bill Dodkins, a Bermondsey furrier, and his wife Sophia, from Somerset, he was born in London on the 11th November 1895 to elder sister, Mary and brothers, Percy and Bill. Sadly his father died when he was just an infant, and mother Sophia brought up the children working as a dressmaker at home. Lionel attended the School from 1907 until 1911, winning athletic distinctions and studying alongside 'Bay' Ryley, Edgar Churcher, and Leslie Sanders. On leaving, he joined the Capital & Counties Bank at Piccadilly, and enlisted on the first day of the war. Through 1915, he served with the 25th London Cyclists protecting East Anglia from sea borne invasion. In 1916, unlike Len Stables, he went to India to defend the North West Frontier. In 1917, he took a commission in India, and was posted to the Border Regiment. He remained here for only three months seizing the opportunity to train as a fighter pilot in Egypt.

By Christmas 1917, he was back in India based at Risalpur with the Royal Flying Corps, flying dangerous solo flights into enemy territory during the 'Mahmud' campaign, and ferrying politicians to meet with regional tribal leaders. This was just the beginning; Lionel, now of flying officer rank, and flying with 31 Squadron Royal Air Force, played a substantial role in the suppression of the

'Gujranwalla riots' in 1918, and a year later, he fought the Afghans in the Khyber pass. In 1920 he returned to England, and whilst home, visited the School. On his return to India, he was appointed supervisor of physical training to the Indian Royal Air Force, as a result of a pamphlet that he had written on the subject.

Despite his fitness, the hard life of Frontier warfare, led to repetitive attacks of malaria, from which he had to recuperate in England. On a trip home in the early summer of 1921, his fever grew worse, and he could not overcome it. He died on the 13th June 1921 aged twenty-five years, with his mother at his side. He is buried at Bandon Hill Cemetery in Beddington, Surrey.

Nine months went by before news was received at the School of the death of Donald Boone. Working as an architect after demobilisation in 1920, he had married Nellie Powell in Oswestry in the autumn, only to find his health had broken down by the following summer. Throughout the following winter, he fought various viral infections but was gradually getting weaker, until he died, suddenly, at home on the 23rd March 1922. Don was only twenty-four, passing away the day before his birthday, with his bride of little more than a year by his side. It had all been so different once.

John William Donald Boone had been a unique boy; eager, enthusiastic with 'natural artistic skill', he had managed to conquer his stammer, and demonstrated an 'indomitable' character. Above all he was unorthodox, a keen oil painter and architectural student. Born in March 1897, the only child of Amy, originally from St Agnes in Cornwall and John Hezakiah Boone, born in Bermondsey and, following a spell as a shopkeeper, later a clerk to the Distress Committee, which was a central Government body helping the unemployed. Don spent ten years at St Olave's, entering the School gates alongside seventeen boys who were later to fall – characters like Ken Harvard, John Carrier and 'Muscles' Procter; He left in July 1915, aged eighteen, deciding to join the International Red Cross.

His first real involvement in the War was as a volunteer ambulance driver for 'Mrs Stobart's Friends' mission to Serbia. British Medical

Missions in Serbia helped counter the massive problems associated with epidemic typhus and other virulent viruses in the region. Total British volunteers number 370 with 64 of them Doctors in late 1914. Anne Mabel St Clair Stobart and her team arrived in Kragujevac in April 1915. Don's work is described in Fortier Jones 1916 book, 'With Serbia into Exile'. He had been held captive by a wounded Serbian officer who demanded a lift at gun point, also requiring him to drop off his other two wounded soldiers. During his two years in the Balkans, he was responsible for saving the lives of many Serbian soldiers, and was awarded the coveted 'Order of Saint Sava'. By October 1915, the Stobart mission had to move to Albania to avoid the advancing enemy armies. Two months later, they managed to get to the Albanian coast from where they were taken by ship to Italy and thence, England.

Throughout the War, however, Don was regularly susceptible to illness and his constitution was very weak by the latter stages. In 1917, he returned to England, and enlisted as a private in the 22nd Battalion, the Rifle Brigade, the Wessex and Welsh Battalion, who were national reservists, based in England on garrison duty.

The final infantry push through the Hindenburg Line had claimed the lives of three Olavians – Stan King, the 'literary loner', Will Oliver, really a desert soldier, and Len Stables, the 'cyclist from Bedford'. Spanish flu had taken three more – the Civil Servant, Arthur Junkison, the 'prize cadet', Harry Wensley, and the science teacher, John Hood. Rheumatic fever, appendicitis and a tumour had accounted for three men on home service, whilst malaria, shell shock and other disturbing experiences of war, had destroyed the post-war health of seven others.

Bibliography

Battle Honours – Anthony Baker
The Royal Flying Corps in France – Ralph Barker
Conscripts – Ilana Bet-el
Two Schools – Dr R.C.Carrington
The Donkeys – Alan Clark
The British Campaign in France and Flanders – Sir Arthur Conan-Doyle
The war the Infantry knew – Captain J.C. Dunne
A Dictionary of Battles – David Eggenberger
Tanks and Trenches – David Fletcher
The Great War and modern memory – Paul Fussell
Battle of the Somme – Gerald Gliddon
Chronicle of the First World War – Randal Gray
Tunnellers – Captain W.G.Grieve and Bernard Newman
The First Seven Divisions – Lord Ernest Hamilton
A Popular History of the Great War – Sir J.A. Hammerton
The Unknown Soldier – Neil Hanson
The World War One Source Book – Philip Haythornthwaite
The Sky their Battlefield – Trevor Henshaw
Battlefields of the First World War – Tonie and Valmai Holt
The Great War at Sea – Richard Hough
Panorama of the Western Front – John Laffin
Six Weeks – John Lewis-Stempel
Somme – Lyn Macdonald
They called it Passchendaele – Lyn Macdonald
1915 – The death of Innocence – Lyn Macdonald
1914 – The days of hope – Lyn Macdonald
Somme – Chris McCarthy
Passchendaele – Chris McCarthy
The First day of the Somme – Martin Middlebrook
The Kaiser's Offensive – Martin Middlebrook

BIBLIOGRAPHY

Bermondsey's 'Bit' in the Greatest War – H.F. Morriss
The Great War Generals on the Western Front – Robin Neillands
The Old Lie – Peter Parker
Fire-Eater – Captain A.O. Pollard VC, MC, DCM.
They fought for the Sky – Quentin Reynolds
Saturday Night Soldiers – A.V. Sellwood
World War I – Peter Simkins
Defeat at Gallipoli – Nigel Steel and Peter Hart
No Man's Land – The story of 1918 – John Toland
Boy Soldiers of the Great War – Richard Van Emden
To what end did they die – Officer died at Gallipoli – R.W. Walker
The Royal Navy – Anthony J. Watts
Kitchener's Army – Ray Westlake
Palestine 1917 – Robert Wilson

Research sources: St Olaves School Library and Foundation, Southwark Library, National Archives (Military records), Commonwealth War Graves Commission, London Gazette, Ancestry.co.uk (UK Census, Birth, Marriage and Death, Wills and Probate and Military records).

APPENDIX I
Cemetery and Memorial Index

NB – No known grave or memorial has been located for the following Olavian Fallen:

Lewis Berrow (died Preston, lived Faversham, Kent)
William Dale James (died Highgate, lived Amersham)
John Weatherston (died Wandsworth)
Leonard Bendixen (died Kondiat el Biad, Morocco, lived Brockley, Kent. Probate 1929)
Donald Boone (died Camberwell)
Gilbert Doyle (died Chilwell, Nottinghamshire).

Belgium – 17 sites – 38 Olavians

Artillery Wood Cemetery – Grave ref. 1X.D.15 (Boezinghe, Ypres) – Curtis E.J.
Artillery Wood Cemetery – Grave ref. X.E.17 – Harvard K.O.
Bedford House Cemetery – Grave ref. Enclosure No 4 11.C.15 (Ypres) – Dubery F.A.
Brandhoek Military Cemetery – Grave ref. 1.C.27 (Ypres) – Talbot C.M..
Lijssenthoek Military Cemetery – Grave ref. X111.B.14 (Ypres/Poperinghe) – Churcher E.
Lijssenthoek Military Cemetery – Grave ref. XV1.A.16 – Jones J.T.
Locre Churchyard – Grave ref. 11.C.21 (Locre, Ypres) – Roberts J.R.T
Mendinghem Military Cemetery –Grave ref. VE17 (Ypres) – Chapman R.S.
Menin Gate Memorial – Panel 12 & 14 (Ypres) – Clifton F.O.
Menin Gate Memorial – Panel 33 – Dell C.S.

APPENDIX I

Menin Gate Memorial – Panel 30 & 32 – Durant J.S.
Menin Gate Memorial – Panel 3 – Edgley L.S.
Menin Gate Memorial – Panel 52 & 54 – Haseldine N.W
Menin Gate Memorial – Panel 52 – Holman W.E.
Menin Gate Memorial – Panel 46, 48 & 50 – Hunt H
Menin Gate Memorial – Panel 52 & 54 – Marriott H.P.G.
Menin Gate Memorial – Panel 49 & 51 – Norris F.
Menin Gate Memorial – Panel 54 – Ryder G.W.
Menin Gate Memorial – Panel 54 – Schulz H.A
Menin Gate Memorial – Panel 54 – Shepherd H.A.
Menin Gate Memorial – Panel 54 – Sutherland J.
Menin Road South Military Cemetery – Grave ref. 111.G.5 (Ypres) – Hamilton C.W.
Perth Cemetery (China Wall) – Grave ref. 111.A.13 (Ypres) – Taylor W.F.
Ploegsteert Memorial – Panel 10 (Berks Cemetery Extension, Ypres) – Benson G.E.
Ploegsteert Memorial – Panel 11 – Chester H.T.
Ploegsteert Memorial – Panel 11 – Clarke E.H.
Ploegsteert Memorial – Panel 10 – Richardson J.B.
Ploegsteert Memorial – Panel 2 &3 – Shore J.H.
Ploegsteert Memorial – Panel 11 – Tait L.S.
Poperinghe Old Military Cemetery – Grave ref. 11.L.51 (Poperinghe, Ypres) – Lovekyn V.I
Potijke Burial Ground Cemetery – Grave ref. N11 (Ypres) – Schooling G.H.
Talana Farm Cemetery – Grave ref. 1E8 (Boezinghe) – Halliwell W.
The Huts Cemetery – Grave ref. IV.A.13 (Ypres) – Kenyon H.T.J.
Tyne Cot Memorial – Panel 86-88 (Zonnebeke, Ypres) – Blencowe C.E
Tyne Cot Memorial – Panel 148 – Falkner C.B.
Tyne Cot Cemetery – Grave ref. 28.H.18 – Halliwell E.
White House Cemetery – Grave ref. 111.F.6 (Ypres) – Gill J.W.
White House Cemetery – Grave ref. 1.D.18 – Robinson E.H.

Egypt – 1 site – 1 Olavian

Chatby Military & War Memorial Cemetery – Grave ref. L91 (Alexandria) – Wells N.

France – 70 sites – 118 Olavians

Abbeville Communal Cemetery Extension – Grave ref. IF28 (Abbeville, Somme) – Evans L.A.
Ancre British Cemetery – Grave ref. V111.F.6 (Ancre, Somme) – Ebsworth H.E.
Arras Memorial – Bay 10 (Faubourg D'Amiens Cemetery, Arras, Pas de Calais) – Butler E.H.
Arras Memorial – Bay 9 – Dennis R.C.
Arras Memorial – Bay 9 & 10 – Hill S.E.
Arras Memorial – Bay 10 – Howett F
Arras Memorial – Bay 7 – Phare D.G.
Arras Memorial – Bay 1 – Shears E.G.
Arras Memorial – Bay 2 – Smith G.W.
Arras Memorial – Bay 10 – Sutcliffe F.M.
Arras Memorial – Bay 7 – Terry S.F
Arras Memorial – Bay 10 – Williams J.M.V.
Arras Memorial – Bay 3 – Wardley M.E.
Arras Memorial – Bay 7 – West H.D.
Arras Flying Services Memorial – Gaskain C.S.
Arras Flying Services Memorial – Mann S.W.
Arras Flying Services Memorial – Stockins W.J.
Arras Flying Services Memorial – Wade O.J.
Aubigny Communal Cemetery Extension – Grave ref. 1.E.20 (Aubigny-en-Artois, {Pas de Calais) – Rule A.G.
Aubigny Communal Cemetery Extension – Grave ref. V.A.12 – Wilson A.C.
Avesnes Le Comte Communal Cemetery Extension – Grave ref. ID22 (Avesnes Le Comte, Pas de Calais) – Castell G.C.
Bagneux British Cemetery – Grave ref. 1V.D.13 (Gazaincourt, Somme) – Vernall A.H.

APPENDIX I

Bailleul Communal Cemetery – Grave ref. J17 (Bailleul, Nord) – Feben E.

Bailleul Communal Cemetery Extension – Grave ref. 111.E.196 (Bailleul, Nord) – Trotman H.

Beacon Cemetery –Grave ref. 111.G.4 (Sailly-Laurette, Somme) – Almond J.E

Beacon Cemetery – Grave ref. V.D.10 – Dunkley W.H.

Boisleux-au-Mont Communal Cemetery –Grave ref. 5 (Arras, Pas de Calais) – Harvard L.DJ.

Bronfay Farm Military Cemetery – Grave ref. 11.G.25 (Bray-Sur-Somme) – Bennett F.B.

Cambrai Memorial – Panel 13 (Louverval Military Cemetery, Louverval, Nord) – Berrow W.R.

Cambrai Memorial – Panel 3 & 4 – Kidney L.E.

Cambrai Memorial – Panel 7 – Knox J.L.

Cambrin Churchyard Extension – Grave ref. J1 (Cambrin, Pas de Calais) – Hoare E.A.

Caudry British Cemetery – Grave ref. 1.D.30 (Caudry, Nord) – Wensley H.W.

Combles Communal Cemetery Extension – Grave ref. 11.B.3 (Combles, Somme) – Jones T.I

Corbie Communal Cemetery Extension –Grave ref. 2.C.90 (Corbie, Somme) – Baker A.G.

Courcelette British Cemetery – Grave ref. 1X.G.2 (Courcelette, Somme) – Laurie A.W.

Crucifix Corner Cemetery – Grave ref. 1B 14 (Villers-Bretonneaux, Somme) – Chubb J.L.

Delsaux Farm Cemetery – Grave ref. 1E13 (Beugny, Pas de Calais) – King S.E.

Delville Wood Cemetery – Grave ref. X1.1.3 (Longueval, Somme) – Blackman H.W.

Dud Corner Cemetery – Grave ref. V.D.9 (Loos-en-Gohelle, Pas de Calais) – Walker W.R.

Duisans British Cemetery – Grave ref. 111.F.39 (Etrun, Pas de Calais) – Hay A.L.

Ecoivres Military Cemetery – Grave ref. 1.F.18 (Mont St Eloi, Pas de Calais) – Maybrook W.R

Ecoivres Military Cemetery – Grave ref. 111.B.3 – Thompson E.W.M.

Epehy Wood Farm Cemetery – Grave ref. 11.A.10 (Epehy, Somme) – Grist P.C.H.

Euston Road Cemetery – Grave ref. 1C40 (Colincamps, Somme) – Hollands W.G.

Faubourg D'Amiens Cemetery – Grave ref. V.H.29 (Arras, Pas de Calais) – Lunn R.W.

Feuchy Chapel British Cemetery – Grave ref. 1V.C.14 (Wancourt, Pas de Calais) – Sprang, F.W.

Fins New British Cemetery – Grave ref. 1V. E.6 (Fins, Somme) – Edmunds C.H

Fins New British Cemetery – Grave ref. V111.K.7 (Fins, Somme) – Wallace G.F.

Fosse 7 Military Cemetery – Grave ref. 11.C.6 (Mazingarbe, Pas de Calais) – Glenn R.J.

Fosse No. 10 Communal Cemetery Extension – Grave ref. 11.D.34 (Sains en Gohelle, Pas de Calais) – Brown C.H.G

Godewaersvelde British Cemetery – Grave ref. 11.D.13 (Godewaersvelde, Nord) – Burwood P.

Ham British Cemetery – Grave ref. 11.C.5 (Ham, Somme) – Lidgett J.C.

Hazebrouck Communal Cemetery –Grave ref. 11.C.3 (Hazebrouck, Nord) – Edwards A.F.

Hebuterne Military Cemetery – Grave ref. 11.N.1 (Hebuterne, Pas de Calais) – Hocking L.H.

Heilly Station Cemetery – Grave ref. V11.B.1 (Mericourt-L'Abbe, Somme) – Deem H.T.S

Heninel-Croisilles Road Cemetery –Grave ref. 11.E.34 (Heninel, Pas de Calais) – Baker H.W.

Heninel –Croisilles Road Cemetery – Grave ref. 11.D.10 – Gray W.J.

Highland Cemetery – Grave ref. V.C.1 (Le Cateau, Nord) – Stables L.T.D.

APPENDIX I

Lapugnoy Military Cemetery – Grave ref. 1C42 (Lapugnoy, Pas de Calais) – Cook A.J.

Lapugnoy Military Cemetery – Grave ref. V111.B.14 – Kiddle R.H.

Le Grand Hasard Military Cemetery – Grave ref. 1.D.1 (Morbecque, Nord) – Oake D.

Le Touret Memorial – Panel 44 (Bethune/Armentieres, Pas de Calais) – Fitzgerald R.

Le Touret Memorial – Panel 45 – Heron J.S.

Le Touret Memorial – Panel 44- Quixley A.N.A.

London Cemetery & Extension – Grave ref. 6.F.22 (Longueval, Somme) – Brittain P.J.

Loos Memorial – Panel 30 & 31 (Loos en Gohelle, Pas de Calais) – Bliss H.E.

Loos Memorial – Panel 87 to 89 – Howett R.P.

Loos Memorial – Panel 15 to 19 – Jones N.A.

Loos Memorial – Panel 69 to 73 – Knifton J.M.

Loos Memorial – Panel 103 to 105 – Ryley D.A.G.B.

Mailly-Maillet Communal Cemetery Extension – Grave ref. D42 (Albert, Somme) – Garrett A.D.

Meaulte Military Cemetery – Grave ref. G24 (Meaulte, Somme) – Lansdale W.M.

Merville Communal Cemetery – Grave ref. 111.K.6 (Merville, Nord) – Walker S.H.

Mory Abbey Military Cemetery – Grave ref. 1.B.4 (Mory, Pas de Calais) – Murray A.A.

Noeux-Les-Mines Communal Cemetery Extension – Grave ref. 111.A.5 (Bethune, Pas de Calais) – Goatcher F.

Peronne Communal Cemetery Extension – Grave ref. 111.K.2 (Peronne, Somme) – Gale P.J.

Philosophe British Cemetery – Grave ref. 1Q6 (Mazingarbe, Pas de Calais) – Cock E.M.

Pozieres Memorial – Panel 37 (Pozieres, Somme) – Ellis C.A.W

Pozieres Memorial – Panel 46 & 47 – Fletcher B

Pozieres Memorial – Panel 10 – Husk F.J.

Pozieres Memorial – Panel 61 to 64 – Plowman O.C.
Pozieres British Cemetery – Grave ref. 1V.P.16 (Albert, Somme) – Ruggles. C.G.
Quatre Vents Military Cemetery – Grave ref. 11.A.1 (Estree-Cauchy, Pas de Calais) – Stubbs R.A.
Quievy Communal Cemetery Extension – Grave ref. B18 (Quievy, Nord) – Oliver W.H.R.
Ration Farm Military Cemetery – Grave ref. 11.C.2 (Chapelle D'Armentieres, Nord) – Roeber D.A.
Roclincourt Military Cemetery – Grave ref. 1.F.26 (Roclincourt, Pas de Calais) – Levy G.
Rue des Berceaux Military Cemetery – Grave ref. 1.A.17 (Richebourg, Pas de Calais) – Taffs, C.R.
Sailly-Saillisel British Cemetery – Grave ref. V11.B.5 (Albert, Somme) – Gant H.H.
Serre Road Cemetery No.2 – Grave ref. XXV.L.8 (Albert, Somme) – Keesey G.E.H.
St Pierre Cemetery – Grave ref. 1X.C.7 (Amiens, Somme) – Finnimore H.J.
St Sever Cemetery – Grave ref. A.15.59 (Rouen, Seine-Maritime) – Doughton W.G.
St Sever Cemetery – Grave ref. B.2.34 – Knight G.B.
Terlincthun British Cemetery – Grave ref. 111.D.14 (Boulogne, Pas de Calais) – Lorey C.C.
Thiepval Memorial – Pier & Face 9D (Bapaume/Albert, Somme) – Carrier J.R.
Thiepval Memorial – Pier & Face 9D – Dawes A.E.
Thiepval Memorial – Pier & Face 11A – Falby E.F.
Thiepval Memorial – Pier & Face 11A & 11D – Hamilton N.C.
Thiepval Memorial – Pier & Face 11C – Harris H.C.
Thiepval Memorial – Pier & Face 5A & B – Mason W.J.
Thiepval Memorial – Pier & Face 13C – Page A.
Thiepval Memorial – Pier & Face 8C,9A & 16A – Procter, A.D.G.
Thiepval Memorial – Pier & Face 9C – Prout A.S

APPENDIX I

Thiepval Memorial – Pier & Face 13C – Riminton P.H.
Thiepval Memorial – Pier & Face 13C – Rowe H.S.
Thiepval Memorial – Pier & Face 14B &14C – Ryley H.B. Jnr
Thiepval Memorial – Pier & Face 13C – Walsh R.W.
Thiepval Memorial – Pier & Face 9C & 13C – Weatherston S.B.
Valenciennes (St Roch) Communal Cemetery – Grave ref. V.D.26 (Valenciennes, Nord) – Cook W.E.
Valenciennes (St Roch) Communal Cemetery – Grave ref. 1D12 – Hood J.W.
Villers-Bretonneaux Military Cemetery – Grave ref. XV1.A.2 (Villers-Bretonneaux, Somme) – Dixson F.
Vimy Memorial – (Vimy, Pas de Calais) – Spencer- Smith H
Vis-en-Artois Memorial –Panel 10 (Vis-en-Artois, Pas de Calais) – Castle E.W.K.
Warlincourt Halte British Cemetery – Grave ref. V1.C.12 (Saulty, Pas de Calais) – Sanders L.Y.
Warlencourt British Cemetery – Grave ref. V1.J.8 (Warlencourt, Pas de Calais) – Trotman F.W.
Wimereux Communal Cemetery –Grave ref. 11.L.9A (Wimereux, Pas de Calais) – Athow W.J.
Wimereux Communal Cemetery – Grave ref. 1R.23A – Goenner F.C.
Y Farm Military Cemetery – Grave ref. A17 (Bois Grenier, Nord) – Junkison A.C.

Germany – 1 site – 1 Olavian

Berlin South Western Cemetery – Grave ref. 1X..D.3 (Stahnsdorf, Brandenburg) – Bishopp S.

Greece – 2 sites – 2 Olavians

Doiran Memorial (Lake Doiran) – Defries F.
Lembet Road Military Cemetery – Grave ref. 1441 (Salonika) – Belcher D.C.

Iran – 1 site – 1 Olavian

Tehran War Cemetery – Grave ref. 111.A.15 (Gulhek, Tehran) – Grant H.A.

Iraq – 2 sites – 2 Olavians

Basra Memorial – Panel 12 – (Basra, Persian Gulf) – Marner G.L.S.
Kut War Cemetery – Grave ref. D18 (Kut, Iraq) – Oxford H.A.

Israel – 5 sites – 5 Olavians

Beersheba War Cemetery – Grave ref. N43 (Beersheba) – Burn E.A.H.
Gaza War Cemetery – Grave ref. X.C.6 (Gaza) – Young H.G.
Jerusalem War Cemetery – Grave ref. N49 (Jerusalem) – Hearn R.C.
Jerusalem Memorial – Panel 52 (Mount of Olives, Jerusalem) – Hollands H.E.
Ramleh War Cemetery – Grave ref. D30 (Jaffa, Israel) – Ryley H.B. Snr

Turkey – 2 sites – 2 Olavians

Green Hill Cemetery – Grave ref. 11.E.21 (Yilghin Burnu, Gallipoli Peninsula) – Grant P.T.W
Helles Memorial – Panel 30 & 31 (Gallipoli Peninsula) – Halliday E

United Kingdom – 12 sites – 14 Olavians

Abney Park Cemetery – Grave ref. M8.RN.24397 (Abney Park, London) – Beecraft W.H.
Bandon Hill Cemetery – Grave Ref. M44 (Beddington, Surrey) – Dodkins L.C.
Brockley Cemetery – Grave ref. W64 (Deptford, London) – Talbot E.

APPENDIX I

Chatham Memorial –Grave Ref. 30 (Chatham, Kent) – Budd V.J
Chatham Memorial – Grave Ref. 30 – Dodson W.A.
Chatham Memorial – Grave ref. 20 – Fairlie J.A.
City of London & Tower Hamlets Cemetery – Grave ref. 10597 (Stepney, London) – Miles F.D.
Crystal Palace District Cemetery – Grave ref. W3.7736 (Anerley, London) – Pearson E.A.
Forest Hill Road Cemetery – Grave Ref. 27.25151 (Camberwell, London) – Le Chavetois G.A.
Fovant (St George) Churchyard – Grave ref. 11.A.11 (Fovant, Wiltshire) – Child A.G.
Hither Green Cemetery – Grave ref. B643 (Lewisham, London) – Royal G.D.
Kingston upon Thames Cemetery – Grave ref. B401 (Norbiton, Surrey) – Barton E.
Netley Military Cemetery –Grave ref. 1738 (Southampton, Hampshire) – Akerman R.P.
Plumstead Cemetery – Grave ref. H556 (Woolwich, London) – Foreman R.J.

APPENDIX II
Name Index

<u>Abbreviation and explanation:</u> The School Prize List records reveal that certain Students won Athletic distinctions for specific sporting achievements. In addition, each prize giving service updated the latest academic achievements of those on the 'Honour List'. These were Students excelling in some form of further education. Both of these groups are highlighted in the Index.

Where two dates appear in bold type in closed brackets, for example.. **(1880–87)**, this signifies the duration of the Individuals time at St Olaves as a Student. Where a specific date is provided, with day, month and year printed in italics, for example, *1/11/14*, this represents the date of the individuals death, from wounds or disease, or the date on which the individuals were perceived to be missing presumed dead.

Akerman, Ralph Portland, 2Lt, 11th Londons... Chapter 4, **Athletic Distinctions, (1901–05),** *3/10/15*
Almond, James Edgar, Pte, 9th Royal Fusiliers...Chapter 22, **(1911–16)** *8/8/18*
Athow, William, Pte, 8th Royal Fusiliers...Chapter 11, **(1890–99)** *1/6/17*
Baker, Albert George, Pte, 5th Londons.....Chapter 15 **(1909–12)** *19/9/16*
Baker, Harold William, Pte, 20th Royal Fusiliers.....Chapter 11 **(1910–15)** *16/4/17*
Barton, Ernest, Lt, Royal Field Artillery....Chapter 23, **(1900–07)** *1/4/19*
Beecraft, William Henry, Pte, 16th Middlesex....Chapter 23, **(1908–13)** *29/7/20*
Belcher, Douglas Charles, L/Cpl, 102nd Sanitary Section, Royal Army Medical Corps...Chapter 7, **(1906–11)** *5/7/18*

APPENDIX II

Bendixen, Leonard, Caporal, French Army....Chapter 2, **Athletic Distinctions, (1905-06)** *24/11/14*

Bennett, Frederick Barberry, Major, C Battery, 84th Army Bde, Royal Field Artillery....Chapter 14, **(1892-95)** *22/10/18*

Benson, George Enoch, Rfn, 2nd Bn, The Rifle Brigade....Chapter 5, **Honour List, (1906-13),** *9/5/15*

Berrow, Lewis Walter, Pte, Yorkshire Dragoons.....Chapter 23, **Honour List, (1903-10)** *19/1/21*

Berrow, William Rushbury, Pte, E Bn, Tank Corps....Chapter 15, **(1902-07)** *23.11.17*

Bishopp, Stephen **M.M**. Pte, 17th Royal Fusiliers.....Chapter 20, **(1901-05)** *7/5/18*

Blackman, Herbert William, Pte, 8th Rifle Brigade....Chapter 10, **(1901-05)** *15/9/16*

Blencowe, Charles Edward, 2Lt, Royal Sussex att'd 1st Wiltshires.... Chapter 18, **(1903-07)** *3/5/18*

Bliss, Harold Edgar, Pte, 7th Norfolks.....Chapter 6, **(1905-10),** *13/10/15*

Boone, John William Donald, L/Cpl, 22nd Rifle Brigade.....Chapter 23, **(1906-15)** *23.3.22*

Brittain, Percy James, Pte, 1/24th Londons....Chapter 10, **(1906-11)** *18/9/16*

Brown, Charles Henry Goullee, Pte, B Coy, Royal Engineers...Chapter 12, **(1909-16)** *19/8/17*

Budd, Victor John, Flight Sub Lt, Royal Naval Air Service....Chapter 3, *School Captain (1916-17)* **(1910-17)** *20/2/18*

Burn, Edmund Alfred Henry, Pte, 2/14th Londons.....Chapter 21 **(1911-13)** *31/10/17*

Burwood, Philip, Pte, 2/23rd Londons....Chapter 22, **(1905-08)** *24/8/18*

Butler, Edmund Hearn, Cpl, 2/9th Londons....Chapter 11, **(1897-1904)** *26/5/17*

Carrier, John Russell, 2Lt, 1/5th Londons....Chapter 10, **(1906-08)** *8/10/16*

Castell, George Charles, 1st Air Mechanic, 12 Sqdn, Royal Flying Corps.... Chapter 17, **(1904-07)** *12/8/17*

Castle, Ewart William King, Rfn, 1/16th Londons....Chapter 22, **(1909-15)** *28/8/18*

Chapman, Robert Stanley, Rfn, 2/5th Londons....Chapter 16, **Honour List, (1904-10)** *22/9/17*
Chester, Harold Thomas, Pte, 1st Royal Guernsey Light Infantry....Chapter 20, **(1910-15)** *13/4/18*
Child, Albert George, Pte, 3/5th Londons.....Chapter 23 , **(1909-12)**, *29/4/16*
Chubb, John Lethbridge, Pte, 19th Canadian Infantry (Central Ontario Regt)...Chapter 19, **(1911-12)** *8/8/18*
Churcher, Edgar, Lt, 32 Sqdn, Royal Flying Corps.....Chapter 17, **(1907-10)** *14/7/17*
Clarke, Ernest Howell, Pte, 95th Coy, Machine Gun Corps...Chapter 15, **(1897-1903)** *13/4/18*
Clifton, Frank Osenton, L/Cpl, 7th East Kents....Chapter 13, **(1905-08)** *3/8/17*
Cock, Edward Millar, Pte, 28th Londons att'd 9th Suffolks....Chapter 18, *School Captain (1915-16)* **(1908-15)** *26/5/17*
Cook, Alleyne James, Rfn, 18th Londons....Chapter 6, **(1907-12)** *25/9/15*
Cook, William Edwin, Lt, 1/2nd att'd 4th Yorkshires....Chapter 20, **(1908-11)** *28/3/18*
Curtis, Ernest John, 2Lt, 5th att'd 7th Royal West Kents... Chapter 18, **(1891-94)** *22/1/18*
Dale-James, William Rushbrooke, Royal Naval Wireless Service...Chapter 3, **(1894-1900)** *18/10/18*
Dawes, Albert Ernest, Rfn, 1/5th Londons...Chapter 10, **(1906-11)** *9/10.16*
Deem, Henry Theodore Samuel, Pte, 15th Londons....Chapter 22, **(1905-06)** *4/9/18*
Defries, Frederick, Cpt **MID**, 5th att'd 3rd Middlesex...Chapter 21, **(1896-1900)** *5/4/18*
Dell, Claude Stanley, L/Cpl, 5th Yorkshires....Chapter 5, **(1901-05)**, *24/4/15*
Dennis, Robert Charles, Pte, 1/2nd Royal Fusiliers.....Chapter 11, **(1905-11)** *3/5/17*
Dixson, Frank, Sgt, No.4 Workshop, Royal Engineers...Chapter 12, **(1905-09)** *29/3/18*

APPENDIX II

Dodkins, Lionel Claud, Flying Officer, 25th Londons + 31 Sqdn, Royal Air Force....Chapter 23, **Athletic Distinctions, (1907-11)** *13/6/21*

Dodson, William Albert, 2nd Air Mechanic, Royal Naval Air Service... Chapter 3, **(1904-06)** *20/1/18*

Doughton, Walter George, Pte, 10th Royal Fusiliers....Chapter 9, **(1905-06)** *21/7/16*

Doyle, Gilbert, Army Blankets Inspector, Ministry of Munitions....Chapter 23, **(1890-94)** *1/7/18*

Dubery, Frank Arthur, Gnr, A Battery, 236 Bde, Royal Field Artillery... Chapter 14, **(1909-14)** *6/6/17*

Dunkley, William Henry, Pte, 7th Londons....Chapter 22, **(1906-11)** *9/8/18*

Durant, John Stride, 1st Canadian Mounted Rifles (Saskatchewan Regt)... Chapter 19, **(1896-99)**, *2/6/16*

Ebsworth, Harold Charles, 2nd Honourable Artillery Company...Chapter 14, **(1907-14)** *7/12/16*

Edgley, Leslie Seymour, Trooper, Royal Horse Guards....Chapter 5, **(1904-05)**, *13/5/15*

Edmunds, Cecil Harry, Lt, 21st Londons....Chapter 20, **(Master 1911-15)** *23/3/18*

Edwards, Albert Frederick, Rfn, 12th Londons....Chapter 5, **(1903-05)**, *5/5/15*

Ellis, Charles Albert William, Rfn, 1st Monmouthshires att'd 10th South Wales Borderers ...Chapter 20, **(1898-99)** *8/5/18*

Evans, Leonard Austin, 2Lt, 15th Bn, Tank Corps....Chapter 15, **(1906-13)** *27/3/18*

Fairlie, John Alwyne, Able Seaman, Royal Naval Volunteer Reserve.... Chapter 3, **(1897-1903)**, *31/5/16*

Falby, Edward Frederick, 2Lt, 1/4th Loyal North Lancashires....Chapter 9, **(1904-07)** *9/9/16*

Falkner, Clarence Beach, Cpt, 2/2nd Londons....Chapter 16, **(1907-11)** *25/10/17*

Feben, Evi, Cpl, 6th Battery, Royal Field Artillery...Chapter 14, **(1892-93)**, *3/3/15*

Finnimore, Henry James, 2Lt, 7th Royal Sussex att'd Royal Flying Corps.... Chapter 17, **(1908-12)** *27/3/18*

Fitzgerald, Robert, L/Cpl, 1/24th Londons....Chapter 5, **(1908–11)**, *26/5/15*

Fletcher, Beaumont, L/Cpl, 13th Royal Sussex....Chapter 20, **(1887–90)** *25/3/18*

Foreman, Roland John, 2nd Waiter, Royal Navy.....Chapter 3, **(1906–11)** *9/2/19*

Gale, Percy James, L/Sgt, 1/24th Londons....Chapter 22, **(1908–13)** *2/9/18*

Gant, Harold Holden, 2Lt, 2nd Royal Fusiliers...Chapter 22, **(1899–1902)** *1/9/18*

Garrett, Arthur Daniel, Pte, 1st Honourable Artillery Company....Chapter 10, **(1891–95)** *15/10/16*

Gaskain, Cecil Stanley, Lt, 29 Sqdn, Royal Flying Corps + RFA.....Chapter 17, **(1902–05)** *7/5/17*

Gill, Jack Woodward, 2Lt, 6th KOYLI...Chapter 6, **Honour List, (1903–13)**, *20/11/15*

Glenn, Reginald James, Pte, 20th Londons....Chapter 5, **(1909–13)**, *16/7/15*

Goatcher, Fred, Lt, 9th Suffolks....Chapter 16 – **Honour List, Athletic Distinctions, (1903–08)** *31/10/17*

Goenner, Frederick Charles, Rfn, 17th Kings Royal Rifle Corps.....Chapter 10, **(1909–11)** *29/10/16*

Grant, Harold Allan, 2Lt, 4th S.Staffs att'd 7th N.Staffs....Chapter 21, **Honour List, Athletic Distinctions, (1890–99)** *22/9/18*

Grant, PhilipThomas Wilson, 2Lt, 8th att'd 5th Wiltshires.....Chapter 4, **(1908–12),** *15/10/15*

Gray, Wallace James, Pte, 20th Royal Fusiliers.....Chapter 11, **(1901–06)** *16/4/17*

Grist, Percival Charles Hugh, Lt, 25th Londons....Chapter 22, **(1899–1901)** *18/9/18*

Halliday, Eric, Pte, 2/4th Royal West Surreys.....Chapter 4, **(1909–12),** *19/8/15*

Halliwell, Ernest, Gnr, D Battery, 232 Bde, Royal Field Artillery...Chapter 14, **(1897–99)** *12/10/17*

Halliwell, William Co Sgt Major, **M.C.**, 1st Rifle Brigade....Chapter 5, **(1898–99),** *6/7/15*

APPENDIX II

Hamilton, Claud William, Cpt, 287th Siege Battery, Royal Garrison Artillery....Chapter 14, **(1905–06)** *6/11/17*

Hamilton, Noel Crawford, 2Lt, 6th Northamptonshires....Chapter 9, **Honour List,** *School Captain (1911–12)* **(1905–12)** *14/7/16*

Harris, Herbert Cecil, Cpt, 6th Royal West Kents....Chapter 8, **Honour List, (1905–09)** *3/7/16*

Harvard, Kenneth O'Gorman, Lt, 2nd Grenadier Guards....Chapter 13, **(1906–10)** *1/8/17*

Harvard, Lionel De Jersey, Cpt, 1st Grenadier Guards....Chapter 20, **Athletic Distinctions, (1904–10)** *30/3/18*

Haseldine, Newton Woollcombe, Rfn, 1/5th Londons...Chapter 5, **(1910–12)**, *2/5/15*

Hay, Arthur Leslie, 2Lt, 4th att'd 10/11th Highland Light Infantry....Chapter 11, **(1908–10)** *26/4/17*

Hearn, Robert Cecil, Cpt, **M.C.**, 2/20th Londons...Chapter 21, **Honour List, (1900–11)** *30/4/17*

Heron, Joseph Solomon, Rfn, 1/21st Londons....Chapter 5, **(1900–04)**, *25/5/15*

Hill, Sidney Ernest, Sgt, 1/20th Londons....Chapter 11, **(1898–1900),** *24/5/16*

Hoare, Ernest Austin, Cpl, 186th Special Coy, Royal Engineers...Chapter 12, **(1909–12)**, *21/9/15*

Hocking, Leslie Harold, Pte, 2/1st London Field Ambulance, RAMC...Chapter 7, **Honour List, (1904–14)** *1/7/16*

Hollands, Harold Evan, Cpl, 2/21st Londons....Chapter 21, **(1905–13)** *20/2/18*

Hollands, Wilfred George, 2Lt, 7th att'd 4th Royal Fusiliers....Chapter 10, **(1903–09)** *12/10/16*

Holman, William Elijah, Pte, 1/2nd Royal Fusiliers....Chapter 11, **(1909–13)** *16/8/17*

Hood, John William, Lt, **MID**, 39th Siege Battery, Royal Garrison Artillery...Chapter 23, **Honour List, (1901–09)** *15/11/18*

Howett, Frank, Co Sgt Major, Londons (Civil Service Rifles)....Chapter 11, **(1894–96),** *21/5/16*

Howett, Robert Plunkett, Sgt, 1/5th Notts and Derby...Chapter 6, **(1895–98),** *14/10/15*

Hunt, Harold, Rfn, 3rd Rifle Brigade....Chapter 13, **(1905-09)** *7/6/17*
Husk, Frederick John, 2Lt, **M.M.**, Royal Garrison Artillery...Chapter 14, **(1904-07)** *21/3/18*
Jones, James Thomas, 2Lt, 20th Londons.....Chapter 13, **School Captain *(1914-15)* (1912-15)** *24/8/17*
Jones, Norman Aldham, Pte, East Kent Regiment...Chapter 6, **(1903-07)**, *13/10/15*
Jones, Thomas Idwal, Lt, **M.M.**, 18th Londons....Chapter 22, **(1908-12)** *31/8/18*
Junkison, Arthur Charles, Pte, 15th Londons...Chapter 23, **(1903-05)** *4/11/18*
Keesey, George Ernest Howard, Cpt, 8th Rifle Brigade...Chapter 9, **Honour List, *School Captain (1904-05)*, (1900-05)** *24/8/16*
Kenyon, Harry Thomas James, Pte, Royal Army Medical Corps....Chapter 7, **(1905-11)** *17/8/17*
Kiddle, Robert Henry, Pte, Liverpool Regt....Chapter 18 **(1910-16)** *15/3/18*
Kidney, Leonard Edwin, Sgt, 9th Royal Fusiliers.....Chapter 18, **(1905-10)** *20/11/17*
King, Stanley Edward, Rfn, 5th Londons......Chapter 23, **(1911-16)** *12/10/18*
Knifton, James McKinlay, 2Lt, 3rd att'd 2nd Royal Sussex....Chapter 22, **(1910-16)** *21/7/18*
Knight, George Bertram, 2Lt, 54 Sqdn, Royal Air Force....Chapter 17, **(1901-07)** *7/4/18*
Knox, John Lawrence, 2Lt, 7th Royal Sussex...Chapter 18, **(1899-1901)** *20/11/17*
Lansdale, William Morris, Cpt, Adj, Royal Army Medical Corps....Chapter 7, **(1902-09)** *26/8/18*
Laurie, Arthur Wyndham, Sgt, 8th Canadian Infantry...Chapter 19, **(1903)** *26/9/16*
Le Chavetois, Grantley Adolphe, Cpt, 22nd Londons....Chapter 21, **Honour List, (1895-1905 as Student, 1912-15 as Master)** *22/1/18*
Levy, Godfrey, Rfn, 9th Londons...Chapter 18, **(1910)** *22/12/17*
Lidgett, John Cuthbert, Lt, South Lancashire Regt....Chapter 20, **Honour List, (1896-1904)** *23 or 31/3/18*

APPENDIX II

Lorey, Conrad Clifford, Sgt, 7th Londons att'd Machine Gun Corps... Chapter 15, **(1906–11)** *9/9/18*

Lovekin, Vyvyan Ivor, Gnr, Canadian Artillery.... Chapter 19, **(1906–11),** *23/4/15*

Lunn, Ralph William, 2Lt, Royal Field and Horse Artillery...Chapter 14, **(1904–08)** *17/6/17*

Mann, Stanley Walter, 2Lt, 9 Sqdn, Royal Flying Corps.....Chapter 17, **(1910–12)** *1/11/16*

Marner, George Lionel Stuart, Cpt, 10th Leicesters....Chapter 21, **Honour List, (1900–1904)** *15/4/17*

Marriott, Herbert Percy Gordon, Rfn, 5th Londons....Chapter 16, **(1909–15)** *20/9/17*

Mason, William John, Cpt, 8th Gloucesters...Chapter 8, **Honour List, (1898–1908)** *3/7/16*

Maybrook, Walter Richard, 2Lt, 1st Wiltshires...Chapter 11, **Honour List, Athletic Distinctions,** *School Captain (1912–13)* **(1908–13),** *24/4/16*

Miles, Frank David, Pte, 28th Londons......Chapter 22, **(1906–09)** *20/9/18*

Murray, Archibald Albert, Gnr, Royal Field Artillery....Chapter 11, **(1910–13)** *15/4/17*

Norris, Frederick, Cpt, 23rd Middlesex....Chapter 13, **Honour List,** *School Captain (1912–13)* **(1905–13)** *7/6/17*

Oake, Douglas, Cpt, **M.C.**, East Yorkshires att'd 92nd Trench Mortar Battery....Chapter 14, **(1900–1906)** *8/10/18*

Oliver, William Henry Rudland, Pte, 20th Londons....Chapter 23, **(1909–13)** *20/10/18*

Oxford, Harry Arthur, Pte, Royal Army Supply Corps....Chapter 23, **(1889–94)** *28/9/18*

Page, Alfred, Pte, 15th Londons att'd Machine Gun Corps...Chapter 15, **(1908–11)** *16/9/16*

Pearson, Eugene Arthur, Sub Lt, Surgeon, Royal Navy....Chapter 3, **(1903–12)** *6/11/18*

Perkins, Douglas, Rfn, 12th Londons...Chapter 18, **(1899–1901)** *28/2/17*

Phare, Dudley Gershom, Lt, 7th Kings Shropshire Light Infantry....Chapter 20, **(1903–04)** *28/3/18*

Plowman, Oswald Cheyney, Pte, Kings Royal Rifle Corps....Chapter 20, **(1906–10)** *28/3/18*

Procter, Alexander Duncan Guthrie, 2Lt, 8th Royal Fusiliers....Chapter 8, **(1906–10)** *7/7/16*

Prout, Arthur Stanley, Pte, 12th Londons.....Chapter 8, **(1902–08)** *1/7/16*

Quixley, Arthur Newman Charles, Pte, 24th Londons....Chapter 5, **(1908–11)**, *25/5/15*

Richardson, James Bert, Pte, 12th Rifle Brigade....Chapter 6, **(1908–10)**, *25/9/15*

Riminton, Percy Henry, Rfn, 16th Londons....Chapter 10, **(1909–11)** *18/9/16*

Rings, Fritz Ludwig, Pte, Royal Sussex Regiment....Chapter 16, **(1907–11)** *27/10/17*

Roberts, James Roderick Trethowan, 2Lt, 2nd Suffolks....Chapter 2, **(1908–13),** *3/3/15*

Robinson, Edwin Hall, Rfn, Kings Royal Rifle Corps....Chapter 16, **(1888–96)** *24/10/17*

Roeber David Arnold, 2Lt, Bedfordshire Regiment...Chapter 9, **(1908–10)** *15/8/16*

Rowe, Henry Shepard, Rfn, 16th Londons....Chapter 10, **(1903–08)** *18/9/16*

Royal, George Dudley, Pte, Royal Army Supply Corps....Chapter 23, **(1906–12)** *3/12/16*

Ruggles, Charles George, Pte, Australian Contingent.....Chapter 4, **(1901–06),** *25/6/16*

Rule, Austin George, Pte, 15th Londons....Chapter 9, **(1911–14)** *7/9/16*

Ryder, Gordon William, Pte, 14th Londons....Chapter 2, **(1898–1900),** *1/11/14*

Ryley, Donald Arthur George Buchanan, Lt, N.Staffordshires....Chapter 18, **Honour List, Athletic Distinctions, (1904–12)** *11/2/17*

Ryley, Harold Buchanan Snr, Lt, 1/5th Suffolks....Chapter 21, **Honour List, (1880–87 as Student, 1895–1901 as Master)** *15/12/17*

Ryley, Harold Buchanan Jnr, 2Lt, 4th att'd 1st North Staffordshires.... Chapter 9, **(1907–11 and 1914)** *7/9/16*

Sanders, Leslie Yorath, 2Lt, Royal Garrison Artillery att'd Royal Engineers

APPENDIX II

Survey Coy...Chapter 12, **Honour List,** *School Captain (1911-12)* **(1907-12)** *10/3/17*

Schooling, Geoffrey Holt, Pte, 16th Londons....Chapter 6, **(1903-06),** *28/12/15*

Schulz, Harry Albert, Cpl, 12th Londons....Chapter 5, **(1904-07),** *24/4/15*

Shears, Edmund George, Ptem Honourable Artillery Company...Chapter 14, **(1909-11)** *22/5/17*

Shepherd, Henry Alick, Pte, 15th Londons.....Chapter 13, **(1901-03)** *7/6/17*

Shore, James Harold, Pte, 14th Warwickshires....Chapter 20 **(1911-14)** *14/4/18*

Smith, George William, 2Lt, Royal Lancaster Regiment....Chapter 20, **(1910-15)** *28/3/18*

Spencer-Smith, Herbert, Pte, Princess Patricia's, 49th Canadians.... Chapter 19, **(1903-08)** *14/9/16*

Sprang, Frederick William, Cpt, 6th Dorsets...Chapter 11, **(1901-08)** *13/4/17*

Stables, Leonard Theodore Drury, Lt, 6th Bedfordshires....Chapter 23, **(1903-10)** *23/10.18*

Stockins, William James, 2Lt, 28th Londons att'd 27 Sqdn, Royal Flying Corps...Chapter 17 **(1906-11)** *6/6/18*

Stubbs, Reginald Arthur, 2Lt, 32 Sqdn, Royal Flying Corps....Chapter 17, **(1900-1907),** *8/6/16*

Sutcliffe, Frederick Malcolm, 2Lt, 8th Londons...Chapter 11, **(1894-1900)** *29/5/17*

Sutherland, John, Pte, 15th Londons.....Chapter 13, **(1909-14)** *3/7/17*

Taffs, Charles Reginald, Lt, 1st Royal Berkshires...Chapter 5, **(1901-06),** *17/5/15*

Tait, Leonard Sidney, Pte, 16th Londons.....Chapter 2, **(1903-06),** *24/12/14*

Talbot, Cecil Melliar, 2Lt, 14th att'd 4th Middlesex Regiment...Chapter 6, **(1902-07),** *27/9/15*

Talbot, Ernest, Sgt, Royal Fusiliers.....Chapter 23, **(1901-05),** *4/1/16*

Taylor, William Frederick, Lt, 3rd East Kents...Chapter 5, **(1906-10),** *7/6/15*

Terry, Sidney Frederick, Cpt, **M.C.**, 1st Wiltshires....Chapter 20, **Honour List, (1905-13)** *24/3/18*

Thompson, Edward William Murray, Pte, 2/13th Londons....Chapter 11, **(1909-12)** *2/7/16*

Trotman, Frank William, Pte, 15th Londons....Chapter 10, **(1897-1903)** *7/10/16*

Trotman, Henry John, Dvr, Royal Field Artillery...Chapter 14, **(1902-05)** *12/9/16*

Veale-Williams, John Marcus, Rfn, 3/5th Londons....Chapter 20, **(1910-14)** *24/3/18*

Vernall, Arthur Humphrey, 2Lt, **M.C.**, 6th Leicesters.....Chapter 22, **(1897-1899)** *23/8/18*

Wade, Oliver John, 2Lt, Royal West Kents att'd 45 Sqdn, Royal Flying Corps....Chapter 17, **Athletic Distinctions,** *School Captain (1914-15)* **(1904-15)** *22/10/16*

Walker, Sidney Herbert, Pte, 6th Seaforth Highlanders...Chapter 5, **(1907-11),** *15/6/15*

Walker, William Richard, Pte, 14th Londons....Chapter 6, **(1907-11),** *25/9/15*

Wallace, George Frederick, 2Lt, 24th Middlesex...Chapter 11, **(1908-13)** *23/5/17*

Walsh, Richard William, Pte, 15th Londons...Chapter 11, **(1908-10)** *15/9/16*

Wardley, Miles Edward, Pte, 15th Londons....Chapter 11, **(1902-07)** *29/4/17*

Weatherston, John Frederick, Able Seaman, Royal Naval Volunteer Reserve....Chapter 3, **(1901-04)** *12/3/19*

Weatherston, Sidney Bowler, Pte, 14th Londons....Chapter 8, **(1902-07)** *1/7/16*

Wells, Neil, Pte, 6th Australian Imperial Force....Chapter 4, **(1895-1902),** *25/6/15*

Wensley, Harold William, 2Lt, 1st Lincolnshires.... Chapter 23, **(1910-17)** *15/11/18*

West, Harold Douglas, 2Lt, 1st Kings Royal Rifle Corps....Chapter 20, **(1896-99)** *25/3/18*

APPENDIX II

Wilson, Albert Cecil, 2Lt, 14th Londons....Chapter 11, **(1898-1903)**, *8/7/16*

Young, Henry George, Pte, 4th Essex.....Chapter 21, **(1901-06)** *26/3/17*

APPENDIX III
Military Unit Index

NB: The London Territorial Regiments are listed first, followed by other Infantry Regiments (alphabetically), then Artillery, Machine Gun Corps, Army Service Corps, Royal Air Force, Royal Flying Corps, Artillery, Medical Corps, Engineers, Navy, Tank Corps, Colonial Regiments/Artillery and French Army.

City of London Yeomanry (Rough Riders) – Berrow William Rushbury No.91863 (Pte) (see also 'E' Battalion, Tank Corps)

2nd County of London Yeomanry – Hay Arthur Leslie No. 2170 (Pte) (see also 4th att'd 10th Highland Light Infantry)

London Regiment – Goenner Frederick Charles No 4065 (see also 13th KRRC) (Pte)

London Regiment – Battalion unknown – Trotman Henry John No. 951151 (see also RFA)

1st London Regiment – Dawes Albert Ernest

2nd London Regiment – Dennis Robert Charles No 232878 (Pte) (see also Machine Gun Corps)

2nd London Regiment – Gant Harold Holden (Pte then O) (see also HAC)

2nd London Regiment – Holman William Elijah No. 245019 (Pte) (see also 9th Londons)

2/2nd London Regiment – Stockins William James (O) (see also 27 Squadron RFC and RAF)

3rd London Regiment – Child Albert George (Pte) died Home Service.

5th London Regiment – Baker Albert George (Pte) (see also Machine Gun Corps)

5th London Regiment – Carrier John Russell (Pte, L/Cpl, CQM Sgt, O)

5th London Regiment – Chapman Robert Stanley (Pte) No 302410 (see also 25th Londons)

APPENDIX III

5th London Regiment – Churcher Edgar No.766 (466 ?) (Pte) (see also Rifle Brigade and 32 RFC)
5th London Regiment – Haseldine Newton Woollcombe No 314 (Pte)
5th London Regiment – King Stanley Edward No305893 (Pte)
'C' Company, 5th London Regiment – Chapman Robert Stanley No 302410 (Pte) (see also 25th Londons)
5th London Regiment – Marriott Herbert Percy Gordon No.303416 (Pte)
3/5th London Regiment – Veale-Williams John Marcus No305327 (Pte)
7th London Regiment – Dunkley William Henry No 350959 (Pte)
'A' Coy, 8th London Regiment – Sutcliffe Fred Malcolm (O)
9th London Regiment – Butler Edmund Hearn No 391910 (Pte)
9th London Regiment – Holman William Elijah No.472440 (Pte)(see also 2 London Regiment)
9th London Regiment – Levy Godfrey No 415193 (Pte)
9th London Regiment – Sanders Leslie Yorath No 3062 (Pte then O)
11th London Regiment – Akerman Ralph Portland (O) (based E.Africa)
12th London Regiment – Edwards Albert Frederick No 2836 (Pte)
12th London Regiment – Perkins Douglas No. 6186 (Pte)
12th London Regiment – Prout Arthur Stanley No 2593 (Cpl)
12th London Regiment – Schulz Harry Albert No 2341 (Cpl)
13th London Regiment – Thompson Edward William Murray No 3018 (Pte)
14th London Regiment – Burn Edmund Alfred Henry No (Pte)
14th London Regiment – Ryder Gordon William No (Pte) (won 14 Star)
14th London Regiment – Walker William Richard No 3928 (Pte)
14th London Regiment – Weatherston Sidney Bowler No. (Pte)
14th London Regiment – Wilson Albert Cecil (O)
15th London Regiment – Deem Henry Theodore Samuel No 532458 (Pte)
15th London Regiment – Howett Frank No. 412 (CQM Sgt)
15th London Regiment – Junkison Arthur Charles No 530445
15th London Regiment – Page Alfred (see also the Machine Gun Corps)
15th London Regiment – Rule Austin George No.2986 (Pte)
15th London Regiment – Shepherd Henry Alick
15th London Regiment – Sutherland John
15th London Regiment – Trotman Frank William No.4762 and 532108 (Pte)

15th London Regiment – Walsh Richard William
15th London Regiment – Wardley Miles Edward(O)
16th London Regiment – Castle Ewart William King
16th London Regiment – Procter Alexander Duncan Guthrie No. 3714 (Pte/L/Cpl) (see also Royal Fusiliers)
16th London Regiment – Riminton Percy Henry
16th London Regiment – Rowe Henry Shepard No.4189 (Pte)
16th London Regiment – Schooling Geoffrey Holt
16th London Regiment – Tait Leonard Sidney
17th London Regiment – Bishopp Stephen M.M.
18th London Regiment – Cook Alleyne James
18th London Regiment – Falkner Clarence Beach
18th London Regiment – Jones Thomas Idwal M.M. (O)
20th London Regiment – Glenn Reginald James
2/20th London Regiment – Hearn Robert Cecil M.C.(O)
20th London Regiment – Hill Sidney Ernest
20th London Regiment – Jones, James Thomas (O)
20th London Regiment – Oliver William Henry Rudland
21st London Regiment – Edmunds Cecil Harry (O)
21st London Regiment – Ellis Charles Albert William No. 654422 (Pte) (see also Monmouthshire Regiment)
21st London Regiment – Heron Joseph Solomon
21st London Regiment – Hollands Harold Evan No.2860 and 650850, (Cpl)
22nd London Regiment – Falkner Clarence Beach (O)
22nd (could be 2/2) London Regiment – Le Chavetois Grantley Adolphe (O)
23rd London Regiment – Burwood Philip
24th London Regiment – Brittain Percy James
24th London Regiment – Fitzgerald/Ball Robert
24th London Regiment – Gale Percy James No 3483 and 721181 (Pte/Cpl)
24th London Regiment – Halliday Eric
24th London Regiment – Quixley Arthur Newman Charles

APPENDIX III

25th London Regiment – Chapman Robert Stanley No 302410 (Pte) (see also 5th Londons)
25th London Regiment – Grist Percival Charles Hugh (O)
25th London Regiment – Stables Leonard Theodore Drury No.1570 and 305 (L/Cpl) (see also 6th Bedfordshire Regt and Northamptonshire Regt)
28th London Regiment – Cock Edward Millar
28th London Regiment – Falby Edward Frederick
28th London Regiment – Hamilton Claude William No. 2340 (Pte) (see also Royal Garrison Artillery and KRRC)
28th London Regiment – Lidgett John Cuthbert
28th London Regiment – Maybrook Walter Richard
28th London Regiment – Miles Frank David
28th London Regiment – Terry Sidney Frederick M.C.
28th London Regiment – Veale-Williams John Marcus
4th Royal Fusiliers (attached from the 7th) – Hollands, Wilfred George (O) (see also Middlesex Regt)
6th Royal Fusiliers – Wardley Miles Edward(O)
8th Royal Fusiliers – Athow William J
8th Royal Fusiliers – Doughton Walter George
8th Royal Fusiliers – Procter Alexander Duncan Guthrie (O) (see also 16th Londons)
8th Royal Fusiliers – Talbot Ernest (CQSM) died Home Service.
9th Royal Fusiliers – Almond James Edgar
9th Royal Fusiliers – Kidney Leonard Edwin No.1136 (L/Cpl, A/Sgt)
10th Royal Fusiliers – Doughton Walter George
20th Royal Fusiliers – Baker Harold William no. PS/10635 (Pte)
20th Royal Fusiliers – Gray ,Wallace James no. G/53109 (Pte)
22nd Royal Fusiliers – Wardley Miles Edward(O)
25th Royal Fusiliers – Blencowe Charles Edward No. (Pte) E.Africa – (see also Royal Sussex and Wiltshire Regiments)
6th Bedfordshire Regiment – Stables Leonard Theodore Drury (O) (see also 25th Londons and Northamptonshire Regiment)
3rd attached 7th Bedfordshire Regiment – Roeber David Arnold (O)

'D' Company, 6th Dorset Regiment – Sprang Frederick William (O)
3rd East Kent Regiment (The Buffs) – Taylor William Frederick (O)
6th East Kent Regiment (The Buffs) – Jones Norman Aldman no. G/246 (Pte/Cpl)
7th East Kent Regiment (The Buffs) – Clifton Frank Osenton
East Surrey Regiment – Battalion unknown – Clarke Ernest Howell No. 28037 (Pte) (see also Royal Sussex Regt and 95th Coy, Machine Gun Corps)
11th East Yorkshire Regiment – Oake Douglas M.C. (O)
4th Essex Regiment – Young Henry George
8th Gloucester Regiment – Mason William John(O)
1st Grenadier Guards – Harvard Lionel De Jersey (O)
2nd Grenadier Guards – Harvard Kenneth O'Gorman. (O)
4th attached 10/11th Highland Light Infantry – Hay Arthur Leslie (O) (see also 2nd County of London Yeomanry)
1st Battalion TheRifle Brigade – Blackman Herbert William No.S/15952
3rd Battalion The Rifle Brigade – Churcher Edgar (O) (see also 5th Londons and 32 Squadron, RFC)
3rd Battalion, The Rifle Brigade – Hunt Harold no. S/31329 (Rfn)
8th Battalion The Rifle Brigade – Keesey George Ernest Howard (O)
12th Kings Royal Rifle Brigade – Richardson James Bert
22nd Kings Royal Rifle Brigade – Boone John William Donald
Kings Royal Rifle Corps – Battalion unknown – Hamilton ClaudeWilliam (O) (see also 28th Londons and Royal Garrison Artillery 287 Siege Battery
1st Kings Royal Rifle Corps – Halliwell William
1st Kings Royal Rifle Corps – West Harold Douglas (O)
5th Kings Royal Rifle Corps – Benson George Enoch
'B' Coy, 13th Kings Royal Rifle Corps – Goenner Frederick Charles no. A/2000089 (Rfn)
13th Kings Royal Rifle Corps – Robinson Edwin Hall no. R/31386 (Rfn)
17th Kings Royal Rifle Corps – Plowman Oswald Cheyney no. A/202333 (Rfn)
7th Kings Shropshire Light Infantry – Phare Dudley Gershom (O) attached from the RASC. (see also Royal Army Supply Corps and Royal

APPENDIX III

Army Medical Corps)
8th Kings Own Royal Lancaster Regiment – Smith George William (O)
3rd attached 6th Leicester Regiment – Vernall Arthur Humphrey M.C.(O)
'B' Company, 2nd Battalion, 10th Leicester Regiment – Marner George Lionel Stuart (O)
1st Lincolnshire Regiment – Wensley Harold William (O)
'Y' Coy, 1/10th The Kings (Liverpool) Regiment – Kiddle Robert Henry No 358315 (Pte)
1/4th Loyal North Lancashire Regiment – Falby Edward Frederick (O)
Manchester Regiment – Battalion unknown – Ryley Donald Arthur George Buchanan (O)
Middlesex Regiment – Battalion unknown – Hollands Wilfred George (Pte) (see also 7th attached 4th Royal Fusiliers)
14th attached 4th Middlesex Regiment – Talbot Cecil Melliar (O)
5th attached (?) Middlesex Regiment – Defries Frederick (O)
10th Middlesex Regiment – Vernall Arthur Humphrey M.C.(O)
14th Middlesex Regiment – Talbot Cecil Melliar (O)
16th Middlesex Regiment – Beecraft William Henry
20th Middlesex Regiment – Wallace George Frederick (O)
23rd Middlesex Regiment – Norris Frederick(O)
24th Middlesex Regiment – Wallace George Frederick (O)
Monmouthshire Regiment – Battalion unknown – Ellis Charles Albert William No.263065 (Pte) (see also 21st Londons)
7th Norfolk Regiment – Bliss Harold Edgar
Norfolk Cycling Battalion – Grist Percival Charles Hugh (O) (see also 25th Londons)
Northamptonshire Regiment – Battalion unknown – Stables Leonard Theodore Drury (O) (att'd from 6th Bedfordshire Regt). (see also 25th Londons and 6th Bedfordshire Regt)
North Staffordshire Regiment – Battalion unknown – Ryley Donald Arthur George Buchanan (O)
4th attached 1st North Staffordshire Regiment – Ryley Harold Buchanan (Jnr) (O)
7th North Staffordshire Regiment – Grant Harold Allan (O)

6th Northamptonshire Regiment – Hamilton Noel Crawford (O)
5th Notts and Derbyshire Regiment – Howett Robert Plunkett
1st Royal Berkshire Regiment – Taffs Charles Reginald (O)
5th Royal Berkshire Regiment – Lansdale William Morris (O) (see also Royal Army Medical Corps)
1st Royal Guernsey Light Infantry – Chester Harold Thomas No1758 (Pte)
4th Royal Munster Fusiliers – Stubbs Reginald Arthur (O)
Royal Sussex Regiment – Battalion unknown – Blencowe Charles Edward (O) (attached to the 1st Wiltshire Regiment and 25th Royal Fusiliers)
Royal Sussex Regiment – Battalion unknown – Clarke Ernest Howell (Pte) 2397 (see also East Surrey Regt and Machine Gun Corps"
7th Royal Sussex Regiment – Finnimore Henry James (O) (see also 28th Londons and 48 Squadron RFC)
3rd attached 2nd Royal Sussex Regiment – Knifton James McKinlay (O) DOE: 19.4.18 Missing 21/7/18
Royal Sussex Regiment – Battalion unknown – Rings Fritz Ludwig (Pte)
7th Royal Sussex Regiment – Knox John Lawrence
13th Royal Sussex Regiment – Fletcher Beaumont
6th Royal West Kent Regiment – Harris Herbert Cecil (O)
5th attached 7th Royal West Kent Regiment – Curtis Ernest John (O)
9th Royal West Kent Regiment – Wade Oliver John (O) (see also RFC)
6th Seaforth Highlanders – Walker Sidney Herbert
11th South Lancashire Regiment – Lidgett John Cuthbert (O)
4th South Staffordshire Regiment – Grant Harold Allan (O) (see also 7th North Staffordshires)
2nd Suffolk Regiment – Roberts James Roderick Trethowan (O)
1/5th Suffolk Regiment – Ryley Harold Buchanan (Snr) (O)
9th Suffolk Regiment – Goatcher Fred (O)
14th Warwickshire Regiment – Shore James Harold
1st Wiltshire Regiment – Blencowe Charles Edward (O) (see also 25th Royal Fusiliers and Royal Sussex Regiment)
1st Wiltshire Regiment – Maybrook Walter Richard (O)
1st Wiltshire Regiment – Terry Sidney Frederick M.C.(O)
8th attached 5th Wiltshire Regiment – Grant Philip Thomas Wilson (O)

APPENDIX III

Yorkshire Dragoons – Berrow Lewis Walter
6th (Kings Own) Yorkshire Light Infantry – Gill Jack Woodward (O)
5th Yorkshire Regiment – Dell Claude Stanley No 632
1/2nd attached 4th, and 8th Yorkshire Regiment (Green Howards) – Cook William Edwin (O)
HAC – Gant Harold Holden (Pte) Battalion unknown (see also 2nd Londons)
1st HAC – Garrett Arthur Daniel No 5145 (Pte)
1st HAC – Shears Edmund George No 10060 (Pte)
1st HAC – Gaskain Cecil Stanley (O) (see also RFA and RFC)
HAC – Ebsworth Harold Charles No 5061 (Pte)
Machine Gun Corps 95th Coy – Clarke Ernest Howell No.70438 (Pte) (see also East Surrey and Royal Sussex Regts)
Machine Gun Corps 2ndBattalion – Lorey Conrad Clifford No42232 (Sgt)
Machine Gun Corps – Battalion unknown, Dennis Robert Charles no. 232878 (Pte) (attached from 2nd Londons)
Machine Gun Corps – Battalion unknown, Baker Albert George no. 9927 (L/Cpl) – (attached from the 5th Londons.)
Machine Gun Corps – Battalion unknown – Page Alfred – (see also 1/15th Londons)
Royal Army Service Corps – 815th Mechanical Transport Coy, Oxford Harry Arthur No M/334631 (Pte)
Royal Army Service Corps – Phare Dudley Gershom (O) (attached to 7th KSLI)
Royal Army Service Corps – Mechanical Transport Section unknown, Royal George Dudley no. MS/3012 (Pte)
Royal Air Force – 31 Squadron – Dodkins Lionel Dodkins (O)
Royal Air Force – 54 Squadron – Knight George Bertram (O)
Royal Flying Corps – 12 Squadron – Castell George Charles (Air Mechanic 1st Class)
Royal Flying Corps – 9 Squadron – Mann Stanley Walter (O)
Royal Flying Corps – 27 Squadron – Stockins William James (O) (see also RAF, 2/2nd Londons)
Royal Flying Corps – 29 Squadron – Gaskain Cecil Stanley (O)
Royal Flying Corps – 32 Squadron – Churcher Edgar (O) (see also 5th Londons and Rifle Brigade)

Royal Flying Corps – 32 Squadron   – Stubbs Reginald Arthur (O)
Royal Flying Corps – 45 Squadron   – Wade Oliver John (O)
Royal Flying Corps – 48 Squadron   – Finnimore Henry James (O)
Royal Field Artillery – Battery unknown – Barton Ernest (O)
Royal Field Artillery – Battery unknown – Gaskain, Cecil Stanley (O)
Royal Field Artillery 'C' Battery, 84th Army Brigade – Bennett Frederick Barberry (O)
Royal Field Artillery 'A' Battery, 236th Brigade – Dubery Frank Arthur
Royal Field Artillery 'D' Battery, 236th Brigade – Trotman Henry John No 951151
Royal Field Artillery 279 Battery – Halliwell Ernest No 179067 (Gunner)
Royal Field Artillery (GL) attached 92 TMB – Oake Douglas M.C. (O)
Royal Field Artillery 'B' Battery 15th Brigade – Lunn Ralph William (O)
Royal Field Artillery 'C' Battery, 291st Brigade– Murray Archibald Albert
Royal Field Artillery – 40th Brigade – Feben Evi
Royal Garrison Artillery 287th Siege Battery –Hamilton Claude William (O) (see also KRRC and 28th Londons)
Royal Garrison Artillery 39th Siege Battery – John William Hood (O)
Royal Garrison Artillery 301st Siege Battery – Husk Frederick John M.M. (O)
Royal Garrison Artillery – Battery unknown – Sanders Leslie Yorath (O) – attached to
Royal Horse Artillery –'B' Battery, 15th Brigade – Lunn Ralph William (O)
Royal Army Medical Corps 102nd Sanitary section – Belcher Douglas Charles
Royal Army Medical Corps 2/1st London Field Ambulance – Hocking Leslie Harold
Royal Army Medical Corps 2/2nd London Field Ambulance – Kenyon Harry Thomas James
Royal Army Medical Corps – Battalion unknown – Phare Dudley Gershom (O)
Royal Army Medical Corps – Battalion unknown – Lansdale William Morris (O) (att'd 5th Royal Berkshires)
Royal Engineers – 'B' Special Company, Brown Charles Henry Goullee No. 186518

APPENDIX III

Royal Engineers- No. 4 Workshop – Dixson Frank (Sgt)
Royal Engineers 186th Special Coy, Hoare Ernest Austin no. 106556 (Cpl)
Royal Engineers – Field Survey Co – Sanders Leslie Yorath (O)
Royal Engineers Field Survey Company. (see also Royal Engineers)
Royal Horse Guards – Edgley Leslie Seymour
Royal Naval Air Service – Budd Victor (O) Flight Sub Lieutenant.
Royal Naval Air Service – Dodson William Albert (HMS Louvain)
Royal Naval Fleet Auxiliary – Dale-James William Rushbrooke (Wireless Officer, Lusitania, Carmania, Marmora, UC Saxon, P&O Palermo, Kaiser-I-hind.)
Royal Navy – Foreman Roland John (HMS Phaeton)
Royal Navy Volunteer Reserve – Pearson Eugene (O) Surgeon Sub Lieutenant (HMS Lysander)
Royal Naval Volunteer Reserve – Fairlie John Alwynne (HMS Queen Mary)
Royal Naval Volunteer Reserve – Weatherston John Frederick (Vessel unknown)
1st Battalion, the Tank Corps – Evans Leonard Austin (O)
Tank Corps – Battalion unknown – Berrow William Rushbury No. 91863 (Pte) (see also City of London Yeomanry)
5th Battalion, Australian Imperial Force – Ruggles Charles George no. 2083
6th Battalion, Australian Imperial Force – Wells Neil no. 2019
49th Battalion, Canadian Infantry – Princess Patricias (Alberta) Regiment – Spencer-Smith Herbert no. 433039
1st Battalion, Canadian Mounted Rifles (Saskatchewan Regiment) – Durant John Stride no. 106205
8th Battalion, Canadian Infantry – Manitoba Regiment, Laurie Arthur Wyndham no. 466252
19th Battalion, 81st Canadian Force (Central Ontario Regiment) – Chubb John Lethbridge no. 158050 (Pte)
9th Battery, 3rd Brigade, Canadian Field Artillery – Lovekin Ivor Vyvyan no. 42523 (Gnr)
French Army – Bendixen Leonard (Caporal)

CHAPTER IV
Western Front Location Index

This index attempts to break down geographically the British sector of the Western Front running from the Flanders coast near Ostend down into eastern France. The line ran from Nieuport in the north to Peronne in the south. The main sectors sub divide from north to south, as follows:

Nieuport to Ypres 1	Ypres to Armentieres 2	Armentieres to Bethune 3
Boesinghe	Armentieres	Aubers
Dixmuide	Gheluvelt	Bethune
Etang (Lake Dickebusch)	Hollebeke	Cambrin
Fortuyn	Menin	Cuinchy
Frezenberg	Messines	Festubert
Langemarck	Quesnoy	Hulluch
Nieuport	St Eloi	La Bassee
Passchendaele	Wormezeele	Laventie
Pilckem	Wulverghen	Lille
Poelcappelle	Wytschaete	Neuve Chapelle
St Jean		Richebourg L'Avoie
St Julien		Vermelles
Ypres		
Zeebrugge		
Zillebeke		
Zonnebeke		

APPENDIX IV

Bethune to Arras
4

Arleux
Arras
Givenchy
Lens
Loos
Mazingarbe
Mont St Eloi
Neuville St Vaast
Oppy
Scarpe River
Souchez
Vimy

Arras to Albert
5

Authuille
Bapaume
Bazentin-Le-Petit
Beaumont Hamel
Boursie
Butte de Warlencourt
Cambrai
Combles
Contalmaison
Courcelette
Croisilles
Eaucourt L'Abbaye
Ervillers
Flers
Fonquevillers
Gavrelle
Ginchy
Gomiecourt
Gommecourt
Grandcourt
Irles
La Boisselle
Le Sars
Les Boeufs
Longueval
Mametz
Miraumont
Monchy au Bois
Monchy le Preux
Montauban
Morval
Ovillers La Boisselle
Pozieres
Sailly Saillisel
Serre

Albert to Peronne
6

Albert
Carnoy
Chaulnes
Clery
Fricourt
Hem
Le Mesnil
Martinpuich
Mont St Quentin
Peronne
Roisel

APPENDIX V
Battles of the Great War by Theatre of War

Military: France and Flanders:

4 Aug 1914: German invasion of Belgium begins.
20 Aug 1914: German troops enter Brussels
23 Aug 1914: Namur captured.
23–24 Aug 1914: Battle of Mons (includes action at Elouges)
26 Aug 1914: Battle of Le Cateau (includes Le Cateau Battery)
24 Aug – 5 Sept: Retreat from Mons (includes actions at Solesmes, Etreux, Le Grand Fayt and Crepy en Valois)
1 Sept 1914: Battle of Nery (includes Nery Battery)
7–10 Sept 1914: Battle of the Marne (includes passages of the Petit Morin and the Marne)
12–15 Sept 1914: Battle of the Aisne (includes passage of the Aisne, capture of Aisne Heights and Chemin des Dames Ridge)
9 Oct 1914: German troops take Antwerp
10 Oct – 2 Nov 1914: Battle of La Bassee
12 Oct – 2 Nov 1914: Battle of Messines
13 Oct – 2 Nov 1914: Battle of Armentieres (includes capture of Meteren)
19 Oct – 22 Nov 1914: Battle of Ypres (includes Langemarck, Gheluvelt, Nonne Boschen)
21–24 Oct 1914: Battle of Langemarck
25–30 Oct 1914: Action at Hollebeke Chateau
29–31 Oct 1914: Battle of Gheluvelt
11 Nov 1914: Battle of Nonne Boschen
23–24 Nov 1914: Battle of Festubert
14 Dec 1914: Action at Wytschaete
20–21 Dec 1914: Battle of Givenchy

APPENDIX V

25 Jan 1915: Battle of Givenchy
10–13 March 1915: Battle of Neuve-Chapelle
17–22 April 1915: Action at Hill 60
22 April– 25 May 1915: Second Battle of Ypres (includes Battles of Gravenstafel, St Julien, Frezenberg, Belewaarde)
22–23 April 1915: Battle of Gravenstafel (includes the German gas attack)
24 April – 4 May 1915: Battle of St Julien
4 May 1915: Counter attack at Hill 60
8–13 May 1915: Battle of Frezenberg
9 May 1915: Battle of Aubers
24–25 May 1915: Battle of Bellewaarde
15–25 May 1915: Battle of Festubert
19 & 30 July & 9 Aug 1915: Actions at Hooge
25 Sept – 8 Oct 1915: Battle of Loos (includes Actions of Pietre, Bois Grenier, Bellewaarde)
25 Sept 1915: Action at Bois Grenier & Pietre
21 Feb 1916: Battle of Verdun begins.
25 Feb 1916: Battle of Douaumont (Verdun)
27 March – 16 April 1916: Actions at St Eloi Craters (Canadian initiative)
2–3 June 1916: Battle of Mount Sorrel
1 July 1916: Battle of the Somme (includes Battles from Albert to Ancre inclusive)
1–13 July 1916: Battle of Albert
1 July 1916: Action at Beaumont Hamel
1 July 1916: Action at Schwaben Redoubt
14–17 July 1916: Battle of Bazentin (includes Actions at Longueval, Trones Wood, Ovillers)
15 July – 3 Sept 1916: Battle of Delville Wood
19 July 1916: Action at Fromelles
23 July – 3 Sept 1916: Battle of Pozieres (includes Action at Mouquet Farm)
3–6 Sept 1916: Battle of Guillemont
9 Sept 1916: Action at Ginchy
15–22 Sept 1916: Battle of Flers Courcelette (includes Action at Martinpuich)

25-28 Sept 1916: Battle of Morval (includes Actions at Combles, Les Boeufs, Guedecourt)
25-28 Sept 1916: Battle of Thiepval
1-18 Oct 1916: Battle of Le Transloy (includes Actions at Eaucourt L'Abbaye, Le Sars, Butte de Warlencourt)
1 Oct – 11 Nov 1916: Battle of the Ancre Heights (includes Actions at Schwaben & Stuff Redoubts, Regina Trench)
24 Oct 1916: Second Battle of Douaumont (Verdun)
13-18 Nov 1916: Battle of the Ancre (includes the capture of Beaumont Hamel)
18 Nov 1916: Battle of the Somme ends.
15 Dec 1916: Battle of Verdun ends
14 Mar – 15 April 1917: German retreat to the Hindenburg line
17 Mar 1917: Battle of Bapaume
9-14 April 1917: Battle of Vimy
19 April – 4 May 1917: Battle of Arras (includes Battles of Vimy, Scarpe, Arleux)
9 April – 4 May 1917: First Battle of the Scarpe (known as Monchy Le Preux)
23-24 April 1917: Second Battle of the Scarpe (known as Gavrelle-Guemappe)
28-29 April 1917: Battle of Arleux
3-4 May 1917: Third Battle of the Scarpe (known as Fresnoy – includes Action at Wancourt Ridge)
3-17 May 1917: Battle of Bullecourt
5 May 1917: Battle of Chemin des Dames
7-14 June 1917: Battle of Messines (includes Action at Wytschaete)
28 June 1917: Battle of Oppy
31 July 1917: Third Battle of Ypres (includes Battles from Pilckem to Passchendaele)
31 July – 2 Aug 1917: Battle of Pilckem
10 Aug 1917: Action at Westhoek
15-25 Aug 1917: Battle of Hill 70 (Canadians)
16-18 Aug 1917: Battle of Langemarck
20 Aug 1917: Second Battle of Verdun

APPENDIX V

22 –27 Aug 1917: Battle of St Julien
20–25 Sept 1917: Battle of Menin Road
26–Sept – 3 Oct 1917: Battle of Polygon Wood
4 Oct 1917: Battle of Broodseinde
9 Oct 1917: Battle of Poelcapelle
12 Oct 1917: First Battle of Passchendaele
26 Oct – 10 Nov 1917: Second Battle of Passchendaele
20 Nov– 3 Dec 1917: Battle of Cambrai (includes the Tank Attack, Actions at Bourlon Wood, German Counter–attacks)
20–21 Nov 1917: Action at Gouzeaucourt
21 Mar – 5 April 1918: Second Battle of the Somme (with 3rd Battle, includes all Actions from St Quentin to the Ancre)
21–23 Mar 1918: Battle of St Quentin
21–22 Mar 1918: Action at Fontaine-les-Clercs
23 Mar 1918: Action at Cugny
24–25 Mar 1918: First Battle of Bapaume
26–27 Mar 1918: Action at Rosieres
28 Mar 1918: First Battle of Arras
4 April 1918: Action at Avre
5 April 1918: Battle of Ancre
9–29 April 1918: Battle of Lys (includes Battles of Estaires, Scherpenberg, Kemmel Ridge)
9–11 April 1918: Battle of Estaires
10–11 April 1918: Battle of Messines
12–15 April 1918: Battle of Hazebrouck (includes Actions at Hinges Ridge and Nieppe Forest)
13–15 April 1918: Battle of Bailleul (includes Action at Neuve Eglise)
17–19 April 1918: First Battle of Kemmel Ridge
18 April 1918: Battle of Bethune
22 April 1918: Action at Pacaut Wood
24–25 April 1918: Action at Villers–Bretonneaux
25–26 April 1918: Second Battle of Kemmel Ridge (known as La Clytte)
29 April 1918: Battle of Scherpenberg
27 May – 6 June 1918: Second Battle of Aisne
6 June 1918: Action at Bligny

6 June 1918: Action at Bois des Buttes
4 July 1918: Action at Hamel
20 July – 2 Aug 1918: Second Battle of the Marne (includes Battles of Soissonais-Ourcq and Tardenois)
20 –31 July 1918: Battle of Tardenois
23 July – 2 Aug 1918: Battle of Soissonais – Ourcq
8–11 Aug 1918: Battle of Amiens
8 Aug 1918: Action at Harbonnieres
21–31 Aug 1918: Battle of Albert (known as Chuignes)
21Aug –3 Sept 1918: Third Battle of the Somme (known as Picardy)
26 Aug – 3 Sept: Second Battle of Arras (known as Queant – includes Scarpe and Drocourt–Queant)
26–30 Aug 1918: Battle of the Scarpe (Monchy Le Preux)
29 Aug 1918: Action at Mont Vidaigne
31 Aug – 3 Sept 1918: Second Battle of Bapaume (known as Mont St Quentin)
2–3 Sept 1918: Battles of Drocourt–Queant
12 Sept 1918: Battle of Sainte-Mihiel
12 Sept– 9 Oct 1918: Battle of the Hindenburg line (includes all Battles from Havrincourt to Cambrai)
12 Sept 1918: Battle of Havrincourt
18 Sept 1918: Battle of Epehy
27 Sept– 1 Oct 1918: Battle of Canal du Nord
28 Sept – 2 Oct 1918: Fourth Battle of Ypres
29 Sept – 2 Oct 1918: Battle of the St Quentin Canal
3–6 Oct 1918: Battle of Beaurevoir
8–9 Oct 1918: Second Battle of Cambrai (includes Actions at Villers Outreaux and the capture of Cambrai)
14–19 Oct 1918: Battle of Courtrai
17–25 Oct 1918: Battle of Selle River
17–18 Oct 1918: Action at Le Cateau
31 Oct 1918: Action at Tieghem
1–2 Nov 1918: Battle of Valenciennes (includes capture of Mont Houy)
4 Nov 1918: Battle of Sambre (includes Actions at Sambre-Oise Canal, Le Quesnoy)
4–11 Nov 1918: Pursuit to Mons

APPENDIX V

Military – Dardanelles (Turkey).

25 April – 6 June 1915: Battle Of Helles (includes landings at Helles and Krithia)
25–26 April 1915: Landing at Cape Helles (includes Action at Sedd el Bahr)
25 April – 30 June 1915: Battle of Anzac (includes landing at Anzac and defence of Anzac.)
25–26 April 1915: Landing at Anzac
28 April 1915: First Battle of Krithia
6–8 May 1915: Second Battle of Krithia
8 May 1915: Defence of Anzac
4June 1915: Third Battle of Krithia (includes two actions at Kereves Dere)
6–15 Aug 1915: Battle of Suvla (includes Battles of Sari Bair, Landing at Suvla, Scimitar Hill)
6–10 Aug 1915: Battle of Sari-Bair (includes Actions at Lone Pine and Russell's Top).
6–15 Aug 1915: Landing at Suvla (includes Actions at Kanakol Dagh and Chocolate Hill)
21 Aug 1915: Battle of Scimitar Hill
27 Aug 1915: Battle of Hill 60 (Anzac)
8 Dec 1915: Evacuation of Dardanelles
8 Jan 1916: Evacuation completed.

Military – Italy

15–24 June 1918: Battle of Piave
24 Oct –4 Nov 1918: Battle of Vittorio Veneto

Military – Balkans (Macedonia)

5 Oct 1915: Allied Landing at Salonika
22 Oct 1915: Fall of Uskub
4 Nov 1915: Battle of Kachanik

2 Dec 1915: Fall of Monastir
7–8 Dec 1915: Battle of Kosturino (includes Actions during retreat from Serbia to Salonika)
1–3 Jan 1916: Cettinje taken
24 Feb 1916: Durazzo taken
17–18 Aug 1916: Action at Horseshoe Hill
30 Sept – 31 Oct 1916: Battle of Struma (includes Actions of Karajaloia, Yenikoi and Barakli Zunaa)
23 Nov 1916: Monastir retaken.
24–25 April 1917: First Battle of Doiran
8–9 May 1917: Second Battle of Doiran
1–2 Sept 1917: Action at Roche Noir
12 Sept 1917: Action at 'P' Ridge
15–25 Sept 1918: Battle of the Vardar
18–19 Sept 1918: Third Battle of Doiran
30 Sept 1918: Uskub retaken

Military – Mesopotamia (Iraq)

6 Nov 1914 – 14 April 1915: Battle of Basra (includes Actions of Saihan and Sahil)
12–14 Mar 1915: Battle of Shaiba
5–24 July 1915: Action at Nasiriya
28 Sept 1915: First Battle of Kut al Amara
22–24 Nov 1915: Battle of Ctesiphon
7 Dec 1915 – 28 April 1916: Defence of Kut al Amara
14 Jan – 24 April 1916: First Battle of the Tigris (three attempts to relieve Kut)
26 Feb 1916: Kermanchah taken by the Russians
6–22 April 1916: Battle of Sanna-i-yat
16 Dec 1916 – 25 Feb 1917: Second Battle of Kut al Amara
25 Feb – 30 April 1917: Battle of Baghdad
11 Mar 1917: British occupy Baghdad
19 Sept 1917: Battle of Samaria
28 Sept 1917: Action and capture of Ramadi

1 Oct – 6 Dec 1917: Second Battle of the Tigris
30 Oct 1917: Battle of Sherghat
26–27 Mar 1918: Battle of Khan Baghdadi
28–30 Oct 1918: Battle of Sharquat (W Battery)

Military – Persia (Iran)

10 Jan – 9 Sept 1915: Battle of the Persian Gulf
26 Aug – 15 Sept 1918: Battle of Baku
1 Nov 1918: Battle of Merv

Military – Southern Arabia

3 July 1915 – 31 Oct 1918: Battle of Aden (includes Actions of Lahej, Sheikh Othman, Jabir, Imad)

Military – Egypt

26 Jan – 12 Aug 1915: Battle of the Suez Canal
3–4 Feb 1915: Defence of the Suez Canal
25 Dec 1915: Action at Waji Majid
23 Jan 1916: Action at Halazin (South Africans forces)
26 Feb 1916: Battle of Agagiya (operations against the Sennussi)
4–5 Aug 1916: Battle of Rumani
23 Dec 1916 – 9 Jan 1917: Battle of Magdhaba –Rafah
9 Jan 1917: Battle of Rafah

Military – Palestine

26–27 Mar 1917: First Battle of Gaza
17–19 April 1917: Second Battle of Gaza (known as Mukhadem)
27 Oct – 7 Nov 1917: Third Battle of Gaza (known as Beersheba)
27 Oct – 7 Nov 1917: Battle of Gaza-Beersheba
8 Nov 1917: Action at Huj
13 Nov 1917: Battle of El Mughar

17–24 Nov 1917: Battle of Nebi Samwill
7–9 Dec 1917: Capture of Jerusalem
26–30 Dec 1917: Defence of Jerusalem
21–22 Dec 1917: Battle of Jaffa
19–21 Feb 1918: Battle of Jericho
8–12 Mar 1918: Battle of Tell' Asur
21 Mar – 11 April 1918: Battle of Jordan
24–25 Mar 1918: Battle Es Salt (or the first 'Trans Jordanian Raid)
27–30 Mar 1918: Battle of Amman
30 April 1918: Battle of Es Salt (or the second 'Trans Jordanian Raid)
19–25 Sept 1918: Battle of Megiddo
19–25 Sept 1918: Battle of Sharon
19–25 Sept 1918: Battle of Nablus
1–26 Oct 1918: Actions at Syria
1 Oct 1918: Battle of Damascus

Military – India

28 Nov 1914 – 10 Aug 1917: Battles of the North West Frontier (includes Actions against the Tochi, Mohmunds, Bunerwals, Swatis, Mahsuds)
2 Mar – 10 Aug 1917: Battle of Waziristan
18 Feb – 8 April 1918: Battle of Baluchistan

Military – Russia

1 Aug 1918 – 27 Sept 1919: Battle of Archangel (includes seizure of the white sea ports and Battle of Troitsa)
29 June 1918 – 12 Oct 1919: Battle of Murman (includes the seizure of the railway and disarmament of the Bolsheviks, plus operations in Karelia)
10 Aug 1919: Battle of Troitsa
23–24 Aug 1919: Battle of Dukhovskaya
8 Aug 1918 – June 1919: Battles of Siberia

APPENDIX V

Military – China & Australasia

23 Sept – 7 Nov 1914: Battle of Tsingtao
12 Sept 1914: Battle of Herbertshohe

Military – East Africa

5–21 Mar 1916: Battle of Kilimanjaro (Actions of Latema, Nek, Kahe)
3–4 Jan 1917: Battle of Beho Beho
19 July 1917: Battle of Narungombe
16–19 Oct 1917: Battle of Nyangao

Military – South West Africa

8–26 Aug 1914: Battle of Gibeon
20 Aug 1914 – 9 July 1915: Battles of South West Africa

Military – West Africa

6 Aug 1914 – 17 Feb 1916: Battles of Cameroon
8–26 Aug 1914: Battle of Kamina (Togoland)
26–27 Sept 1914: Battle of Duala (includes capture of Duala, Actions at Nsana Kang, Yabasi, Edea, Kuyuka, Buea, Cameroon Mountains)
31 May – 10 June 1915: Battle of Garua
4–6 Nov 1915: Battle of Banyo

APPENDIX VI
Medal Awards Index

Abbreviation and explanation:

VM – Victory Medal
Authorized in 1919 to commemorate the victory of the Allies over the Central Powers in the seven theatres of operation.

ARMY – the medal was granted to those who served on the establishment of a unit within a theatre of war between 1914 and 1919 – Officers, men, staff of military hospitals. Members of recognized organisation that handled the sick and wounded; Members of women's formations who were enrolled under a direct contract of service with HM Imperial Forces.

ROYAL NAVY – granted to those who were mobilised and gave service at sea between 4th August 1914 and 11th November 1918. Royal Navy, Royal Marines, RNAS, Royal Indian Marine, RNR, RNVR, Royal Naval Auxiliary Sick Berth Reserve, Dominion/Colonial Naval Forces, Officers and men, Royal Naval Air Service employed in actual flying from home air stations on overseas missions, Mercantile Marine Officers and men. Women's Royal Naval Service, Queen Alexandra's Royal Naval Nursing Service and Royal Naval Nursing Service Reserves, Canteen Staff who served in a ship of war at sea.

ROYAL AIR FORCE – Officers and men serving overseas in a theatre of war, those serving in an operational unit at home who were actively engaged in the air against the enemy, those who flew new planes from Britain to France, and those who formed part of the complement of an aircraft-carrying ship.

APPENDIX VI

Example of Victory Medal

BWM – British War Medal

To commemorate some of the most terrible battles the world has ever known. The medal was instituted by George V in 1919 to mark the end of the Great War and record the service given.

ARMY – for those who entered a theatre of war on duty or who left their places of residence and rendered approved services overseas between 5th August 1914 and 11th November 1918, including Officers and men, members of Women's formations enrolled under direct contract to HM Imperial Forces, staff of military hospitals and organisations handling sick and wounded, enrolled and attested followers on the establishment of units of the Indian Army.

ROYAL NAVY – for those who performed 28 days of mobilized service or lost their lives in active operations before completing that period between 5th August 1914 and 11th November 1918; Categories as above with Victory Medal plus non-nursing members of medical units eg. dispensers, store-keepers, clerks, ward maids serving in a hospital ship at sea, or proceeded overseas and served in a naval hospital abroad.

ROYAL AIR FORCE – for Officers and men of the RAF, RFC and RNAS, including those actively engaged in the air against the enemy whilst borne on the strength of an operational unit at home, employed in flying new aircraft to France and part of a complement of a aircraft-carrying ship.

14S – 1914 Star
Authorized in April 1917, to be awarded to those who served in France or Belgium on the strength of a unit, or service between 5th August and midnight on the 22nd/23rd November 1914. In October 1919, the King sanctioned the award of a bar to this star to all who had been "under fire" in France or Belgium during, or between the above dates. The bar is of bronze 31mm x 5mm and has small holes at each corner, enabling it to be sewn onto the ribbon. Recipients of the bar were entitled to wear a small silver rose on the ribbon, when the star itself was not worn. The only personnel of the Royal Navy to be awarded this star were those who served at Antwerp. 378,000 stars were awarded.

Example of 1914 Star with Bar and Rose, British War Medal and Victory Medal

15S – 1915 Star
Authorized in 1918 and awarded to those who saw service between 5th August 1914 and 31st December 1915. Those eligible for the 1914 star were not eligible for the 1914-15 star. Officers and men of the Army, Navy, Marines, Mercantile Marine, Medical services and RNAS were eligible. This star was not awarded for service which qualified for the African General Service Medal or the Sudan Medal 1910. Approximately, 2,366,000 stars were awarded.

Example of 1915 Star

APPENDIX VI

MM – Military Medal
Awarded to personnel of the British Army and other services, below commissioned rank, for bravery in battle on land. Established on 25th March 1916, it ranked below the Distinguished Conduct Medal (DCM), which was also awarded to non-commissioned members of the Army.

Example of Military Medal

MC – Military Cross
Awarded to commissioned Officers of the substantive rank of Captain or below and for Warrant Officers. The award was created on the 28th December 1914 and is granted in recognition of an act or acts of exemplary gallantry during active operations against the enemy on land. Bars were awarded in recognition of the performance of further acts of gallantry.

Example of Military Cross and 1914 Star Trio

MID – Mentioned in Despatches
A soldier mentioned in despatches (MiD) is one whose name appears in an official report written by a superior officer and sent to the high command, in which is described the soldier's gallant or meritorious action in the face of the enemy. Soldiers of the British Empire who are mentioned in dispatches but do not receive a medal for their action, are nonetheless entitled to receive a certificate and wear a decoration. For 1914–1918 and up to 10 August 1920, the decoration consisted of a spray of oak leaves in bronze. This decoration was only established in 1919, but it had retroactive effect.

Akerman, Ralph Portland, 2Lt, 11th Londons... ......VM, BWM, 14S
Almond, James Edgar, Pte, 9th Royal Fusiliers..........VM, BWM.
Athow, William, Pte, 8th Royal Fusiliers..........VM, BWM.

Baker, Albert George, Pte, 5th Londons................VM, BWM.
Baker, Harold William, Pte, 20th Royal Fusiliers.......VM, BWM
Barton, Ernest, Lt, R.F.A.....VM, BWM
Beecraft, William Henry, Pte, 16th Middlesex......VM, BWM
Belcher, Douglas Charles, L/Cpl, 102nd Sanitary Section, R.A.M.C. ....VM, BWM
Bendixen, Leonard, Caporal, French Army........Porte a l'ordre du regiment, Cor de chasse en or.
Bennett, Frederick Barberry, Major, C Battery, 84th Army Bde, R.F.A...VM, BWM
Benson, George Enoch, Rfn, 2nd Bn, The Rifle Brigade....VM, BWM
Berrow, Lewis Walter, Pte, Yorkshire Dragoons.....VM, BWM, 15S
Berrow, William Rushbury, Pte, E Bn, Tank Corps.....VM, BWM, 15S
Bishopp, Stephen, Pte, 17th Royal Fusiliers......VM, BWM, MM.
Blackman, Herbert William, Pte, 8th Rifle Brigade.....VM, BWM
Blencowe, Charles Edward, 2Lt, Royal Sussex att'd 1st Wiltshires....VM, BWM, 15S
Bliss, Harold Edgar, Pte, 7th Norfolks......VM, BWM, 15S
Boone, John William Donald, L/Cpl, 22nd Rifle Brigade......VM, BWM
Brittain, Percy James, Pte, 1/24th Londons.......VM, BWM
Brown, Charles Henry Goullee, Pte, B Coy, Royal Engineers.....VM, BWM
Budd, Victor John, Flight Sub Lt, R.N.A.S.......VM, BWM.
Burn, Edmund Alfred Henry, Pte, 2/14th Londons......VM,BWM
Burwood, Philip, Pte, 2/23rd Londons.........VM, BWM
Butler, Edmund Hearn, Cpl, 2/9th Londons.......VM, BWM
Carrier, John Russell, 2Lt, 1/5th Londons......VM, BWM, 14S
Castell, George Charles, 1st Air Mechanic, 12 Sqdn, R.F.C..VM, BWM, 15S
Castle, Ewart William King, Rfn, 1/16th Londons....VM, BWM
Chapman, Robert Stanley, Rfn, 2/5th Londons.....VM, BWM
Chester, Harold Thomas, Pte, 1st Royal Guernsey Light Infantry....VM, BWM
Child, Albert George, Pte, 3/5th Londons – VM, BWM.
Chubb, John Lethbridge, Pte, 19th Canadian Infantry (Central Ontario Regt)....VM, BWM.
Churcher, Edgar, Lt, 32 Sqdn, Royal Flying Corps.....VM, BWM, 15S

APPENDIX VI

Clarke, Ernest Howell, Pte, 95th Coy, Machine Gun Corps....VM, BWM
Clifton, Frank Osenton, L/Cpl, 7th East Kents.......VM, BWM
Cock, Edward Millar, Pte, 28th Londons att'd 9th Suffolks......VM, BWM
Cook, Alleyne James, Rfn, 18th Londons........VM, BWM, 15S
Cook, William Edwin, Lt, 1/2nd att'd 4th Yorkshires.....VM, BWM, 15S
Curtis, Ernest John, 2Lt, 5th att'd 7th Royal West Kents.....VM, BWM
Dale-James, William Rushbrooke, Royal Naval Wireless Service...VM, BWM
Dawes, Albert Ernest, Rfn, 1/5th Londons.....VM, BWM
Deem, Henry Theodore Samuel, Pte, 15th Londons........VM, BWM
Defries, Frederick, Cpt, 5th att'd 3rd Middlesex.....VM, BWM, 15S, MID
Dell, Claude Stanley, L/Cpl, 5th Yorkshires......VM, BWM, 15S
Dennis, Robert Charles, Pte, 1/2nd Royal Fusiliers......VM, BWM
Dixson, Frank, Sgt, No.4 Workshop, Royal Engineers......VM, BWM
Dodkins, Lionel Claud, Flying Officer, 25th Londons + 31 Sqdn, R.A.F.....VM, BWM
Dodson, William Albert, 2nd Air Mechanic, R,N.A.S.....VM, BWM.
Doughton, Walter George, Pte, 10th Royal Fusiliers......VM, BWM, 15S
Doyle, Gilbert, Army Blankets Inspector, Ministry of Munitions.....VM
Dubery, Frank Arthur, Gnr, A Battery, 236 Bde, R.F.A......VM,BWM, 15S
Dunkley, William Henry, Pte, 7th Londons.......VM, BWM, 15S
Durant, John Stride, 1st Canadian Mounted Rifles (Saskatchewan Regt)....VM, BWM
Ebsworth, Harold Charles, 2nd H.A.C...VM, BWM, 15S
Edgley, Leslie Seymour, Trooper, Royal Horse Guards....VM, BWM, 15S
Edmunds, Cecil Harry, Lt, 21st Londons......VM, BWM
Edwards, Albert Frederick, Rfn, 12th Londons......VM, BWM, 15S
Ellis, Charles Albert William, Rfn, 1st Monmouthshire's att'd 10th South Wales Borderers......VM, BWM
Evans, Leonard Austin, 2Lt, 15th Bn, Tank Corps......VM, BWM
Fairlie, John Alwyne, Able Seaman, R.N.V.R.....VM, BWM
Falby, Edward Frederick, 2Lt, 1/4th Loyal North Lancashires.....VM, BWM
Falkner, Clarence Beach, Cpt, 2/2nd Londons.....VM, BWM, 14S
Feben, Evi, Cpl, 6th Battery, R.F.A......VM, BWM, 14S
Finnimore, Henry James, 2Lt, 7th Royal Sussex att'd R.F.C.......VM, BWM

Fitzgerald, Robert, L/Cpl, 1/24th Londons...VM, BWM, 15S
Fletcher, Beaumont, L/Cpl, 13th Royal Sussex.......VM, BWM
Foreman, Roland John, 2nd Waiter, Royal Navy.......VM, BWM
Gale, Percy James, L/Sgt, 1/24th Londons.........VM, BWM, 15S
Gant, Harold Holden, 2Lt, 2nd Royal Fusiliers.......VM, BWM
Garrett, Arthur Daniel, Pte, 1st H.A.C.......VM, BWM
Gaskain, Cecil Stanley, Lt, 29 Sqdn, R.F.C + R.F.A......VM, BWM, 14S
Gill, Jack Woodward, 2Lt, 6th KOYLI.......VM, BWM, 15S
Glenn, Reginald James, Pte, 20th Londons........VM, BWM, 15S
Goatcher, Fred, Lt, 9th Suffolks.......VM, BWM
Goenner, Frederick Charles, Rfn, 17th K.R.R.C......VM, BWM
Grant, Harold Allan, 2Lt, 4th S.Staffs att'd 7th N.Staffs........VM, BWM
Grant, PhilipThomas Wilson, 2Lt, 8th att'd 5th Wiltshires.......VM, BWM, 15S
Gray, Wallace James, Pte, 20th Royal Fusiliers......VM, BWM.
Grist, Percival Charles Hugh, Lt, 25th Londons...............VM, BWM
Halliday, Eric, Pte, 2/4th Royal West Surreys......VM, BWM, 15S
Halliwell, Ernest, Gnr, D Battery, 232 Bde, R.F.A.......VM, BWM
Halliwell, William Co Sgt Major, VM, BWM, 14S, MC.
Hamilton, Claud William, Cpt, 287th Siege Battery, R.G.A....VM, BWM, 15S
Hamilton, Noel Crawford, 2Lt, 6th Northamptonshires........VM, BWM
Harris, Herbert Cecil, Cpt, 6th Royal West Kents.......VM, BWM, 15S
Harvard, Kenneth O'Gorman, Lt, 2nd Grenadier Guards.....VM, BWM
Harvard, Lionel De Jersey, Cpt, 1st Grenadier Guards.........VM, BWM
Haseldine, Newton Woollcombe, Rfn, 1/5th Londons.........VM, BWM, 15S
Hay, Arthur Leslie, 2Lt, 4th att'd 10/11th Highland Light Infantry......VM, BWM, 15S
Hearn, Robert Cecil, Cpt, 2/20th Londons.......VM, BWM, 15S, MC
Heron, Joseph Solomon, Rfn, 1/21st Londons.......VM, BWM, 15S
Hill, Sidney Ernest, Sgt, 1/20th Londons........VM, BWM, 15S
Hoare, Ernest Austin, Cpl, 186th Special Coy, Royal Engineers.....VM, BWM, 15S
Hocking, Leslie Harold, Pte, 2/1st London Field Ambulance, RAMC.....VM, BWM
Hollands, Harold Evan, Cpl, 2/21st Londons......VM, BWM

APPENDIX VI

Hollands, Wilfred George, 2Lt, 7th att'd 4th Royal Fusiliers.........VM, BWM
Holman, William Elijah, Pte, 1/2nd Royal Fusiliers........VM, BWM
Hood, John William, Lt, 39th Siege Battery, Royal Garrison Artillery......
  MID, VM, BWM.
Howett, Frank, Co Sgt Major, Londons (Civil Service Rifles)........VM, BWM, 15S
Howett, Robert Plunkett, Sgt, 1/5th Notts and Derby.......VM, BWM, 15S
Hunt, Harold, Rfn, 3rd Rifle Brigade..........VM, BWM
Husk, Frederick John, 2Lt, R.G.A.......VM, BWM, MM, MID
Jones, James Thomas, 2Lt, 20th Londons......VM, BWM
Jones, Norman Aldham, Pte, East Kent Regiment.....VM, BWM
Jones, Thomas Idwal, Lt, 18th Londons.......VM, BWM, MM
Junkison, Arthur Charles, Pte, 15th Londons......VM, BWM
Keesey, George Ernest Howard, Cpt, 8th Rifle Brigade........VM, BWM, 15S
Kenyon, Harry Thomas James, Pte, R.A.M.C......VM, BWM
Kiddle, Robert Henry, Pte, Liverpool Regt.......VM, BWM
Kidney, Leonard Edwin, Sgt, 9th Royal Fusiliers.......VM, BWM, 15S
King, Stanley Edward, Rfn, 5th Londons.......VM, BWM
Knifton, James McKinlay, 2Lt, 3rd att'd 2nd Royal Sussex........VM, BWM
Knight, George Bertram, 2Lt, 54 Sqdn, R.A.F.......VM, BWM
Knox, John Lawrence, 2Lt, 7th Royal Sussex.......VM, BWM
Lansdale, William Morris, Cpt, Adj, R.A.M.C.......VM, BWM
Laurie, Arthur Wyndham, Sgt, 8th Canadian Infantry........VM, BWM
Le Chavetois, Grantley Adolphe, Cpt, 22nd Londons.......VM, BWM
Levy, Godfrey, Rfn, 9th Londons........VM, BWM
Lidgett, John Cuthbert, Lt, South Lancashire Regt.......VM, BWM
Lorey, Conrad Clifford, Sgt, 7th Londons att'd Machine Gun Corps......VM, BWM
Lovekin, Vyvyan Ivor, Gnr, Canadian Artillery........VM, BWM
Lunn, Ralph William, 2Lt, R.F.A & R.H.A.........VM, BWM
Mann, Stanley Walter, 2Lt, 9 Sqdn, R.F.C........VM, BWM
Marner, George Lionel Stuart, Cpt, 10th Leicesters........VM, BWM
Marriott, Herbert Percy Gordon, Rfn, 5th Londons.........VM, BWM
Mason, William John, Cpt, 8th Gloucesters............VM, BWM, 15S
Maybrook, Walter Richard, 2Lt, 1st Wiltshires ....VM, BWM, 15S

Miles, Frank David, Pte, 28th Londons.......VM, BWM
Murray, Archibald Albert, Gnr, R.F.A......VM,BWM
Norris, Frederick, Cpt, 23rd Middlesex............VM, BWM
Oake, Douglas, Cpt, East Yorkshires att'd 92nd T.M.B...VM, BWM, 15S, MC
Oliver, William Henry Rudland, Pte, 20th Londons......VM, BWM, MID
Oxford, Harry Arthur, Pte, Royal Army Supply Corps......VM, BWM
Page, Alfred, Pte, 15th Londons att'd Machine Gun Corps.....VM, BWM, 15S
Pearson, Eugene Arthur, Sub Lt, Surgeon, Royal Navy.......VM, BWM.
Perkins, Douglas, Rfn, 12th Londons.......VM, BWM
Phare, Dudley Gershom, Lt, 7th Kings Shropshire Light Infantry.......VM, BWM
Plowman, Oswald Cheyney, Pte, Kings Royal Rifle Corps........VM, BWM
Procter, Alexander Duncan Guthrie, 2Lt, 8th Royal Fusiliers........VM, BWM
Prout, Arthur Stanley, Pte, 12th Londons......VM, BWM, 15S
Quixley, Arthur Newman Charles, Pte, 24th Londons.......VM, BWM,. 15S
Richardson, James Bert, Pte, 12th Rifle Brigade........VM, BWM, 15S
Riminton, Percy Henry, Rfn, 16th Londons.......VM, BWM
Rings, Fritz Ludwig, Pte, Royal Sussex Regiment............VM, BWM
Roberts, James Roderick Trethowan, 2Lt, 2nd Suffolks.......VM, BWM, 15S
Robinson, Edwin Hall, Rfn, Kings Royal Rifle Corps.........VM, BWM
Roeber David Arnold, 2Lt, Bedfordshire Regiment..........VM, BWM, 14S
Rowe, Henry Shepard, Rfn, 16th Londons..............VM, BWM
Royal, George Dudley, Pte, R.A.S.C........VM, BWM, 14S
Ruggles, Charles George, Pte, Australian Contingent.........VM, BWM
Rule, Austin George, Pte, 15th Londons...............VM, BWM
Ryder, Gordon William, Pte, 14th Londons..........VM, BWM, 14S
Ryley, Donald Arthur George Buchanan, Lt, N.Staffordshires.....VM, BWM, 15S
Ryley, Harold Buchanan Snr, Lt, 1/5th Suffolks..............VM, BWM
Ryley, Harold Buchanan Jnr, 2Lt, 4th att'd 1st North Staffordshires...VM, BWM, 15S
Sanders, Leslie Yorath, 2Lt, Royal Garrison Artillery att'd Royal Engineers Survey Coy......VM, BWM, 15S
Schooling, Geoffrey Holt, Pte, 16th Londons........VM, BWM, 15S
Schulz, Harry Albert, Cpl, 12th Londons........VM, BWM, 15S

APPENDIX VI

Shears, Edmund George, Pte H.A.C.........VM, BWM
Shepherd, Henry Alick, Pte, 15th Londons........VM, BWM, 15S
Shore, James Harold, Pte, 14th Warwickshires.......VM, BWM
Smith, George William, 2Lt, Royal Lancaster Regiment......VM, BWM
Spencer-Smith, Herbert, Pte, Princess Patricia's, 49th Canadians......VM, BWM, 15S
Sprang, Frederick William, Cpt, 6th Dorsets........VM, BWM, 15S
Stables, Leonard Theodore Drury, Lt, 6th Bedfordshires........VM, BWM
Stockins, William James, 2Lt, 28th Londons att'd 27 Sqdn, R.F.C.....VM, BWM
Stubbs, Reginald Arthur, 2Lt, 32 Sqdn, R.F.C.,....VM, BWM
Sutcliffe, Frederick Malcolm, 2Lt, 8th Londons.........VM, BWM
Sutherland, John, Pte, 15th Londons.........VM, BWM
Taffs, Charles Reginald, Lt, 1st Royal Berkshires........VM, BWM, 15S
Tait, Leonard Sidney, Pte, 16th Londons........VM, BWM, 14S
Talbot, Cecil Melliar, 2Lt, 14th att'd 4th Middlesex Regiment......VM, BWM, 15S
Talbot, Ernest, Sgt, Royal Fusiliers........VM
Taylor, William Frederick, Lt, 3rd East Kents.........VM, BWM, 14S, 15S
Terry, Sidney Frederick, Cpt, 1st Wiltshires............VM, BWM, 15S, MC
Thompson, Edward William Murray, Pte, 2/13th Londons.......VM, BWM
Trotman, Frank William, Pte, 15th Londons........VM, BWM
Trotman, Henry John, Dvr, R.F.A........VM, BWM
Veale-Williams, John Marcus, Rfn, 3/5th Londons.........VM, BWM
Vernall, Arthur Humphrey, 2Lt, 6th Leicesters........VM, BWM, 15S, MC
Wade, Oliver John, 2Lt, Royal West Kents att'd 45 Sqdn, R.F.C.....VM, BWM
Walker, Sidney Herbert, Pte, 6th Seaforth Highlanders.......VM, BWM, 15S
Walker, William Richard, Pte, 14th Londons.......VM, BW.15S
Wallace, George Frederick, 2Lt, 24th Middlesex.........VM, BWM, 15S
Walsh, Richard William, Pte, 15th Londons........VM, BWM
Wardley, Miles Edward, Pte, 15th Londons........VM, BWM, 15S
Weatherston, John Frederick, Able Seaman, R.N.V.R.........VM, BWM
Weatherston, Sidney Bowler, Pte, 14th Londons.........VM, BWM
Wells, Neil, Pte, 6th Australian Imperial Force.........VM, BWM
Wensley, Harold William, 2Lt, 1st Lincolnshires........VM, BWM

West, Harold Douglas, 2Lt, 1st Kings Royal Rifle Corps.......VM, BWM
Wilson, Albert Cecil, 2Lt, 14th Londons.......VM, BWM
Young, Henry George, Pte, 4th Essex.........VM, BWM, 15S

APPENDIX VII
School Years Index

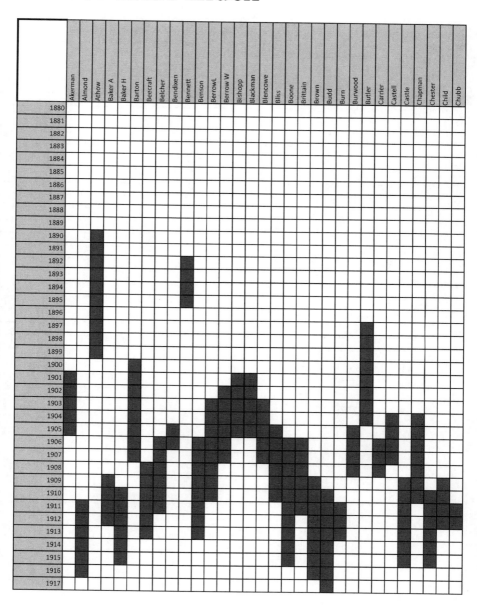

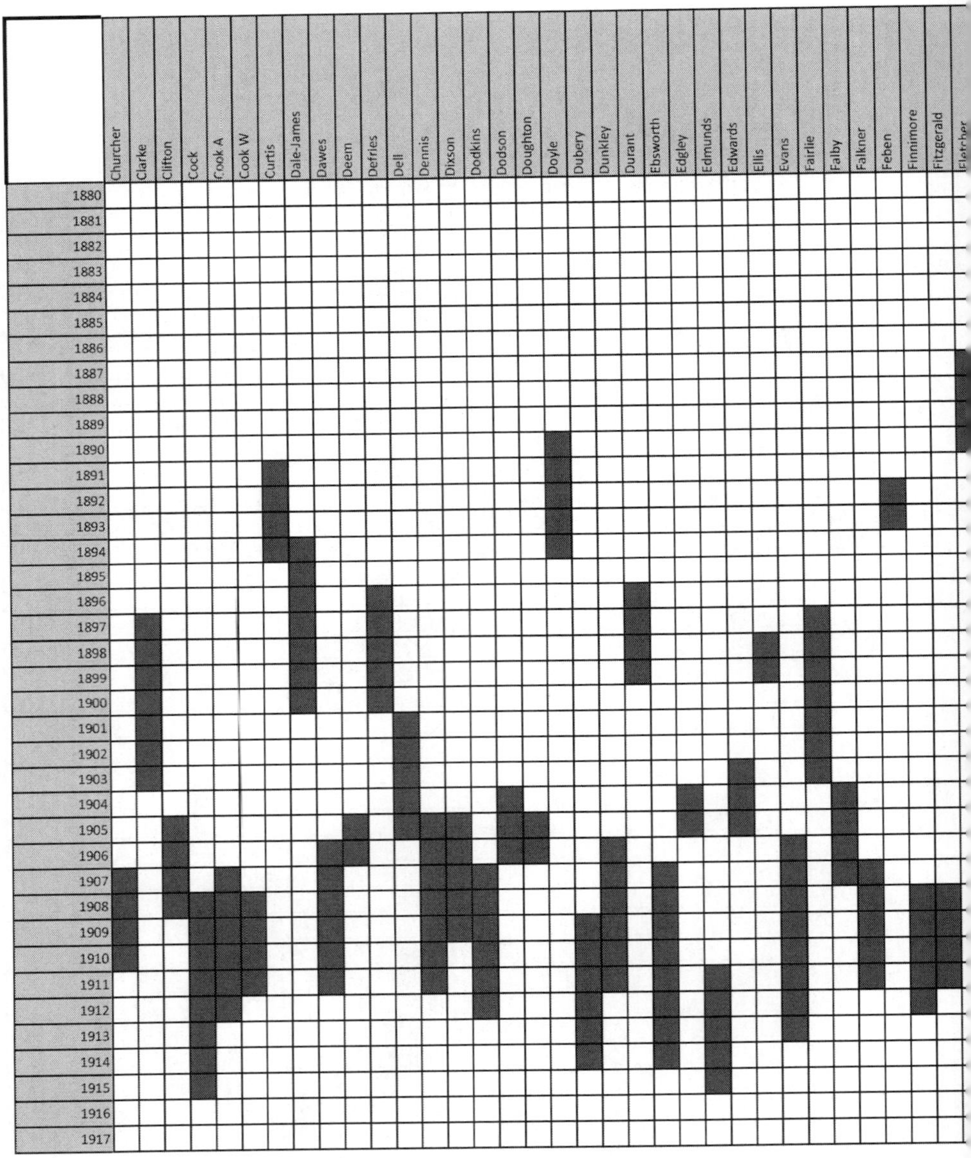

Churcher
Clarke
Clifton
Cock
Cook A
Cook W
Curtis
Dale-James
Dawes
Deem
Defries
Dell
Dennis
Dixson
Dodkins
Dodson
Doughton
Doyle
Dubery
Dunkley
Durant
Ebsworth
Edgley
Edmunds
Edwards
Ellis
Evans
Fairlie
Falby
Falkner
Feben
Finnimore
Fitzgerald
1880
1881
1882
1883
1884
1885
1886
1887
1888
1889
1890
1891
1892
1893
1894
1895
1896
1897
1898
1899
1900
1901
1902
1903
1904
1905
1906
1907
1908
1909
1910
1911
1912
1913
1914
1915
1916
1917

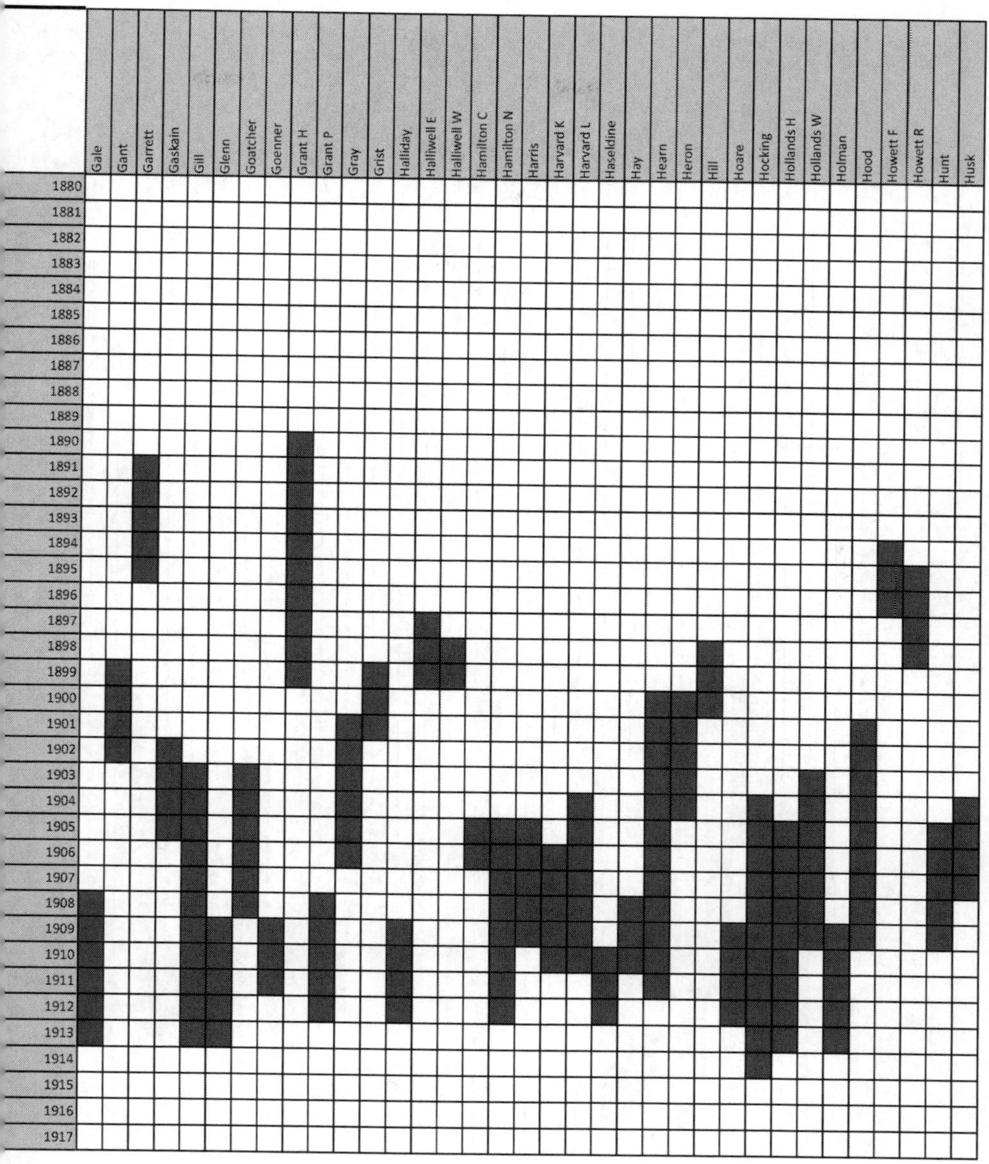
Gale
Gant
Garrett
Gaskain
Gill
Glenn
Goatcher
Goenner
Grant H
Grant P
Gray
Grist
Halliday
Halliwell E
Halliwell W
Hamilton C
Hamilton N
Harris
Harvard K
Harvard L
Haseldine
Hay
Hearn
Heron
Hill
Hoare
Hocking
Hollands H
Hollands W
Holman
Hood
Howett F
Howett R
Hunt
Husk
1880
1881
1882
1883
1884
1885
1886
1887
1888
1889
1890
1891
1892
1893
1894
1895
1896
1897
1898
1899
1900
1901
1902
1903
1904
1905
1906
1907
1908
1909
1910
1911
1912
1913
1914
1915
1916
1917

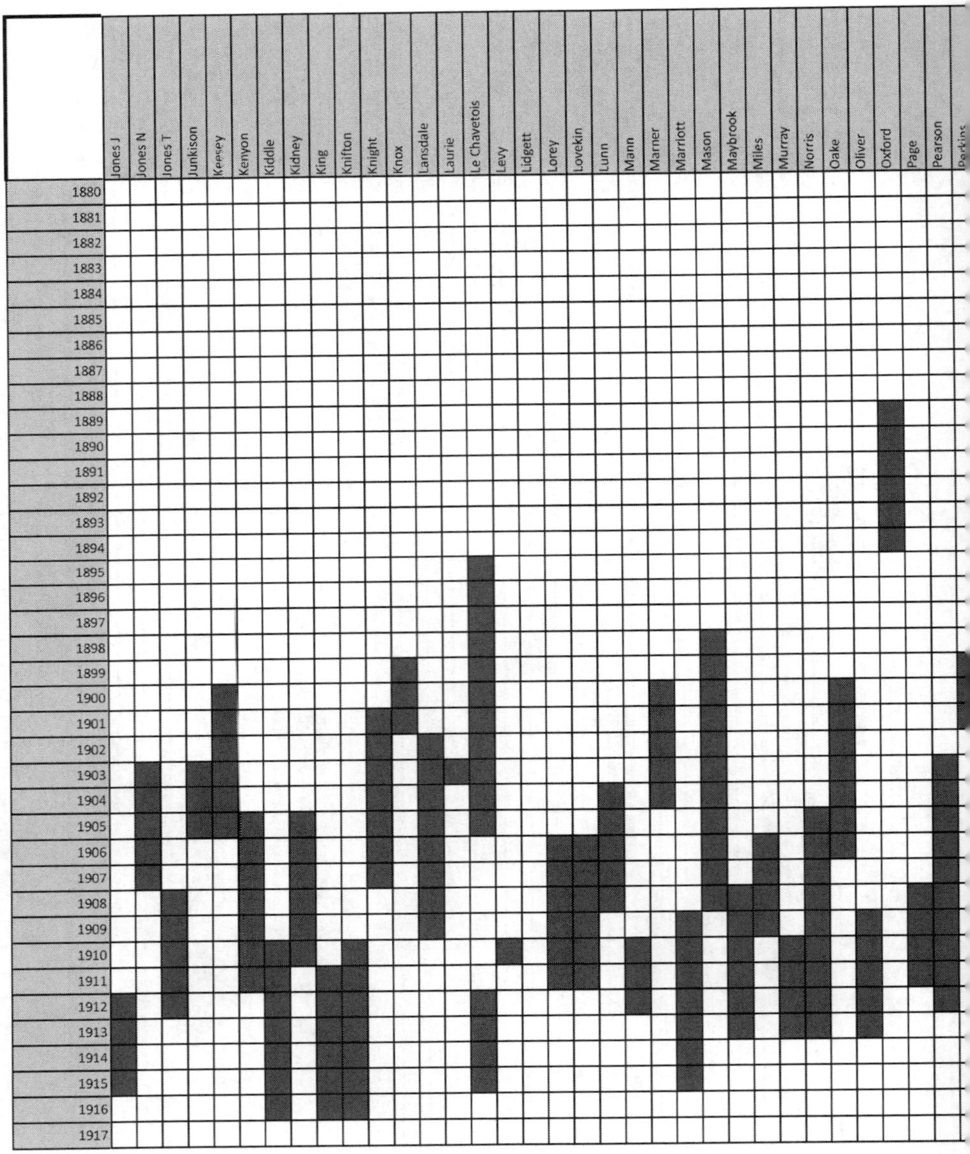
Jones J
Jones N
Jones T
Junkison
Keesey
Kenyon
Kiddie
Kidney
King
Knifton
Knight
Knox
Lansdale
Laurie
Le Chavetois
Levy
Lidgett
Lorey
Lovekin
Lunn
Mann
Marner
Marriott
Mason
Maybrook
Miles
Murray
Norris
Oake
Oliver
Oxford
Page
Pearson
1880
1881
1882
1883
1884
1885
1886
1887
1888
1889
1890
1891
1892
1893
1894
1895
1896
1897
1898
1899
1900
1901
1902
1903
1904
1905
1906
1907
1908
1909
1910
1911
1912
1913
1914
1915
1916
1917

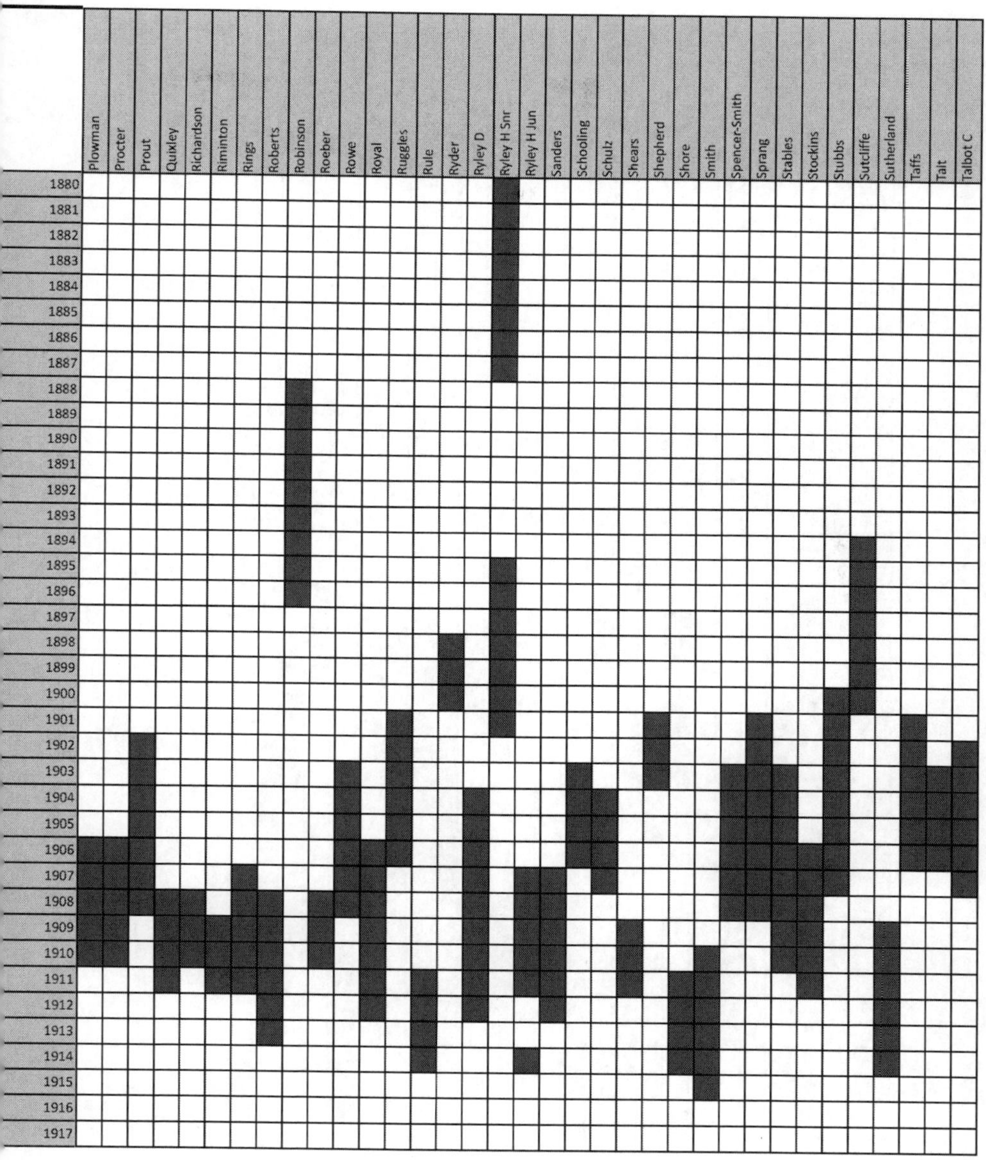
Plowman
Procter
Prout
Quixley
Richardson
Riminton
Rings
Roberts
Robinson
Roeber
Rowe
Royal
Ruggles
Rule
Ryder
Ryley D
Ryley H Snr
Ryley H Jun
Sanders
Schooling
Schulz
Shears
Shepherd
Shore
Smith
Spencer-Smith
Sprang
Stables
Stockins
Stubbs
Sutcliffe
Sutherland
Taffs
Tait
Talbot C
1880
1881
1882
1883
1884
1885
1886
1887
1888
1889
1890
1891
1892
1893
1894
1895
1896
1897
1898
1899
1900
1901
1902
1903
1904
1905
1906
1907
1908
1909
1910
1911
1912
1913
1914
1915
1916
1917

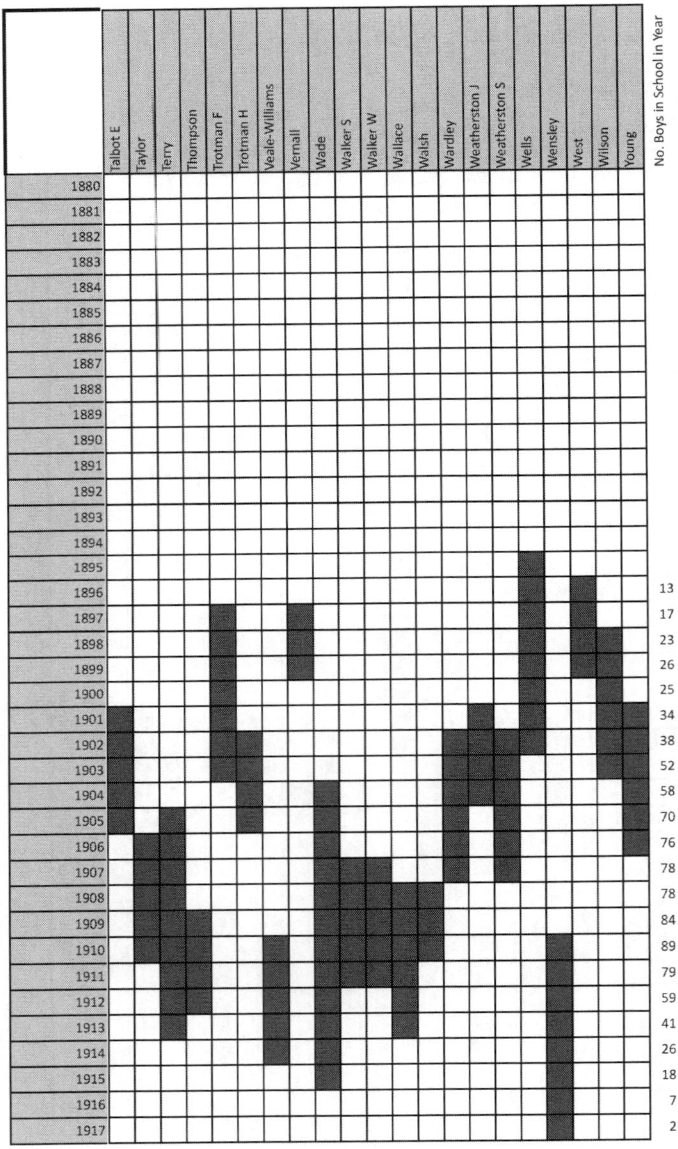

TILL ALL OUR FIGHT BE FOUGHT

Year	No. Boys in School in Year
1880	
1881	
1882	
1883	
1884	
1885	
1886	
1887	
1888	
1889	
1890	
1891	
1892	
1893	
1894	
1895	
1896	13
1897	17
1898	23
1899	26
1900	25
1901	34
1902	38
1903	52
1904	58
1905	70
1906	76
1907	78
1908	78
1909	84
1910	89
1911	79
1912	59
1913	41
1914	26
1915	18
1916	7
1917	2

Columns: Talbot E, Taylor, Terry, Thompson, Trotman F, Trotman H, Veale-Williams, Vernall, Wade, Walker S, Walker W, Wallace, Walsh, Wardley, Weatherston J, Weatherston S, Wells, Wensley, West, Wilson, Young

408

APPENDIX VIII
Fathers and Brothers Index

Surname	First	Father's Name	Father's Occupation	Brothers of Olavian Fallen (260) (many who would have served)
Almond	James	James Almond	Bookbinder	Leonard H.
Akerman	Ralph	Portland Akerman	Solicitor	Jack Philipps
Athow	William	Charles Athow	Hatters Manager	Charles, Alfred, Frank
Baker	Albert	George Baker	Not Known	None
Baker	Harold	William Baker	Booksellers Manager	None
Barton	Ernest	William Barton	Labourer	William Henry, Edward John, Charles Sidney
Beecraft	William	Joseph Beecraft	Dining Rooms Keeper	Clifford Joseph
Belcher	Douglas	Charles Belcher	Greenhouse Maker	None
Bendixen	Leonard	Julien Bendixen	Leather Manufacturer	Charles S
Bennett	Frederick	Ernest G	Clerk to Thames Conservancy Board	Charles EM, George B, Arthur C
Benson	George	Joseph Benson	Leather Shaver	Arthur F, Joseph
Berrow	Lewis	William Berrow	Foreign Office Registrar	William Rushbury, Philip John
Berrow	William	William Berrow	Foreign Office Registrar	None
Bishopp	Stephen	Stephen Bishopp	Buildings Manager	Leslie Graham
Blackman	Herbert	Alfred Blackman	Law Clerk	Alfred Reginald
Blencowe	Charles	JEB Blencowe	Accounts Clerk	Frederick J
Bliss	Harold	Edward Thornycroft	Clicker in Shoe Trade (Uncle)	Joseph CF, Ernest R
Boone	John	John Boone	Clerk to District Distress Committee	None
Brittain	Percy	Frank Brittain	Builders Foreman	None
Brown	Charles	William Brown	Bookseller, Minister Wellington College Mission church	William JG
Budd	Victor	Leonard Budd	Licensed Victualler	Leonard George, Ernest Frank
Burn	Edmund	Henry William Burn	Law Clerk, Board of Guardians	None
Burwood	Philip	Philip Burwood	Seaman, Master, Mate	Charles Leonard
Butler	Edmund	John Butler	Vellum Bookbinder	Alfred J W
Carrier	John	John Comley	Law Clerk - Step-father	Seymour Thomas, Stepbrother Dennis Comley
Castell	George	George Henry Castell	Foreman, Grocers	None
Castle	Ewart	William Frederick Castle	Builder and Decorator	None
Chapman	Robert	Robert John Chapman	General Merchants Clerk	None
Chester	Harold	John Tate Chester	Confectioner	Charles John
Child	Albert	James Child	Sawyer	James Ernest
Chubb	John	Thomas Chubb	Secretary, Ironworks	Thomas A, Richard.
Churcher	Edgar	Alfred Churcher	Stockbroker's Clerk	Herbert, Athelstan
Clarke	Ernest	Elijah Clarke	Minister	William E.
Clifton	Frank	Frank Clifton	Restaurateur	Alan Newell
Cock	Edward	Edward J Cock	Seaman of Lighterman Barge	None

409

TILL ALL OUR FIGHT BE FOUGHT

Surname	First	Father's Name	Father's Occupation	Brothers of Olavian Fallen (260) (many who would have served)
Cook	Alleyne	Edward Cook	Leather Dresser, Currier	Charles E, Frank S, George M.
Cook	William	William John Cook	Cooper at Docks	Sydney
Curtis	Ernest	Ernest Curtis	Foreman at Grain and Seed Warehouse	Bertie G
Dale James	William	William Dale James	Doctor	Kenneth
Dawes	Albert	Albert Dawes	House Decorator	None
Deem	Henry	Henry Deem	Billposter	None
Defries	Frederick	Albert Defries	Book keeper for County Council	Reginald, Gerard
Dell	Claude	Frederick Dell	Grocer Tea Merchant	Frederick, Leighton, Charles
Dennis	Robert	Herbert Dennis	Butcher	None
Dixson	Frank	William George Dixson	Lighterman on Barge	Owen
Dodkins	Lionel	Percival Henry Dodkins	Assurance Clerk	None
Dodson	William	Albert Ernest Dodson	Fishmonger	Ernest, Ralph
Doughton	Walter	Walter Doughton	Checker at Wharf	None
Doyle	Gilbert	J M Doyle	Master Scale Maker	John, Martin, Leonard, Vincent.
Dubery	Frank	Alfred Dubery	General Labourer	Alfred, Harry, Robert
Dunkley	William	Henry Dunkley	Carpenter	None
Durant	John	Luke Lee Durant	Commercial Traveller	None
Ebsworth	Harold	Frederick Ebsworth	Chartered Accountant	None
Edgley	Leslie	Robert W Edgley	Builder	Harold, Percy, Laurence
Edmunds	Cecil	Alfred Edmunds	Corn Flour Merchant	John, Alfred
Edwards	Albert	Frank J M Edwards	Auctioneer and Valuer	Frank, Walter, Horace, Stanley, Douglas
Ellis	Charles	William Albert Ellis	Labourer	None
Evans	Leonard	Charles H. Evans	Assistant Inspector, G.P.O	Charles F, Arthur E.
Fairlie	John	Percy M G Fairlie	Bank Cashier	Hugh, Gerald
Falby	Edward	Frederick Falby	Grain Sampling Agent	Frederick Charles, Richard, Arthur
Falkner	Clarence	Alfred Beach Falkner	Builder	Alfred Cecil
Feben	Evi	Henry Feben	Bricklayer	Minett, Septimus, Henry, Caleb
Finnimore	Henry	James Alfred Finnimore	Grocer	Bernard Nelson, John William
Fitzgerald	Robert	David Fitzgerald	Postman	None
Fletcher	Beaumont	Alfred E. Fletcher	Author and Journalist (Daily Chronicle)	Ruskin, Alfred, Cavendish, Wilfred
Foreman	Roland	George Foreman	Silk Warehouseman	George, Percy, Frederick
Gale	Percy	William Henry Gale	Bricklayer	Walter, Maurice, William, Cecil
Gant	Harold	Arthur Sidney Gant	Manufacturer, Ladies Dressing Gowns	Alfred Arthur.
Garrett	Arthur	William Garrett	Not known	None
Gaskain	Cecil	Denis H. Gaskain	Hop and Seed Factor/Agent	Albert, William, Walter.
Gill	Jack	Robert W. Gill	Bankers Clerk	Hugh, Harry Norman, Laurence
Glenn	Reginald	James T. Glenn	Auto Gas Collector	William Owen, Horace Morgan
Goatcher	Frederick	Arthur Goatcher	Elementary Teacher, LCC	William, Arthur, Herbert
Goenner	Frederick	Frederick Charles Goenner	Engineer/Manager - Steam Packing Manufacturers	Augustus
Grant	Harold	Alexander Grant	Doctor	Alexander
Grant	Philip	Philip Grant	Butcher	None

APPENDIX VIII

Surname	First	Father's Name	Father's Occupation	Brothers of Olavian Fallen (260) (many who would have served)
Gray	Wallace	James E. Gray	Grocer's Manager	Thomas, Albert, Sidney
Grist	Percival	Arthur A. Grist	Sanitary Inspector	Arthur, Herbert
Halliday	Eric	William Halliday	Civil Service Commissioners – Clerk	Laurence
Halliwell	Ernest	Thomas Halliwell	Secretary of the Licensed Victuallers Society	Archibald, Albert, Harold, Sidney, William
Halliwell	William	Thomas Halliwell	Secretary of the Licensed Victuallers Society	Archibald, Albert, Harold, Sidney, Ernest
Hamilton	Claude	Frederick Hamilton	Clergyman – Church of England	Frederick, Noel
Hamilton	Noel	Frederick Hamilton	Clergyman – Church of England	Frederick, Claude
Harris	Herbert	Henry Harris	Clerk.	Henry, Charles, John
Harvard	Kenneth	Thomas Mawson Harvard	Rubber Merchant	Lionel, John
Harvard	Lionel	Thomas Mawson Harvard	Rubber Merchant	Kenneth, John
Haseldine	Newton	George Haseldine	Jeweller and Watchmaker	Bertrand
Hay	Arthur	Arthur W Hay	Leather Merchant	None
Hearn	Robert	Charles H. Hearn	Commercial Traveller, Vinegar Making	Charles, Thomas
Heron	Joseph	Albert Jacob Heron	Manager of Leather Dressers	None
Hill	Sidney	Frederick W. Hill	Oil and Colour Man	William, Frank, Harry
Hoare	Ernest	John Hoare	Police Constable	Jack.
Hocking	Leslie	William John Hocking	Assistant Superintendent, Royal Mint	William Stanley, Leonard Charles.
Hollands	Harold	Alfred Christy Hollands	Shopkeeper	Wilfred
Hollands	Wilfred	Alfred Christy Hollands	Shopkeeper	Harold
Holman	William	Elijah John Holman	Dust Inspector, Southwark Council	Herbert Charles.
Hood	John	John Johnson Hood	Printers Compositor	Arthur Frederick.
Howett	Frank	John Howett	Engineer Fitter	Walter, Herbert, Horace, Harold, Edgar, Robert
Howett	Robert	John Howett	Engineer Fitter	Walter, Herbert, Horace, Harold, Edgar, Frank
Hunt	Harold	William Hunt	Vellum Binder	Edward, James, George
Husk	Frederick	John Husk	Sugar Manufacturer	None
Jones	James	David Rees Jones	Not known	None
Jones	Norman	John Jones	Club Steward	None
Jones	Thomas	John T.Jones	Dairy Manager	Hywel Glyn
Junkison	Arthur	William Junkison	Insurance Broker	None
Keesey	George	George W Keesey	Congregational Minister	Walton M, Edward W.
Kenyon	Harry	Harry Kenyon	Leather Bag Maker	None
Kiddle	Robert	John H Kiddle	Surveyor, HM Customs Service	Thomas Walker
Kidney	Leonard	Edwin Kidney	Insurance Agent	John S
King	Stanley	James David King	Printer (Numerical) at Stationers	Arthur James, Sidney William.

TILL ALL OUR FIGHT BE FOUGHT

Surname	First	Father's Name	Father's Occupation	Brothers of Olavian Fallen (260) (many who would have served)
Knifton	James	John Knifton	Schoolmaster, London School Board	Charles WM, Alfred
Knight	George	Bertram G E Knight	Assistant Master, St Olave's Grammar School	Norris
Knox	John	John Knox	Stockbrokers Clerk	Andrew, Clifford, Harold Garthorne
Lansdale	William	William Lansdale	Physician and Surgeon	None
Laurie	Arthur	Arthur Laurie	India Civil Service	None
Le Chavetois	Grantley	Adolphe Le Chavetois	Not Known	None
Levy	Godfrey	Samuel Levy	Tailor	Isadore
Lidgett	John	John Scott Lidgett	Reverend	None
Lorey	Conrad	Heinrich Lorey	Baker (Adopted Father)	None
Lovekin	Vyvyan	Alfred Lovekin	Not known	Alan Bernard, Cyril
Lunn	Ralph	William Henry H. Lunn	Quantity Surveyor and Architect	Percy Reginald
Mann	Stanley	W.Mann	Market Gardener	None
Marner	George	George Marner	Brass Founder	Reginald G MS, Sidney S
Marriott	Herbert	Herbert J Marriott	Superintendent of Warehouse	Charles A, Leonard
Mason	William	Bowler George Mason	Clerk at Board of Education	George Bowler.
Maybrook	Walter	Walter R Maybrook	Schoolmaster	None
Miles	Frank	David Miles	Joiner	None
Murray	Archibald	Archibald Murray	Foreman Packer	None
Norris	Frederick	W.Norris	Oven Builders Labourer	Harry, Victor Lawrence
Oake	Douglas	Joseph Oake	Councillor, Mayor	Cyril
Oliver	William	Henry Oliver	Provisions Agent	Sidney G, Norman R, Leslie JR, Laurence ER
Oxford	Harry	Henry Oxford	Factory Manager, Hatmakers	None
Page	Alfred	Henry Page	Timekeeper	Harry.
Pearson	Eugene	JC Pearson	Rector, Leguan, British Guiana.	George, Cecil, Maurice, Clarence.
Perkins	Douglas	George W. Perkins	Corn Dealer	William, Alfred, George, Stephen, Wilfred
Phare	Dudley	George Rowe Phare	Associated Accountant, Chairman Bible Crusade	None
Plowman	Oswald	Albert Percy Plowman	General Draper	None
Procter	Alexander	Charles Procter	Not known	None
Prout	Arthur	Alfred S. Prout	Draper's Traveller	George, Herbert, Frank.
Quixley	Arthur	Arthur Quixley	Commercial Traveller	None
Richardson	James	Luther Joseph Richardson	Grocer and Sub Post Master	Horace Monte, Luther John.
Riminton	Percy	William Riminton	Clerk in the Hide trade	Ernest William.
Rings	Fritz	Fritz Hubert A. Rings	Architect and Engineer	Franz Wilhelm
Roberts	James	William Roberts	Journalist	William Evelyn
Robinson	Edwin	Thomas Robinson	Oilman	Harry
Roeber	David	Albert Oscar Roeber	Market Clerk, Leather Trade	Colin, George, Rudolph.
Rowe	Henry	John Rowe	Butcher	John, Frederick, Leonard, Frank.
Royal	George	William Royal	Engine Fitter	Charles

APPENDIX VIII

Surname	First	Father's Name	Father's Occupation	Brothers of Olavian Fallen (260) (many who would have served)
Ruggles	Charles	Harry Ruggles	Engineer's Factor	William, Frank.
Rule	Austin	John Rule	Examing Officer, HM Customs and Excise	John Henry
Ryder	Gordon	Arthur Ryder	Clerk, Visar-General's Office	Arthur
Ryley	Donald	Harold B Ryley	Headmaster Emmanuel School, Master St Olaves	Harold
Ryley (Senior)	Harold	George B Ryley	Independent Minister - Hannover Chapel	Cyril L.
Ryley	Harold	Harold B Ryley	Headmaster Emmanuel School, Master St Olaves	Donald
Sanders	Leslie	Charles Sanders	Civil Servant Superintendent Wrecks & Loss of life at sea	Reginald Yorath
Schooling	Geoffrey	Henry Schooling	Commercial Traveller	Terence Holt
Schulz	Harry	Gottlieb Schulz	Furskin dresser	Frederick
Shears	Edmund	Willie Shears	Schoolmaster	None
Shepherd	Henry	Alick Shepherd	Compositor - Paint	None
Shore	James	James Shore	Brewers Storekeeper	Benjamin, Charles
Smith	George	George Smith	Provisions Dealer	Charles James
Spencer-Smith	Herbert	Percy Ledger Smith	Doctor	Ernest
Sprang	Frederick	Frederick H Sprang	Indian Rubber Manufacturer	None
Stables	Leonard	Walter Stables	Doctor	Walter William Godfrey, John Gordwood Ingham
Stockins	William	WJ Stockins	House Decorator	E. B, LJ, GH, WE
Stubbs	Reginald	George B Stubbs	Civil Service Staff Clerk	Stanley George
Sutcliffe	Frederick	Joseph Sutcliffe	Physician and Surgeon	Joseph, John, William, Percy, Richard
Sutherland	John	William Sutherland	Police Constable (Metropolitan)	William
Taffs	Charles	Leslie H Taffs	Headmaster	Arthur Leslie
Tait	Leonard	Edward Tait	Warehouseman	Percy Edward, Archibald Campbell
Talbot	Cecil	Francis Thomas Talbot	Bargebuilder Owner	Francis John, Albert Edward, Ernest Arthur.
Talbot	Ernest	James Talbot	Builder Merchant Lime and Cement Maker	James, Arthur, John
Taylor	William	William Taylor	Assistant School Teacher, London County Council	None
Terry	Sidney	T.Terry	Company Secretary	Ernest William, Thomas Cuthbert
Thompson	Edward	William Thompson	Not known	None
Trotman	Frank	George Trotman	Grocer	Walter George
Trotman	Henry	Henry Trotman	Draper and Shirt cutter	Edward, Eric
Veale Williams	John	John Veale-Wiiilams	Manufacturing Chemist and Alderman	Conrad
Vernall	Arthur	George Vernall	Compositor	William Edward, George
Wade	Oliver	John Wade	Doctor of Science, Investigator and Lecturer	None
Walker	Sidney	William Walker	Master Baker, employer	James B
Walker	William	William Walker	Master Baker, employer	James B

TILL ALL OUR FIGHT BE FOUGHT

Surname	First	Father's Name	Father's Occupation	Brothers of Olavian Fallen (260) (many who would have served)
Wallace	George	William Frederick Wallace	Sub-Inspector City of London Police 1911	Charles William, Arthur Thomas
Walsh	Richard	Richard Walsh	Inspector Engineers Dept GPG	Alfred, Sidney
Wardley	Miles	Joseph Wardley	Machine Ruler	Joseph Albert
Weatherston	John	John T Weatherston	Foreman of Hop Warehouse	Harold Arthur
Weatherston	Sidney	John T Weatherston	Foreman of Hop Warehouse	Harold Arthur
Wells	Neil	Neil Wells	Tanyard Manager	William, Thomas Benjamin
Wensley	Harold	Frederick Porter Wensley	Detective Scotland Yard	Frederick Martin
West	Harold	John S. West	Tea Dealer and Grocer	Cyril
Wilson	Albert	William Sherry Wilson	Printer Manager	Arthur Henry
Young	Henry	George Young	Labourer	Edward William, Frank Anthony

APPENDIX IX
Date of Death Index

YEAR	JANUARY	FEBRUARY	MARCH	APRIL	MAY	JUNE
1914 3 men						
1915 30 men			3. Feben 3. Roberts	23. Lovekin 24. Dell 24. Schultz	2. Haseldine 5. Edward 9. Benson 13. Edgley 17. Taffs 25. Heron 25. Quixley 26. Fitzgerald	7. Taylor 15. S. Walker 25. Wells
1916 43 men	4. E. Talbot			24. Maybrook 29. Child	21. F. Howard 24. Hill 31. Fairlie	2. Durant 8. Stubbs 25. Ruggles
1917 46 men		11. D. Ryley 28. Perkins	10. Sanders 26. Young	13. Sprang 15. Marner 15. Murray 16. H. Baker 16. Gray 26. Hay 29. Wardley	3. Dennis 7. Gaskain 22. Shears 23. Wallace 26. Butler 26. Cock 29. Sutcliffe	1. Athow 6. Dubery 7. Hunt 7. Norris 7. Shepherd 17. Lunn
1918 59 men	20. Dodson 22. Curtis 22. Le Chavetois	20. Budd 20. H. Hollands	15. Kiddle 21. Husk 23. Edmunds 24. Terry 24. Veale Williams 25. Fletcher 25. West 27. Evans 27. Finnimore 28. W. Cook 28. Phare 28. Plowman 28. Smith 29. Dixson 30. L. Harvard 31. Lidgett	5. Defries 7. Knight 13. Chester 13. Clarke 14. Shore	3. Blencowe 7. Bishopp 8. Ellis	6. Stockins
1919 3 men		9. Foreman		12. J. Weatherston	1. Barton	
1920 1 man						
1921 2 men	19. L. Berrow					13. Dodkins
1922 1 man			23. Boone			

YEAR	JULY	AUGUST	SEPTEMBER	OCTOBER	NOVEMBER	DECEMBER
1914 3 men					1. Ryder 24. Bendixen	24. Tait
1915 30 men	6. W. Halliwell 16. Glenn	19. Halliday	21. Hoare 25. A. Cook 25. W. Walker 27. C. Talbot	3. Akerman 13. Bliss 13. N. Jones 14. R. Howett 15. P. Grant	20. Gill	28. Schooling
1916 43 men	1. Hocking 1. Prout 1. S. Weatherston 2. Thompson 3. Harris 3. Mason 7. Procter 8. Wilson 14. N. Hamilton 21. Doughton	15. Roeber 24. Keesey	7. Rule 7. Bay Ryley 12. H. Trotman 14. Spencer Smith 15. Blackman 15. Walsh 16. Page 18., Brittain 18. Riminton 18. Rowe 19. A. Baker 26. Laurie	7. F. Trotman 8. Carrier 9. Dawes 12. W. Hollands 15. Garrett 22. Wade 29. Goenner	1. Mann	3. Royal 7. Ebsworth
1917 46 men	1. Doyle 5. Belcher 21. Knifton 23. Vernall 24. Burwood 26. Lansdale 28. Castle 31. T. Jones	8. Almond 8. Chubb 9. Dunkley 9 Lorey 13. Grist 20. Miles 22. H. Grant 29. Oxford	1. Gant 2. Gale 4. Deem 20. Oliver 22.Bennett 23. Stables	8. Oake 12.King 18 Dale James 15. Wensley	4. Junkison 6. Pearson 15. Hood	
1918 59 men	20. Dodson 22.Curtis 22. Le Chavetois	20. Budd 20. H. Hollands	15. Kiddle 21. Husk 23. Edmunds 24. Terry 24. Veale Williams 25. Fletcher 25. West 27. Evans 27. Finnimore 28. W. Cook 28. Phare 28. Plowman 28. Smith 29. Dixson 30. L. Harvard 31. Lidgett	5. Defries 7. Knight 13. Chester 13. Clarke 14. Shore	3. Blencowe 7. Bishopp 8. Ellis	6. Stockins
1919 3 men						
1920 1 man	29. Beecraft					
1921 2 men						
1922 1 man						

APPENDIX X
Home Area Index

HOME AREA	SURNAME	FIRST	PART OF LONDON
Balham	Haseldine	Newton	South
Battersea	Barton	Ernest	South
Battersea	Ryley	Don	South
Battersea	Ryley (Senior)	Harold	South
Battersea	Ryley	Bay	South
Beckenham	Castle	Ewart	South
Bermondsey	Athow	William	South
Bermondsey	Beecraft	William	South
Bermondsey	Benson	George	South
Bermondsey	Boone	John	South
Bermondsey	Burwood	Philip	South
Bermondsey	Child	Albert	South
Bermondsey	Dawes	Albert	South
Bermondsey	Foreman	Roland	South
Bermondsey	Halliwell	Ernest	South
Bermondsey	Halliwell	William	South
Bermondsey	Hunt	Harold	South
Bermondsey	Husk	Frederick	South
Bermondsey	Kenyon	Harry	South
Bermondsey	Lidgett	John	South
Bermondsey	Marner	Lionel	South
Bermondsey	Oake	Dug	South
Bermondsey	Schulz	Harry	South
Bermondsey	Smith	George	South
Bermondsey	Stables	Leonard	South
Bermondsey	Stockins	William	South
Bermondsey	Talbot	Ernest	South
Bermondsey	Trotman	Henry	South

HOME AREA	SURNAME	FIRST	PART OF LONDON
Bermondsey	Veale-Williams	John	South
Bermondsey	Wells	Neil	South
Bermondsey	Dennis	Robert	South
Bermondsey	Doughton	Walter	South
Bermondsey	Ellis	Charles	South
Bermondsey	Falby	Eddie	South
Bermondsey	Royal	George	South
Bermondsey	Taylor	William	South
Blackfriars	Fitzgerald	Robert	North
Bow	Almond	James	East
Bow	Miles	Frank	East
Brixton	Knox	John	South
Brixton	Berrow	Lewis	South
Brixton	Berrow	William	South
Brixton	Dubery	Frank	South
Bromley	Sprang	Frederick	South
Bromley	Hoare	Ernest	South
Camberwell	Bendixen	Len	South
Camberwell	Clifton	Frank	South
Camberwell	Quixley	Arthur	South
Camberwell	Durant	John	South
Camberwell	Gray	Wallace	South
Camberwell	Hill	Sidney	South
Camberwell	Lorey	Conrad	South
Camberwell	Rings	Fritz	South
Camberwell	Falkner	Clarence	South
Catford	Maybrook	Didi	South
Catford	Spencer-Smith	Herbert	South
Clapham	Evans	Leonard	South
Clapham	Roberts	James	South
Clapham	Sutcliffe	Frederick	South
Clapham	Weatherston	John	South
Clapham	Weatherston	Sid.	South

APPENDIX X

HOME AREA	SURNAME	FIRST	PART OF LONDON
Coulsden	Wade	Olly	South
Cricklewood	Heron	Joe	North
Croydon	Grant	Harold	South
Croydon	Phare	Dudley	South
Deptford	Dell	Claude	South
Deptford	Hearn	Bob	South
Deptford	Chapman	Bob	South
Deptford	Chester	Harold	South
Deptford	Cock	Teddy	South
Deptford	Levy	Godfrey	South
Dulwich	West	Harold	South
Dulwich	Prout	Arthur	South
East Ham	Young	Harry	East
Finchley	Defries	Fred.	North
Forest Hill	Goenner	Frederick	South
Forest Hill	Grist	Percy	South
Forest Hill	Procter	Alexander	South
Forest Hill	Roeber	David	South
Greenwich	Talbot	Cecil	South
Greenwich	Glenn	Reginald	South
Greenwich	Plowman	Oswald	South
Grove Park	Gaskain	Cecil	South
Hackney	Garrett	Arthur	East
Hackney	Hamilton	Claude	East
Hackney	Hamilton	Noel	East
Hampstead	Chubb	Jack	North
Hatch End	Gill	Jack	North
Herne Hill	Tait	Len	South
Hither Green	Oliver	William	South
Hornsey	Lovekin	Vyvyan	North
Ilford	Kiddle	Bobbie	East
Ilford	Rule	Austin	East
Ilford	Walker	Sid	East

HOME AREA	SURNAME	FIRST	PART OF LONDON
Ilford	Walker	Bill	East
Isleworth	Akerman	Ralph	West
Isleworth	Burn	Eddie	West
Kennington	Norris	Fred	South
Kennington	Perkins	Douglas	South
Kennington	Walsh	Richard	South
Lambeth	Halliday	Eric	South
Lambeth	Goatcher	Fred	South
Lambeth	Blencowe	Charles	South
Lambeth	Brittain	Percy	South
Lambeth	Churcher	Edgar	South
Lambeth	Hood	John	South
Lambeth	Trotman	Frank	South
Lambeth	Gale	Percy	South
Lambeth	Oxford	Harry	South
Langley, Bucks	Taffs	Charles	North
Lewisham	Bishopp	Stephen	South
Lewisham	Robinson	Edwin	South
Lewisham	Ruggles	Charles	South
Leyton	Jones	Thomas	East
Leyton	Sanders	Leslie	East
Leytonstone	Knight	Bert	East
Loughton	Mason	William	East
Merton Park	Harvard	Lionel	South
Mile End	Shore	James	East
Mortlake	Budd	Vic	South
New Cross	Blackman	Herbert	South
New Cross	Edwards	Albert	South
New Cross	Harris	Herbert	South
New Cross	Hay	Arthur	South
New Cross	Jones	Jimmy	South
New Cross	Ebsworth	Harold	South
New Malden	Harvard	Ken	South

APPENDIX X

HOME AREA	SURNAME	FIRST	PART OF LONDON
Newington	Keesey	Howard	South
Newington	Dodkins	Lionel	South
Newington	King	Stan.	South
Newington	Sutherland	John	South
Newmarket	Edmunds	Cecil	North East
Palmers Green	Wensley	Harold	North
Peckham	Belcher	Douglas	South
Peckham	Cook	Alleyne	South
Peckham	Cook	William	South
Peckham	Howett	Frank	South
Peckham	Howett	Robert	South
Peckham	Junkison	Arthur	South
Peckham	Murray	Archibald	South
Peckham	Fletcher	Monte	South
Plumstead	Finnimore	Harry	South
Plumstead	Knifton	Jimmy	South
Plumstead	Le Chavetois	Grantley	South
Plumstead	Shears	Edmund	South
Richmond	Carrier	John	South West
Rotherhithe	Bliss	Harold	South
Rotherhithe	Castell	George	South
Rotherhithe	Clarke	Ernest	South
Rotherhithe	Deem	Henry	South
Rotherhithe	Jones	Norman	South
Rotherhithe	Kidney	Leonard	South
Rotherhithe	Richardson	James	South
Rotherhithe	Dixson	Frank	South
Shepherd's Bush	Dodson	William	West
South Norwood	Riminton	Percy	South
South Norwood	Stubbs	Reg.	South
Southwark	Butler	Edmund	South
Southwark	Curtis	Ernest	South
Southwark	Hollands	Harry	South

HOME AREA	SURNAME	FIRST	PART OF LONDON
Southwark	Hollands	Wilf	South
Southwark	Lansdale	William	South
Southwark	Page	Alf	South
Southwark	Wallace	George	South
Southwark	Doyle	Gilbert	South
Southwark	Dunkley	William	South
Southwark	Edgley	Leslie	South
Southwark	Rowe	Henry	South
Southwark	Shepherd	Henry	South
Steyning	Laurie	Arthur	South
Stockwell	Grant	Philip	South
Streatham	Lunn	Ralph	South
Streatham	Terry	Sid	South
Sydenham	Pearson	Tot	South
Thornton Heath	Baker	Albert	South
Tonbridge	Dale James	William	South
Tooting	Thompson	Edward	South
Twickenham	Mann	Stanley	South West
Upton Park	Bennett	Frederick	East
Wallington	Baker	Harold	South
Wallington	Ryder	Gordon	South
Walthamstow	Vernall	Arthur	East
Walworth	Brown	Charles	South
Walworth	Wardley	Miles	South
Walworth	Wilson	Albert	South
Walworth	Feben	Evi	South
Walworth	Holman	William	South
Wandsworth	Schooling	Geoffrey	South
West Norwood	Fairlie	Alwynne	South
Westham	Marriott	Herbert	East
Whitechapel	Hocking	Leslie	East
Woodside Park	Gant	Harold	East

APPENDIX XI
Epitaphs Index

66 of the 192 Fallen have Gravestones with Epitaphs which have been researched and collected here, courtesy of Mr Robert Gardner, Old Olavian.

ALMOND J E	AN OLD STOG ALWAYS FAITHFUL, ALWAYS READY
BAKER A G	DEUX LIGNES POUR VOUS, MOURER OU JE ME RESTE
BARTON E.	WITH FOND MEMORIES FROM YOUR LOVING WIFE AND CHILDREN
BEECRAFT W B	BRAVE AND TRUE
BELCHER D C	THERE IS A LINK WHICH DEATH CANNOT SEVER. SWEET REMEMBRANCE
BENNETT F B	FAITHFUL UNTIL DEATH
BLACKMAN H W	WITH CHRIST WHICH IS FAR BETTER
BRITTAIN P J	TELL ENGLAND WE LIE HERE CONTENT
BURN E H A	DEAR EDDIE, COOL AND COURAGEOUS, EVER READY
BURWOOD P	HIS MEMORY LIVETH
CASTELL G.C.	GREATER LOVE HATH NO MAN THAN THIS
CHAPMAN R S	I AM THE RESURRECTION AND THE LIFE. LOOKING UNTO JESUS
COCK E M	TRUE LOVE BY DEATH, TRUE LOVE LIFE IS TRIED, TRUE THOU FOR ENGLAND, AND FOR ENGLAND DIED
COOK AJ	HE PLAYED THE GAME

TILL ALL OUR FIGHT BE FOUGHT

COOK W E	*TAKE HEART WHO BEARS THE CROSS TODAY, SHALL WEAR THE CROWN TOMORROW*
CURTIS E J	*FOR A SURE AND CERTAIN HOPE, OF A GLORIOUS RESURRECTION*
DEEM H T S	*ASLEEP IN JESUS*
DOUGHTON W G	*FOR FREEDOM AND HONOUR*
DUBERY F A	*GREATER LOVE HATH NO MAN THAN THIS*
DUNKLEY W H	*O HAPPY SAINT FOREVER BLESSED, AT JESUS FEET HOW SAFE YOU REST*
EBSWORTH H E	*HE SHALL HIS LORD IN RAPTURE SEE, AND BE WITH HONOUR CROWNED*
EDMUNDS C H	*BELOVED HUSBAND OF C. A. EDMUNDS AND SON OF MR & MRS EDMUNDS OF SOHAM*
EDWARDS A F	*DIED A HERO FOR KING COUNTRY AND ALL*
EVANS L A	*GREATER LOVE NO MAN HATH THAN HE LAY DOWN HIS LIFE FOR HIS FRIENDS*
FOREMAN R I	*ALWAYS REMEMBERED BY WHAT THEY HAVE DONE*
GALE P J	*GREATER LOVE HATH NO MAN*
GANT H H	*GREATLY LOVED, A GOOD SON, A GOOD BROTHER, A GOOD SOLDIER*
GARRETT A D	*I HAVE CALLED THEE BY THY NAME. THOU ART MINE CHOSEN OF GOOD AND PRECIOUS*
GOENNER F C	*THY WILL BE DONE*
GRIST C H	*THY WILL BE DONE REST IN PEACE*
HALLIWELL E	*HE GAVE HIS LIFE SO THAT OTHERS MIGHT LIVE, THY WILL BE DONE*
HALLIWELL W	*AND HOW CAN MEN DIE BETTER THAN FACING FEARFUL ODDS*

APPENDIX XI

HAMILTON C W	*WITH CHRIST WHICH IS FAR BETTER*
HAY A L	*HE GAVE HIS ALL*
HOARE E A	*HIS DUTY DONE NOW AT REST*
HOCKING L H	*PERFECT PEACE AND AT SUCH A TIME*
HOLLANDS W G	*ONLY BROTHER OF H. E. HOLLANDS. AGED 21. KILLED IN ACTION PALESTINE FEB 20 1918*
HOOD J W	*FAITHFUL UNTO DEATH*
KEESEY G E H	*TO HIS EVER LIVING MEMORY*
KIDDLE R H	*DEAD ERE HIS PRIME YOUNG LYCIDAS AND HATH NOT LEFT HIS PEER*
KING S E	*LIFE'S RACE WELL RUN, LIFE'S WORK WELL DONE, LIFE'S CROWN WELL WON*
LANSDALE W M	*DARE QUAM ACCIPERE*
LEVY G	*HE BUILDED BETTER THAN HE KNEW*
LIDGETT J C	*UNDERNEATH ARE THE EVERLASTING ARMS*
LOREY C C	*NEVER FORGOTTEN*
LOVEKIN V L	*PRO PATRIA REST IN PEACE*
LUNN R W	*IN VERY DEAR AND SACRED MEMORY A BELOVED HUSBAND*
MAYBROOK W R	*A GENTLEMAN UNAFRAID*
OLIVER H W R	*FAITHFUL UNTO DEATH LOVED BY ALL*
PEARSON E A	*I LAID ME DOWN AND SLEPT*
ROBINSON E H	*FOR OF SUCH ARE THE KINGDOM OF HEAVEN*
ROEBER D A	*HE DID HIS DUTY*
ROYAL G D	*AT REST*

SANDERS L Y	GLAD DID I LIVE AND GLADLY DIE AND LAID ME DOWN WITH A WILL
SCHOOLING G H	MORS NON MORA LAUDI
STABLES L T D	THEY SHALL BE MINE IN THAT DAY WHEN I MAKE UP MY JEWELLS MAL. 3. 17.
STUBBS R A	OH BRAVE TRUE HEART! FOR THY DEAR LIFE WE GIVE HIGH PRAISE
TAFFS C A	MEMBER OF LINCOLN'S INN, ONE OF THOSE WHO DIED SO WE MIGHT LIVE
TALBOT E	FATHER IN THY GRACIOUS KEEPING LEAVE WE NOW OUR DEAR ONE SLEEPING
TAYLOR W F	OUR GOD IS LOVE, HIS WILL IS JUST, TO HIM WE LEAVE OUR SON IN TRUST
THOMPSON EWM	SAFE IN GOD'S KEEPING
TROTMAN F W	THIS HAPPY STARRED FULL BLOODIED SPIRIT SHOOTS INTO THE SPIRITUAL LAND REST IN PEACE
TROTMAN J T	HE DIED FOR US
VERNALL A H	FOR HIS COUNTRY HE DIED THAT OTHERS MIGHT LIVE. NEVER FORGOTTEN
WENSLEY H W	YOU AND FRED MADE A NOBLE SACRIFICE. BOTH LIE WITH THE GLORIOUS
YOUNG H G	FAITHFUL UNTO DEATH